THE ROYAL NAVAL DIVISION

[*Photo by F. A. Swaine.*

Major-General Sir Archibald Paris, K.C.B.

[*Frontispiece.*

THE ROYAL :: ::
NAVAL DIVISION
By Douglas Jerrold
With an Introduction by the Right
Hon. Winston S. Churchill :: ::

Printed & bound by Antony Rowe Ltd, Eastbourne

AUTHOR'S PREFACE

THIS history of the Royal Naval Division does not claim to record all the doings of the many separate units which served in the Division. Selection is essential to the writing of history, and the idea that the history of a division should provide an exception to a very golden rule is one which I do not share, and for the same reason as that for which I feel the terms " Divisional History," and, still more, " Divisional Historian," to be misconceived. A history of the evolution of the division as an administrative and tactical unit might perhaps, for want of a better epithet, be called " divisional." But there should be nothing *sui generis* about the history of the officers and men who go to make up a particular division at a particular time. Their deeds must surely be weighed and judged by the same standards as those of other men, by the quantity they achieved, but most of all by the quality they touched.

And so I have endeavoured to see and to write of the Naval Division from the standpoint of the historian rather than the chronicler, and I have unhesitatingly selected for the most detailed treatment those episodes which bear on the widest issues.

By reason of its origin and its organization, of its prominent share in two famous military operations, and because among its officers was more than one famous personality, representative of the culture of an age on which the future will look back at least with interest, the name of the Royal Naval Division will live in history. I have tried so to write this book that round the name may linger some flavour of the quality of its exploits, some reflection of the several tragic if splendid scenes among which its lot was cast.

I am conscious of omissions and imperfections. This book has been written in the intervals of a rather scanty leisure, and it is too much to hope that it contains no inaccuracies. I can only trust that they will be brought to my notice, and that there will be an opportunity of correcting them.

My main authorities have been the War Diaries of the different units and, in particular, of the General Staff of the Divisions. The detailed contemporary reports on operations which these Diaries contain have made it unnecessary to consult many to whom otherwise I should have had to refer constantly. This is particularly true of the Divisional Commanders and their staffs. As regards some of the earlier operations, however, even the General Staff Diaries are incomplete, and in all cases the records of lower formations are barren of much detail essential if the actual experiences of the infantry battalions are to be understood. In these circumstances my thanks are due to many for invaluable assistance in supplementing the available written records.

In particular I must express my gratitude to Lieut.-General Sir Herbert Blumberg, K.C.B., Major-General Sir Archibald Paris, K.C.B., Brigadier-General A. M. Asquith, D.S.O., Colonel Commandant H. C. du Pree, C.B., C.M.G., Captain H. D. King, C.B.E., D.S.O., R.N.V.R., M.P., Lt.-Colonel Bernard Freyberg, V.C., C.M.G., D.S.O., Commander A. W. Buckle, D.S.O., R.N.V.R., Major H. D. Lough, D.S.O., R.M.L.I., Lieut.-Commander R. Blackmore, M.C., R.N.V.R., and Lieut. F. W. Sowerby, R.N.V.R., for assistance in connection with particular operations, and to Mr. Gordon H. N. Inman, A.R.I.B.A., and Mr. G. M. C. Taylor, M.C., A.M.I.C.E. (both of them former officers of the Division), for their help with the maps. Finally, my especial thanks are due to Brigadier-General J. E. Edmonds, C.B., the official historian of the Military Operations of the late war, and to his staff, for their unfailing assistance in helping me to fill the gaps in the Divisional War Diaries, to my mother for reading the proofs, and to my wife for compiling the index.

Those who have helped me by lending me documents and maps are so many that I cannot attempt here to thank them individually. I hope to do so later.

February, 1923.   DOUGLAS JERROLD.

CONTENTS

ILLUSTRATIONS

The illustrations facing pages 212, 220, 224, 260 and 290, are from official photographs and are reproduced by the courtesy of the Imperial War Museum. The remaining illustrations, except the Frontispiece and those facing pages 86, 240 and 300, are from photographs taken by Surgeon A. H. Crook, R.N., who has kindly given his consent to their reproduction. The portraits are reproduced by the kind permission of the Artist, Mr. Ambrose McEvoy.

INTRODUCTION

THE foundations of the Royal Naval Division were laid before the War began. It was perceived that on mobilization there would be at least twenty or thirty thousand men belonging to the Reserves of the Royal Navy for whom there would not be room on any ship of war which went to sea. It had already been proposed on the Committee of Imperial Defence to form from these elements one Brigade of Marines and two Naval Brigades to increase the Forces available for Home Defence, or for any special purpose, such as the seizure of an advanced naval base, for which they might be needed by the Admiralty. On the outbreak of War these three Brigades were assembled and formed into the Royal Naval Division. In those August and September days our Military resources were on a very small scale. Six regular Divisions were going to France, two others were being collected from the garrisons of the Empire, and only the first six Divisions of Lord Kitchener's new Army had yet been planned. The addition of another Division of men of high quality, of prolonged if partial training, and of considerable discipline, for whom weapons were available, was, therefore, an appreciable factor. Lord Kitchener was delighted to include the Division in our Military Forces. He welcomed the Admiralty's intention, and announced its creation to the House of Lords in one of the earliest speeches which he made as Secretary of State. Afterwards, when many hundreds of thousands of eager volunteers had swarmed in to the recruiting stations, and when over seventy British Divisions were being organized and trained, the relative importance of the Naval Division diminished proportionately, and by the time that it was definitely incorporated with the Armies under the War Office, it bulked much smaller than at its birth.

The three Brigades were formed with almost incredible rapidity. *Cadres* were created from the Petty Officers of the Navy, from the Instructors and Sergeants of the Royal Marines and with a sprinkling of retired regular officers of high quality, mostly belonging to the Brigade of Guards.   On this structure it was easy to build the men of the Royal Naval Volunteer Reserve, of the Royal Naval Reserve and of the Royal Fleet Reserve, and of the Royal Marines, in suitable proportions.

At a later stage several thousand recruits who could not at that time be handled by the New Armies, mostly Tyneside miners, were added to the Battalions and maintained consistently the reputation of the North Country.

The method employed in forming the units may be studied in detail by those who care to read the two or three operative Minutes by which this process was regulated.   These are reprinted as an appendix to this history.

The Royal Naval Volunteer Reservists and many others in the various elements of which the Division was composed had set their hearts on serving afloat, and it was with much disappointment and many heartburnings, but with boundless and unflinching loyalty, that they devoted themselves to the deadly work ashore.   The pressure of the opening events of the War was so intense that it was not easy to forecast or measure what would happen after the first decisive battles on land; whether the War would be long or short, or what character its secondary phases would assume.   The overwhelming numbers of volunteers who joined the Army in the latter part of 1914 made this small Admiralty contribution seem superfluous. On the other hand, the vast expansion of the flotillas and small craft of the Navy, together with the need of increasing the complements of the Grand Fleet caused by the conditions of protracted War and by the German submarine campaign, would have afforded five or six months later ample scope in the Naval Service and afloat for all these keen and valiant would-be sailors.   Others were forthcoming when the time came to take their places in the Navy, but the original elements of the Royal Naval Division, who certainly had the first claim to the coveted service afloat, were by that time locked in the heart of the land grapple.   All criticisms on these and kindred grounds were, however, to be swept away by the extraordinary achievements and almost incomparable prowess which this small band of men continued to display in every theatre where they fought during the whole course of the War.

By their conduct in the forefront of the battle, by their

character, and by the feats of arms which they performed, they raised themselves into that glorious company of the seven or eight most famous Divisions of the British Army in the Great War. Their reputation was consistently maintained in spite of losses of so awful a character as to sweep away three or four times over the original personnel. Their memory is established in history and their contribution will be identified and recognized a hundred years hence from among the enormous crowd of splendid efforts which were forthcoming in this terrible period. Deriving as they did their nomenclature, their ceremonial, their traditions, their inspiration from the Royal Navy, they in their turn cast back a new lustre on that mighty parent body of which it will ever be proud and for which it must ever be grateful.

The chronicles which these pages unfold put on faithful record the episodes by which all this work was accomplished. From " Dunkirk to Belgrade," from Antwerp to Gallipoli, from the Somme and Ancre in 1916 to the Drocourt–Quéant switch in 1918, through every bloody battle and in the brunt of it, they marched and suffered. Again and again shot to pieces, always rising anew unconquerable, never failing, never faltering, until in the end their story stands out as an epic ineffaceable in national gratitude and long fortified against the ravages of time.

The great majority of the original Company are dead. The gallant Guards Officers were among the first to fall. The meteor brightness of Rupert Brooke was extinguished almost as soon as his rays began to light the storm. Arnold Quilter, Denis Browne, Charles Lister, of the Hood ; Tisdall and Grant of the Anson ; W. L. Maxwell and Frank Wilson, the Brigade-Majors of the two Naval Brigades* ; Evelegh of the Nelson, Luard of the Portsmouth Marines, Spearman of the Collingwood,† Barker and Lancelot Cherry of the Drake, were among those cut down and swept away before a year of the War had run its course. But their spirit lived on, their example was emulated, their names and memories were cherished, and here and there an Asquith or a Freyberg, a Hutchison, a Ramsay

* Lt.-Colonel W. L. Maxwell (Indian Army) and Major F. Wilson, R.M.L.I., killed on the 11th and 18th May, 1915, respectively.

† Commander A. Y. Spearman, R.N., was killed in action at Gallipoli on June 4th, Lt.-Colonel E. G. Evelegh, R.M.L.I., on July 13th, and Lt.-Colonel F. W. Luard, R.M.L.I., on July 14th, 1915.

Fairfax, a Beak, or a Buckle, salamanders born in the furnace, survived to lead, to command, and to preserve the sacred continuity. The long list of bright names grew with every month that passed. Burge of the Nelson, Tetley of the Drake,* Vere Harmsworth and William Ker of the Hawke, F. S. Kelly of the Hood, were among the many officers of fine promise and attainment who fell in the Ancre Valley. Cartwright† of the 1st Marines was killed at Gavrelle and Sterndale Bennett was mortally wounded at Passchendaele. Patrick Shaw Stewart and Alan Campbell fell on Welsh Ridge, and Farquharson of the 2nd Marines, Kirkpatrick of the Anson and Ellis of the Hawke,‡ till then unscathed, in those resolute engagements in which the Division stemmed the tide of the German advance in March, 1918. Jones of the Hawke,§ Surgeon Pocock of the Drake, Fish of the Hood, fell in the final and triumphant advance.

When the Division went to France in the spring of 1916 a new set of difficulties began to assail it and even to menace its existence. It was a Naval Division. It had different rates of pay, different ranks, different customs, different methods, different traditions, from those of the British Expeditionary Army. Its officers and men used consistently the Naval parlance on every possible occasion. To leave their camps, in which the White Ensign flew and bells recorded the passage of time, men requested " leave to go ashore ; " when they returned they " came aboard," and when they did not they were reported as " adrift." Men were " rated " and " disrated," and for Sergeants and Lance-Corporals they had Petty Officers and Leading Seamen. Anchors were stencilled on their limbers and emblazoned on their Company flags, and their regimental badges were in the form of the crests of the Admirals whose names their Battalions bore. When ill or wounded they attended " Sick bay ; " field kitchens were the " galley ; " the King's health was drunk sitting in the " ward-

* Lt.-Colonel N. O. Burge, R.M.L.I., and Lt.-Colonel A. S. Tetley, R.M.L.I., were both killed on the morning of November 13th, 1916.

† Lt.-Colonel F. J. W. Cartwright, D.S.O., R.M.L.I., died on April 30th, 1917, of wounds received in the second battle of Gavrelle. Commander W. Sterndale Bennett, D.S.O., R.N.V.R., died on November 7th, 1917.

‡ Lt.-Colonel C. G. Farquharson, M.C., R.M.L.I., was killed on the 23rd, and Lt.-Colonel Kirkpatrick, D.S.O. (The Buffs), and Commander Bernard Ellis, D.S.O., R.N.V.R., on the 25th March, 1918.

§ Commander S. G. Jones, R.N.V.R., killed on August 25th, 1918.

room "—where Officers wanting salt are even reported to have been heard asking their neighbours to " give it a fair wind ; " all Wrights were " Shiner," and all Clarks were " Nobby." Many of the men and some of the Officers requested " leave to grow," and paraded creditable beards in the faces of a clean-chinned Army.*

It need scarcely be said that these manifestations inspired in a certain type of military mind feelings of the liveliest alarm. To this type of mind anything which diverged in the slightest degree from absolute uniformity according to the sealed pattern was inexpressibly painful. Yet these very peculiarities of the Naval Division, this consciousness they had of partnership with the great traditions of the Royal Navy, these odd forms and ceremonies, this special nomenclature, which were cherished and preserved so punctiliously by officers and men, few of whom had ever been to sea, were in fact the mainspring of their exceptional prowess. It is strange how men deprived of everything that makes for happiness and pleasure in human life, confronted with the cruellest trials and under the constant menace amounting almost to certainty of death, find comfort and revivifying strength in little things which to others, freed from these circumstances, living in an easy and exalted sphere, only appear trivial and, perhaps, absurd.

Two remedies for the shocking spectacle which the Naval Division presented to the eyes of martinets were alternately and repeatedly proposed. The first was to break them into uniformity, the second was to disband them. When at last General Paris, whose proved sagacity had led the Division from the outset, had fallen wounded, the first of these remedies was tried. An Army officer with unexceptionable credentials for the task was placed in command. For six months in 1916 he laboured to force the officers and men of the Royal Naval Division to amend their ways, to drop their naval vogue, to forget their naval tradition, and even to shave their beards. Army officers selected for this express purpose were placed in command of many of the battalions over the heads of those who had won their way to these situations by continued

---

* When going aboard the train which was to take them from Dunkirk to Antwerp in 1914, the Anson and Hood Battalions were warned that in case the train was attacked during the night the Anson Battalion was to fall out on the " port " and the Hood on the " starboard " side of the train.

promotion under the fire of the enemy. But so stubborn was the resisting power which all ranks developed in a perfectly obedient and respectful manner, and so high was their conduct in action, that after six months the essential character of the Division was unchanged. Under a new commander they re-entered a period in which their only troubles were provided by the Germans.

The second remedy, which would naturally occur to the particular type of military mind which has been referred to, was next attempted. A concerted and vigorous effort was made in the spring of 1917 both by General Headquarters and the War Office to disband the Division. The first remedy had failed through the obstinacy of the troops and their fine performances against the enemy. The second encountered a not less effective opposition in the person of Sir Edward Carson, then First Lord of the Admiralty. Wielding at that time ample political influence and gifted with not less ample controversial powers, he was able to repulse the attack in a decisive fashion. The War Office and General Headquarters accepted their defeat this time with good grace, and hence-forward the Royal Naval Division, confirmed in all its pre-rogatives, was permitted to go forward without molestation. Neither to the enemy in their front, nor to their pedantic friends in the rear, had they yielded in any respect. Even the Artillery, purely military in their origin, who were attached to the Division, adopted with the utmost punctilio its naval customs, and so continued to the end of the War.

It would be impossible to pass from this aspect without referring to those Army units who, with unfailing con-stancy and comradeship shared the fortunes of the Division throughout all the campaigns n France and Belgium. The 223rd and 317th Brigades of the Royal Field Artillery sustained the Division from midsummer, 1916, until the Armistice under a succession of skilful and intrepid Com-manders, and the exploits of the 190th Infantry Brigade, which included the Honourable Artillery Company and the 4th Bedfords, were a shining part of the record of the Division.

* * * * * * *

It was a long road to tread. Few there were who survived from· first to last. Two, whose names have been mentioned,

Asquith and Freyberg, rose from Sub-Lieutenants to Brigadier-Generals across a succession of battlefields on which they gained every distinction prized by fighting men and sustained between them more than a dozen wounds. For these and others like them the story of the Royal Naval Division must indeed seem a vivid panorama of changing scenes and unforgettable episodes. All is recounted in Mr. Douglas Jerrold's faithful and moving pages with the sincerity and accuracy of one who saw and endured. Antwerp and its seething, cheering crowds when these young soldiers arrived on their desperate errand of succour; Antwerp under bombardment; Antwerp evacuated, with its streams of refugees pouring over the bridges and along the roads, huddled together, hurrying on, impelled by the crash of the cannonade and lighted on their way by the blaze of the great oil reserve flowing in rivers of fire along the ditches. The retreat—the fateful moment at the Dutch frontier : Sub-Lieutenant Grant under arrest for refusing to cross into neutral territory; hanging back until his superior officer, by himself crossing it, had forfeited authority, and then, by byways, leading through the night thirty-five men to safety and freedom. The retreat again : the train load of refugees and Marines intercepted in the night by German riflemen and machine guns : Colonel Luard and Major French extricating their weary men who had already marched thirty-five miles and breaking through. Such was their first experience.

Then to the Mediterranean. On the scented Island of Skyros the little band of friends, themselves nearly all marked for death, gathered at the grave in which they buried Rupert Brooke and his dawning genius. The landing on Gallipoli : Freyberg's midnight swimming exploit in the Gulf of Xeros; Tisdall's repeated journeys to and from the *River Clyde* saving the wounded on the terrible beach, surviving incredibly the intense rifle fire only to perish a few days later, his life no longer charmed. Warwick and other Anson officers leading forward to the recapture of their positions Senegalese troops, all of whose French officers were killed. The sunsets behind Samothrace, seen from the front lines in the rising heatherland of the peninsula, bathing the Troad in golden light ; night by the calm Aegean, illuminated by the red and green lights of the hospital ships and the fitful flashing of artillery.

B

The fierce scenes of battle in the cruel, cramped positions at Cape Helles; the awful midsummer of dust, flies, dysentery, and the nausea of corruption; the rigours of the November blizzard; the sorrow of the final evacuation. Then an interlude of peace, unshelled, and the quiet beauty of early spring in the Greek Islands.

The scene shifts to France. The November attack at Beaucourt in the fog and mist of the Ancre Valley, when the Royal Naval Division, at the cost of more than a third of its strength, in the words of Sir Douglas Haig, "advanced further and took more prisoners than any Division had done in one day." Here Freyberg, twice wounded, but still continuing to lead the attack, took every objective, and, pressing on beyond the furthest, gained his immortal V.C. All this was but a prelude to 1917, which brought a new series of bloody trials to the inexhaustible Division : the night attack in the bitter frost and brilliant moonlight of February 3rd. The storm of Gavrelle after the Arras battle, Sterndale Bennett leading the Drake in column of route between the only gap of wire on his front, and Surgeon McCracken, in a mist of red brick dust and of the yellow and black shell fumes, leading the survivors of his own stretcher bearers and of captured German Red Cross men to clear the village streets of wounded under withering fire : the capture of the Gavrelle Windmill by Captain Newling of the Marines and its brilliant defence.

Then Passchendaele, with its daily and nightly flounderings through the swamp, and ghastly struggles in the dark for enemy pill-boxes. Welsh Ridge after the Cambrai disaster, with the German storm troops attacking white-clad across the snow, securing a lodgment in the vital second line, hurled out of it again by the Anson counter-attack.

At last 1918 is reached with its terrific 21st of March, its difficult and exhausting retreat leading up to the brilliantly sustained engagements of March 25th, when at Les Bœufs, at High Wood and at Courcelette, the Naval Division stood in the van of the Vth Corps and saved the line of the Ancre.

And so all through the long summer struggle till the victorious advance. Still the Division is in the forefront—taking part in the storming of the redoubtable Drocourt–Quéant switch of the Hindenburg Line (September 3rd) with the Anson and the Marines on the flank of the Canadian advance, and Beak, with the dash and exploiting enterprise of the born leader, thrusting forward to Pronville and opening the way to the banks of the Canal du Nord. On September 30th, begins that astonishing advance of the Division towards Cambrai, when, with Beak and Buckle once more in the front of the battle, we see them forcing the passage of the Canal du Nord, carrying Anneux and Graincourt, storming the almost impassable defences of the St. Quentin Canal, capturing the village of Niergnies and repelling with a captured field gun and captured German anti-tank rifles a German counter-attack made with captured British tanks—an extraordinary inversion. They were fighting still in the neighbourhood of Mons when 11 o'clock struck on the morning of November 11th, and the annals of the Royal Naval Division came in honour to a close.

Long may the record of their achievements be preserved, and long may their memory be respected by those for whom they fought.

April, 1923.   WINSTON S. CHURCHILL.

THE ROYAL NAVAL DIVISION

CHAPTER I

THE FORMATION OF THE ROYAL NAVAL DIVISION

LEGEND has been busy with the origin and the fortunes of the Royal Naval Division. It tells us how it was hurriedly formed by the Admiralty of a number of recruits, on the outbreak of the war, and thrown into Antwerp without any realization of its inadequacy. It returned from there, after heavy losses, with an impaired *moral*, and was faultily trained—so the legend goes—to take a premature share in the Gallipoli campaign. After these misadventures the Naval Division went to France, and was " taken over by the Army " !

If the legend were true, there would be little excuse at this date for compiling the history. But the truth about the Naval Division is something different, and the respects in which it differs from the legend bear upon important issues. It is not the case that the Division was improvised to gratify the whim of any statesman, or that, once it had been formed, it was used by the Admiralty to enable them to dabble in matters left by prescriptive custom to the Military authorities. Still less is it the case that the successes achieved by the Naval Division in France were due to any overhauling of its organization, or to the fact that its individuality was lost.

A military history must not be allowed to degenerate into a polemic, and as far as the criticisms which are still levelled at the Naval Division have as their aim the scarification of this or that statesman or soldier, they will find no answer in this history—they have, indeed, long ago had the answer they deserve. In so far, however, as public attention has been called to the work of the Division as exemplifying the results of an unsound policy, of faulty organization, of the miscalculation of the effective value of troops employed under specific conditions, the historian, while remembering always that his principal duty is to record the achievements of the Division, to keep alive its traditions, and hand down to the future not only a name but a memory, cannot stand wholly aside from political or even military controversy.

The origin of the Naval Division is to be found in the plans prepared some years before the outbreak of the war, at the instance of the Committee of Imperial Defence, for the formation on the outbreak of war of a force of Royal Marines to operate under the direction of the Admiralty. This force was to be called the "Advanced Base Force," and its object was the seizure, fortification, or protection of any temporary Naval Bases which might be necessary to the employment of the Fleet, or the provisioning of an army in the field.

The plan provided for a Royal Marine Brigade of four infantry battalions (one from each of the R.M.L.I. Divisions, and one from the depot of the Royal Marine Artillery). When war broke out, this Brigade was duly formed and was the only land force at the disposal of the Admiralty till August 16th.

On that date the Admiralty decided to strengthen the Advanced Base Force by adding two brigades of Naval Reservists.* The measure was a tentative one. There was no intention of expanding unnecessarily the land force at the disposal of the Admiralty. It was intended, on the contrary, to concentrate the surplus reservists at Walmer only for such time as the needs arising out of the military situation were more urgent than the requirements of the fleet. At the moment when the decision was taken, the difficulty of finding employment and accommodation for some of the reservists there was considerable, and though, eventually, their employment on shore service was not only a legitimate grievance to the men, but was regrettable from the point of view of the Navy afloat, it had, and could have had, no immediate effect on naval efficiency. Nevertheless, the wording of the Press communiqué issued on September 7th lent an easy handle to the critics. The statement that "After providing for all

* See Appendix A for the text of Mr. Winston Churchill's instructions.

present and foreseeable future needs of the fleet there remained available a large number of men " of the different Naval reserves was a controversial one, and the ignorance of the public and the Press of the responsibilities laid on the Admiralty under the pre-existing plan for the Advanced Base Force, an ignorance which it was impossible to dispel, made it more than difficult for the critics to see the problem in its true perspective.

These responsibilities could not, however, be shelved. While the two Royal Naval Brigades were concentrating, German cavalry approached the outskirts of Ostend, and on August 26th it was necessary to send the Marine Brigade across the Channel to assist the garrison of that town in case a descent should be made in greater force on this important coast line, the loss of which would be a fatal blow to our communications with our army in the field. As we shall see, when we come to the narrative of the early operations of the Division, the threat did not at the time materialize, but the progress of events on the main front, and the necessity which now became evident for establishing on the Belgian coast a base for the Naval Air Service, made it clear that the threat could not be ignored. If the enemy was less immediately audacious than had been feared, it remained probable that considerable forces would be directed in the near future against the Belgian coast. It thus became necessary to prepare for military action on the Belgian front on a more elaborate scale. The War Office were not only unable to find the troops, but, just at this time, were pressing the Admiralty to accept for service (in the Naval Brigades) some thousands of the recruits whom the Army could neither train nor equip. In these circumstances the important decision was taken on September 3rd to train and equip the two brigades of Naval Reservists, and the hitherto independent Marine Brigade, as an Infantry Division. The decision met with the full approval of Lord Kitchener.

Such was the origin of the Royal Naval Division. Obviously, it is easy to imagine a division composed of more homogeneous elements, and less likely by its nature to create administrative difficulties. But such a division in 1914 would have been purely a work of imagination. Unlike the journalist, or even the historian, the statesman and the administrator have to subdue their hands to the stuff they work in. Few can be ignorant of the difficulties of securing agreement among a number of men on any question of policy. Such difficulties may indeed be adduced as one more proof of the impotence of humanity to meet the problems it creates, but they are there, nevertheless, and can only be overcome by compromises which are as easy to criticize as they are impossible to avoid. The problem before the statesman or the administrator lies, seldom in deciding what to do, always in getting anything at all done in a world where the support of other men and other interests is a prerequisite of successful enterprise. And so if we find that, in the stress of a great crisis, the problem of strengthening the only land forces available for the special duty of safeguarding naval and air bases was solved, it is idle to cavil too much at the imperfections of the particular measures taken. These were many, and have never been denied. The simple question is whether other measures could have been taken at the time, or, if they could have been but were not, whether, on this ground alone, the Admiralty should have let a paramount naval interest go by default. The answer to this question is reasonably clear.

The administration of the Naval Division was entrusted to an Admiralty standing committee, presided over by Mr. Winston Churchill the then First Lord, with Captain Sir R. Williams Bulkeley, R.N.R. (Chairman of the Admiralty Volunteer Committee), the Director of Naval Personnel, the Adjutant-General, Royal Marines, and Major Ollivant, R.A. (Staff Officer to the Division), as members. This Committee was responsible for the selection of the personnel of the force, for the many detailed arrangements necessary to concentrate, house and feed them, and for the selection of officers to command the different battalions and brigades. The orders of the Committee were issued through the Admiralty Secretariat.

The War Office could render very little assistance in the way of personnel, and none whatever in the almost equally important matter of equipment (of which so much was to be heard later). Yet these difficulties, it was felt, so far from condemning the experiment, were its primary justification. The War Office were straining every nerve to place and maintain our main expeditionary force in the field. Any other force which might be required for service overseas, if an emergency should arise in the immediate future, must be provided elsewhere. To provide it, in spite of difficulties, however great, was the task of the Admiralty Committee.

It found ready to its hand the Marine Brigade which had returned from Ostend on September 1st, and, at Walmer, 128 officers and 3,400 petty officers and men of the R.N.V.R., 2,000 Royal Fleet Reserve stokers, and 1,500 selected ratings of the Royal Naval Reserve. In addition, there had been drafted to the force 17 retired officers, R.N., 288 chief petty officers, petty officers and leading seamen, R.N., and 320 petty officers from the R.F.R.

The training of the Marine Brigade gave rise to no problems. When it was decided to incorporate it in the Naval Division, the only change considered necessary was the disbanding of the R.M.A. battalion,* and the formation of a fourth R.M.L.I. battalion. This was done by drawing one company and one platoon from the battalions provided by the three Marine Divisions at Chatham, Portsmouth and Plymouth. These battalions were commanded by Lt.-Colonel R. McN. Parsons, R.M.L.I., Lt.-Colonel Luard, R.M.L.I., and Lt.-Colonel Matthews, C.B., R.M.L.I., and the new (Deal) Battalion by Lt.-Colonel Beith, R.M.L.I. The whole Brigade, after a short period under Major-General McCausland, had been placed under Brigadier-General Sir George Aston, K.C.B., and, when they returned from Ostend, they went into active training at Portsmouth, till they were ordered overseas again, this time to Dunkirk, at the end of September.

These battalions had, of course, a large number of recruits to absorb, but they had at their disposal trained instructors and regular officers, and the machinery for barrack square training of the most orthodox character. They were thus, in effect, trained, both now, before Antwerp, and in the months following, independently of the rest of the division, of which they became an integral part only when divisional training began in January, 1915.

Very different was the problem of organizing and training the rest of the Division. The first thing had been to reduce to military shape the heterogeneous force of naval reservists who poured into Walmer between the 22nd and 26th August.

---

* It was intended to use the personnel of this battalion to form divisional artillery, but the scheme had to be abandoned owing to difficulties of supply and training.

This force, divided into two, and separated into two camps,* became the 1st and 2nd Naval Brigades, commanded by Commodore Wilford Henderson, R.N., and Commodore Oliver Backhouse, R.N. The rudimentary battalions were known first of all by prosaic numbers, but later by the names of eight famous admirals, a stroke of genius which had an incalculable influence in keeping alive some elements of the naval tradition to the very end of the war. The first definite organization of the two Brigades was as follows :

1ST R.N. BRIGADE—G.O.C. : Commodore W. Henderson, R.N. Brigade Major : Major Cunningham. Staff Captain : Captain Dyke.

1st (Drake) Battalion—O.C. : Commander V. A. L. Campbell, R.N. 2nd in Command and Adjutant : Major F. Wilson, R.M.L.I.

2nd (Hawke) Battalion—O.C. : Commander Fargus, R.N. 2nd in Command : Major Bryce (Scots Guards).

3rd (Benbow) Battalion—O.C. : Commander Beadle, R.N. 2nd in Command : Major Fletcher.

4th (Collingwood) Battalion—O.C. : Lt.-Colonel Aymer Maxwell (Coldstream Guards). 2nd in Command : Major Trefusis.

2ND R.N. BRIGADE—G.O.C. : Commodore O. Backhouse, R.N. Brigade Major : Major Maxwell. Staff Captain : Captain Saunders.

5th (Nelson) Battalion—O.C. : Commander C. D. Bridge, R.N. 2nd in Command : Major Murray (Grenadier Guards).

6th (Howe) Battalion—O.C. : Commander Viscount Curzon, R.N.V.R. 2nd in Command : Major Dalrymple Hamilton (Scots Guards).

* The 2nd R.N. Brigade moved from Walmer to Lord Northbourne's park at Betteshanger on September 9th.

7th (Hood) Battalion—O.C. : Lt.-Colonel Quilter (Grenadier Guards). 2nd in Command : Major Viscount Bury (Scots Guards).

8th (Anson) Battalion—O.C. : Lt.-Colonel George Cornwallis West (Scots Guards).

The establishment of the battalions* was fixed for the time being at 937 other ranks, made up as follows :—

> Petty Officers—(R.N.)............... 28
> Petty Officers—(R.F.R.).......... 48
> Petty Officers, Leading Seamen and
>   Seamen—(R.N.V.R.) 424
> Stokers—(R.F.R.) 250
> Seamen—(R.N.R.) 187

Had it been possible to maintain this establishment of disciplined men, progress in the matter of training might have been rapid. Almost at once, however, the needs of the fleet made it necessary to withdraw many of the better trained personnel and to substitute for them the new army recruits who had been taken over, at the request of the War Office, from the surplus enlistments of several North Country regiments. The number of recruits coming in from the army swamped the under-officered battalions, and it became necessary in the middle of September to open a divisional depot at the Crystal Palace. This depot was placed under the command of Commodore Sir Richard Williams Bulkeley, R.N.R.

This problem of providing officers for the depot and to complete the establishment of the battalions could only be met, as in the army, by commissioning men from civil life.† The new officers had, for the most part, no sort of training, but they were urgently needed for duty with the battalions in camp, and there the majority had to go, without even a day's preparation for their new profession.

The progress made in training the Naval Brigades turned

---

* For the text of the orders issued by Mr. Winston Churchill, see Appendix A.

† These officers were chosen by a selection committee under the chairmanship of Sir Richard Williams Bulkeley. The Press notice asking for candidates to come forward gave as the required age " between 25 and 85." This wise variant of the usual practice had exceptionally good results.

necessarily on the personalities of the few regular officers available with the battalions and at the depot for the fourfold task of training officers, training recruits, creating the administrative machine and at the same time making a beginning with platoon and company training. On the whole, and with the inevitable exceptions, the progress was surprisingly good. To the 2nd Naval Brigade, in particular, Major Maxwell and Colonel Quilter (of the Hood Battalion) were a tower of strength. A serious difficulty, however, was that of providing suitable training for the officers. The officers with permanent commissions in the R.N.V.R. were, of course, as uninstructed in land war as the newest joined civilian, and, as these officers were often of considerable seniority, the difficulty was a real one.

To attempt to train officers for responsible military duties in a short time was contrary to the whole tradition of the pre-war Army. It was soon realized that to do so was essential, but it was not so soon realized that a special system of training was necessary. In the Naval Brigades in September, the idea was, too often, that the function of junior officers was to receive and carry out orders. There is no better method, perhaps, of learning to command than by learning to obey. But it is a slow method. We shall see that the peculiar problem was recognized and solved a little later (and solved exceptionally well), but it is necessary to say here what has been said if some of the difficulties experienced by the Naval Brigades at Antwerp are to be understood.

The other difficulties arose from a more obvious source. For all their admitted shortcomings, the Naval Brigades, in the course of September, took on quite definitely the character of military formations. Of a divisional organization, however, there was little sign. There was not even a Divisional Commander.

The administrative machine consisted of four staff officers (Lt.-Col. Forster, Major Micklem, Major G. S. Richardson and Major Ollivant) working with an improvised assortment of clerks at 41, Charing Cross, under the orders of a departmental Committee. At least one of these officers, Major Richardson, had the highest administrative abilities, but, as luck had it, both he and Major Ollivant had to go overseas in the middle of September with the Marine Brigade. In the result, the task of organizing even the nucleus of a mobile Division, while at the same time organizing a depot and training and equipping two infantry brigades, proved to be an impossible one. There was indeed a principal medical officer (Fleet-Surgeon Gaskell, F.R.C.S., R.N., had been appointed to this post in succession to Fleet-Surgeon Mesden, R.N. on September 22nd), and some divisional engineers were being recruited. There was, however, no trained administrative staff, no signal company, no artillery, no supply train and no field ambulances available at this time for duty with the Division in the field.

It was the absence of such essentials as these, far more than the lack of training of the infantry personnel, which retarded the progress at Walmer and Betteshanger. Military history abounds in instances of decisive successes achieved by relatively untrained troops, certainly by troops less disciplined than the majority of those in the Naval Brigades. But defects of individual proficiency and inexperienced leading can be overcome only by a rigid and scientific organization under the hand of a keen, dominating and experienced commander. The Brigades of the Naval Division in September, 1914, had no commander and formed part of no effective organization.

The office at Charing Cross did all that could be done in the circumstances, but it was not enough, and when, very wisely, it was decided on October 1st to transfer the administrative control of the Naval Division to the Marine Office, it was too late. The hour of crisis was dawning ; the Naval Brigades, for all their unpreparedness, had to take the field, and the missing divisional organization had to be improvised under the guns of Antwerp.

The order to move overseas reached the camps at Walmer and Betteshanger at 2 a.m. on the morning of October 4th. In what circumstances the desperate decision was taken we shall see in the next chapter. Before turning to the controversial story of the operation in Belgium in August, September and October, we must, however, say something of the personal quality of the officers and men of the three Brigades who were thus signalled out, from the many other newly-raised formations, to be the first to face in the field the legendary strength of the German armies.

From the first, the Division attracted men of a remarkable quality. Those from the R.N.V.R. Divisions, whether they had joined before the war, or were recruited after the war, were easily distinguishable. The R.N.V.R. comprised in its ranks both before and during the war men of no inconsiderable education, inspired by an enthusiasm which more than made up for that lack of mere physical stamina inevitable in men whose daily life is one of office routine.

In sharp contrast were the newly-joined recruits taken over from the War Office, men who had enlisted in the very first days of the war, mostly in the Durham Light Infantry, the Northumberland Fusiliers and the King's Own Yorkshire Light Infantry. These men, of truly remarkable physique, inexhaustible patience and endurance, and unfailing courage, were almost all miners from Durham and Northumberland. They had none of the somewhat mercurial optimism of London troops, still less had they the positive zest for fighting which characterizes some regiments north of the Tweed. But they had a courageous acquiescence in even the most outrageous fortune.

In many ways resembling these North Country recruits, and particularly in their patience, endurance and fighting quality, were the men of the Royal Fleet Reserve, who, adding to their inherent qualities those others which come only from discipline and technical training, were the real backbone of the Division from the date of its formation to that of their withdrawal for service with the Fleet in June, 1915. The quality of these men was all the more remarkable because they were possessed of some superficially less attractive characteristics. They never became " smart " soldiers. Like all men worth their place in the firing line, they were resentful of incompetence in their officers, and they were inclined to assume it in any newly joined officer till the contrary was proved. Many officers can recall with some amusement, but without much pride, their early efforts to exercise authority over " the stokers." Military (or naval) discipline had no terrors for them : they knew the regulations better than most, and the appropriate penalty for any minor delinquency had, one soon came to know, been taken into account as just, or more than, worth while before the particular breach of discipline was decided on. In these circumstances, it need hardly be said, the one unforgivable crime in the eye of the stoker was to neglect to impose it.

These peculiarities were, however, only superficial. As

a body, these men were possessed of a remarkably high sense of duty, all the more compelling, perhaps, in that it was only completely evoked under the most trying conditions. Finer fighting men on the day of battle the Division never knew. Their magnificent example in the first serious engagements in which the Division was to take part was the foundation of the fighting tradition of the Naval Brigades.

The R.N.V.R. officers were drawn from too many places, too many professions, to give them any marked corporate characteristics. The majority, no doubt, of those from the Clyde, Mersey, and Tyneside Divisions were engaged, in one capacity or another, in the shipping industry, and not a few had served their apprenticeship in the Merchant Service before settling down on shore. But the life of cities produces much the same characteristics all over the world, and there was, probably, less difference than was thought at the time between these officers and their admittedly civilian colleagues who joined the Division throughout September.

Some, indeed, of the most recently joined officers were to play a predominant part in the training or organization of the Division, and from the very first figured largely in its life, and became part of its tradition. Such were Arthur Asquith, Rupert Brooke and Denys Brown, who were appointed as sub-lieutenants to the Anson Battalion early in September. Bernard Freyberg was already appointed to the Hood, which he was to command with so much distinction. F. S. Kelly, an old Oxford rowing blue, and holder of the record for Diamonds, who combined with these achievements a brilliant musical talent, was with the Drake. There were others less well known to the public, who came to the front equally soon. Indeed, if ever there was a military formation with a " *carrière ouverte au talent* " it was the Naval Division, and the most remarkable thing about it was that in every battalion were found men to take advantage of the opportunity when it came. Most of these men were unknown before the war, and were forgotten six months after it was over, but they were the rank and file of the officers of a Division which had no use for supermen, and they won such distinction as came their way merely by the exercise in unfamiliar surroundings of the ordinary qualities of mind and character which bring success in civil life.

The characteristics of the officers of the Naval Brigade which were developed in their early days were, indeed, the result of other influences than the peace-time training which the majority had undergone.

There was, of course, in each battalion more than one officer with a regular military training, and on these officers all alike depended for such strictly technical knowledge as they found it essential to possess. But, broadly, the junior officers had to teach themselves anything they wanted to know about the art of war, and to learn from experience the habit of command. The two camps were, from the young officers' point of view, two vast experimental stations containing all the material for successful improvisation, unhampered by any limiting conditions prescribing the line of development. Under these conditions audacity and initiative were at a premium, and the more conventional qualities of junior subalterns less in request. The desire to mould the different patterns of men to one type of officer may have existed in the minds of some in authority, but, if so, circumstances were against its realization, and more particularly because the senior officers of the R.N.V.R., who had a very strong *esprit de corps* of their own, were at first by no means anxious to adopt more than was essential of military technique. In a sense this was unfortunate, but it had in the end a not unsatisfactory result, for it gave an enduring quality to the early traditions of the Naval Battalions, who remained, to the very end of the war, resolute in their determination to do things always as seemed best to their judgment, and never to sacrifice their independence to the outward forms of discipline. Discipline there was, but it was the discipline which bowed to superior judgment or ability more readily than to superior rank, and bowed to rank against its judgment only when the exigencies of the situation strictly demanded it, as the alternative to more serious ills. This made the Naval Battalions and Brigades always and admittedly difficult to command, but perhaps also it made them, in some ways, rather well worth commanding. What at any rate is indisputable is that the traditions, which were born of these early days of experiment, gave to the Naval Division an individual quality which it preserved to the end, and which assisted it to more than one historic success.

CHAPTER II

THE operations in Belgium in August and September, 1914, are overshadowed by the more spectacular struggle which opened on August 23rd at Mons. The dramas of the retreat from Mons, of the Marne and of the Aisne, engrossed the attention of the world at the time, and have since almost monopolized the interest of historians. Not till after the Aisne, when the race for the sea began, did the eyes of Europe turn to the Channel ports, for which the struggle seemed only then to be beginning. On this reading, even the siege of Antwerp was an isolated episode, in which we were unwise to intervene, an irrelevant side issue which should not have distracted our attention from the battle of main armies.

Macaulay's schoolboy might welcome this interpretation of events, for it would spare his overburdened memory the recollection of many minor operations controversial in their inception, confusing in their brevity, and of an influence in the campaign as a whole which, if not disputable, is at any rate disputed.

Yet the determining triumph of the Allies in the first three months of the war did not consist only in the very important facts that Paris was saved and that the battle front was stabilized on a line running North and South, rather than on a line running East and West, but in the fact that, as late as October 10th, the Belgian coastline was still in our possession, and that we were thus enabled permanently to retain the more important Channel ports. Had the ports fallen in August or September, Paris could not have been saved. Had the Germans reached the Belgian coast in the first days of October, our victories on the Marne and Aisne would have lost their strategic significance ; in the outflanking race northwards we should have been beaten. Neither the French ports nor the Belgian coast could be directly defended by our original expeditionary force, or by our allies. Why were they not seized by the enemy ? How did it happen that the greatest opportunity ever offered to the Germans on the Western front was missed ? The truth is that the safety of the Channel ports was an essential of British naval strategy, and that it is, in great part, to the efforts of the Admiralty, in co-operation with the War Office and the French General Headquarters staff, that we must look for the explanation of the inaction of the German High Command.

In their efforts the Allies were assisted undeniably by the caution of the leaders of the enemy forces in Belgium, but the salient and determining fact is that the enemy were given reason for caution, and persistently encouraged to exercise it. Had it been otherwise the Channel ports would not have been saved.

The formation of the Advanced Base Force by the Admiralty, on the outbreak of war, was the initial step taken by them for the defence of these ports. The second step was taken on August 25th when the Marine Brigade under Brigadier-General Sir George Aston, K.C.B., was ordered to Ostend. The move was, as we have seen, prompted by no sudden vagary of the First Lord of the Admiralty, but by the news that, on the evening of the 24th August, German patrols had approached Ostend. The Marine Brigade, though hardly at the time capable of offensive action (the battalions had been returned from camp to their divisions for further training only a few days before), was embarked on the morning of the 26th, the Chatham Battalion on four Channel Fleet battleships under Rear-Admiral Currey, and the Plymouth Battalion in four Channel Fleet battleships under Admiral Bethell. These last (*Vengeance*, *Goliath*, *Prince George* and *Cæsar*), with the light cruiser *Proserpine*, six destroyers and three monitors, formed the covering force.

Owing to difficulties of co-ordinating the movement of the different squadrons, bad weather and delays off Ostend, the force was not landed in its entirety till the morning of the 28th.

Sir George Aston's orders were to take up a defensive position round Ostend, keeping close to the coast, so as to enjoy the protection of the Fleet, and to facilitate re-embarkation should events necessitate it. His force proceeded to entrench on the perimeter of the town, forming an outpost line, with bicycle patrols linking up the positions. The force was not mobile; it had no cavalry, no supply train, no engineers and no artillery; moreover, the lie of the land deprived it of the intended support of the guns of the fleet.* It was capable, however, of doing what was required, for its presence meant that the enemy must send a properly equipped force against Ostend if they wished to occupy it. Meanwhile, it provided an effective covering force to the landing of any French or Belgian troops who might be sent to garrison it, or to take the offensive against the enemy's communications. In fact, a very considerable force of somewhat disorganized Belgian troops from Havre were landed on August 31st under cover of this Brigade, and, had the situation developed as was feared on the 25th, there is no doubt that more effective forces would have followed. In short, the Allies retained the option of defending the town should they so decide.

By the end of August, however, the intelligence reports made it fairly clear that no immediate descent on the Channel ports need be feared, and, partly for this reason, partly to free the Naval covering force for more urgent tasks, the Marine Brigade was suddenly ordered on the night of the 31st–1st to re-embark. Though the force was deployed on a seven-mile front, and two hundred tons of baggage and stores had to be loaded on the transports, the task was accomplished in just over twelve hours. Reporting on the operations as a whole, the Admiralty stated that "the promptitude with which the Brigade was embarked, landed and re-embarked was highly creditable." Considering the limitations of the force in the matter of training and organization the tribute was well earned.

Sir Julian Corbett speaks of this expedition—it was really hardly more than an excursion—as having had little "material effect on the campaign."† As a statement of fact no one will quarrel with this verdict. The measure was one of precaution. When the threat to Ostend did not materialize, the precaution of providing cover for a landing of trained troops at that point became superfluous, and the Marine Brigade was naturally withdrawn.

By the middle of September the situation had profoundly

* Corbett, "Naval Operations," Vol. I., page 98.
† Corbett, "Naval Operations," Vol. I., page 124.

changed—for the better, as far as concerned the operations of
our own expeditionary force, but for the worse, as regards the
threat to the Channel ports. These were now clearly menaced
from two quarters. The Germans in their advance had, according to their original plan, left behind in Belgium a strong
force under General Von Beseler to engage and defeat the
Belgian Field Army, and, having done so, to lay siege to Antwerp. This force (consisting of the 3rd Reserve Corps, the 4th
" Ersatz " Division, a " Marine Division," three " Landwehr "
Brigades and a strong quota of army troops and siege artillery)
had by now taken the field, and the Belgian Field Army was
falling back on Antwerp. In view of the Belgian losses and of
the numerical superiority of the German containing forces,
there would have been reason to fear for the safety of the ports,
even if there had been no question of co-operation between Von
Beseler and the German main armies. But, in fact, such co-
operation was just what there was reason to fear. On
September 15th the left flank of the main allied battle line was
at Noyon. The German positions on the Aisne had proved
impregnable to frontal attack, and the only way in which a
further allied advance could be effected was by repeating against
the German right the tactics of the Marne. There was, however, little or no hope that the manœuvre, so successful
before, would have any similar results. Then, the enemy's
right, attacked by Manoury, could not be reinforced. Foch in
the centre had seen to that. The result was a rapid and immediate retreat ; the alternative would have been disaster.
Now, it was almost certain that any threat to the German right
would lead only to a counter turning movement, executed by
troops drawn from other parts of the German line. This, as we
know, is precisely what happened, and, within a few hours of the
opening of the attack near Noyon, it became clear that the opposing armies were so evenly balanced, and so equally served
by their communications, that the position would not be stabilized till one army or the other reached the coast. Who would
reach the coast first and at what point ? If the French ports
were to be saved, we must prevent the junction of the German
right and Von Beseler's force until our own left had reached
the Belgian coast.

It was in these circumstances that Sir John French drew the
attention of the authorities at home to the necessity for safe-

guarding the Belgian coast,* and that on September 18th† the French Government made a formal request to London for the intervention of a British force, based on Calais or Dunkirk, to demonstrate against the menacing German right. To the British Admiralty, as well as to the War Office, the plan commended itself, for our short experience of St. Nazaire had strengthened the conviction that the Channel ports alone provided a satisfactory base for our growing army overseas. Seldom indeed was the inter-relation of naval and military strategy more complete. The military situation required a threat to the German communications : the naval situation made it imperative to relieve the threat to our own. Where, however, were to be found the troops necessary for even the most audacious demonstration against Von Beseler and the German right ?

The enterprise and enthusiasm which had raised and equipped the two Naval Brigades in a week was not to be damped by the request to organize a field force in the same time. The Naval Brigades themselves were still immobile. The men were there, but the organization, the training, the mobility were lacking. The Marine Brigade had, however, been reorganized with success : the more elderly reservists had moreover been replaced by younger men (though some of them were only recruits), and the force had enjoyed the benefits of a fortnight's field training. The War Office offered the necessary army troops (including the Oxfordshire Hussars, a famous yeomanry regiment), and a detachment of Royal Engineers. This force was ordered to Dunkirk, and was disembarked by September 21st. Sir George Aston was again in command, with Major Powys Sketchley, R.M.L.I., afterwards, and until his death in the summer of 1916, so well known a figure in the Naval Division as Brigade Major, and Lt.-Colonel H. D. Farquharson as A.A. & Q.M.G.

To enable the force to demonstrate over a wide area, and so keep the enemy in doubt as to the size of the concentration, extreme mobility was essential. A force of armoured cars belonging to the R.N.A.S., but manned by two hundred specially selected men of the R.M.A. and R.M.L.I. (fifty from

* For a fuller account see " 1914 " by the Earl of Ypres, 2nd Edition, pages 155-156.

† Corbett : " Naval Operations," Vol. I., pages 169-170.

each Marine Division), under Major Armstrong, R.M.L.I., which had been operating independently under Commander Samson at Dunkirk since September 12th,* was placed under Sir George Aston's command; arrangements were made for more cars and motor transport to follow. Among this motor transport were a number of motor omnibuses from London, whose drivers had been hurriedly enlisted as Royal Marines at Chatham.†

The idea underlying the operations of this heterogeneous force recalls, and was perhaps prompted by, the historic exploits of Stonewall Jackson and Stewart in the Shenandoah Valley. The almost insuperable administrative difficulties created by the despatch of a composite force for which the War Office was not responsible, and which had no regular supply service of its own, marred in some degree the execution of a very promising conception. Things improved when Major Richardson went over a few days later, and gave the force the benefit of his wider experience of practical administration; but the infantry force remained necessarily almost immobile. The presence in the Marine Brigade of 687 recruits partly accounted for their inactivity : mainly, it was the absence of any reliable information of the enemy movements which held them to their ground, since, with its ponderous administrative arrangements, the force could not afford a false move.

The armoured cars were, however, faced with no comparable difficulties. Till the composite force arrived, they had been based on Dunkirk, and had patrolled a very wide area, embracing Amiens, Albert, Arras, Courtrai and Ghent. Later, their headquarters were moved to Morbecque near Hazebrouck, from which advanced base patrols, operating in sections of from three to ten cars each, went out continuously searching for German cavalry detachments, and engaging them wherever possible. In one such action near Douai, towards the end of September, Lieut. Williams, R.M.A., was wounded.

---

* These cars had been sent overseas in the first instance to protect the R.N.A.S. base at Dunkirk, from which point Commander Samson was operating against the German air bases nearest to England. The employment of armoured cars was a new departure destined to have very far-reaching results.

† These buses remained in France attached to the Army until the Autumn of 1915, and were the pioneers of the Army 'bus companies. Their record is of interest as that of another singularly fruitful and sensible improvisation in which the Admiralty was first in the field.

Meanwhile, the Infantry had remained at Dunkirk, except for the Portsmouth Battalion, which had been sent, at the urgent request of the French, to Lille, to cover the withdrawal of a number of isolated French detachments. At the end of the month, however, Sir George Aston was invalided, and Colonel Paris, C.B., R.M.A., was sent out to take his place. He at once (September 27th) moved his headquarters to Cassel, and there concentrated all three battalions of his Brigade, less the recruits whom he left at Dunkirk. Cassel was a commanding position across the Belgian frontier, far better suited to form the advanced base for the more serious operations which seemed now likely to develop ; and, by shedding his recruits, Col. Paris further strengthened his force.

The dominating facts in the situation on the evening of September 30th were that the main armies in the race for the sea had reached Lens, that the Germans were closing on Antwerp, and that the effects of their bombardment on the outer forts showed that it was only a question of days before these positions would have to be abandoned. The French had, in these circumstances, already offered to send a force of 15,000 men to operate against the flank of the besieging army, if the British Government would co-operate, and Lord Kitchener, through Sir Francis Villiers (British Minister at Brussels), had suggested despatching as soon as possible the 7th and 3rd Cavalry Divisions, if the French support could be relied on. Neither Division (nor indeed the promised French contingent) was ready for immediate service, but till October 2nd the plan held the field.

On that day the situation changed suddenly for the worse. The Germans broke through the outer line of the Antwerp forts, driving the Belgian Field Army back on the line of the Nethe, and the Belgian Government decided to abandon the defence of the position to the fortress troops. This decision was tantamount—so much can be said with conviction in the light of the happenings on October 9th—to the surrender of the fortress within at most three days, and probably sooner.*

The surrender of Antwerp at this juncture would have involved the gravest possible danger of losing the Channel

* For a detailed account of the capacity of the fortress troops and of their actual performances on October 8th and 9th, see " La Défense de la position fortifiée d'Anvers en 1914," by Lieut.-General Deguise, the Governor of Antwerp from September 8th till its surrender.

ports; for the junction of Von Beseler and the main German army (by this time at Lille), which must have meant the definite outflanking of the allied line, could hardly then have been prevented. " It was a position which, for naval reasons alone, could not be accepted without an effort to prevent the breakdown of our plans."*

There was one way out of the difficulty, though one only. If the Belgian Government could be induced to modify their decision to withdraw the Field Army, the German plans, which were clearly based on an attack from the East, and not on an enveloping movement culminating (in accordance with the plan prepared in peace time by the German staff) in an attack from the South, would be inevitably delayed for a definite number of days. The reason for this was that the Belgians would have to be driven from the line of the Nethe before the guns could be got into position to bombard the inner forts, the ramparts and the city. Insufficient attention has been paid to this fortunate modification of the German plan, which had so signal an influence on the situation at this date. Yet the reason of it is avowed in the German monograph on this campaign.† Von Beseler was afraid of the menace to his flank, constituted by the presence of allied troops at Ostend and Dunkirk, and the threat of a further intervention. The activities of the Marine Brigade and, perhaps still more, of Commander Samson and his " motor bandits," as they had come to be known, had had in fact precisely the intended effect. Thus the time was now come to take advantage of the delusions under which the enemy was labouring, to bring into operation, if possible, even at the eleventh hour, the plan already in being for the relief of Antwerp; or, in any event, by delaying the fall of the fortress, to perform the more vital service of saving the ports.

It was in these circumstances, not to initiate an unpremeditated adventure, but to save from premature abandonment a plan of operation inaugurated at the instance of the French High Command, that the First Lord of the Admiralty undertook, at the request of the Government as conveyed to him by

* Corbett: "Naval Operations," Vol. I., pages 183-184; the "plans" were, of course, those for the employment of the 7th and 3rd Cavalry Divisions in conjunction with the French in the relief of Antwerp.

† " Antwerpen, 1914," Erich von Tschischwitz: Berlin, 1921.

Lord Kitchener, his much discussed visit to Antwerp, on the evening of October 2nd.

Concrete promises of support were required of Mr. Winston Churchill before the Belgians were induced to hold their hand. But, on the understanding that the Marine Brigade was to go immediately to reinforce the line of the Nethe, that the two Naval Brigades from England would follow at once, and that, if no more substantial aid could be sent, the Belgian Government should be free to review the situation in three days' time (on October 6th), the matter was arranged. In these circumstances, and anticipating Government approval which was subsequently forthcoming, General Paris received orders, early on the morning of October 3rd, to take his infantry to Antwerp.

The Brigade entered Antwerp, without difficulty, by the railway running through Ghent, Lokeren, and St. Nicholas, and detrained at Edeghen, a suburb some four miles due south of the town, at 1 a.m. on October 4th. They moved at 9 a.m. into trenches on the Western bank of the Little Nethe, immediately north of Lierre, where they relieved the 21st Belgian Regiment.

The position in which the Brigade found themselves formed, with the line of the Scheldt as far as Termonde, the key to the remaining Antwerp defences; for the line covered the breach made by the enemy in the main (outer) defensive position. Once the river lines had fallen, nothing could save the town from intensive bombardment. On the contrary, while they held, the position was less definitely hopeless than has been imagined. The trouble was that the Belgian Field Army was exhausted, that there was virtually no efficient artillery support for the infantry, and that the trenches, at any rate on the line of the Nethe, were not only inadequate to sustain a fierce bombardment, and without any covered communications, but so sited as not to command the crossings of the river. It is, nevertheless, clear that the forcing of the line of the Nethe and the Scheldt by Termonde was a task to which the enemy would have to devote serious attention, so long as those lines were resolutely defended.

The battle on the Nethe was already in progress when the Marines entered the trenches, on the morning of October 4th, but the line was intact. The forces under General Paris's command consisted, in addition to the Marine Brigade, of the 7th Regt. Belgian Infantry, the 1st Carabineers, some machine-gun

detachments of the R.N.A.S. and a detachment of Royal
Engineers under Captain Rooke, R.E. The 7th Regiment and
the Chatham, Plymouth and Deal Battalions R.M.L.I. took
over the front-line trenches, each battalion forming its own
local reserve ; the 1st Carabineers and the Portsmouth Battalion were in Brigade reserve. October 4th passed quietly;
but, during the night of the 4th-5th, the enemy brought up
field guns to the opposite bank of the river, and, firing into our
advanced trenches at close range, compelled a retirement to
the main line of defence, 300 yards further back. At the same
time, enemy scouts crossed the river into Lierre, in the sector
held by the 7th Belgian Regiment. On the afternoon of the
5th, the enemy achieved a more important success, when they
crossed the Great Nethe (which was not under fire from the
trenches on the west bank) in force, and drove back the Belgian
troops on General Paris's right flank. Later in the afternoon,
the position was partially restored, on the initiative of General
Paris, the original line of trenches being retaken by the
Belgians, in a counter attack " gallantly led by Colonel Tier-
chon, 2nd Chasseurs ; "* but the Germans could not be dislodged
from their holding on the west bank of the river. Later, on
the same day, the enemy crossed the Lower Nethe north of
Lierre—on the left of the sector held by the Deal Battalion.

The situation was at once reviewed by the Belgian General
Staff, but it was decided, very late on the evening of the 5th,
to fight on, and to make a determined attempt to throw the
enemy back across the Nethe. This decision was taken, and
the orders consequent on it were issued, without consultation
with General Paris. An attack to have had any chance of
success would have had to be carefully organized, well supported
by artillery, and carried out by fresh troops. As it was, the
order for the attack reached General Paris at 1.15 a.m. The
troops under his command formed the only body of troops in
the line who were not exhausted by previous fighting ; but they
were also there, primarily, to stiffen the defence, and, in the last
resort, to cover a retreat. To risk this small body of troops in
a night attack, for which no preparations had been made, seemed
in the circumstances impossible. In the result, the attack was
carried out by the Belgians alone, and was at first partially
successful. By 11 a.m., however, on the 6th, German counter-

* General Paris's dispatch to the Admiralty dated October 31st, 1914.

attacks deprived us of our gains, and the line of the Nethe became untenable.

General Paris decided at once on a withdrawal to a position intermediate between the river line and the inner forts, and the retirement was begun, under a very heavy bombardment, at 11 a.m. This was, superficially, a disappointing issue, and the German account goes so far as to express surprise that the British and Belgians did not persist further with their counter-attack on the night of the 5th-6th. The facts are, however, unquestionable. There were insufficient troops to fight, without adequate artillery support, more than a delaying action. Only by keeping his forces, and the Belgian troops under his command, intact, could the game of delay be at all prolonged. In the circumstances, the fact that the enemy did not dare to follow up the retirement, on the morning of the 6th, is ample justification for the decision to retire. The salient point was that, at this date, three days after that on which the Belgian Government had determined originally to withdraw the field army, the field army was still in being in front of Antwerp, holding a position sufficiently defensible at any rate to give the Germans reason to pause before renewing their advance. The share of General Paris and his force in bringing about this situation was certainly not inconsiderable. It was not on the front held by the Marines that the decisive break-through had taken place.

It will be remembered that the Marine Brigade was not the sum total of the immediate assistance promised by Mr. Winston Churchill. He had also undertaken, subject to the consent of the Cabinet, that the two untrained Naval Brigades from Walmer and Betteshanger should follow at the earliest possible date. This undertaking also had been carried out, and on this same morning the Brigades had begun to detrain at the city station.

The decision to send these Brigades cannot be seriously challenged. The promise to send them had indeed justified itself by the time it was fulfilled, for the Belgian resistance had been prolonged. If it is fairly certain that this could not have been done but for the timely arrival and judicious handling of the Marine Brigade, it is also true that the effort would not have been made but for the definite promise of further reinforcements. Moreover, the actual arrival of the Brigades created the greatest enthusiasm, and undoubtedly counteracted to some extent the then prevailing depression.

The Naval Brigades were, however, a slender asset from a military point of view, and their capacity for service in an emergency had been considerably weakened by their experiences since they left camp two days before. After a long march to Dover, the Brigades had loaded their own stores (of which too many were taken, including the men's kit-bags and officers' uniform cases), and embarked late in the evening on transports so over-crowded that many of the men were compelled to stand almost the whole time on board. Not till 12 noon, on the 5th, had the transports been able to get into Dunkirk Harbour. Since leaving camp more than twenty-four hours before, the men had had only one meal (at Dover at about noon), and that an improvised one, and when they reached Dunkirk they had to set to work at once unloading the transports, and loading up the waiting trains. In the interval, an attempt had been made by the base staff to remedy the more glaring deficiencies in kit and equipment, and 120 rounds of ammunition (which had to be carried in pockets for the most part, as few had bandoliers or haversacks) were served out. The absence of a trained staff, and the inexperience of some of the battalion and company commanders, had made the business of disembarking, issuing stores and entraining exceptionally long and tedious, and the men were thoroughly exhausted by the time they had started for Antwerp. Even in the train, the men had the strictest injunctions not to sleep lest the train was attacked. Rupert Brooke summed up a day of chaotic improvisation as a " very tragic and amusing affair," from which we may infer that for some at least of the junior officers the day brought a certain measure of disillusion.

The first train for Antwerp, consisting of advance parties, had left the quayside at 9 p.m., but it was not till 11.30 p.m. that the last battalions of the 2nd Brigade got away.

The trains began to arrive at Antwerp in the early hours of the 6th, and the 1st Brigade, as soon as they were formed up, were marched off again to Wilryk, an eastern suburb a few miles from the station. As the men passed the station barriers many had been given tinned meat, sardines, or coffee by the civil population, and when, on arrival at Wilryk, orders were given to arrange billeting accommodation, it looked

Men of the Naval Brigades in trenches near Vieux Dieu, Antwerp,
October 7th, 1914.

as though they were going to get the essential rest. Almost
at once, however, they were ordered by Major Richardson
to Vieux Dieux, another suburb further east, near which
ran the line of the inner forts. Here, while the Brigade
were breakfasting, Mr. Winston Churchill came on the scene,
and spoke to many of the officers of the intended plan, which
was still, at this time, to hold the Germans on the line of the
Nethe, till the 7th Division and the expected French divisions
could join hands on the west of Antwerp and attack the flank
of the besieging army.

After breakfast, the Brigade got orders from the Belgian
staff to move forward to some dismantled trenches, between
the line of the inner forts and the line of the Nethe, there to
remain in reserve to what was still (at 10 a.m.) our line of
resistance.

Meanwhile the 2nd Brigade had detrained. By the time
they were ready to move off the whole city was astir, and the
scene was one of poignant humour, of romantic excitement, of
that unintelligible optimism which comes to men in any brief
respite from an incalculable menace. To the station had
come the Civic Guard and numerous officials ; as the Brigade
marched away (in this case direct to Vieux Dieux), the shops
were open, and, as in all times of public excitement, the whole
population was in the streets, fearful lest solitude might
perhaps reveal for a moment the face of truth. "Every
one cheered," writes Rupert Brooke, "and flung themselves
on us, and gave us apples and chocolate and kisses"—another
more prosaically-minded eye-witness includes also jugs of
beer in this Homeric catalogue of gifts—"and cried ' Vivent
les Anglais ' and ' Heep ! Heep ! Heep ! ' "

The enthusiasm was infectious. The doubts of the evening
dusk had given way to the resilient optimism of midday,
and so these raw battalions, without any orders, without
equipment, with but few senior officers skilled in the control
of troops in the field, and few junior officers who had been
taught anything save to be controlled with a good grace,
marched through Antwerp without more, perhaps, than a
subconscious repudiation of the cheers which acclaimed
them as seasoned troops, possessing in their bayonets the
veritable means of deliverance to a great city.

The 2nd Brigade halted on the way to Vieux Dieux for

breakfast, and eventually arrived there at about 4 p.m.
Here they found part of the 1st Brigade, which had been brought
back from the trenches in front of Vieux Dieux, on its way
to join the Marine Brigade on the new advanced position,
now being consolidated.

The retirement of General Paris's force from the Nethe
line was now completed, and the Marine Brigade and the
Belgians were entrenching on a line from Vremde to Bouchout.
General Paris had learnt of the arrival of the Naval Brigades
while the retirement was in progress, and, as soon as the situation was clearer, not knowing, of course, of the literally continuous activities of the 1st Brigade since 9 a.m. on October 4th,
he had ordered it to come up on the left of the Marines,
and extend the line across the Malines Railway.

The scene in Vieux Dieux as the 2nd Brigade arrived, and
the 1st Brigade re-entered it on the way to the front, was
a memorable one. The two brigades of British troops filled
the Square, yet, through the ranks, came endless Belgian troops
returning from the trenches. Excited staff officers shouted
indiscriminately to everybody to keep cool, guns galloped in
all directions, motor cyclists rushed through with apparently
endless dispatches, and, threading their way in humble, pitiful
groups, by by-streets and on the edges of crowds, the refugees
from the outlying villages fled from the certain, to the uncertain,
disaster. Here, too, the brigades had their first sight of war-
weary troops. Later, the Division came to know well enough
that look, which marks out men exhausted by desperate and
long-continued exposure to the risks of imminent and horrify-
ing death. The sight of the Belgian troops in Vieux Dieux
was their first introduction to the realities of war.

Amid these scenes of excitement, Commodore Henderson's
Brigade moved forward to the new position, the Drake and
Benbow Battalions going into line on the right of the Chatham,
and the Hawke and Collingwood Battalions into support to
the Marine Brigade near Château Weyninex. On the right of
the Benbow Battalion were some Belgian troops, who, however,
retired later in the evening.

More fortunate than their fellows, Commodore Backhouse's
Brigade, though less exhausted, were able, on arrival at Vieux
Dieux, to go into billets, where for a time they remained.
Already, however, grave decisions had been taken, which made

it necessary before the night was out to reconsider the dispositions of the force.

It must be understood that there were, on the morning of the 6th, no fewer than four separate bodies of troops fighting in and round Antwerp. There was the Belgian Field Army, under H.M. the King of the Belgians, the garrison of the fortress of Antwerp, under the immediate command of Lieut.-General Deguise, General Paris's advanced base force (with Belgian units attached for tactical purposes), and the two Naval brigades, who did not know, till after they arrived in Antwerp, that they were to come under General Paris's command. There were also present in Antwerp Mr. Winston Churchill, who, as First Lord of the Admiralty, stood in a special relation to the Naval and Marine brigades, and Sir Henry Rawlinson, who had been sent by Lord Kitchener to command the force which was assembling at Ostend, and which had been originally intended for the relief of Antwerp.

During the early part of October 6th, the future arrangements for the defence of Antwerp remained undecided. In pursuance of the agreement arrived at with Mr. Churchill on the 3rd, the Belgian General Staff, under whose orders came General Paris's force, had, as we have seen, continued a vigorous defence on the Nethe and, subsequently, on the Vremde line. They had also strengthened their forces on the Scheldt, and had beaten off very determined efforts of the Germans to cross the river at Schoonaerde. During the forenoon, however, the Belgian authorities had met Mr. Winston Churchill and General Rawlinson to discuss the future. The arrival of General Rawlinson's force had been delayed owing to naval difficulties, and it was not to be concentrated now till the 8th at the earliest. There was also no news of the expected French force. All this meant, in effect, that the Belgians were free to decide whether to continue the defence, or to revert to their original plan of withdrawing the Field Army. Eventually a compromise was arrived at. The Army, less the 2nd Division, would at once withdraw across the Scheldt, and ultimately, if necessary, fall back in the direction of Ostend ; but it would defend the crossings of the Scheldt as long as possible, while General Deguise, with the help of the 2nd Division of the Field Army and of General Paris's force (now increased to three brigades), would continue to man the eastern defences of the fortress. Under this arrangement, General Paris, who had now been promoted Major-General, was left in independent command of the British troops in the fortress.* The scheme for relieving the fortress was not definitely abandoned, but the loss of the line of the Nethe, and the withdrawal of the Field Army, made it virtually certain that the defence could not be prolonged sufficiently to make the scheme practicable.

During the afternoon of October 6th, the rumour of the impending departure of the Belgian Army began to circulate, and the effect on the *moral* of the remaining Belgian troops was deplorable. In these circumstances, General Paris had to consider whether it would not be wise to withdraw his force that night to the inner defences. As the afternoon drew on, the reports regarding the Belgian troops became more and more alarming, and, by the time the final decision regarding the future defence of the fortress was arrived at, the General's mind was made up, and orders were issued to Brigade Commanders for a further withdrawal to take place at 2 a.m.

While these orders were being written, Mr. Winston Churchill and General Rawlinson were with General Paris, and, after the decision had been taken, both expressed their agreement with the latter's view of the situation.

The front to which General Paris had decided to withdraw was the line of the inner forts, a very strong prepared position, consisting of eight forts covering Antwerp from the east and north-east. The right of the line was protected by the Scheldt, and the left by inundations. Between the forts were trenches, well wired and solidly constructed, with a perfect field of fire of five hundred yards. On the other hand, the trenches were old-fashioned and quite useless against modern artillery ; there were no communication trenches, and the forts could not be relied on, either as to the quality of their armament or the resolution of the garrisons. The line, however, was the best there was ; the trenches could be deepened ; and, above all, the position could, at least, not be carried by infantry assault. To hold it meant, at any rate, to impose on the enemy the delay necessary for him to bring up his guns ; or, alternatively, to

---

* His improvised Divisional Staff now consisted of Colonel Ollivant and Major Sketchley, General Staff Officers, and Major Richardson as A.A. & Q.M.G. Colonel Seely and Major Bridges were also lent to General Paris temporarily for staff duties. Beyond these officers there was no divisional organization.

force the line of the Scheldt and cut off the retreat of the garrison.

To rest the Marine Brigade, General Paris put the two Naval brigades into the trenches, the 1st R.N. Brigade on the left (Forts 2 to 5), and the 2nd R.N. Brigade on the right (Forts 5 to 8). Between Fort 8 and the Scheldt were Belgian fortress troops, relieved later by the Chatham Battalion.

The night of October 6th-7th passed off quietly, there being very little shelling, and that directed mainly against the houses behind the line. The only " incident " was on the Anson front, where two guns in the fort on their left flank burst, causing an ominous and significant panic among the Belgian garrison. The remaining guns in the fort were then manned by naval gun crews, picked from the ranks of the battalion.

Still the Germans hesitated to follow up the retirement, and, on the morning of the 7th, the staff were able to send up rations to the men in motor-buses, which drew up in front of our lines. So quiet, indeed, was the situation that many officers drove back into Antwerp on derelict carts, which were to be found behind the lines, to buy food and drink for their company messes. Meanwhile, officers of greater seniority unburdened their minds by writing field messages with ceaseless activity. Throughout the day, men were kept busily engaged, under the superintendence of the engineers, in digging shrapnel trenches in the rear of the main position, though the shortage of tools prevented any great progress being made except on the right. Only an occasional shell passing overhead into Antwerp reminded the troops of the stern realities of their situation. Remote, however, as its dangers still appeared at the time, the position of the Brigades was far from comfortable. They had no suitable cooking arrangements ; the men had nowhere to sleep, the trenches themselves were overcrowded ; there was no support line, and meals were irregular and scanty. Moreover, the entire ignorance of active service conditions on land, which was common to all ranks of the Brigades, made the situation, which to trained troops would have appeared comparatively peaceful, unnecessarily trying. The men in some battalions were being worked too hard, having regard to what they might be called on to face ; and the golden rule that a soldier, on front-line duty, when he is not working should be sleeping, was not being, and had not been, observed. Particularly was this true of the officers, many of whom, for absolutely no reason, came back to England, after the Antwerp expedition, without a single proper eight hours' rest to their credit.

The first half of the night of October 7th-8th brought no change in the local situation. The front was still clear, and there was no suspicion of any attack. Towards 2 a.m., however, a German patrol was seen in front of our wire on the Drake Battalion front, and the firing from the Drake trenches led to an outburst of rapid fire along the front of several battalions to the right and left. This incident, reported to have led to the death of one cow, did little credit, no doubt, to the measure of control exercised by some of the officers; but many parallels could be found for it in early experiences of most formations, and it certainly cannot be regarded as a conclusive proof that few of the men in the Division knew how to load or fire a rifle.

Order had barely been restored after this incident, when a desultory bombardment was opened on our trenches, which continued for some hours. The shelling was mostly by six and eight inch howitzers, but was neither heavy nor well directed ; on the 2nd Brigade front, in fact, the casualties were extremely light—only some half-dozen men being wounded. The 1st Brigade lost rather more, one officer, Lt.-Colonel Maxwell (commanding the Collingwood Battalion) and three men being killed, and some twenty men wounded; but, thanks largely to the progress made in improving the trench system on this front, the damage was less than might have been expected.* The bombardment, however, finally shattered the *moral* of the remaining fortress troops in this part of the line, and Forts 2, 3 and 4 had to be taken over, wholly or in part, by officers and men from the Naval Brigades.

Nevertheless, there was nothing in what had occurred on this front to make our position untenable. The serious happenings were those on the Scheldt at Schoonaerde, where the Germans, after severe fighting, had secured a footing across the river on the evening of the 7th, and, during the night, had thrown across more than a brigade. It was this that made

* The medical arrangements were in the skilled hands of Fleet-Surgeon Finch, R.N., and, when tested on this occasion, proved excellent.

it clear to General Paris that the Belgian Field Army was
nearing the limits of its powers of resistance, and that the
time when it would be necessary to withdraw was therefore
approaching. Accordingly, at 7 a.m. on the morning of the
8th, he informed General Rawlinson by telephone that he would
probably be forced to withdraw that night. Already, the
previous day, the Brigade staffs had been warned to reconnoitre the routes to the lower (pontoon) bridge at Burght,
and Colonel Bridges had, in conjunction with Major Richardson,
made certain preliminary arrangements, and had secured
boats to take the Division across, in the event of the bridges
being destroyed. The only thing that remained was to secure,
if possible, trains to meet the Division outside Antwerp, and
this was put in hand by General Rawlinson, who sent Colonel
Fairholme to the Belgian (Field Army) Headquarters at Selzaete to make the best possible arrangements.

It was not, however, necessary as yet for General Paris
to make an irrevocable decision. Belgian rearguards were
still covering the approaches to the main roads and railways leading from Antwerp to the coast, and the longer his
force could stay the better. The only immediate danger,
indeed, seemed to be from the north, where, according to the
Belgian reports which reached General Deguise, the Germans
had got round the flank of our line and captured Forts 1 and
2. Colonel Seely and Major Bridges found, however, on going
personally to the 1st Brigade line, that no Germans had been
seen, and that the forts, though abandoned by the Belgians,
had been taken over by Naval gunners from the ranks of the
Brigade. In the circumstances, there still seemed a hope of
prolonging the defence for a little time; and it was agreed
that, so long as the flanks were safe, and the bombardment
along the line not sufficiently serious to necessitate withdrawal
on that ground alone, the Division would remain. Only in
the event of any change for the worse in the situation on
the northern bank of the Scheldt, or on the left of the 1st
Brigade, would the Division withdraw.

There was indeed every reason for remaining to the last
possible moment. The popular idea that the position was
untenable, and that it was only by good fortune that anyone
escaped, has no shadow of foundation in fact. The lines of
the inner forts, and the Belgian positions across the Scheldt,

could be held for a good many hours (if not for two or three days) longer, if only the Belgians were ready to remain in their trenches, to man their forts, and to fire their guns. Moreover, though nothing could have saved the city from ultimate destruction except a further intervention, such intervention was still possible. General Paris was, in the circumstances, bound to remain as long as the Belgians stood to their remaining positions, and so safeguarded for him a line of retreat.

During the afternoon of the 8th, however, General Paris, who had moved his headquarters so as to be in the closest touch with General Deguise, saw reports coming in of continual defections of the Belgian fortress troops, which made it clear that the conditions, on which alone he could remain, were no longer being fulfilled. His written instructions (which he had received from Mr. Winston·Churchill) were imperative. " He will exert his utmost efforts to secure the prolongation of this defence . . . and, secondly, he will insist on being excluded from any capitulation or surrender, and will in all circumstances keep and consider himself and his force free to make their way to the left bank of the Scheldt in order to rejoin Sir Henry Rawlinson's command or any other British force, naval or military." If the retreat of the Division were further postponed, the freedom to withdraw across the Scheldt would be lost, and the exclusion of the force from the now inevitable surrender would become impossible.

At 5 p.m. on the 8th, therefore, the final decision was taken, and reported to Mr. Winston Churchill by telephone, as the decision of the Commander on the spot, and accepted as such by him without question.

The order for retirement was issued between 5.30 and 6 p.m. The original of the order cannot be traced, though it was sent to the Admiralty by General Paris. The tenour of the instructions is, however, known. The 1st Brigade was to go by the Malines Gate to the ·city pontoon bridge, and thence to the rendezvous—Zwyndrecht ; the 2nd and Marine Brigades were to go their direct routes to the pontoon bridge at Burght, and then to Zwyndrecht. The Portsmouth Battalion of Marines was to act as a rearguard, moving off in rear of all details. All Brigades were to leave *on receipt of the order*.

The order for retirement had not been unexpected. The

different commanding officers had already been warned on the 6th and 7th to reconnoitre the road to the pontoon bridge, and the new route now assigned to the 1st Brigade, being through the town, was easy to find. Unfortunately, the staff officer, charged with the duty of delivering this order to Commodore Henderson, delivered it instead to Commander Campbell, of the Drake Battalion ; and intimated to him, at the same time, that his brigade had already been notified and were on the point of departure. The result was that, whereas the 2nd Brigade, the Marine Brigade and the Drake Battalion left as soon as possible, Commodore Henderson and the Hawke, Benbow and Collingwood Battalions only learnt of the order to retreat, as the result of a visit from Colonel Ollivant* at about 7.15, and were, even then, not informed as to the vital point that the retirement was to take effect on its receipt.

The result of these mistakes was that, while the 2nd and Marine Brigades were able to reach the bridge at Burght at about 9.30 p.m. in good order, and, while the Drake Battalion reached the lower bridge as early as 9 o'clock, Commodore Henderson did not arrange to retire till 9.30, and, for various reasons, did not start till even later. The Portsmouth Marines, detailed as rearguard to the division, were, of course, longer delayed, and did not leave till some short time after 10.30 p.m.

The order had been for all three brigades to rendezvous at Zwyndrecht, a western suburb of Antwerp, about 14 miles from the centre of the line of the forts. From there, General Paris had intended to march to Beveren-Waes, not more than seven miles ahead, in the hope of getting a train, and, failing that, to continue his march westwards, through Stekene and Moerbeke. This plan was based on incorrect information regarding trains, for a message sent by Colonel Dallas from Selzaete (telling General Paris that the line from St. Nicholas was not safe because of the presence of Germans at Lokeren, and that he must therefore go to St. Gillaes-Waes), had unfortunately miscarried. The true situation became known to General Paris only during the course of the retreat.

The march of the two brigades and of the Drake Battalion

---

* Colonel Ollivant was the staff officer detailed to take the order to the Marine Brigade. It was after doing this that he had called at the 1st Brigade H.Q.

to the river, a distance of some seven or eight miles, had been accomplished without much difficulty, and there was no interference whatever by the enemy. This was perhaps because a detachment, which had approached our lines just before the retreat, had been fired on, and had retired, with the conviction that the defence of the fortress was being continued. Yet the occasional shells falling in Antwerp, the theatrical reflection of great fires, and the noise of continuous explosions, seemed to cast over the deserted streets an atmosphere of calamity, and gave to the weary battalions some faint warning of what they might have to face across the river.

Here, on the roads to Zwyndrecht, was a scene not indeed unparalleled in the annals of modern savagery but never surpassed in the pity it inspired. It seemed as if the whole population of Antwerp, women and children, priests and nuns, the sick, the aged and the infirm, had fled from their homes, and yet, momentarily indifferent to the consequences, they must halt ever and again to look back at the burning ruin of their hopes and their aspirations. To the other sorrows of exile, was added the threat of an armed and hostile pursuit. Mixed up with the procession of fugitives, were men driving cattle, and mules and peasants' carts, fleeing in an interminable procession along the same road; and each man, in his haste, impeding the progress of the others.

Amid these scenes it was impossible, from the start, to maintain any military formation. Battalions got separated from each other, and, as the hours passed, companies and even platoons had to fight their way along for themselves. Officers and men had been exhausted (to some extent needlessly, it is true, but the fault was not theirs) before they started. By the time they reached Zwyndrecht, about 11.30 p.m., they had marched, under the most impossible conditions, for nearly six hours. Some of the men had no water-bottles, and all carried ammunition in their pockets, which chafed unbearably as time went on. Acting on very correct instructions, many started the retreat carrying also boxes of ammunition, trench stores not lightly to be abandoned to the enemy, and these boxes were carried many miles, with a remarkable fidelity.

Yet, by the time the rendezvous was reached (the Drake Battalion arrived first, but was closely followed by the other brigades), the limit of endurance seemed near.

After a halt (during which time General Paris received reports from his staff officers that all three brigades were present), the column marched on along the St. Nicholas Road; and it was not till two hours' later, when they got past Beveren-Waes, that they learnt that they could only get trains from St. Gillaes-Waes.

Now the worst of the journey began. The new line of march was off the main road along narrow lanes, and the press and confusion was redoubled. As buses and motors made futile endeavours to pass along the line of march, and only succeeded in driving the men off the road, and then coming to a standstill themselves, the confusion soon bordered on chaos. To understand the scene in these last hours, we must see through the enveloping darkness not battalions of trained men, used to the unceasing fatigues of war, marching along recognizable roads; but, rather, groups of tired and hungry men, painfully cutting out a path for themselves along narrow lanes, through the throng of refugees, to which every hour and every path opening into the line of march added its tale of panic and confusion.

Inevitable that, in scenes such as this, stories should spread of men throwing away their equipment, of officers losing their men, of men refusing to acknowledge constituted authority. Almost all such stories were false. The battalions that started the march finished it, and finished it without loss. The head of the columns reached St. Gillaes-Waes at 7 a.m., and the last had entrained by nine o'clock. Having regard to the incalculable circumstances, the lack of adequate equipment and food, the raw condition of the men, and the utter inexperience of many of the senior and junior officers, there was much that was creditable in this achievement. Save for the mistake already explained, which lost the best part of four battalions, but was due in no way either to any defect in General Paris's plans for the retreat, or to the admitted fact that the battalions themselves were untrained, the dispatch of the Naval Brigades to Antwerp would not have excited popular criticism. What is still more important, it would not have obscured so fatally the true history of the Antwerp operations, in which the Naval brigades played only a small part, and that not a part which depended for its execution on any military qualities. They were sent by request to fulfil a promise, and they fulfilled it.

3*

The less equable fortunes of the Hawke, Collingwood, Benbow and Portsmouth Marine Battalions must now be told.

As we have said, Commodore Henderson, after Colonel Ollivant's visit, had ordered the 1st R.N. Brigade to retire at 9.30 p.m. Some delay occurred in arranging for the Portsmouth Marines to cover this retirement, but eventually a start was made, at about 10.15 p.m. The Hawke Battalion got away first and crossed the river (though by the upper bridge at Burght and not as intended by the city bridge) at about midnight. The departure of the Benbow and Collingwood Battalions was, however, delayed still further, and by the time Commodore Henderson and his staff, who were with these battalions, reached the river, the bridge had been destroyed. Colonel Bridges' foresight in providing boats for an emergency saved the situation, and it was in these that the party crossed, followed shortly afterwards by Colonel Luard's battalion.

The road from Burght to Zwyndrecht, where Commodore Henderson still hoped to find the rest of the Division, was by now comparatively clear; and all might yet have been well, if the three Naval battalions had not halted at Zwyndrecht for more than two hours, while Commodore Henderson, whose car had been commandeered by a staff officer, and who was thus without any means of getting into personal touch with General Paris, tried to get news. When, at last, the three battalions started for St. Gillaes-Waes, it was nearly 5 a.m. From the available records it appears that partly as the result of the confusion on the roads, partly, perhaps, owing to the variable quality of the staff work, carried on under almost impossible conditions, mainly owing to the extreme physical exhaustion of the men,* these battalions lost all cohesion. This must certainly have been the case, if we are right in stating that details of the 1st Brigade reached St. Gillaes as early as 11.30 a.m. on the 9th, while others did not reach till 3.45 p.m. This may have been unavoidable; but it is, nevertheless, certain that had the 1st Brigade—only some 1,500 men in all—maintained as much cohesion as did the 2nd and Marine Brigades, they might have begun to entrain at St. Gillaes-Waes at 2 p.m.,

---

* This brigade had throughout been subjected to more severe exertions than the 2nd Brigade, and the reckless way in which the strength of the men had been used was now a fatal element in the situation.

and have got away before the enemy threat to the railway had developed sufficiently to be regarded as a menace to their line of retreat. As it was, a report (not, as it turned out, a correct one) reached St. Gillaes just as the 1st Brigade had entrained, that the enemy had crossed the southern railway at Lokeren, and had already cut the line at Moerbeke, a station a little way down the line.

Meanwhile the rearguard (Portsmouth) battalion, which had taken a different route, had arrived at St. Nicholas, only to learn, as General Paris had learnt some ten hours before, that the Germans were at Lokeren. Colonel Luard decided to march to Kemseke, *i.e.*, one station further than St. Gillaes, acting on information, received from Belgian sources, that no trains were running from any nearer station. His battalion, curiously enough, had picked up some six hundred stragglers from the Naval battalions, under Lieut. Crossman, R.N., but the column, though naturally exhausted by their experience, managed to reach Kemseke some time after 8 p.m.

Almost at this hour, the 1st Brigade, which had undertaken the shorter march to St. Gillaes, crossed the Dutch frontier, with the result that the Hawke, Benbow and Collingwood battalions, with the Brigade Staff, were interned. Acting on information, misleading, as it turned out, as to the strength of the threat to his line of retreat, Commodore Henderson had felt it his duty to save his command from useless casualties and apparently inevitable surrender. His decision was subsequently upheld by the Admiralty and the Government.

It would, indeed, have been one of the ironies of war had the stragglers from his command, who were at almost the same hour entraining at Kemseke, made good their escape. But this was not to be. The train from Kemseke had only got as far as Moerbeke (reached about 10 p.m.) when it was derailed. The Marines, who formed no more than half the complement of the train, at once got out, and rallied round their officers. The R.N.V.R. details, without officers, and, for the reasons already described, in a hopeless state of physical exhaustion, mostly remained asleep in the train. A few, however, under Lieut. Crossman, R.N., got out, and joined a party of Marines under Major French and Captain (then Lieut.) Gowney, who had opened fire on the German detachment.

Under cover of the fire, Colonel Luard and a number of his men marched forward along the railway, and many more could have escaped. Unfortunately, however, the majority had got out on the far side of the train, and, hurrying in the wrong direction, were surrounded and captured. In the circumstances, Major French and the covering party were compelled to retire, leaving behind some wounded, including Lieut. Crossman, and the R.N.V.R. details, who, to the number of 7 officers and 950 men, were captured by a hardly superior German force, which immediately retreated with its prisoners.

The train itself, with the refugees, was taken on later into safety by a Belgian officer, and many Belgian troops passed down the line as late as the morning of October 10th.

Colonel Luard, Major French (who was awarded the D.S.O. for his services on this occasion), Captain Gowney (who was awarded the D.S.C.), and approximately half the other officers and men of the Portsmouth Battalion made good their escape by road to Selzaete, a fact which shows that the German threat to the line of retreat was even now, on the night of October 9th-10th, not very serious. Further evidence of this is to be found in the success with which Lieut. Grant, R.N.V.R.,* and forty men of the Benbow Battalion made their way along the frontier, and also reached Selzaete on the 10th.

As regards the general conduct of the operations, Sir John French's dispatch says the final word. " From a comprehensive review of all the circumstances," he gave it as his opinion that " the force of Marines and Naval Brigades which assisted in the defence of Antwerp was handled by General Paris with great skill and boldness."†

And, after all, what was the cost of these operations in comparison with their results ? Antwerp did not fall, thanks to British intervention, till October 10th; by that time Sir Henry Rawlinson was in position at Ghent with a substantial

---

* This officer was awarded the D.S.C. for a fine exploit in bringing these men through. Sub-Lieut. Modin, of the same battalion (who also came through on the 10th), was awarded the same distinction for displaying a similar resolution.

† The question of the Naval Division is, of course, quite independent of the merits or demerits of the plan for relieving Antwerp. If the scheme advocated by the Earl of Ypres in his book " 1914 " had been adopted, it would still have been essential to prolong the defence of Antwerp in order to give the scheme a chance of success.

force, the Belgian Field Army had retreated and rested, and the left wing of our Expeditionary Force was at Bailleul. The result was that the three forces could stand on the line of the Yser, and bar for ever the road to Calais, Boulogne and Dunkirk. For this decisive success had been sacrificed the lives of 7 officers and 53 men ; 3 officers and 135 men had been wounded ; 37 officers and 1,442 men had been interned, and 5 officers and 931 men had fallen into the hands of the enemy. It is impossible to speak lightly of such losses, but the sacrifice, less than was exacted in many minor and fruitless engagements, was certainly not in vain.

CHAPTER III

THE TIME OF PREPARATION

WHEN the Naval Division returned from Antwerp (they had been re-embarked from Ostend on the 10th and 11th), and their losses became known, there was a virulent outcry. The true facts of the situation in Belgium and of the movement of our main army to the North could not be made public, and critics were able to point to the fall of Antwerp, and the loss of some three thousand officers and men, as evidence of the inefficiency of the Division, and the incompetence of those who directed its employment.

Challenging this ill-informed criticism, Mr. Winston Churchill issued to the Division the following message :

" The First Lord welcomes the Royal Naval Division home, on its return from active service. Officers and men of all ranks and ratings have acquitted themselves admirably, and have thoroughly justified the confidence reposed in them. The loss of a portion of the 1st Brigade, through a mistake, in no way reflects upon the quality or character of the Division.

" The Brigade of Royal Marines, throughout the operations, sustained fully—by their firmness, discipline and courage— the traditions of the corps. It is not necessary to say more than this. The Naval Brigades bore themselves admirably under the artillery fire of the enemy, and it is to be regretted that no opportunities of closer contact with his infantry were afforded them.

" The dispatch of the Naval Brigades to Antwerp has interrupted, for a time, the progress of their instruction and training. They were chosen because the need for them was urgent and bitter ; because mobile troops could not be spared for fortress duties ; because they were the nearest and could be embarked the quickest ; and because their training, although incomplete, was as far advanced as that of a large portion, not only of the forces defending Antwerp, but of the enemy forces attacking.

" The Naval Division was sent to Antwerp, not as an isolated incident, but as part of a large operation for the relief of the city. Other and more powerful considerations prevented this being carried through. The defence of the inner lines of Antwerp could have been maintained for some days ; and the Naval Division only withdrew when ordered to do so in obedience to the general strategic situation, and not on account of any attack or pressure by the enemy. The prolongation of the defence, due to the arrival of the Division, enabled the ships in the harbour to be rendered useless and many steps of importance to be taken.

" It is too early yet to judge what effect the delaying, even for five or six days, of at least 60,000 Germans before Antwerp may have had upon the fortunes of the general battle to the southward. It was certainly powerful and helpful. Apart from the military experiences, which have been invaluable, the Division have been the witnesses of the ruthlessness of the German foe towards a small and innocent State. These facts should inspire all ranks to fit themselves in the shortest possible time for further service in the field, not merely as fortress, but as mobile units.

" The Belgian people will never forget that the men of the Royal Navy and Royal Marines were with them in their darkest hour of misery, as, please God, they may also be with them when Belgium is restored to her own by the Armies of the Allies."

This pronouncement failed to convince the First Lord's political opponents, but set at rest present uncertainty as to the future of the Division. The decision to train the Naval and Marine Brigades as a mobile division was to be persisted in.

The first step was to open recruiting for three new battalions, to take the place of the interned Hawke, Collingwood and Benbow Battalions, and to organize the Divisional depot for their training. The next was to create, at the same depot, reserves to supply the Division in the field ; and then to provide for the reinforcement, reorganization and training of

the five Naval battalions which remained in being. Last, but
not least, it was necessary to organize and equip the Divisional
troops.   When the time came, it was proposed to concentrate
the entire Division for brigade and divisional training at a new
camp at Blandford.   This, it was hoped, would be early in the
new year.

The twofold task, which fell to the Crystal Palace Depot
under this programme, of training officers and non-commissioned
officers, and specialists of all kinds, as the nucleus of an instructional staff ; and of organizing simultaneously three new
battalions and three reserve battalions, was a heavy one.   The
fact, however, that the whole Division could be served by one
depot* meant that, with skilful organization, the minimum of
administrative and instructional staffs could produce the
maximum result.   To Sir Richard Williams Bulkeley, the Commodore in charge of the Crystal Palace Depot, to Lt.-Colonel
Ramsden, R.M., the Chief Military Instructor, and above
all to Lieut. (now Lt.-Colonel) J. H. Levey, the Adjutant
of the instructional staff, no small measure of praise is due for
the way in which the many problems were solved.   It would
no doubt have been possible (and to have done so might well
have modified the rather indifferent attitude of the military
authorities) to beg, borrow or steal a nucleus of trained officers
and N.C.O.'s from elsewhere, and to drill the thousands of
untrained civilians into something resembling a military formation.   This course was often suggested, but happily it was
not adopted.   Instead, it was decided to find among the
thousands of keen and physically well-equipped civilians
waiting training at the depot, not only the subaltern and the
private with a rifle, but the leaders of companies and battalions,
regimental sergeant-majors, quartermasters, drill sergeants,
musketry instructors ; the brains and sinews, and not merely
the flesh and blood, of battalions, brigades and depots.   In
short, it was decided to create a self-supporting Division, whose
strength would come from within, not from without.

In these circumstances, the Training School of Instruction
was organized by Lieut. Levey.   N.C.O. instructors were
obtained from the Royal Navy and Royal Marines and, later,

---

* Though full advantage was not taken of this at once, for actually the
Marine Brigade drew on the Marine Depots for recruits and reserves of
officers and men until late in 1915.

from the Brigade of Guards. The first course was for officers only, but the second marked an important development when a number of "Candidates for Commissions" were selected from the recruit battalions, and, after a preliminary instruction in general subjects, were given a month's training as officers, with a view to testing their fitness for commissions. This experiment is believed to have been the origin of the Cadet battalions, organized so much later by the military authorities. It was only another step to extend the benefits of the course to the rank and file, with a view to creating an adequate reserve of N.C.O.'s. For this purpose, a training company of about two hundred men was attached to all the courses held after 1914.

It would be absurd to suppose that the stock of Cæsars and Napoleons multiplied with every course, or that every officer and man, who completed his training there, was turned out a complete expert in the art of war. But it would not be wrong to suppose that there was a very real difference between the training given to raw civilians there and elsewhere, which made up, almost at the start, and, in the end, more than made up, for the lack of regular officers on the establishment of the Division.*
It was partly a difference of atmosphere, partly of technique : at the time, probably, the atmosphere seemed the more important ; later, those who had been trained there came to realize that technically, also, their training had been remarkably sound.

In the new army battalions, the civilian, whether a newly-commissioned officer or a recruit, was a minnow among tritons. Sent from all parts of the country to join battalions at once, these men had to learn the elements while they were actually serving with their units. They had little confidence, they had but a slight idea of their duties, and no preparatory grounding in the first principles of war. There were above them, below them (if they were officers), around them, men who had made a lifelong study, so it must be presumed, of the very subjects of which the civilian was ashamedly ignorant. "Mine not to reason why" was inevitably, if only for the sake of peace and quiet, the motto of the civilian, plunged into such an atmosphere. And, indeed, it was a reasonable one. There was plenty to learn, and many ready to teach.

* After Antwerp, many of the very few, who had accompanied the Division there, were recalled by the Army, and were not replaced.

The atmosphere at the Crystal Palace was rather different : the officer's time of training there was emphatically not a period in which he learnt how to carry out orders, but what orders to give, and how to get them executed; not a period in which he learnt his drill and his musketry, but how to teach drill and musketry; not a period in which he was taught elementary tactics, but rather the underlying principles, knowing which he could not only solve minor tactical problems himself, but could face, with a certain measure of confidence, the practical business of training troops.

If the training of officers was, perhaps, a little ahead of that provided elsewhere in 1914 and 1915, that given to candidates for commissions was actually without parallel till the Cadet battalions were formed nearly two years later, and that given to aspirant N.C.O.'s was in advance of anything attempted throughout the war.

The system evoked the very best that was in the men to whom it was applied. Its very existence gave an incentive to all ranks, and, above all, there was no false barrier created between the officer and the N.C.O. Each knew exactly what the other had learnt in order to qualify for his position, and each, in this way, got confidence in himself and in the other. The organization was very largely based on promotion by merit, proved in competitive examination. Naturally, very many officers were commissioned without prior service in the ranks ; but, literally, scores of such officers were passed, in the first three months of their training, by men who, as candidates for commissions, had shown greater aptitude for command. And these candidates for commissions were not selected on any ground save that of merit. Commissions in the Naval Division were not only open to, but were obtained in the very earliest days by, men of all walks of life. Naturally, the advantages of early education could not be, and were not, overlooked, but the equal advantages of experience, endurance, and the habit of supervision were not ignored. The bright, young, public schoolboy or undergraduate, so dear to the heart of the novelist, and so excellent an ornamentation of less anxious days, was taken at no more than his true valuation.

From the training schools were drawn the officers and petty officers for the new Hawke, Benbow and Collingwood Battalions, which were gradually re-formed in December and

January, 1915, under Lt.-Colonel Leslie Wilson, D.S.O., M.P., R.M. (Hawke), Colonel J. Oldfield, C.B., R.M.L.I. (Benbow) and Commander Spearman, R.N. (Collingwood).

The Hawke Battalion was fortunate enough to be allowed to absorb, as one of its companies, the Public Schools Battalion, raised originally by Commander the Hon. Victor Gibson for service in the Army, and later re-enlisted in the R.N.V.R. for service with the Naval Division. The senior officers of the Battalion could not, of course, be absorbed in the Hawke Battalion, and were transferred to service elsewhere ; the men transferred were under the command of Lieut. Wolfe Barry, R.N.V.R., who thus became O.C. "D" Coy. in the new Hawke Battalion.

The Hawke Battalion had, as its second in command, Commander Ramsay Fairfax, R.N., one of the few officers of the Naval Division who had, prior to joining the Division, seen active service afloat. Commander Fairfax was, later, to command the Howe Battalion in France with great distinction.* The second in command of the Collingwood Battalion, Lt.-Commander West, R.N.V.R., was also, curiously enough, destined later to command the Howe Battalion.

Very wisely, the technical training of officers, N.C.O.'s and specialists, the training of recruits, and of the active service companies were kept wholly distinct from the administrative and disciplinary control of the depot. The former was left almost entirely to Lt.-Colonel Ramsden and Lieut. Levey, assisted by the best products of their training school; the latter, to the Commodore and his staff, and the regular R.N. and R.N.V.R. officers of the executive, medical and accountant branches, who provided the senior officers of the depot.

The organization and disciplining of a huge depot in London was no light task, but it was well done. The chief needs of the private soldier, hard work, good food and clothing, warmth, sleep, and leave, and amusement, were all provided. The provision of the necessaries of life never seems to call for comment ; only when the machine breaks down, do we remember the man at the wheel. Indeed, in more ways than one, the senior officers of the depot had a thankless task in feeding, clothing and equipping, in the months from October, 1914, to February, 1915, many thousands of men, that they might be ready to go out as

* Later still, Commander Fairfax commanded a brigade of Tanks.

complete units or as drafts, often under other commanders. Of all those who commanded battalions at the depot in 1914, only Captain Spearman, R.N. (Collingwood), took his battalion to the front. The rest, from reasons of age, health, or seniority, had to remain behind : it was the same with very many of their officers, who, nevertheless, played an important part in the creation of the reorganized Division.

While the organization of the new battalions and the training of the reserves was thus proceeding, the nine battalions which had survived the Antwerp expedition were being overhauled. The Marine Brigade was placed under the command of Brig.-General Trotman, R.M.L.I.,with Captain M. C. Festing, R.M.L.I., as Brigade Major, and Captain C. F. Jerram, R.M.L.I., as Staff Captain. After a brief period of training at the different Marine Barracks, the Brigade went to stations at Gravesend, Browndown, Tavistock and Deal, till the Blandford Camp was ready. The 2nd Brigade had returned to their summer camps at Bettyshanger, where drafts of officers and men from the depot at the Crystal Palace were ordered to join them and complete their establishment. Early in November, the Brigade went into barracks at Portsmouth (Nelson), Chatham (Anson), Plymouth (Hood) and Portland (Howe). During this period, considerable changes were effected. The Commanding Officers of the Nelson, Anson and Howe Battalions were all transferred to different appointments during the three months following on the Antwerp expedition ; their places were taken by Lt.-Colonel Eveleigh, R.M.L.I., Lt.-Colonel Moorhouse and Commander Collins, R.N.V.R., the first two being regular officers, and the last a company commander in the Hood Battalion. At the same time it became necessary to make changes in the personnel of the battalion staffs and among the company commanders, owing to the transfer of a number of the senior R.N.V.R. officers to sea service, and the withdrawal by the Army of several Army officers. The opportunity was taken to promote to responsible positions those who had done good service at Antwerp, or who had joined the battalions from the depot with good records of service elsewhere.

Of the 1st Brigade, the Drake was the only surviving unit, and, while the other three were being re-formed at the depot, Commander Campbell's battalion went to Alnwick, for coast defence duty. In succession to Commodore Henderson, Brigadier-

General Mercer* was appointed to command the 1st Brigade, with Captain F. Wilson, R.M.L.I., who had been attached to the Drake Battalion at Antwerp, as Brigade Major.

Meanwhile, the divisional troops were being recruited and trained, under arrangements inaugurated by the Admiralty, and carried out by the Marine Office. The Engineers were commanded by Major Carey, R.E., who became C.R.E. of the Division; and the Divisional train by Lt.-Colonel Chaytor, an officer of the New Zealand forces. The Field Ambulances were officered mainly by regular Naval Surgeons (under the command of Fleet-Surgeon Gaskell, R.N., who became A.D.M.S. of the Division); a few of the N.C.O.'s of the Medical Unit were supplied from the Marine Shore establishment, and the military training of the unit was entrusted to Captain Casement, R.A.M.C., later D.D.M.S. of the Division. With these exceptions, the divisional troops were recruited direct from civil life, the Medical Unit through, and mainly from, the ranks of the St. John Ambulance Corps, and the first three companies (the Signal Company and two Field Companies) of Engineers directly from the three Institutes of Civil, Mechanical and Electrical Engineers, though later a limited number of qualified tradesmen were enlisted.

In a field off the road from Dover to St. Margaret's Bay, near Martin Hill Station, was the first camp of Naval Divisional Engineers. Recruiting for this force had begun on September 16th, and the establishment for three companies was nearly completed by the end of the month. Of this remarkable unit, in which many even of the sappers were qualified professional engineers, Lieut. (later Brig.-Gen.) G. H. Harrison was the first Adjutant; the first and second Field Companies were organized under Major Chivers (with Captain Morgans second in command) and Major Adams (with Captain Rugg second in command); and the Signal Company under Major Spittle, R.M. Other officers gazetted in the early days, were Major Aveling, Major Revel and Major Teale, the last of whom took the Third Field Company (formed in February, 1915) to Gallipoli. These companies of trained specialists were a tower of strength to the Division, not only by virtue of the quality of their work for the field, but of

---

* The late Major-General Sir D. Mercer, K.C.B., who relinquished command of this brigade in 1917 to become Adjutant-General of the Royal Marines, in which office he rendered many services to the Naval Division.

their unrivalled efficiency in work outside the scope of the ordinary Field Company, for which the varied training and wide experience of the rank and file proved invaluable. In the First Field Company alone ninety per cent. of the men rose, after a short time at the front, to commissioned rank.

After enduring the Dover mud till the end of November, 1914, the Corps went into billets at Walmer and Deal till the Blandford Camp was ready.

The Medical Unit of the Royal Naval Division was first put into training at the Crystal Palace, under Captain Casement, on the 3rd December, 1914. From them, the complements of three Field Ambulances were selected, and Fleet-Surgeon Finch, Staff-Surgeon Stanford and Staff-Surgeon Fleming were appointed to command them.

Almost at the same time that the Medical Unit went into training, the Divisional train was formed at the Crystal Palace, from volunteers from the R.N.V.R. and R.M. battalions at the different depots. Major F. Holmes, R.M., was appointed Senior Supply Officer. A little later, the Ordnance Company was raised by Col. Lord Bangor (late R.A.) from men at the Marine depots not fit for general service, and Lord Bangor was appointed D.A.D.O.S. of the Division.

There remained only the Naval Divisional Cavalry and the Divisional Artillery. Ambitious schemes for the former had been drawn up, even before the Antwerp expedition, and for some time it was rumoured that, under the title of the Royal Naval Hussars,* yet another new Corps was to be formed. The Admiralty records contain even a descriptive account of the uniform of this remarkable organization, which was to be built up on the lines of the Boer Commandos. Such a unit would have been invaluable, but perhaps political considerations decided its fate. Anyway, it was not formed ; but instead a Divisional Cyclist Company was formed at Forton Barracks on the 1st December, 1914, under Major French, D.S.O., R.M.L.I. No such substitute was, however, available for the missing artillery, which, owing to the very successful, but, on the whole, unfortunate stone-walling policy of the War Office, was never formed.

By the close of 1914 the Naval Division was, nevertheless, well on the way to becoming a mobile unit. The Antwerp

* I fear the name is apocryphal.

battalions, reinforced and reorganized, several of them under new commanders, all with a stronger *cadre* of officers, were ready for serious brigade and divisional training, and, with the organization of the Divisional Troops and the completion of Blandford Camp, such training was now practical.

The first infantry unit of the Division to enter Blandford Camp was the Nelson Battalion, which arrived there from Portsmouth on November 27th. The rest of the 2nd R.N. Brigade, the Drake Battalion, and some of the Divisional Troops followed. The Marine Brigade, whose lines were not ready for occupation, arrived during the last days of January, and went into billets in Pimperne, Iwerne Minster and Shilling-stone. By this time, too, General Paris and his staff had taken up their residence at Stud House. The Hawke, Benbow and Collingwood Battalions had not, however, yet completed their preliminary training at the Crystal Palace, and the division at Blandford was thus short of three infantry battalions. To equalize matters between the Brigades, the 1st Brigade, of which General Mercer assumed command as from January 1st, was strengthened by the transfer of the Nelson Battalion from the 2nd Brigade. In the result, the nucleus of three Brigades, a Signal Company, two Field Companies of Engineers, and a complete establishment of other Divisional troops, were available for divisional training by January 28th.

As the concentration of the Division neared completion, there came an improvement in discipline and efficiency. This was the result partly of the rivalry of the different battalions and brigades, and, to a greater extent, of the belief that, once the spade work had been done and the equipment completed, the departure of the Division overseas would only be delayed until all units had reached fighting efficiency. Moreover, the issue in December of active service uniform and equipment to all ranks (up to this time the Naval infantry battalions had been fitted out in blue, with that rather primitive equipment which had startled the critics at Antwerp) had immensely improved the appearance of the troops, and was thus in itself a great aid to discipline.

At this point the history of the preliminary training of the Naval Division comes to an abrupt end. The whole force was never actually concentrated, much less trained, as a Division. Events moved too rapidly.

The story of those events, the why and wherefore of those orders, which once more sent the Division overseas so unexpectedly, will be sketched in the next chapter. These orders mark, however, the beginning of the Division's second period of active service, which lasted till March, 1919, and before relating the story of those years it is necessary to say something of the organization which the Division, proceeding overseas, left behind it, and the influence of this organization on the spirit and the efficiency of the fighting units.

The Crystal Palace had begun, as we have seen, as a regimental depot for the two Naval Brigades. Even at that time the fact that, as in the case of the Guards Division later in the war, the whole of the first-line battalions supplied from the depot served together in the field, gave to it an exceptional importance in relation to the Division, and bred a more uniform technique, and a more instinctive habit of co-operation, than might otherwise have been achieved. This alone would call for comment. The difference between the Naval Division and the ordinary Army organization became even greater when, first, the Crystal Palace was expanded into a depot, not only for certain infantry battalions, but for the Divisional troops ; and, secondly, when, shortly after the Division went overseas, the whole of this enlarged depot was transferred to Blandford, further expanded to be the depot for all units of the Naval Division, including the Royal Marines, and placed under a general officer responsible to the Admiralty.

Under these arrangements, Commodore Sir R. Williams Bulkeley remained in charge of what became a purely naval depot at the Crystal Palace, and with him remained most of the R.N. and R.N.V.R. officers, who had commanded the training battalions at the Crystal Palace in the early days. The principal exception was Captain Hunter, R.N., who commanded the Fourth Reserve Battalion at Blandford, till he went to sea in 1918.

To write the history of the innumerable developments in training and organization of the divisional depot, subsequent to 1915, would involve telling of the evolution of methods of instruction and training throughout the war. Such a history should perhaps be written, but our only concern here is to emphasize what there was, in the home organization of the

Naval Division, which helped to create in the Division overseas qualities which were distinctive, and which did, in fact, distinguish the Division from other equally famous fighting formations.

To the Blandford organization English military experience afforded no precise parallel. When the "new army" divisions went overseas, they left behind them no visible embodiment of their existence. They drew drafts from innumerable depots. Their casualties went back to different depots, and, when they returned to the front, they returned as often as not to a different division. Such modifications of training, as the experience of a division in the field showed to be necessary, had to be achieved through the machinery of the War Office, if at all. Nor were they in fact ever adopted, unless it was possible, and considered desirable, to make them of general application throughout the whole army. Still more serious was the potential reaction on the *esprit de corps* of the division. Neither men nor officers could count on joining or rejoining any particular division. Each time they went to the front, they had to meet new faces, to learn new ways, to obey new whims, to learn the practice of alternative theories, to imbibe, very often, new standards of efficiency and conduct.

The Naval Division was more fortunate. If, in its surface routine, it was in no way different from hundreds of other camps in 1915 and 1916, in almost every other respect the Blandford depot was, certainly, unique. Its situation, on high ground in the open country, at any rate appeared to have been selected for reasons of health; and it was, in fact, incomparably healthier than most other camps. It was entirely self-contained, and it was isolated from all other troops in training in the Southern Command. The Camp thus became, even geographically, a little township of its own, with a life shut off entirely from other regiments and corps. When the Marines sent their reserve battalion there in 1915, the depot became the Division in miniature; all units were represented there, and each supplied each other's wants. It provided its own engineering services, its own medical services, its own hospital, its own rifle range, its own chaplains, its own supply and transport, all responsible solely to the Camp Commandant. It was not in 1915 even technically subject to Army jurisdiction, and its organization at home was, to all intents and purposes, that of

4*

a mobile unit in the field, with the General in command responsible only to the authorities in Whitehall.

Thus there was maintained at home the divisional spirit, fostered by what was, in theory as well as in fact, a divisional organization, after the Division had gone overseas. And thus was maintained that strong individuality, that sense (only half-justified, but none the less valuable) of being " not as other men," which is the origin of all *esprit de corps*, and which, in the Naval Division, was so fortunately centred round what was not merely a temporary or a sentimental association but an effective fighting organization. One further point—not the least important—must be noticed. The Division had had to find from within its ranks not only its leaders in the field, but its administrators and instructors at home. When the time came for reinforcements to be sent out, there were thus available officers and N.C.O.'s, not only well trained, but fully accustomed to responsibility, and better versed in administration than those who first went overseas; and who, at the same time, were not unfitted by age, seniority, or temperament for the command of men in the firing line, which meant in the mud and dust, the heat and the blizzards, of an uncertain Eastern climate. Their places on the depot staffs were taken by officers returning from the front; thus that essential interchange between the firing line and the training ground became an accomplished fact, not only, as elsewhere, among the rank and file and the junior officers, but among the battalion commanders, the adjutants and the instructors. The General at home and the General in the field could and did co-operate, and, perhaps to a greater extent, the interchange of adjutants and company commanders meant that traditions and customs which grew up under the stress and strain of battle experience took root, as a matter of course, at the depot. Thus the traditions and the lessons of Gallipoli and the Somme were insensibly inherited by later drafts of officers and men, who saw their first fighting at Arras or Passchendaele. Indeed, some of the finest officers who ever served in the Division came from the depot late in 1915 and in 1916.

It was not only among the officers that tradition and *esprit de corps* was fostered by this organization, but even more was it so among the rank and file. From the Crystal Palace and Blandford there went out literally tens of thousands of men, many of them again and again, to rejoin the Division. The history of the Division is the record of what these men did. They, like the officers, had seen the Division growing. They knew exactly how much more their officers knew than their N.C.O.'s and their N.C.O.'s than themselves, for they had all started together ; this knowledge created an automatic discipline at the front or on parade, which was not relaxed in leisure hours, but which, in the circumstances, could be tempered by a measure of friendly intercourse which was never fatal to discipline. This acquaintance was not, as elsewhere, broken but strengthened by the ebb and flow of war. Very many, probably the majority of the men, never changed their companies, let alone their brigades or battalions, throughout the whole of their service at the front. When they came back wounded or sick and returned eventually to the depot, they would join up again with some, at least, of the old officers, the old N.C.O.'s, the old platoon.

A striking instance of the reality of this friendly atmosphere is to be found in the history of the Durham and Northumberland miners who came to the Division. The first contingent, barely two thousand, had, as we have seen, come accidentally, They had enlisted in different northern regiments in August. 1914, and had been transferred to Walmer, Betteshanger and the Crystal Palace, because of the breakdown of the arrangements for their accommodation in the North. But this contingent was followed by thousands of others from the same mining villages, voluntary enlistments in every case. At least a third of the best fighting men of the Division came from these villages, and they came because of the reputation which the Division enjoyed among the men already enlisted.

That, for all their experiments in training and organization, the Division could not have reached efficiency without the ordinary drill, discipline and technical training common to all units of the British Army, is so obvious as to be hardly worth saying, and that any other form of divisional organization would have provided these essentials is equally clear. But it is not fanciful to think that the finest technical training will not come to full fruition without other qualities, which the organization we have described did undoubtedly foster to an exceptional degree, and which we can sum up in two simple phrases as *esprit de corps* and a genuine friendship between officers and men.

And so, behind the Division in the field we must remember always the depot. But for the depot, the following chapters of this history, when we speak of the Division moving from battlefield to battlefield, from campaign to campaign, would have only a specious unity. Between every battle, often between one phase of a battle and the next, there is some vital change among the individual personalities who form the Division. When we compare campaign with campaign these changes become more numerous, more far-reaching. Far-reaching as far as the individual is concerned, but as far as the Division is concerned, wholly devoid of significance. Why ? Only because, behind the flux of the battle-front, there remained always, for the Naval Division, a divisional organization at home. To this plain fact the continued existence of the Naval Division through four years of war is pre-eminently due. There was no bond of local patriotism such as made the 51st Division so living an organism, no age-long tradition such as stimulated the Guards Division. In place of these traditional spurs to enthusiastic action the Naval Division had, in addition to youth and enthusiasm, a scientific organization. The two together spelt victory.

NOTE

In reply to a request for his "impressions" of the Crystal Palace and Blandford depots in 1915, my friend Mr. Hugh Lunn sent me the amusing notes which I print here *in extenso.* They seem to me to recall very fully the atmosphere of those strenuous, but amusing, days.

I arrived at the Crystal Palace on November 23rd, 1914, to begin my training as an officer of the R.N.D. Already in the train from Victoria the shadow of him who at that time dominated the Crystal Palace was cast over me, and chilled me to the bone. My fellow-passenger, an R.N.D. officer, was a melancholy, refined young man, not at all communicative. To his resentment, for he gazed at me as at a new boy inclined to be unseasonably familiar, I pressed him with questions. However, he revenged himself adequately with a curt description of Lieutenant Levey, the military instructor to whose charge I would presently be committed—a man without bowels, an expert in insults, a flail, a tempest, a tiger.

Presently I found myself in a lecture-room. The lecture was already in progress when I crawled in. The audience appeared to me, in my demoralized state, to consist of an extraordinarily brilliant body of young men, superbly at ease. They were actually laughing, and no wonder ; for the lecturer, whom I now took courage to examine, was extremely witty, animated and charming —a dark, good-looking man, seething with vitality. What a delightful fellow ! I thought, and my spirits rose. But where was Lieutenant Levey ? Probably, I thought, that powerful, forbidding person in the corner, who is keeping an eye on us lest our attention to the lecture should relax.

As we left the lecture-room, I sought to confirm this guess by a question to another officer. He was contemptuously amused. "That's old Quinlan," he answered; "the lecturer is Levey." "Why, he's delightful," I protested, but my companion advised me to wait till I had experienced Levey on the parade ground, before I passed a final opinion on his charm.

Lieutenant Levey had joined the Scots Guards as a private, and rose to be a sergeant-major before the outbreak of war. It would be difficult to exaggerate his prestige at the Crystal Palace towards the close of 1914. The R.N.D. was a rough-hewn body in those days. The officers commanding the various battalions were retired Naval Captains or R.N.V.R. Commanders, conversant, I doubt not, with the arts of tacking, trimming, studding sails, and the like, but very much at sea, on land. Now here was a man who, from earliest youth, had been preoccupied with the technique of loading in the standing position, of advancing in fours from the right, of forming close columns of platoons, a man who could slope arms like a thunderbolt, and order them like the crack of doom. Students of Carlyle, the senior officers at once recognized "how indispensable everywhere a *King* is, in all movements of men." With a kind of stern joy they submitted to learn from Lieutenant Levey, and, when I arrived at the Crystal Palace, they had most of them passed through his class. It was now the turn of younger persons to realize, again in Carlyle's words, that what "the Commander over men tells us to do must be precisely the wisest, fittest, that we could anywhere or anyhow learn ; the thing which it will in all ways behove us, with right loyal thankfulness, and nothing doubting, to do." Of course, that "right loyal thankfulness" is a little overpitched. I will try to reconstruct as well as I can a typical scene in the Crystal Palace grounds. The class of officers is standing easy : out of the corner of his eye Colour-Sergeant Ashton* watches for Lieutenant Levey's approach. "Squad ! " Instantly the class is standing-at-ease, eyes front, rigid. Each officer swells, in his own imagination, to grotesque proportions, the others dwindling in proportion ; his tunic appears to be unbuttoning itself, his puttees gape and wriggle, his tie will presently be shaking in the wind ; his hands are wool, and he is unable to die.

* Colour-Sergeant Ashton helped us through many an awkward moment, whispering and pushing the careless and the confused into the way they had been directed to go. Napoleon might not have approved of Colour-Sergeant Ashton ; but neither would Colour-Sergeant Ashton have very greatly relished Napoleon.

Five minutes pass, crammed with passionate exertion. A roar of pain and rage ! Lieutenant Levey hurls himself at No. 4 in the front rank. The two faces almost touch. " You, you ! What's your name ? Never heard of such a thing ! Got a little boy at home . . . order arms better'n you."

The agony begins again. Another roar ! Lieutenant Levey hurls himself at No. 7 in the rear rank. The two faces almost touch. " You, you ! What's your name ? Where d'you come from ? I've been in the Army twenty years —never seen such an exhibition ! Fall about like a sack of potatoes ! Never heard of such a thing."

An officer drops his rifle. " What the HELL are you doing, that officer at the end of the rank. Drop a rifle on parade ! I've been in the Army twenty years. Never heard of such a thing ! Got a little boy . . ." etc., etc.

The best drill instructor is he who can deal with every lapse or negligence, however trivial, as though it were an unprecedented phenomenon, a demonstration deliberately planned to sap loyalty, to sow dissension in the ranks, to debauch the nation, to enhearten the enemy, and to bring the Empire crashing to the ground. Such a drill-instructor was Lieutenant Levey.

All the same, most of us, I think, acquired in time a kind of tremulous regard for Lieutenant Levey, and, without rancour, learnt in suffering what we afterwards taught in extremely broken prose.

At lunch and dinner, in the mess, the talk was largely Levey. Men find it hard to imagine a throne without a power behind it : Monsieur Mendel, for example, behind Clemenceau ; General Weygand behind Marshal Foch. Was Colonel Ramsden, we subalterns would ask each other, the brain behind Lieutenant Levey ? Or was Lieutenant Levey the brain in front of Colonel Ramsden ?

Technically, Lt.-Colonel Ramsden was the Chief Military Instructor, and Lieutenant Levey his second-in-command. Hence these debates.

We did not see the Colonel often, but were content to picture him sitting in his office, meditating on the larger issues of war, or brooding over the psychology of the temporary officer. He must have had misgivings, for once, when we were sitting down to a written examination, a presence loomed in the doorway, uttered two words : " No cheating," and retired.

A subaltern, having passed through the class, was attached to a battalion Innumerable imitations of Lieutenant Levey were in the course of a few weeks scattered over the grounds of the Crystal Palace, roaring like doves at tough, sardonic miners. It is difficult to roar with conviction when the end of the sentence does not present itself clearly to the roarer. Fortunately, in those early days sick leave was granted in a generous and unpedantic spirit. I remember a note from the M.O. which ran : " You are not to return till you feel perfectly fit ; " and a conversation between J—— and myself. " Are you applying for sick leave to-day ? " I asked him. " No," he replied, " I am not feeling well enough."

In those days, the war was still a strange and exciting phenomenon, and the routine of an army not yet become a habit to the civilian soldier. The mess was very mixed in its composition. But the general level of character and intelligence was high. Beyond doubt the '14 vintage was the best, though even then, I concede, some curious specimens were bottled. Ker and Harmsworth stand out in my memory as types of the finest young officer of the new army.

Another type of new army officer was, I believe, more fully represented in the Naval Division than elsewhere : the man who had knocked about and seen life in the raw, planted tea in Ceylon, and daggers in recalcitrant cannibals, built bridges in India, and blown them up in South America. This kind of officer was apt to be unduly affronted by the luxury of a sleeping bag, or the elaborate fittings of a dug-out. However, with one or two exceptions, this type did well : I should say " made good."

At the high table, in mess, sat the Sea-Captains, the C.M.I., Lieutenant Levey, and our Commodore, Sir Richard Williams Bulkeley, with his second-in-command, Commander Roberts Wray. Sir Richard did not, as far as I know, concern himself too closely with detail, but he was great on discipline, and caused a pamphlet to be distributed, in which he set forth the reasons that led him to consider discipline as of paramount importance. One saw him at times pacing the quarter-deck of H.M.S. *Crystal Palace* with Commander Roberts Wray, and divined the brief interchange of words :

" Discipline, Wray, discipline. It all comes back to that."

" Ay, ay, sir."

A fortnight's intensive training at Blandford, in Dorsetshire, completed, more or less, the young officer's military education. I went there in June, '15. The heat was terrific, and the daily papers, read hurriedly at breakfast, annoyed us with pictures of Londoners retreating to underground cellars with an assortment of iced drinks.

In spite of field days, the defence of Pimperne, open order drill, picketing and night operations, this second course was far less agonizing than the first. I except, as far as I am concerned, my attempt to march the officers' squad on to a given point, and halt them in close columns of platoons. That was an awful experience. I remember well the curt casualness with which Captain Levey (for Captain he had now become) informed me that he wished me to carry out the above movement ; the roar with which I opened, the tentative suggestions with which I continued, and my subdued return to the ranks.

Some officers were not at all alarmed by Captain Levey. A subaltern in A 4 Lines told us one day in mess how he had tamed the Captain.

" He called me out and told me to march the squad on a given point, you know—began shouting at me—I didn't like it—turned to him, and said : ' Captain Levey, do you notice that my hand is shaking ? Captain Levey, it is shaking not with fear but with anger. Out East, where I have just come from, I shoot men who talk to me as you have just talked. Drop it ! ' From that moment," he concluded, " I had no more trouble with Levey."

It always used to delight me to hear from a subordinate how he had browbeaten a superior officer ; but I never had the luck to be actually present during the beating of a superior officer's brow.

We finished the fortnight at full strain, with a field day, night operations lasting till breakfast the following morning, and, after a few hours' repose, a written examination. The field day exhibited the full scope of Captain Levey's genius. His generalship was excellent ; but his tact was superb. At one time it looked as if nothing could save his army from gaining an overwhelming victory over the force commanded by Colonel Ramsden. But at long last the Captain's passionate energy and consummate resource were rewarded by a drawn battle, slightly in the Colonel's favour.

The night operations were like other night operations, superficially annoying and uncomfortable, but with wonderful moments when the scent of the pine woods and the warm earth revived, for the last time in many, the forgotten magic of the world.

The dawn that broke on these particular night operations was one of the loveliest I have ever seen. Did Captain Levey feel its influence, and retire to a grove, weeping, he knew not why ? Almost certainly not. But all great men have their limitations ; and great he was, beyond doubt. I refrain from a technical estimate of his extraordinary talent as a military instructor. Here I have tried simply to describe the personal impression he made on the raw subaltern ; a very remarkable impression, even when the novelty and excitement of the time have been allowed for.

The other day (November, 1921) I read in a newspaper that the house of Colonel Levey (for Colonel he has now become) had been broken into by burglars, who subsequently returned him his war medals. " I cannot help thinking," Colonel Levey remarked to the interviewer, referring to the restitution, " that the thief was an ex-Service man." No doubt ; but the journalist missed, and Colonel Levey ignored, the tragic pith of the situation : the biter bit, the expert in night operations dished by a fellow practitioner. Where were your pickets, Colonel Levey ? Where were your outposts ? " Never heard of such a thing ! "

CHAPTER IV

THE VOYAGE TO THE EAST

THE second departure of the Naval Division overseas was as unexpected as the first. We have seen how the whole Division, less one Field Company of Engineers and the Hawke, Collingwood and Benbow Battalions, had finally been concentrated for Divisional training by January 28th. The next day came the first orders for overseas. They affected only two battalions, the Plymouth and Chatham R.M.L.I. battalions, and the Staff of the Marine Brigade,* but the event is noteworthy, not only because through the issue of these orders the last chance of concentrating the whole Division for serious divisional training passed away, but still more, perhaps, because it gave rise for the first time to those rumours that the Division would never again be employed as a separate formation in the field, which, from that date, hardly ever ceased to be current, and were hardly ever wholly without foundation.

That the Naval Division should never have been concentrated except under fire, is merely an incident in its history. It was in the most literal sense a fighting Division. The rumours which made up the mess-room gossip through the whole course of the war, rumours of dispersal, transfer to the army or to sea service, or condemnation to garrison duties, were, however, more than an episode in the history of the Division : they were part of its daily life, the very atmosphere it breathed.

The two Marine Battalions which left Blandford for Plymouth on February 1st, under Brigadier-General Trotman, sailed

---

* Captain M. C. Festing, R.M.L.I. (Brigade Major), and Captain C. F. Jerram, R.M.L.I. (Staff Captain). Brigadier-General Trotman was in command of the force.

for an unknown Eastern destination on February 6th. The general belief was that the balance of the Division would be dispersed on different independent operations, and rumour gave East Africa as the destination of a number of battalions. Not till the 17th February, when Mr. Winston Churchill inspected it, did the hopes of the Division revive. The inspection was held in pouring rain, under the most unfavourable conditions, but the verdict of the First Lord must have been a favourable one, for the next day the orders came for the rest of the troops at Blandford to prepare to follow the Marine Battalions. Exactly a week later, the Division was again inspected by the First Lord, and two hours later by H.M. the King. On this occasion the inspection was unusually detailed, Mr. Winston Churchill inspecting every battalion, except the Nelson battalion, which he had seen on his visit the week before. At 11.30 the Royal Standard was hoisted and the King's inspection began; after which, the Division marched past the saluting point in column of companies, and later marched again past His Majesty on their way back to camp in double column of fours.

This was the end of the Division's training. The 26th and 27th, the last two days spent by these units at Blandford, were occupied with the distribution of ammunition and iron rations, and the overhauling of equipment and kit, and on the evening of the 28th the whole of the Division, with the exception of the partially trained Collingwood Battalion, the Third Field Company of the Engineers (by now at Blandford, but also untrained) and the Hawke and Benbow Battalions (still at the Crystal Palace), marched out of camp by Black Lane to the town station. The next day the troops embarked at Avonmouth, and sailed the same day; General Paris and the Headquarters Staff, General Mercer and the 1st Brigade Staff, the Drake, Nelson and Deal Battalions, the 1st Field Ambulance, and the Motor Machine Gun detachment of the R.N.A.S., on board the *Franconia*, and other units in the *Braemar Castle*, the *Gloucester Castle*, the *Grantully Castle*, the *Minnetonka* and the *Astrian*.

The decision to send the Division overseas was, as we have said, unexpected. It is doubtful, however, if it was premature. Officers and men had everything to learn of the things which active service alone can teach, but it is a reasonable view that

they were otherwise adequately trained. Those who consider
no training adequate which is not comparable in its duration
to that considered necessary for the corresponding ranks of the
regular army overlook, perhaps, one very vital difference between
a professional and a volunteer formation. The average civilian
soldier must usually learn the business of soldiering in less
time than that required by regular officers who join their
regiments virtually straight from school. After all, the con-
verse holds : no one expects a regular officer, who retires and
goes into the City, to begin as an office boy, and it would be
strange if a really competent professional or business man
were to find serious difficulty in mastering the work of a company commander. The same, *mutatis mutandis*, holds good of
lower ranks. There were cases where this was hardly appreciated, with the result that units, brigades, even whole divisions,
became routine-bound, over-trained, stale. This danger was
avoided in the case of the Naval Division, and, in this sense, it was
right to regard all, save the three recruit battalions, as already
in February, 1915, fit for service overseas. If, however, it is
reasonable to assume that, in marked contrast to the Division
which went to Antwerp in 1914, the Division which left Blandford on this occasion was fit to take the offensive, it would be
idle to pretend that the decision to send it to the East
was equally uncontroversial. Nothing in the war (not even
excepting the Antwerp expedition) has been the subject of
weightier criticism than the decision reached in February, 1915,
to embark on extensive military operations in the Near East.

To understand the operations in which the Naval Division
was so soon to begin to play its part, the circumstances leading
\'p to them must be briefly outlined.

At the end of 1914, the dominant facts in the general situation were the staying of the German offensive on the West,
and the ominous threat of a decisive German victory in the
East. Turkey, known to our military advisers to be still one
of the most formidable military powers in Europe, had declared
war on the Allies on October 31st, and must be expected at
any time to make her presence felt on the Russian flank unless
her armies could be engaged elsewhere. This in itself was
serious enough, for the Russians were already sufficiently hard
pressed by the Germans and Austrians ; but it was only
part of the story. Serbia was threatened with an Austro-

German invasion, and such a threat, if it materialized, might be expected to bring to the aid of the Central Powers the armies of Bulgaria and Rumania. In such an eventuality, would Italy feel herself able to intervene on the side of the Allies, a step which she was at the time actively contemplating? These dangers were so grave that they could not be ignored. They had to be faced, on the contrary, with energy and resolution. Whatever may have been the faults of the Allied strategy, the errors of generals or politicians, the need for some action to prevent the threatened disasters in the East is, if not un-challenged, at least unchallengeable. Those who attempt to review the 1915 situation in the light of our success in 1918, and still suggest that, because the war had to be won on the Western front, it had to be fought on that front, forget that the drain imposed on the German, Austrian and Turkish re-sources in 1915 and 1916 by the vigorous prosecution of the war in the East, was as decisive in the battle of armies as the battles of attrition in France and Flanders in 1916 and 1917. Is it seriously arguable that disaster could have been averted if Italy had remained neutral, if Serbia had been crushed, and if Russia had been faced by a German-Austrian-Turkish offensive, before the British armies were sufficiently power-ful (which was not till 1916) to initiate a vigorous and continuing offensive in France? These considerations in themselves afford no argument for, and are not mentioned here in defence of the Gallipoli expedition, its strategy, its tactics, or the adequacy of the preparations made for it; but they are unanswerable as arguments in support of the Cabinet decision (arrived at on February 16th, 1915) to send substantial forces to the Near East.* It was in pursuance of this decision that the main body of the Royal Naval Division were ordered overseas later in the month.

The decision to employ the new " Mediterranean Expedi-tionary Force " (as it came to be known) in the historic attempt to force a passage for the fleet through the Dardanelles, by seizing the Gallipoli peninsula, was more controversial. This operation had been considered directly Turkey came into the war, but had been put aside, in view of the then success of the

---

* See, for a fuller discussion of this point, Corbett: " Naval Operations," Vol. II., pp. 66-69.

Russian armies and of the critical situation in the West. No
more had been heard of the Dardanelles till January 2nd,
when the now menacing situation in the East was brought
urgently to the notice of the Government by a request from
the Russian Commander-in-Chief for an early demonstration
against Turkey, with a view to relieving his armies from pressure
on their flank. Lord Kitchener, through the Foreign Office, at
once agreed; and the Admiralty immediately sought the views
of the Admiral Commanding in the Eastern Mediterranean
(Vice-Admiral Carden), on the possibility of rushing the Dardanelles, an attack on the Straits being clearly the most
direct threat which a naval Power could bring to bear on
Turkey. Admiral Carden replied by telegram that, in his view,
the Straits could not be rushed, but could be forced by extended
operations directed to the systematic reduction of the forts.

It would be outside the scope of this history to examine
the tangled story of the manner in which the Government
finally, on January 28th, committed themselves to endorsing
this project. It is sufficient for our purpose to record their
decision, which was arrived at independently and prior to the
decision to assemble in the Near East a substantial military
force. The only military movement to which this decision,
by itself, gave rise was the dispatch of the two Marine Battalions
to the East on February 6th in advance of the rest of the
Division. These battalions were not to form part, as has been
often assumed, of any military force, but were to act under the
fleet in what were definitely assumed to be purely naval operations, involving the landing only of reconnaissance patrols or
demolition parties, operations normally within the province of
a naval commander.

Towards the end of February, the position was that the
preparations for the naval attack (assisted only by the Marine
Battalions) were well advanced, and that the concentration of
troops to exploit any naval success, or to operate in the Balkans,
if that theatre should appear later more profitable, was proceeding. If the naval attack had succeeded, there would, of
course, have been no Gallipoli campaign; but when the naval
attack, begun at last on February 18th, proved inconclusive,
and then had to be broken off because of the weather, Admiral
Carden suggested speeding matters up by a military landing
on the peninsula. The proposal was rejected by the War

Office as involving an irrelevant diversion; the assumption still was that the main work of reducing the forts could be achieved by the Navy alone. The Admiralty appear to have endorsed this view, and Admiral Carden was so informed, but he was asked, at the same time, to confer with General Birdwood, and told that " if he was of opinion that the army could help him, he was at liberty to submit suggestions."* The same evening (February 24th) the War Office sent out similar instructions to General Birdwood.

This development marked the first definite step towards the decision to attempt to force the Straits by conjoint naval and military operations, and, for this reason, February 24th is one of the critical days in the history of the war; and not for this reason only, but also because, on this day, the Government appeared first to be moving towards the conclusion that the Dardanelles operations must somehow or other be carried to a successful conclusion,

There was, however, still a firm belief in the chances of a purely naval success. It was not till the beginning of March that events at the front, in which the Plymouth Marine Battalion took a gallant if unsuccessful share, brought about a decisive change in the prospects of the purely naval campaign. Admiral Carden's plan had been to force a passage through the Straits, by a series of progressive bombardments against the forts which guarded the whole length of the Straits on either side. The long range guns would keep down the fire of the forts, while the ships with lighter armament closed in to effective range and destroyed them. The long range bombardment would then lift and come down on the next group of forts, and in due course these also would be closed and put out of action. The same procedure would be applied, and of course at the same time, to any mobile batteries which the enemy might bring, in support of his permanent defences.

The first naval attack, on February 19th, had had, as we have seen, to be broken off before the merits of the plan could be tested, but, when the attack was renewed on February 25th, the fleet, standing in close, compelled all the outer forts to cease fire. Next day, demolition parties from the fleet, covered by Marine detachments, were put ashore to complete the work of destruction. These parties, which displayed the utmost

* Corbett: " Naval Operations," Vol. II., p. 156.

gallantry and energy, did no small amount of damage, and further landings on February 27th and March 1st and 2nd added to the tale of destruction. As far as the outer forts were concerned, everything indeed seemed to be proceeding according to plan. It was quite otherwise with the more important attack on the inner forts, which had been begun on the 26th, and had proceeded as weather permitted, but without any sort of success. The main objectives of the fleet were, of course, the groups of forts at Chanak and Maidos, guarding the entrance to the Narrows. Before, however, these could be effectively bombarded, the smaller " Dardanos " group had to be subdued, and the minefields at the entrance to the Narrows (by Kephez Point) had to be swept. Despite all efforts, neither task had been accomplished, nor had any material progress been made by the evening of March 3rd. The fire of the forts, indeed, whose position was accurately known, could be kept down, but all attempts to deal with the mobile batteries had failed. It was becoming increasingly clear that without the occupation of some commanding position on shore, which would enable the fire of the ships' guns to be effectively controlled, or the forts to be taken in reverse, no further progress could be confidently expected. General Birdwood, who had by this time conferred with Admiral Carden, appears to have advised Lord Kitchener in this sense, and the next day's operations made the situation even more clear. These operations consisted of landings by the Plymouth Battalion at Kum Kale and Sedd-el-bahr. Both landings were unsuccessful, and their failure was significant. The plan in each case was much the same. The parties landed in open boats without much opposition, but, once landed, they were unable to make any headway. The idea was to advance inland and hold a line in each case some two miles in length, on the Asiatic side from Kum Kale pier to Yeni Shehr, and on the peninsula from Morto Bay to Cape Tekke. These lines were to be held for three hours, while an exhaustive search was made for guns, gun positions and ammunition dumps, and while the work of destruction and survey, hitherto undertaken piecemeal, was carried to completion. Instead, the landing parties, though consisting of two companies each, found themselves held up almost on the beaches, while the Turks were occupying strongly entrenched positions in the neighbourhood of the different objectives.

Against these it was found impossible to advance, even with the assistance of the ships' guns.

In the circumstances, there was nothing for it but to withdraw, and even this proved to be difficult, though, in the end, it was successfully accomplished.

This failure was important because of the light it shed on the prospects of the purely naval attack. The destruction of the outer forts, at least, had been considered, until now, to have been relatively satisfactorily achieved. It was now seen that the Turks were not only undismayed at our success but still in a position to maintain by force of arms their hold on the coast-line even at the entrance to the Straits, and even there to bring mobile batteries to bear at their pleasure on our fleet and transports.

In spite of this it was decided to persist, and the attacks on the inner forts were renewed on March 5th and the following days. These, like the former attacks, were, at the very best, negative in their results, and the situation was thus dubious when the War Council met on March 10th, to take a final decision regarding the question of the military force to be sent to the Near East.

The crux of this question was the 29th Division, which it had been agreed to send out in February, but which Lord Kitchener had since felt unable to release. Though it is clear that no definite proposal to abandon the naval attack in favour of joint naval and military operations was under consideration at this date, there can be little doubt but that the decision, now finally reached, to send the 29th Division, marked the definite acceptance by the Government of the Near East as an important military theatre. It meant, in particular, that, if the naval attack failed, the Government were by this date determined to push the attack home by military measures, if such were recommended by the authorities on the spot. The necessary corollary to these decisions was the appointment of a Commander-in-Chief, and Sir Ian Hamilton was selected almost immediately after the meeting of March 10th. Sir Ian's written instructions* make the Government's position unmistakable. " Having entered on the project of forcing the Straits there can be no idea of abandoning the scheme." It is, of course, equally clear from the instructions

---

* Second Report of the Dardanelles Commission, paragraph 18.

that the Government still hoped that military intervention would not be necessary to subdue the forts, and that, as Sir Ian Hamilton puts it in his Diary,* " the Cabinet did not want to hear anything of the army till it had sailed through the Straits." But these were pious wishes. The written instructions above quoted (reinforced by a subsequent telegram from Lord Kitchener) decided the issue. The only essential precaution enjoined by Lord Kitchener was that extensive operations should wait on the arrival of the 29th Division.

The fact that the Government had by this date definitely faced the possibility of combined operations did not mean, however, that in their view the naval attack need not be pressed. On the contrary, high hopes were now entertained of extensive Russian co-operation against the Turkish forts on the Bosphorus and the Turkish armies if we could force the Dardanelles; and Admiral Carden was urged on March 11th to further efforts. Only in preference to an attempt to rush the Straits across unswept mine-fields were combined operations on an extensive scale to be undertaken this side of Constantinople. Admiral Carden agreed to the Admiralty proposals, and the plans for a final attempt on the Narrows were put in hand and were ready by March 15th. The next day Admiral Carden was forced under medical orders to resign his command, and the date of the attack was postponed while the Admiralty exchanged telegrams with the new naval commander, Vice-Admiral de Robeck, who was able to assure them that he was satisfied that the proposed attack was sound, and that he was anxious to carry it out.

In these circumstances, the historic action of March 18th was decided on, and with that decision the active participation of the Naval Division in the Gallipoli operations begins.

It must not be imagined, though it is indeed hard in the light of events to imagine otherwise, that the situation seemed, to those on the spot, anything but reasonably promising at this time. It is indeed poignant to recall the high hopes with which the Naval Division had started out to the scene of war. Rupert Brooke has left on record his own peculiar enthusiasm : " I had not imagined," he wrote, " that fate could be so benign. . . . I am filled with confident and glorious

---

* " Gallipoli Diary," Vol. I., p. 8.

hopes."* He was not alone in his excitement. The English-
man's protective irony could not indeed be expected to survive
the splendour of that voyage through the Mediterranean,
when the first breath of spring was in the air, the sea was
brilliant like a jewel, and " sunset and dawn divine blazes of
colour."

Not even Malta, that suburb of the East, could break the
spell. Africa lay behind them, the Greek islands and Constantinople lay before them. The spirit of adventure was in
the air of spring, and no jarring note intruded on the Eastern
scene as the transports worked up the Mediterranean from
Malta in the second week in February and weighed anchor
in Mudros harbour. Later, with the too facile genius of our
race, even these primitive islands of the Aegean Archipelago
became Anglicized, but as yet those tranquil shores were the
embodiment of a classic, if somewhat arid, simplicity. Thucy-
dides' description of primitive Attica comes inevitably to mind
as we wander in memory among these barren but fragrant
hills, and see the scattered peasants eking out a peaceful
existence from the small patches of cornland and vineyard
which they had won in the course of a struggle with nature
extending through many sunny, if penurious, centuries.

And in the harbour itself the scene was not only unfamiliar,
but without parallel in the modern annals. Indeed, as John
Masefield says, you might have thought that all the ships
of the world were gathered there. From the *Queen Elizabeth*,
then the pride of the fleet, to the smallest variety of tramp
steamer that ever carried yeast from Edinburgh to Grimsby,
every type of craft was represented. Coming to rest in such
an anchorage, the battalions of the Naval Division suffered no
sense of anticlimax.

At 6 p.m. on March 18th, the Division, still in the original
transports, sailed out of the harbour eastwards. Steering W.
and N. of Imbros, the transports arrived off the western shore
of the peninsula at 5.80 a.m. on the morning of the 19th.
Down the coast, the flotilla moved on to Cape Tekke, and came
up with H.M.S. *Dublin* at 6 a.m. There, at the entrance of
the Straits, destroyers went cruising round, and *Queen Elizabeth, Dublin, Glory, Albion* and *Inflexible* were keeping up a
desultory bombardment on the Turkish forts. The first

* " Rupert Brooke : A Memoir," by Edward Marsh, p. 187.

5*

sight of these historic waters, famous beyond all other channels of the world, held out, to the untrained and enthusiastic eyes of the young officers and men on board the transports, the promise of early developments. The great ships, gathered off the entrance, appeared in truth to dominate the scene. Every moment the men expected orders to disembark. From the decks of the troopships the Turkish infantry could be seen lining the cliffs. The hour of battle seemed at hand.

But in fact the movement of the transports, a demonstration planned to divert the attention of the enemy from what should have been the closing and critical stage of a great naval attack, was no longer required. The great naval attack had failed, and within two hours of their first sight of the enemy, the Naval Division received orders to return to Lemnos.

There was in one sense no reason why the failure of this naval attempt on the Straits should have been regarded as decisive. The disaster which had led to the breaking off of the engagement, though believed at the time to be due to floating mines, was caused, so it has since been established, almost accidentally, by a minefield laid by the Turks on the night of the 17th and 18th in waters which we could have cleared. Unaccountably, this minefield had been missed by our sweepers, and the result was a heavy loss in capital ships, but the loss need not have been regarded as likely to recur if the operations were renewed : in other words the original plan was not necessarily shown to be incapable of fulfilment.

The Admiral, however, was not long in deciding not to make any further unsupported attacks on the Straits, and, on March 21st, he formally notified Sir Ian Hamilton of his decision. The effect was to commit the Army to an attack on the Gallipoli peninsula. Sir Ian Hamilton's instructions from Lord Kitchener were such as to compel him to undertake such military operations as were necessary to enable the fleet to reach Constantinople, unless he was convinced that no operations of the kind were possible ; and, after a personal reconnaissance, he was already reasonably satisfied that this object could be achieved by military operations against the Gallipoli peninsula.

When, therefore, the Admiral notified him, on the 21st, that he would require military assistance if he was to get the fleet to Constantinople, the only question left open was the

time and the place of the military attack. The time was the
immediate question. The chance of a surprise had been jeo-
pardized by the naval operations. A further delay would
render a surprise impossible. Despite the grave difficulties,
General Birdwood was in favour of an immediate landing.
Admiral Wemyss held similar views. In addition to the
Naval Division, there was on the spot approximately the
strength of an Australian Division. An immediate landing,
it was urged, might be comparatively unopposed, and might
mean the capture of Achibaba almost without a struggle.
Meanwhile other troops could be brought on the scene. But
Sir Ian Hamilton had no hesitation in rejecting the plan.
The 29th Division could not be expected for a fortnight or
longer; the Naval Division transports were not suitably
loaded for landing operations; troops from Egypt could
not arrive for some days. The force might indeed reach
Achibaba, but what chance had they of remaining there,
unsupported by artillery (save a few Australian guns), without
Engineers' stores, periscopes and tools ? In the absence of
detailed preparation for the landing, the supply and the transport arrangements for even twenty thousand men must
inevitably be inadequate; if bad weather arose they must
break down completely, and weather conditions could not be
expected to become settled till mid-April at earliest. Above
all, there was Lord Kitchener's precise instruction that no
extensive military operations should be undertaken till the
arrival of the 29th Division.

In these circumstances it was decided to postpone the attack,
and to make, in the interval, the most careful and detailed preparations; and on the 22nd March the Naval Division transports
sailed from Mudros to Port Said, where they were to re-ship
their stores, and await the concentration of the remainder of
the force.

The disembarkation of the Division was completed by Monday, March 29th, and on that and the following days the R.N.D.
S.A.A. column (Major Carter), the R.N.D. Supply Column
(Major J. D. Buller, A.S.C.), the R.N.D. Sanitary Section and
the 19th Mobile Veterinary Section joined the Division. On
the 1st April, orders were received by General Paris to send a
detachment to take over a section of the trenches at Kantara
on the Suez Canal defences, and a composite force consisting

of two half-battalions from each of the 1st and 2nd Naval
Brigades (Drake, Nelson, Howe and Anson Battalions), under
General Mercer, left for Kantara by rail at 7 a.m.

On April 3rd, the Division was inspected at Port Said by the
Commander-in-Chief, Admiral Pierce and his Flag Captain
(Captain Burmester, R.N.) being present. The inspection
passed off successfully, at least according to Sir Ian Hamilton,
who notes in his Diary the next day that the Division " marched
past very well indeed." For a division, not by any means at its
best on a parade ground, this was satisfactory. The day has,
however, a painful significance, as it marked the beginning of
Rupert Brooke's illness, an illness not then, or for some days,
diagnosed as serious, but which was to lead to the untimely
death of one of the most brilliantly gifted Englishmen of his
day. It is easy to find defects in the writings of men of genius—
because they set in their own works a standard which inevitably
they cannot always maintain—but only poets of the younger
generation have ever doubted that by the death of Brooke
England lost not only the greatest of her younger poets, but a
voice which would have championed the cause of humane
justice without discrimination in a world where, later, such
voices were to be few.

Two days later the arrangements for the transport of the
Naval Division had taken shape, and the re-embarkation of
stores began. On this day, also, the Anson Battalion were
ordered to Alexandria to act as beach parties for the 29th
Division, who had just arrived, but whose transports, like those
of the Naval Division, had been loaded as for a peace-time
change of station. The Anson left Alexandria at 4 p.m. It
is interesting to recall that this battalion, which, as it happened,
had the most honourable part of any in the Naval Division at
the landing on April 25th, was detached and sent to Alexandria,
in the belief that it would be required solely for routine fatigue
duties. Nothing but disappointment was felt by the Anson
officers, at this time, with the task believed to be before them.

The remainder of the Division proceeded at top speed with
the work of re-embarkation. Time was indeed pressing. It
was now a fortnight since the last naval attack ; and the Admiral
had consented to break off further active operations, only on the
understanding that they would be renewed again by April 14th
at earliest. A slight interruption to the embarkation was

caused by a reported attack on the Canal defences at Kantara,
on the 7th, with the result that at 11 a.m. all troops in
Alexandria were ordered to " stand by." The attack proved,
however, to be nothing more than a reconnaissance by a
mounted patrol, some sixty strong, which was beaten off without
loss, the enemy not venturing within effective range ; and, at
2 p.m., the division was able to " carry on."

The next day, 8th April, the first Naval Division transport
(the *Braemar Castle*) sailed for Mudros. On board, were General
Trotman and his staff, and Colonel Matthews and the Plymouth
Battalion of Marines. The *Braemar Castle* was followed by the
Cawdor Castle (Chatham Battalion), the *Gloucester Castle* (Portsmouth Battalion), the *Inkonka* (Motor Machine Gun Squadron),
the *Royal George* (Commodore Backhouse, R.N., and staff, and
the Howe Battalion), the *Grantully Castle* (Hood Battalion),
and the *Somali* (1st and 3rd Field Ambulances and details
R.M.A.). All the transports had their tow of lighters, not for
the disembarkation of the Division (even at this eleventh hour,
when every element of surprise had been sacrificed to completing
the preparation and equipment of the force, there were not
enough lighters to enable the whole force to be landed simultaneously), but for the use of the 29th Division. The departure
of these transports left in Egypt only the headquarters of the
Division, and General Mercer's 1st Naval Brigade, who were
required for the re-embarkation of horses and mules. As soon
as this had been completed, the Brigade and the divisional troops
embarked on the *Alnwick Castle* (Deal Battalion R.M.L.I.), the
Ayrshire (R.N.D. Engineers), the *Franconia* (D.H.Q. and H.Q.
1st Brigade, Drake Battalion, Div. Cyclist Company and Signal
Sections), the *Minnetonka* (Nelson Battalion, S.A.A. Column
and No. 2 Field Ambulance) and the *Astrian* (Divisional Train).
As the transports arrived at Mudros, they were ordered to proceed to Trebuki Bay, Scyros, in conformity with the detailed
plan of campaign which had by now been decided on.

CHAPTER V

THE GALLIPOLI LANDINGS

UNLIKE the Grecian Islands and the peninsulas of Italy and Spain, fellow survivors of that prehistoric inundation which buried beneath the Black Sea and the more placid waters of the Marmora, the Aegean and the Mediterranean a once fertile and sunlit Continent, the Gallipoli peninsula has an almost accidental importance. It is no more than a chain of rugged uplands and mountain peaks running down from the Thracian mainland between the Aegean and the Sea of Marmora ; a narrow strip of land nearly fifty miles in length, but only a few miles in width, where many nations have passed, many historic events have taken place, and where, for all this, no culture has taken root and no civilization has endured. But beneath the cliffs of its eastern shore, and dominated by its once mountainous peaks, still rising above the level of the sea to a height of seven or eight hundred feet, lies the narrow channel which we know as the Straits of the Dardanelles.

From the first dawn of history the control of the Straits has been the foremost aim of one or more of the great Powers of Asia or Europe. Opposite the southern extremity of the peninsula lie buried the seven cities of Troy, and when the control of the Straits was finally wrested from Persia by the Ionian Greeks, the history of Mediterranean civilization begins. With the loss of the control of the Straits by Athens to Sparta at Aegospotami, the power of the Athenian Empire hastened to its premature decline. The assertion of Roman superiority in these same waters was the historic service of Sulla to the cause of Roman imperialism. On the control of the Straits the Byzantine Empire depended through a thousand years for its amazing stability, amid a world relapsed into barbarism. To her control of these waters, won by her naval supremacy,

Venice owed her greatness; and with the defeat of Venice by the
Turks off the entrance to the Straits the renascence of Mediterranean civilization came to an end. Through their control of
the Straits the Turks had maintained themselves in Europe
for more than five hundred years.

And so history was only repeating itself when the seizure of
the Gallipoli peninsula became for a little, perhaps for too short
a time, an avowed aim of British strategy. But history had no
lessons to teach us as to the manner in which we could establish
a footing on that inhospitable and barren shore. However old
the strategy, new tactics must be brought into play. The
greater battles of the past had been fought on the sea ; following
precedent, we too had attempted a decision at sea, and we had
failed. The science of earthwork defences had, as in purely land
warfare, so in amphibious warfare, outrun the development of
destructive explosives, and, where the wooden hulks of Lysander
had been supreme, the *Queen Elizabeth* had proved ineffective.

It was now the turn of the Army. The point where the naval
operations had broken down was in the reduction of the forts
guarding the approaches to the Narrows. The object of the
military operations was to succeed where the Navy had failed.
To this end they had either to reach, and hold for so long as
might be necessary, some position on the European or Asiatic
shore of the Straits, from which not only these forts but those at
Chanak, and Kilid Bahr and beyond, could be dominated and
silenced, or so to manœuvre as to cut off the Turkish garrison
in Gallipoli and enforce its surrender.

The alternative plans, discussed at the time and subsequently,
were many. Broadly, however, the choice appeared to Sir Ian
Hamilton to lie between a landing in Asia to secure the eastern
shore of the Straits, a landing on Gallipoli with its objective the
Kilid Bahr Plateau,* a landing at Bulair, or a landing in the
Gulf of Xeros. The last two projects, particularly popular with
amateur strategists, are attractive only on a misreading of the
situation and were never very seriously considered.

Looking at the map, we see Bulair to be the narrowest point
of the peninsula, and the mistaken impression has prevailed
that the seizure of this position would isolate the Turkish forces

---

* A dominating feature running inland almost due west from Kilid Bahr
for a distance of some four miles, which is at its broadest two miles in length,
and from 600 to 800 feet above sea-level throughout.

on the peninsula itself and compel their surrender. But the fact
is that the main communications of the Turkish divisions in the
peninsula did not run through or anywhere near Bulair, but down
and across the Straits to the town of Gallipoli. The most
northerly point from which the land communications of the
force guarding the Narrows could be threatened was the Sari
Bair bridge, south-east of Suvla, and commanding the road
from Gallipoli to Maidos. But if this position were aimed at,
it would be folly to attack it from Bulair, twenty miles to the
north.   The distance, in fact, could never be traversed in
hostile country, with a large Turkish army in the rear round
Adrianople, and the consequent need for a large force not only
to maintain communications but to protect the base. ,

The same objection, with even more force, applies to the
proposal to land north of the Bulair lines, in the Gulf of Xeros.
From there, only one objective was possible, and that was the
main European military centre of the Turks at Adrianople.
But such an objective implied warfare on a wide front, with no
assistance from the fleet, if it was to be anything more than a
futile, if spectacular, diversion.   For extensive land operations,
we had not the troops : for a diversion, there was no occasion.

The plan for landing in Asia was more attractive, and, in
one of its most vital assumptions, it was shown to be justified.
A landing at Kum Kale was proved to be a practical, military
operation, and the Turks did not expect us to land there.   A
substantial advance up the Asiatic shore of the Straits might,
it was urged, enable the fleet, fired at from one side only, to
get through the Narrows. The objection to the plan, and
one which, in the light of the gallant and determined
character of the Turkish reaction, history will probably regard
as decisive, was that we could not, with any certainty, maintain
ourselves on the Asiatic shore against a strong enemy attack.
The advantages of the narrow front, of the constant support of
the guns of the fleet at all stages of an advance, which enabled
us to maintain ourselves on the peninsula against the most
determined assaults, would not have entered into the situation
had we landed on the Asiatic coast.   Instead of the guns of the
fleet, we should have had the guns of the enemy on our left
flank.

The question before Sir Ian Hamilton narrowed itself
down to this. Was it possible, with the forces at his disposal,

to reach and hold the Kilid Bahr Plateau? The plateau was protected from a force attacking it from the western beaches (Gaba Tepe, or Anzac Cove) by the Sari Bair ridge, and from a force based on the southern beaches by the hill of Achibaba. Both these carefully prepared positions were formidable, if not actually impregnable, should it be necessary to attack them when once the main Turkish forces were concentrated for their defence. The Turks had, so it was correctly thought, four first-line divisions on the peninsula, and they were within easy reach of reinforcements from Asia, where they had another four second-line divisions immediately available. Sir Ian Hamilton had at his disposal only four divisions (with not even a ten per cent. margin for casualties in the 29th or Naval Divisions) and the French force, less than two divisions, mainly of African troops. Could we neutralize the overwhelming advantages of the enemy, in position, in preparation, in numbers, by immobilizing the bulk of his reserves while we were making good our hold on the shore of the peninsula? Having landed, could we hope to hold the enemy in suspense as to the direction of our main attack sufficiently long for us to concentrate our army before he could concentrate his?

Even if we succeeded so far, were our resources in men, in guns, in ammunition, in equipment, sufficient to enable us to take the offensive with a reasonable chance of immediate success? And, even then, could we maintain ourselves—even on the defensive—with lengthened communications crossing impossible country, without roads, docks, or landing stages, against the full strength of the Turkish reserves?

No man living could have answered these questions with any great degree of conviction in either sense. Yet they had to be faced. The only alternative would have been the abandonment of the whole campaign, in view of its admittedly dubious issue. This course was, indeed, in the first instance definitely recommended by General Hunter Weston, in an " appreciation " written at Malta, and neither General Birdwood nor General Paris definitely excluded this possibility from his consideration. Indeed, as the Extracts quoted by Sir Ian Hamilton from the Memoranda submitted by these commanders clearly indicate, there was no unreasonable optimism among the higher command in the days immediately preceding the landing. Looking back on these forebodings, in particular on General Hunter Weston's remark that " there is not in present circumstances a reasonable chance of success," and General Paris' less definite but depressing opinion that " To land . . . would be hazardous in the extreme under present conditions," it may seem a matter for regret that their prudent counsels did not prevail.

Although, however, the situation was anxious and obscure, and although no considered estimate of the requirements of an army attempting the seizure of the Gallipoli peninsula had been put before the Cabinet, Sir Ian Hamilton had, nevertheless, been given instructions which he could hardly interpret otherwise than as requiring him to attempt the task with the forces at his disposal. The result was, as it happened, fatal to the success of the operation, for, when the first check occurred, the necessary reinforcements and the still more necessary guns, material and ammunition were not available in time to retrieve the initial failure. By the time we were reinforced, sickness had taken its hold of what had become a beleaguered garrison, and the reinforcements were inadequate. The necessary guns and ammunition were never sent. Here, probably, and not in any tactical mishandling of the forces available, or in any fallacious strategy, was the primary cause of our failure; but it is a cause which redeems the campaign from insignificance as a military achievement. Whatever else may be said, the divisions that fought at Gallipoli (maintained at great expense indeed, but starved of all essential military supplies, denied reinforcements, and forced to fight when, to a man, they would, in France, have been considered medically unfit even for the quietest part of the line), engaged the power of the Turkish armies, and, in the war of armies, if not in the war of positions, they were victorious. This consideration is relevant not only to an historical verdict on the results of the campaign, but in abatement of any criticism which the legion of those who never fail to be wise after the event may think fit to bring against the undoubted miscalculations which preceded it. To have failed in a great adventure through lack of meticulous estimating of requirements (if, indeed, that was the governing factor) was lamentable. To have let the issue of the war in the Near East go by default would have been an irretrievable disaster. It is with that thought uppermost in his mind, that we must imagine Sir Ian Hamilton to have flung his doubts to the wind in deciding to attempt to seize the peninsula with the slender forces on the spot, and to trust to the military authorities at home for that loyal support which every Commander-in-Chief has the right to expect.

Having reached his decision, the question was to decide on the best means to give effect to it. The essential problem was to prevent, by a number of simultaneous attacks, whether simulated or actual, the concentration within forty-eight hours of the four Turkish divisions on Gallipoli and their reinforcement from Asia. To do this, it was necessary not only to land in Asia, as well as on the peninsula, but to threaten directly the real objective, the Kilid Bahr Plateau, from more than one side. Any landing or demonstration which did not threaten this position, would, if things went badly for the enemy, be inevitably ignored.

With this object it was decided to make two landings in force—at Gaba Tepe and in the toe of the peninsula—and to detach the French corps for a demonstration in Asia, and the Naval Division for a demonstration at Bulair. This involved a division of forces, but there was no means oi avoiding it; on the available beaches only a small covering force and no guns could be landed in the first instance, and subsequent progress must be slow. To land the whole force on either front would have taken longer than it could have taken the enemy to concentrate their own forces, had their reserves not been held to their ground. The only hope was to immobilize their reserves at points as widely separated as possible; and to trust to our fleet to concentrate our forces quicker than the enemy, working across the endless hills and gullies of the peninsula, could concentrate his.

So the plan finally took shape. The main landings were assigned to the Australian and New Zealand Army Corps (in the neighbourhood of Gaba Tepe) and to the 29th Division (south of Achibaba). The Asiatic diversion (to take the form of a temporary landing of at least a brigade) was assigned to General D'Amade's Force, and the bloodless Bulair demonstration to the Naval Division. It was for the purpose of this demonstration that this Division, less the Plymouth and Anson Battalions (attached to the 29th Division for the Southern landings), had been ordered to rendezvous at Scyros.

    *   *   *   *   *   *   *

The date first fixed for the landing was April 23rd, and it was on April 21st, after a further conference with the Naval Commander on the morning of the 21st, that the first operation order of the Naval Division in the campaign was issued. The previous days had been spent in practising landing operations, in case of eventualities, and, with the issue of the detailed orders, nothing but calm weather was now needed for the operations to proceed. Unfortunately on the evening of the 21st a strong wind sprang up, and continued through the following day and night, with the result that the landing was postponed forty-eight hours.

On the 23rd, the day first planned for the landing, Rupert Brooke died ; he was buried the same evening in an olive grove, some five thousand yards up the valley that runs north-east from the Beacon on the north shore of Trebuki Bay. There the curious, or the faithful, may find his resting-place marked by fragments of white marble piled above his grave by Charles Lister, Denis Browne, F. S. Kelly, Arthur Asquith, Bernard Freyberg and Patrick Shaw-Stewart. The news of his death was telegraphed to the Admiralty from Lemnos, and Mr. Winston Churchill's tribute in *The Times* of April 26th recalls across the years the position which Rupert Brooke filled in the eyes of thousands of his countrymen at a great crisis of their fate. The lapse of time and the nakedness of the literary horizon have only emphasized the truth of that striking tribute.*

* "Rupert Brooke is dead. A telegram from the Admiral at Lemnos tells us that his life has closed at the moment when it seemed to have reached its springtime. A voice had become audible, a note had been struck, more true, more thrilling, more able to do justice to the nobility of our youth in arms engaged in this present war, than any other—more able to express their thoughts of self-surrender, and with a power to carry comfort to those who watched them so intently from afar. The voice has been swiftly stilled. Only the echoes and the memory remain ; but they will linger.

"During the last few months of his life, months of preparation in gallant comradeship and open air, the poet-soldier told with all the simple force of genius the sorrow of youth about to die, and the sure triumphant consolations of a sincere and valiant spirit. He expected to die ; he was willing to die for the dear England whose beauty and majesty he knew ; and he advanced towards the brink in perfect serenity, with absolute conviction of the rightness of his country's cause, and a heart devoid of hate for fellow men.

"The thoughts to which he gave expression in the very few incomparable war sonnets which he has left behind will be shared by many thousands of young men moving resolutely and blithely forward into this, the hardest, the cruellest, and the least-rewarded of all the wars that men have fought. They are a whole history and revelation of Rupert Brooke himself. Joyous, fearless, versatile, deeply instructed, with classic symmetry of mind and body, he was all that one would wish England's noblest sons to be in days when no sacrifice but the most precious is acceptable, and the most precious is that which is most freely proffered."

While the Division was at Scyros, General Paris was asked to supply, for beach duties in connection with the impending landings, a further three hundred ratings with sea experience. These were drawn from the Hood and Howe Battalions, and the party, under Sub-Lieut. (later Lt.-Colonel) J. O. Dodge, R.N.V.R., left for Mudros the same day.

On the evening of the 24th the transports sailed north towards the peninsula. The transports of the 29th Division were at the same time moving out from Mudros Harbour, to the accompaniment of those enthusiastic cheers which echo now with so ironic a significance. With them, and in particular with the Plymouth and Anson Battalions, to whom, as it happened, fell the earlier share in the active operations, went the thoughts of all on board the Naval Division transports, as they steamed north to their solitary but peaceful rendezvous five miles west-south-west of Xeros Island.

The fleet of transports, escorted by H.M.S. *Canopus* (on board which were General Paris and his staff), *Dartmouth* (G.O.C. and the Staff Officer 2nd Naval Brigade), *Jed* and *Kennet*, reached the rendezvous at daylight; at 5.45 a.m. H.M.S. *Dartmouth* and *Doris* began a bombardment of the Bulair lines, which continued throughout the day; two hours later, Colonels Ollivant and Richardson on board H.M.S. *Kennet* carried out a detailed reconnaissance of landing-places on the north shore of the gulf. The *Kennet* was stood in close to shore, and was but once fired on—sustaining no casualties. All this time, the fleet of transports was lying ostentatiously in the background, but there was no evidence that the feint was being taken in any way seriously. For the same evening, a more realistic enterprise was decided on, and a platoon of the Hood Battalion was ordered to effect a landing under cover of darkness, to light flares upon the beaches and shoot off machine guns and rifles, and, by great activity and in the manner of a stage army, impersonate a force many times their size, and thus to give the threatened invasion the hall-mark of reality. The fact that the fleet of transports had been demonstrating for several hours opposite the point to be invaded insured a warm if not cordial reception, which would in all probability spell disaster to the force involved. This was pointed out by Lt.-Commander Freyberg, who volunteered himself to swim alone to light flares

upon the hostile shore. His bold offer was accepted. The
night was dark, with a touch of frost in the air, and there was
a slight sea running in the Gulf of Xeros when Freyberg, painted
black and greased to keep out the cold, was lowered into the
water with a little canvas raft of flares. He was armed with
a small revolver, with sheath knife slung round his waist, and
wearing a small luminous wrist compass for direction in case
the stars became obscured. A start was made at 10 p.m. ;
it was dark and unattractive, save for the phosphorescent
splash from the muffled oars of the ship's boat. By some miscalculation, in the dark, of the distance, two miles had to be
swum, and it was midnight before a landing was effected.
The raft was hidden while a reconnaissance of the enemy
position above the cliff was carried out.

Crawling about, naked, on an open and exposed cliff after
two hours' swim on a cold, windy, April night was not a very
cheerful occupation, but Freyberg was able, in spite of the
noise from his chattering teeth, to get close up to the enemy
trenches on the cliffs. After a few minutes of searching, the
raft was recovered and the first flare was lighted on the beach.
Immediately machine-gun fire was opened from the picket
boats all round and the British war ships bombarded the
beaches. Freyberg had to take refuge in the water to avoid
fire, but swimming in the direction of the Bulair line, was
able to light two other flares on the beaches, a quarter of a mile
apart. When this had been accomplished the mission was at
an end. The stars were all covered by clouds, and so, on a
compass bearing due south, he made a start from the inhospitable shore, in the hope of being picked up in the dark
by a destroyer or picket boat. The ships, of course, showed
no light, and there were no flashes from the guns, which were
by now silent. It was a meagre chance ; but after two hours'
swimming Commander Freyberg was retrieved, cramped and
nearly dead with cold.

The effect of these operations was substantial. As we
have seen, there were four Turkish divisions on the peninsula ;
two were allocated to the defence of the Bulair lines, and
two to the Southern defence systems hingeing on Kilid Bahr
and Achibaba. The headquarters of the Southern defensive
system was at Maidos, of the Northern at Gallipoli. When
the Naval Division feint began, the coast against which they

Brig.-Géneral Bernard Freyberg, V.C., C.M.G., D.S.O.

(From the portrait by Ambrose McEvoy in the possession of the Imperial War Museum.)

were operating was in truth but lightly held. But no sooner had the transports been sighted, than one of the divisions based on Maidos was moved northwards, another was held ready to join it, and General Liman van Sanders took up his post of command on a height near the central front of the Bulair lines. Not till nightfall did he even suspect that the operation was a feint—but by this time the landings which the reinforcement of the Southern force might have prevented had been achieved.

The story of these landings (Sir Ian Hamilton had decided on no less than five) must now be told.

*   *   *   *   *   *   *

The enemy south of Achibaba held one well-sited line of trenches, strongly wired, which ran across the southern slopes of Achibaba in front of Krithia. This was his line of resistance. His outpost line, known to be held in force, consisted of still more elaborately wired earthwork defences on three small knolls which lay at intervals of about a mile from each other, and not more than 500 yards inland, on a line running roughly parallel with the southern coast of the peninsula from Cape Tekke to Sedd-el-bahr. Linked up with these defences, were advanced posts, guarding the only two beaches on the southern shore at which a landing could be anticipated. The first was the bay below Sedd-el-bahr, where the tall and precipitous cliffs give place for some 350 yards to a green amphitheatre of crumbled and grass-grown slopes, falling away to the sea and ending in undulating ridges of sand. The second was nearer the entrance to the Straits, west of Cape Helles, where the line of cliffs is broken by a small gully, opening on to a strip of beach 40 yards deep at its widest point, and the whole not more than 250 yards long. There were also small detachments watching Morto Bay and Gully Beach.

The main Turkish line on the slopes of Achibaba was our first objective. To enable an attack on this line to be developed effectively, the two main beaches must be stormed. Once the beaches were secured by the covering forces, further troops were to be landed, and the advance was to begin. To ensure the immediate success of this advance, a third landing

6

was to be made at a small cove almost exactly on the left flank of the Turkish position.   This force was to join in the pursuit of the Turks as they were dislodged, or in the preliminary attack, should any untoward event make it necessary. The finishing touch to the Turkish *débâcle* was to be given by two flanking parties, landed a couple of miles behind the Turkish position on either flank.   These parties, though small in numbers, were expected to harass the retreating Turk, and prevent anything like an orderly retirement.   As the main line advanced, the flanking parties would join in the assault on the main Turkish position.   The places selected for the landing of the flanking parties were the north of Morto Bay (" S " beach) in the Straits, an ideal landing-place for a small force, but impracticable for a large one because of its exposure to artillery fire from Asia ; and " Y " beach on the Aegean shore.   In the case of these two landings there was to be only a covering force :   *i.e.*, no more troops were to be landed than those required to carry the position in the face of, what was expected to be, a very slight opposition.

The forces detailed for the five landings were as follows :

	" V " Beach	1st Dublin Fusiliers
		1st Munster Fusiliers
		2nd Hampshires
		" A " Coy. Anson Battalion
		1 Platoon " D " Coy. Anson Battalion
Main attack	" W " Beach	1st Lancashire Fusiliers
		4th Worcesters
		1st Essex
		" B " Coy. Anson Battalion
		Battalion H.Q. Anson Battalion

	" X " Beach	2nd Royal Fusiliers
		1st Inniskillings
Subsidiary attack		1st Border Regiment
		" D " Coy. Anson Battn. (less 1 Platoon)
		" C " Coy. Anson Battalion

Flanking
parties
{
Morto Bay   2nd South Wales Borderers
(less 1 Coy.)

" Y " Beach Plymouth Battalion R.M.L.I.
1st K.O.S.B.
1 Coy. 2nd S. Wales Borderers
}

The Morto Bay party landed without much opposition, and soon occupied three lines of trenches above de Tott's battery, which was evacuated by a small Turkish detachment. In this they were assisted by sailors and marines from the covering ship. Once safely established on shore, the detachment stood to its ground, waiting till some movement of the enemy should give them an opportunity for effective intervention without risking the loss of touch with their line of supply (and retreat). In this position the detachment was found when the line was finally advanced.

The " Y " Beach party met at first with little opposition ; the actual landing was made from trawlers at 5.45 a.m. without covering fire, and the crest of the steep cliffs had been gained without loss by 6.30. Touch with the enemy was shortly obtained about 800 yards to the north, and a defensive flank was formed facing north-east, to the defence of which Lt.-Colonel Matthews, C.B., R.M.L.I., of the Plymouth Battalion (who was in command of the whole force) detailed two companies of the Marines. The remainder of the force advanced to the east over a wide front. Crossing the deep Gully Ravine, when a few prisoners were taken, Colonel Matthews took up a position on a ridge running roughly parallel to it, a few hundred yards beyond. Here, 300 Turkish infantry were seen moving south, and two field guns taking up a position east of Krithia. For two hours the forces remained unmolested and stationary, waiting for signs of the expected advance from the south. There were none. A further advance with this limited force was hardly practicable, if any touch was to be maintained with the left flank, and, as a Turkish attack in some force was expected, failing the success of the Southern landings, it was decided to withdraw to a defensive position covering the original landing-places, with the right flank only thrown forward across the gully, to give immediate support to any advance from the south. By 3 p.m. this withdrawal

6*

was completed, and at dusk, when the Turks first began to threaten the position, the right flank also was withdrawn to the shore. The new position was a rough semicircle, with each flank resting on the sea, and the centre thrown forward some five hundred yards. The Marines held the flanks, each with two companies, and the K.O.S.B. and South Wales Borderers held the centre.

The decision to remain on the defensive was well-reasoned, and was indeed almost inevitable, having regard to the fact that, although Colonel Matthews had reported the unopposed landing to General Hunter Weston, he had received no acknowledgment and no information of the happenings at the other beaches.

It remains, however, true that a bolder policy would, in all human probability, have had far-reaching results ; what those might have been will appear when we turn back to the more splendid, if more tragic, story of the operations which had been going on simultaneously on the southern shore of the peninsula.

As in the case of the other small detachments, the Royal Fusiliers landed at " X " beach without serious opposition. So effective, indeed, was the support afforded to the covering force by H.M.S. *Implacable* that the Turkish infantry lining the cliffs above the beach were driven back on their main position, while the infantry scaled the cliffs without a casualty. Immediately the heights had been made good, Colonel Newenham secured his left and front with half his battalion, and, holding one company in reserve, threw the other forward towards Hill 114, where he hoped to gain touch with the main landing force at " W " beach. He was met, instead, by a heavy and well-directed fire from an enemy clearly still in undisturbed possession. There was nothing for it but to wait till the whole of his force was ashore, and then, instead of moving forward on Krithia, as he had hoped, to turn south-east to secure his flank. This set-back was, of course, a reaction from the partial check experienced at " W " beach, owing to the dominating position above Sedd-el-bahr being still in the hands of the enemy. The reason for this was that the landing at " V " beach had failed.

" V " beach was of all the beaches selected for landings the most suitable for defence. The beach itself was not more than ten yards wide, and edged by a small but perpendicular bank of sand not above five or six feet high : beyond, was a green amphitheatre rising over a gentle slope of some two hundred yards to a height of two hundred feet above the level of the sea. Not only was the whole beach commanded from Sedd-el-bahr Castle, but these green and peaceful slopes were themselves covered with trenches and dug-outs invisible from the shore, and beyond reach of damage from the preliminary bombardment—for the dug-outs were cut back in the slopes of the hill, and the trenches themselves so deep as to be immune from any save a plunging fire.

At the first hint of dawn, three companies of the Dublin Fusiliers and the 4th Platoon of the Anson Battalion (Lieutenant Denholm, R.N.V.R.) were disembarked from the sweepers, which had brought them from Mudros, and took their places in the boats, the whole force of six hundred men being borne in six tows (each made up of a pinnace and four cutters) in line abreast. On the right of the line of tows was the *River Clyde*, carrying the remaining company and the headquarters staff of the Dublins, the Munster Fusiliers, half the Hampshire Regiment, and Sub-Lieut. Tisdall's 13th Platoon of the Anson Battalion, accompanied by Lieut.-Commander Smallwood, R.N.V.R., the Second in Command of the battalion.

The *River Clyde* grounded almost at the same time as the men in the open boats reached the shallow waters, but, owing to the strength of the current, some delay occurred in fixing up the " bridge " of lighters. Meanwhile the Dublins, landing from open boats,* had been almost annihilated. Of three companies of this fine battalion, barely a hundred and fifty men reached the shore alive. A few of these, in the fury of their first attack, climbed the low ridge of sand which edged the beach, and were seen to disappear into the ruins of Sedd-el-bahr. The rest clung desperately to the slender shelter of the sand-bank, waiting.

* It was to assist in manning the numerous auxiliary craft (tugs, lighters, etc.), which had to play their part in this unprecedented operation of landing a modern army on a hostile beach from open boats, that the naval ratings from the Hood and Howe battalions had been lent to the Navy. These ratings were scattered in small parties and had no independent task assigned to them. Sub-Lieut. Dodge was, however, appointed an assistant Naval Landing Officer at "V" beach and accompanied the Dublin Fusiliers in their first assault. He was wounded before reaching the shore, but remained on the beach throughout the 25th and until the afternoon of the 26th. He was subsequently awarded the D.S.C. for his services at this landing.

Where was that tide of men which should have swept before now from the *River Clyde* to overwhelm the enemy by concentrated weight of numbers ? Throughout the morning, indeed, the little company of the living below the sandbank, almost on the water's edge, were joined by others from the ship.* But they came only in ones and twos, through a hurricane of fire. For every man that stepped ashore from that floating bridge of lighters, six or seven had fallen as they crossed the short fifty yards which lay between the ship and the shore. The wounded fell most often from the lighters as they were hit, and lay in the clear waters, visible but beyond reach of help. The dead lay beside them, or on the lighters or by the water's edge. On that shore, and round the wreckage of those wounded boats, only the living were conspicuous.

Among the foremost of these, were Lieut.-Colonel Doughty Wylie and Captain Walford, who were to lead the desperate and successful assault on the following day, and whose monument, put up by the French in memory of a brilliant feat of arms, still stands, as it stood throughout the campaign, amid the ruins of Sedd-el-bahr. No less conspicuous were those officers and men of the Navy who superintended the operations on the *River Clyde*. Keeping the landing parties between decks to avoid useless slaughter, Commander Unwin and his officers worked for continuous hours on the lighters and in the water, in the first instance making fast the bridge of boats, later repairing it, as the connecting hawsers were shot in half ; later still, rescuing those of the wounded who had fallen above the water's edge or on to the lighters. Only now and then did their labours cease for a moment, when, in Commander Unwin's judgment, the time had come for another party to attempt the passage ashore. Then, without a moment's delay, the work of repair and rescue would begin again.

In the work of rescue Commander Unwin was assisted not only by all those under his immediate command, but also by Sub-Lieut. Tisdall's detachment of the Anson Battalion. Tisdall's heroism must have been noteworthy even on that day and at that place, for it was noted. The official account

---

* Among these was Lieut.-Commander Smallwood, R.N.V.R., who, like Sub-Lieut. Dodge, was wounded coming ashore but remained on the beach till late on the 26th.

"V" Beach Landing, seen from the *River Clyde*, 11 a.m., April 25th, 1915.

(From a photograph taken by Lieut.-Commander E. G. Boissier, D.S.C., R.N.V.R.)

of his exploits, for which later he was awarded the Victoria Cross, is as follows :

" During the landing from the S.S. *River Clyde* at ' V ' beach in the Gallipoli Peninsula, Sub-Lieut. Tisdall, hearing wounded men on the beach calling for assistance, jumped into the water, and pushing a boat in front of him, went to their rescue. He was, however, obliged to obtain help, and took with him on two trips Leading Seaman Malia, and on other trips Chief Petty Officer Perring and Leading Seamen Curtiss and Parkinson. In all, Sub-Lieut. Tisdall made four or five trips between the ship and the shore, and was thus responsible for rescuing several wounded men under heavy and accurate fire."

For their share in these gallant exploits C.P.O. Perring, the platoon sergeant of Tisdall's platoon (promoted on the field a few days later to commissioned rank), Leading Seaman Malia and Leading Seaman Parkinson were awarded the Good Conduct Medal.

But no amount of individual gallantry could make good the heights of Sedd-el-bahr that day. It was clear that it was only under cover of darkness that sufficient troops could be landed to afford any chance of a successful assault. All that could be done was to keep down the Turkish fire, and prevent the enemy leaving their defences and annihilating the heroic survivors of the ill-fated assault. Even this was only made possible by the machine guns on the *River Clyde*.

" W " beach was longer and less deep than " V " beach, and was no less strongly defended. The two sides of the gully which runs down in the centre of the beach were as deeply entrenched as the amphitheatre at Sedd-el-bahr, and the entanglements actually low down to the water's edge. Moreover, there was no *River Clyde* to hold out the hope (though, as it turned out, a fallacious hope) of instant and overwhelming reinforcement to the detachments landing in open boats.

Nevertheless, the attack on the actual beach was instantly successful. The covering force (the 1st Battalion Lancashire Fusiliers), with whom were Lieut.-Colonel Moorhouse and his adjutant (Lieutenant Newman), with " B " Company of the Anson Battalion, approached the shore in four lines of cutters, eight abreast, towed by eight picket boats. When within a few yards of the beach, the tows were cast off and the boats rowed to the shore. Whether by a happy inspiration or by singular good fortune the boats on the left of the line diverged a little from the direct line of advance, and their occupants landed on a small ledge of rock immediately under the cliff at Tekke Burnu. Here they escaped the cross-fire which was brought to bear on other parts of the beach, and were able in their turn to assist the main assault by flanking fire ; the war-ships also closed in and began an intensive bombardment. Thus assisted, the main body of the Lancashire Fusiliers cut their way through the wire and collected under the cliffs at either side of the beach. There the companies were hastily reorganized and then led to the assault. By 9.30 a.m. the trenches up the gully were taken, and the beach was in our hands. In all this early fighting, the Anson platoons and the detachments from the Hood and Howe took part, and not until the heights had been gained were they reformed and assigned to their duties as beach parties, when their first tasks were to mount a guard on the Turkish prisoners, to clear the beach of wire, and to collect tools, ammunition and rifles from the casualties. In the course of the first hour's fighting, Sub-Lieut. T. F. Melland, R.N.V.R., was wounded.

The capture of " W " beach gave the army by 9.30 a.m. a temporary security of tenure on the peninsula, for at least the remaining battalions of the 29th Division could be landed ; but an advance on Krithia was impossible, for, as things were, it was necessary first to reduce from " W " beach the prepared positions on the Turkish left centre and left, which should, on the original plan, have been penetrated by the forces detailed for the " V " beach landing. Unfortunately, even the gallantry of the Worcester and Essex Regiments, who had arrived to the support of the Lancashire Fusiliers in the firing line by 10 a.m., proved unequal to this task. Though the twin positions of Hill 114 on the left and Hill 138 on the right of " W " beach were in our hands by 4.30 p.m., the heavy fighting had taken a grievous toll of casualties, and, with tired troops, a further advance was judged impossible. In the result the Turks remained in possession of the heights of Sedd-el-bahr.

Thus the night of the 25th found the detachments at Morto Bay and " Y " beach still exposed to independent attack, and the main force in the south still unable to advance from the shore. Daylight, the aimed fire of ships' guns and re-

View from the bridge of the *River Clyde*, early autumn, 1915

inforcements were necessary to any further attempt against Sedd-el-bahr. Could the flanking parties hold their ground so long without support ? Could the main body maintain itself where it was until dawn ? And what of the heroic survivors of the ill-fated " V " beach landing ? Could this small party, crouching still under the shelter of the sand hills only a hundred yards or so from the water's edge, protected only by the naval machine guns on the *River Clyde*, be reinforced during the night, so that they could attack with any hope of success at dawn on the 26th ?

On such a scene of tragic anxiety and suffering fell the brief twilight of the Eastern evening. The isolation of the scene was, indeed, a thing for pity. In Egypt were the troops whose presence would have made the landing a sure and swift success. On the *Albion*, with his staff, was the Commander-in-Chief, held to his post of command, without news, without even a sight of the newly-won positions. And on these stricken shores, where the dead were being buried with that hurried and tremulous silence so much more eloquent of human limitations than any funeral panegyric, the scattered relics of twelve battalions were keeping a ceaseless vigil. Till light came, they were beyond reach of the fleet, with no supports behind them but the Anson beach companies, and in front of them the whole strength of the enemy, able in darkness to mass unobserved and fall perhaps in overwhelming strength on any point which he might choose.

Throughout the whole of the day, the men of the Anson Battalion on " W " beach had been occupied without interval in the unloading of stores, the transport of ammunition and water to the firing line and the burying of the dead. The company which had shared in the first assault had been reinforced during the morning by three more platoons of " A " Company (diverted from " V " beach), under Lt.-Commander Peter McCirdy, and with this party came the Reverend H. C. Foster, the Chaplain to the 2nd Naval Brigade, the first Anglican Chaplain to land on the peninsula. Now when night fell, this small party found themselves the only reserves available on " W " beach in case of a Turkish counter-attack. No less wearing, no less responsible, was the lot of " C " and " D " Companies of the Anson (Lt.-Commander Gordon Grant, D.S.C., and Lieut. Spencer Warwick) at " X " beach.

To attempt to rest within sight of the lights from the firing line, to wake up to a noise of rapid fire only a few hundred yards away, to hear shells passing over you, or dropping round you, and to know nothing, except that your company or battalion may be called at any moment for any duty, and that, unless you rest, you may not be ready when the time comes— that was the everyday experience of the regimental officer for many weeks throughout the campaign. How far more wearing the experience of the beach parties on that first night, when the firing line was barely two hundred yards away, when there were no reserves, when the dead were as yet unburied and the wounded unattended, when there was no place to lie in, which was not under rifle fire, when, through the thinly-held line of shallow trenches, manned by tired men and with but few senior officers surviving, might pour down upon the beach without more than a moment's warning the whole force of the enemy.

It was, indeed, almost a relief when, in the middle of the night, the expected attack took place, and cries for ammunition came down from above. Soon the whole Anson detachments were in the firing line, and the beaches were left to the chaplains, the doctors, the wounded and the dead. The scene in the firing line was less terrifying than the desolation of the beaches. True, the trenches were wide and shallow, there was no wire and no cover; but to troops fighting their first night-battle the risk of death is less alarming than the sense of isolation, the feeling of ignorance, the harassing fear of the unknown.

The Turkish attack was, in fact, not made in force. Skilled beyond all other European armies, except our own, in the art of rapid fire, the Turks attacked more often than not as a measure of defence. Their method throughout the first months of the Gallipoli campaign was to open up and maintain an almost unbelievable volume of fire, generally high, but sufficiently well directed to make close or prolonged observation from the front line a matter of extreme danger. Under cover of what was in effect a formidable barrage, small parties would go forward, and attempt to enter our lines.

The chief damage done by these tactics was in the back areas, where the ceaseless fusillade of " overs " exacted a nightly toll of casualties among working parties, ration parties, and reliefs on the beaches, or, later on, in the gullies. So it

was on this first night, and the somewhat alarmist reports
which reached the beaches, and from thence no doubt perco-
lated to General Headquarters, were probably due rather
to the unexpected nature of the Turkish tactics than to the
severity of the actual attacks.

The force at " Y " beach was subjected to much the same
tactics, though carried out with greater success. We have
seen that Colonel Matthews had completed his retirement to
the cliff by 6 p.m. on the 25th. No sooner had he done so
than a strong force of Turks came into action against his
left and centre, having taken up a position some three
hundred yards away from our line in the dense scrub. Heavy
rifle fire began at dusk, and, owing to the semicircular position
which had to be taken up, the effect was unusually severe, the
fire directed from the left of the position at effective range not
only taking toll of the Marines guarding the left flank, but
taking the Marine companies on the right in reverse.

As soon as darkness came down, the Turks, under cover of
their cross rifle fire, made repeated attempts, as usual in small
groups, to break through our line, and the K.O.S.B. in the
centre were heavily engaged for some hours. The crowning
horror of the scene was the fate of the wounded, who,
having been taken to a position half-way down the cliff, were
attacked (whether with a calculated disregard of the laws of
war and humanity or in the confusion of the night-battle) by
a party of Turks, who crawled through the thick scrub on the
cliff face and came in behind our lines. Meanwhile, the rifle
fire from the main enemy position took constant toll of the
front-line troops, who were compelled, by the daring of the
Turkish patrols working in and out of the scrub to expose
themselves almost continuously. Time and again, these patrols
would get into our line, only to be driven out again at the
point of the bayonet. Only once, at 5.30 a.m. on the 26th, was
a serious breach effected. This, as often happens, was at the
junction of two units, the K.O.S.B. and the left-flank companies of the Marines, but the line was soon restored by a
counter-attack, in which Lieut. F. C. Law, R.M.L.I., took
a distinguished part.*

This was the final thrust. In the half-light before dawn,

* In the fighting of this night, Lieut. J. F. May, R.M.L.I., of the Plymouth
Battalion, was killed.

the Turks, who had suffered probably nearly as heavily as the
invading force, withdrew to a distance, and only the shelling
served as a reminder to the tired troops of the horrors of the
night. But by now supplies were short, the force had lost
a third of their slender effectives (less than two thousand rifles
to start with), the K.O.S.B. had lost most of their senior
officers, and the experience of the night had made it clear that,
failing support from the south, the position could not be maintained without reinforcements, at least not without ammunition and water. Accordingly, at 7.80 a.m., Colonel Matthews
signalled his appreciation of the situation to the covering
ship, suggesting at the same time a withdrawal, if it should be
impossible to replenish his supplies.

It was in answer to this signal that boats at once left for
the beach, and simultaneously the right flank and centre, *i.e.*,
the K.O.S.B., the company of the South Wales Borderers,
and two companies of the Marines were ordered to the beach to
re-embark. Colonel Matthews, who was on the extreme left
at the time, was unaware of what was taking place until the
re-embarkation was almost completed. In his judgment,
however, a withdrawal was necessary, failing reinforcements
and supplies, and having throughout the operations received
no message from General Hunter Weston, he withdrew with
the remaining companies of Marines some two hours later,
after collecting and embarking the wounded. By 9.80 a.m.
on the 26th, " Y " beach, so gallantly held against the most
desperate attacks, was abandoned to a defeated enemy.

Sir Ian Hamilton himself assumed that orders for the retirement, of which he was an irritated eye-witness, had been issued
by General Hunter Weston. General Hunter Weston, however, was not responsible for a decision which was defended
by Lt.-Colonel Matthews at the time, and subsequently before
the Dardanelles Commission.

But if the night of April 25th–26th brought to weary
troops at Cape Helles and " Y " beaches their first and, therefore, their most terrifying experience of the Turkish night
attack, and if the dawn saw the inexplicable end of the adventure of Colonel Matthews' force, the gathering darkness on
the 25th brought a welcome interval of relief to the sorely-
tried forces at Sedd-el-bahr, and the dawn of the 26th witnessed
their final and amazing triumph.

Under cover of darkness, and perhaps also because the enemy were already preparing for the inevitable retreat, the remaining troops on the *River Clyde* came ashore without loss, and took up a position, marked down during the day as affording the best cover available, under the shattered earthworks of the old castle on the extreme right of the beach. Here they were joined by the survivors of the first landing, who crawled across the enemy's front under cover of the ridge of sand which had sheltered them through the day. At daybreak the force advanced to the assault assisted by a heavy fire from the ships, and, capturing the village, the old castle and the dominating Hill 141 in a succession of brilliant, if costly, open order skirmishes, were in possession of the entire position by 2 p.m. The retreating Turks, retiring through the wooded country round Morto Bay, suffered heavily from the fire of the *Albion*, off Sedd-el-bahr, and of the *Lord Nelson*, keeping watch over the Morto Bay detachment.

Now was the time for an advance. But the beaches behind our line were bare of reinforcements, and, of the slender force which had been landed, nearly half were supplementing the efforts of the Anson beach parties in getting stores, ammunition and water ashore. In these circumstances, it appeared a regrettable necessity to wait for fresh troops and more supplies, and to allow an opportunity for rest to the 29th Division before a further advance. It was decided to devote most of the day to the disembarkation of the French at " V " beach, where Lt.-Colonel Moorhouse and the rest of the Anson Battalion had now landed as a beach party. The Commander-in-Chief decided at the same time to release, from his slender reserve, the Drake Battalion of the Naval Division. Orders to this effect reached General Paris in the Gulf of Xeros at 1 p.m., and the Drake sailed for Cape Helles at once.

The landing of this battalion, at 8.30 p.m. on April 26th, was in its way as significant as were the heroic landings of the day before. The beaches had been hardly won ; even now the line lay only a few hundred yards inland, and it was but thinly held by tired men. But the separate and organized life of the beaches was already beginning. From this night onward, at least until the end of the July battles, the same scene was to repeat itself. The army which was not sufficiently prepared for victory was showing itself as ever impenetrably

armed against defeat. The staff, which failed for so long to
reduce order out of chaos in the peaceful atmosphere of Mudros,
turned the battlefield of the Lancashire landing into a tolerable
office while the shells were still falling and the dead were still
unburied. This was the night of the transition. From now
onward the nightly scene on " W " beach was one of silent but
ceaseless activity. As dusk fell, the sweepers would come in
from Mudros, and would be directed by signal from the shore
to their allotted anchorage, or, if their draught allowed, to a
berth alongside one of the floating piers improvised already
from the wreckage of lighters and ships' boats, and strengthened
with every unconvincing but effective device which sailors and
engineers could concoct without material of any kind. As
soon as the sweepers were made fast, staff officers of the
different departments would come on board and receive
reports of the troops and stores. Then, while any troops
would be brought ashore and handed over by the military
landing officer to guides from their own formations, beach
parties would go on board to unload stores and dispose of
them under orders of the different administrative officers.
Meanwhile, it would be bitterly cold for troops called on, within
a few hours, to exchange the meretricious comfort of a passenger
ship for the sombre desolation of the very edge of a battlefield.

It was this sudden change, unparalleled in any other
campaign of the present war, a change singularly dramatic,
which so heightened the impression left by the first night
on the peninsula. For, on the very edge of those indifferent
waters, there remained to the end the wreckage of boats
and stores ; the once green slopes of the gully which closed
the view were scarred with trenches and shell holes, and
worn to the colour and substance of dust by the ceaseless
passage of men. Here and there were gathered in pitiful
heaps rifles and equipment, salvage from the wounded and
the dead, and amid this wreckage, across the sand still
strewn here and there with the remains of rusted entanglements, men moved about with that brisk solemnity which one
meets but seldom beyond range of the guns, which contrasts so
markedly with the lackadaisical formalism of the base. In
the near distance, indeed, could be heard, almost every
night for the first four months of the campaign, the ceaseless
rifle fire of the Turks, and, occasionally, the sound of artillery

bombardment, brought very close by the proximity of our heavy guns.

Of the extent of ground which, in fact, separated the beach from the firing line after the very first days of the campaign, nothing could be guessed by the newly-arrived troops, who could see no further than the sloping walls of the gully, honey-combed with dug-outs. No wonder that, at the first glance, the narrow beach seemed the embodiment of desolation, a strange wilderness peopled by flitting figures stumbling against each other sometimes in the darkness, but more usually moving about with the precision of ghosts in a world of shades. And this was no idle fancy, for under the sand and up the sides of the gully many men were buried, and an impalpable atmo sphere of death and decay was in the very air men breathed

CHAPTER VI

THE MAY BATTLES

THE situation south of Achibaba on the morning of the 27th April was a curious one. We held the Turkish outpost line, linking up the three small hills overlooking the entrance to the Straits. On the beaches at Cape Helles and Sedd-el-bahr we were busy disembarking not only the stores and guns of the 29th Division but also the French Expeditionary Force, whose operations at Kum Kale, brilliantly executed and maintained for as long as was necessary, were now at an end. For two miles in front of our line was an open plain, clear of the enemy as far as the eye could see ; our advance over this plain must moreover be effectively covered from the left flank by the guns of the fleet, and from the right by the flanking force north of Morto Bay. Seeing our troops sitting (or more often standing at their ease) in the shallow trenches overlooking this wide stretch of open and undefended country, an inexperienced observer landing in the peninsula for the first time on this day must have wondered at the stories he had heard of the bitter fighting of the preceding forty-eight hours. When, at 4 p.m., the French having come into line on the right of the 29th Division, an unopposed advance carried our line forward a distance of no less than two miles, his wonder must have increased. The campaign south of Achibaba, which had threatened throughout the 25th to end in disaster, seemed indeed to have taken an almost miraculous turn for the better. No little wonder that, to the short-sighted, April 28th was expected to see our troops entrenched on our first objective. Little less is it to be wondered at that critics who look back on this period of the campaign in the light of subsequent events have actually been found to suggest that the Turks were anxious for us to consolidate our position, and land our guns, stores and reinforcements, if only to ensure that we thus committed ourselves to wasting our strength in a subsequently fruitless struggle.

The explanation of the dramatic advance of the 27th is, however, simple. The Turks had planned two positions south of Achibaba. The first was on the lower slopes of the hill covering Krithia, with their left resting on the Kereves Dere (a deep ravine running, roughly, across our front, inland from a point on the shore of the Straits a mile and a half north of Morto Bay). The second was the line commanding the beaches, a line which we had finally captured at dawn on the 26th. The average distance between the two lines was about four and a half miles. There is no valid reason for thinking that our capture of the first position was anything but a great military victory, the truth being that the enemy was thus committed to a defensive campaign in barren and inhospitable country which must last as long as we wished, and which must, while it lasted, prove a disastrous drain on those resources which he had hoped to employ in a decisive offensive. In these circumstances, our initial success decided the enemy to retire as soon as might be on to his second prepared position at Krithia, rather than risk his as yet slender forces by standing on an intermediate position, the defence of which might prove more costly. This was only elementary military commonsense. But there was a further consideration, equally important to the enemy : this was time. He had been perilously delayed in his concentration by the Bulair and the Kum Kale demonstrations. The forces ultimately available for garrisoning the Krithia defences were not as yet south of Achibaba. Moreover, the Krithia defences were incomplete. It was necessary accordingly to delay our advance as far as possible with a skeleton force. For this, the country for nearly two miles in front of our line of the 26th was unsuitable, and so our advance on the 27th was unopposed ; the remainder of the ground might, on the contrary, have been designed for delaying actions.

A line drawn from Gully beach to de Tott's Battery would show roughly our position on the morning of April 28th. Behind us was open plain, unsuitable for our communications. In front of us, the country up to the lower slopes of Achibaba was far less open and was split by three gullies down which mountain streams flowed in winter from the heights of Achibaba ; of these gullies, the widest and deepest, known as Gully ravine, runs down parallel to the western coast of the peninsula, till it opens out abruptly to the sea at Gully beach, midway between "X" and "Y" beaches. The others, known as the Krithia and Achibaba nullahs, divide the rest of the peninsula into three roughly equal sectors, until they open out into the plain, at the point reached by us on the evening of the 27th. These gullies were the key to the Turkish tactics. They provided covered communications through which their rearguards, undetected by our infantry, unassailable by the fleet, could harass any further daylight advance.

The unexpected ease of our progress on the 27th, might have been expected to give, and perhaps gave, a clue to the enemy plans. The country in front of us should certainly have confirmed our suspicions if we had had any. The forces opposed to us must moreover be slender; the strength of the Turks at Anzac and other information from prisoners told us that. Yet in spite of all we rested on our gains on the early evening of the 27th, and prepared an elaborately staged " attack " for 8 a.m. on the 28th. The argument for a daylight advance of a formal character was that the losses in officers made a night advance unsafe. If, however, there was a chance of reaching Achibaba before the enemy's reserves were concentrated, we must get in touch with his main body at once, and defeat it. The question was whether a frontal attack in daylight, across country perfectly adapted for a delaying action conducted with the minimum of force, was the most likely method of achieving this result.

The course of the battle (in which the Drake Battalion attached to the 87th Brigade was the only battalion of the Naval Division to be engaged), suggests only one answer. The attacking force consisted from left to right of the 87th Brigade, the 88th Brigade and five French battalions. In reserve was the 86th Brigade. At 8 a.m. the battle opened.

As on a field day, the front battalions advanced in open order by short rushes, their bayonets glistening in the sun. The supporting battalions followed in artillery formation. The Turks offered, at first, no resolute resistance to that part of the advance which lay over open ground, covered by the ships' guns, and the left flank advanced at the outset for a mile or so, over the high, hilly ground on either side of Gully ravine. In the centre, however, the 88th Brigade made slower progress on a front which included the narrower Krithia and Achibaba nullahs, and on the right, the French, trying to fight up the steepish slope that leads to the Kereves Dere, were checked at the start. Even on the left, the Turks advanced more than once to counter-attack, and elsewhere their rearguards took a heavy toll of our troops, from positions mostly concealed in the long grass and scrub.

The defence is brilliantly organized. In and out of the gullies are little concealed trenches, cunningly sited. We take one ; it is commanded by another. Where are the men to take the next ? Another company comes up, and takes it, only to find it empty ; but the rifle and machine-gun fire still takes its toll, the performance has to be repeated again and again, and yet, in as costly a battle as many first-class engagements on the Western front, many in the centre and on the right never see a Turk. All this time we have been advancing on the left, but the line has become thin, and now the Turks, heartened by their success in the centre, come on again. Then orders come to Commander Campbell to take the Drake through the 87th Brigade, with the South Wales Borderers, and reinforce the firing line. This much they do, but the advance is at a standstill. In the centre the line is thinning, and the 86th Brigade, the shattered but still heroic battalions of the landing, have been thrown in. Scattered parties of the Munster Fusiliers even come up against the Krithia defences, but a fighting patrol is not a match for an army corps in prepared, albeit incomplete, positions ; the isolated units fall back, and when they retreat the Drake and the South Wales Borderers can do no more than stand fast. For there are no reserves. One fresh division at least, almost certainly two, are wanted.

We dug in on the night of the 28th-29th on a line nearly a mile beyond the gully on the left, but bending back to our original position in the centre and on the left. It was the first of those " to-morrows " which were to see us entrenched on Achibaba. It was the most hopeless and the least successful. No sooner, indeed, were we dug in, than the Turks drove back the French on the right almost to Sedd-el-bahr, and two Drake companies* had to be withdrawn from the firing line to guard

* With them went Commander Campbell; Major Barker, R.M.L.I. (the adjutant), was left in command in the front line. This fine officer was unfortunately killed by a shell during the night.

7*

General Hunter Weston's headquarters above " W " beach.
So little had we broken the Turkish resistance.

While the battle of the 28th was in progress, the remainder
of the R.N.D. transports were ordered to Gaba Tepe to disembark the Marine Brigade (Brigadier-General C. Trotman,
R.M.L.I.) and the 1st Naval Brigade (Brigadier-General D.
Mercer, R.M.L.I.). These Brigades, each only two battalions
strong (for the Plymouth and Drake Battalions remained with
the Anson attached to the 29th Division), were to reinforce the
Australian and New Zealand Army Corps.*

The losses at Cape Helles in the attack of the 28th made the
reinforcements of that front no less imperative ; and as soon as
the disembarkations at Anzac were completed (by about 8
p.m. on the 29th) the transports were ordered back to Cape
Helles for the disembarkation there of the Divisional and 2nd
Brigade Headquarters, and the Hood and Howe Battalions. At
the same time was disembarked the bearer sub-division of
3rd Field Ambulance under Surgeon Rivers, R.N. The 2nd
Brigade was now concentrated under Commodore Backhouse,
R.N., and was placed in corps reserve under General Hunter
Weston ; the Drake and Plymouth Battalions were assigned to
beach duties, and General Paris temporarily had no executive
responsibilities. This was a disappointment for the Division.
It was also the deliberate, though inevitable, throwing away of
a fighting organization, which, had circumstances allowed of its
employment as a whole on the southern front immediately after
the first landing, might possibly have helped to achieve an
historic success.

The fighting value of the Division for subsequent operations
was inevitably weakened by the decisions taken on April
28th and 29th. By the time it was re-formed, many officers,
many men, had become casualties, yet the sacrifices made
had gone but a little way to the formation of a fighting
tradition. The tradition came in time, but if it is asked why
the Naval Division never in Gallipoli achieved the same reputation which it held later in France, the answer is, not that it
was better trained in 1916 than in 1915 (it was, but not
relatively to other new divisions), but that the fruits of its
first period of training at Blandford were never gathered,

* The story of the early days at Anzac and the doings of these brigades is
told in the next chapter.

but scattered to the winds at the bidding of an imperious
necessity which was imposed on the Dardanelles army by
the superior tactics of the enemy. He had succeeded in coun-
tering our strategy by fighting south of Achibaba a series of
brilliantly effective rearguard actions, and so preventing the
junction of the two halves of our force. Our failure in this
respect carried with it the division of our slender, and therefore
indivisible, reserve.

The release of the remaining battalions of this reserve to
reinforce General Hunter Weston had not been premature, for
on the night of May 1st-2nd the great Turkish counter-attack
against our southern line was launched. Abandoning their
usual tactics, presumably because of the failure of our
advance on the 28th and the consequent easing off of our
pressure, the Turks came on with determination, their first
line without ammunition that they should rely solely on the
bayonet.

The 2nd Naval Brigade were bivouacking at this time
among the derelict trenches taken from the Turks in the first
advance from " W " beach. This was the corps reserve line.
The Turkish attack broke out at 10.30 p.m., and the brigade,
called out by the Brigade-Major, Lt.-Colonel Maxwell, at once
moved off. The Anson Battalion was sent up independently
to support the French on the extreme right of the line, and the
Hood and Howe Battalions went into support trenches across
the Achibaba nullah. Thus it was, on this night, that Commodore Backhouse established his headquarters for the first time
at (or at least near) the point in the nullah known throughout
the campaign as Backhouse Post, and that the men of the Naval
Division for the first time set their feet in that strange valley,
which was to be the scene of so many of their more laborious
exploits, of so much tragedy and suffering, of sacrifices so
freely exacted. Along that mile and a half of scrub and
heather was already formed the dusty track which runs from
Skew Bridge, when the bed of the mountain stream turns
north to Achibaba, past Backhouse Post, and into the glade
beyond. Across the glade, not half-way up, and on the
higher ground to the left, where the 86th Brigade was standing fast against the Turkish attack, the front line now lay.
The shelling and the rifle and machine-gun fire was heavy
still, the trenches afforded but little cover, and the casualties

were considerable. By dawn, however, the front was quiet, and only small bodies of the enemy could be seen falling back on a wide stretch of front. With the exception of Cox's Indian Brigade, just landed, all the reserves had been drawn into the line, which even then was but thinly held ; but it was decided to counter-attack, and at 10 a.m. the whole line moved forward.

The essential conditions of success were lacking, and the Hood and Howe Battalions found themselves engaged in a futile and hopeless task. Advancing up the gully, and on the left, with the greatest resolution, their casualties made it essential to dig in, if at all, not more than four hundred yards in advance of the old position. Seeing them halt and not knowing the reason, a General some distance behind the line sent up reinforcements. These were the 2nd Hampshire Regiment, and this fine battalion came up under heavy fire with a smartness and precision which was a remarkable example, not lost on the Naval battalions, of the power of discipline and training to rise superior to the most disastrous conditions. As they came up, however, the enemy artillery not unnaturally increased their activity, and Lt.-Colonel Quilter had no alternative but to order the Hood to fall back. The Hampshires retired at the same time and for the same reason. The Howe Battalion conformed. What such an order means to men fighting their first fight in the open is not hard to imagine. It is pleasant to recall that Charles Lister, who was wounded in this unfortunate engagement, was able to write home that the men in his brigade " showed great steadiness for raw troops." Much good work was done also by the bearer subdivision of the 3rd Field Ambulance, and by Surgeon Shaw and Sergeant Roberts (C section) in particular, in withdrawing the wounded from the advanced position. But Sir Ian Hamilton has written the true epitaph of this operation, which came to an inconclusive end along the whole British front, when he says it " was half heroic, half lamentable."

In the evening of the 2nd, the Naval battalions were withdrawn to their bivouacs on " W " beach, near the Drake Battalion ; but on the night of the 3rd the Turks renewed their attack on the French, and the Anson was again called on to go to the support of their extreme left flank. In this position they stayed throughout the 3rd and 4th, fighting continuously and doing much to restore the confidence of the French native troops, who had not as yet got acclimatized to the strange conditions. For their fine work with the Anson at this time, Lieut. Davidson and Lieut. Warwick were awarded the D.S.C. The part played by the Anson Battalion in the first days of the campaign has not received due recognition. They had been fighting at this time almost continuously since the landings, in three of which they had taken part, and in the intervals had been employed on fatigue duties. If their share in the heavy fighting of April 25th had been less arduous than that of the 29th Division, their intervals of leisure since then had been even fewer.

On the 5th, the Anson was withdrawn from the front line trenches, but neither for this nor for the other naval battalions was there any rest in store. After the fruitless attacks of May 2nd, 3rd and 4th,* General Liman von Sanders decided to revert to the defensive, and the result was soon evident in numerous working parties busily strengthening the Krithia line throughout the 4th and 5th. In these circumstances, it was decided to make one more effort to reach and engage the main body of the enemy before they were finally secure in their defences. To reinforce the British troops, seriously depleted by casualties, an Australian and a New Zealand Brigade were brought from Anzac to Cape Helles. These two Brigades, and a Composite Brigade consisting of the Drake and Plymouth Battalions of the Naval Division and the 1st Lancashire Fusiliers, under the command of Lt.-Colonel Casson, C.M.G., were formed into a Composite Division operated by the Naval Division staff and under the command of General Paris : a Brigade of the 42nd Division (arriving from Egypt, but not yet concentrated) was attached to the 29th Division, and the 2nd Naval Brigade, under Commodore Backhouse, was lent to General D'Amade. The Composite Division, less the Composite Naval Brigade, and Cox's Indian Brigade were placed in reserve ; the troops for the attack were the 29th Division (with the Brigade of the 42nd Division attached) on the left, the Composite Naval Brigade in the centre, and the French Expeditionary Corps (with the 2nd R. N. Brigade attached) on the right.

This was a stronger attacking line with more adequate

---

* It was during the fighting on this day that Lieutenant M. D. Campbell, R.N.V.R., of the Howe Battalion, was killed.

reserves than on April 28th. But it must have been expected that the enemy would be reinforced to an equal extent, and they were known to have strengthened their defences. Moreover, the problem which faced us on the 28th, the problem of dealing with the scattered enemy rearguards without exposing our whole force to merciless fire from concealed machine guns, still remained for solution ; although we had now a few more guns, we had not sufficient to put down anything in the nature of an intensive bombardment in depth. Nevertheless, the orders for the battle as planned for May 6th, gave the main enemy position in front of Krithia as the first objective only, and actually contemplated two further phases. In the second, the 29th Division on the left was to push forward to two hills to the west and north-west of Krithia, and so enforce a Turkish retreat from Krithia itself. In the third, the whole force was to close in on Achibaba from west, south-west and south simultaneously.

We read these orders with a certain surprise.

Sir Ian Hamilton had suggested (as before the battle of the 28th) that the advance should be made at night, or, at any rate, that the troops should be led to assembly positions in advance of the line held by them, with a view to an attack at dawn. The Corps Commander was determined, however, on a daylight operation, though half an hour's spasmodic bombardment from some fifty eighteen-pounders was all that could be afforded : the plea was the shortage of regular officers and of trained troops. The plea was perhaps hardly adequate, for, if it was impossible to make even a local advance by night because of the inexperience of the troops, why should daylight (with its accompaniment of aimed fire) enable the same officers and men to achieve the spectacular success which the orders foreshadowed ?

The battle opened at 11 a.m., the first advance being made by the French on the right and the 29th Division on the left, and in the centre, up the Achibaba (right centre) and Krithia (left centre) nullahs, by the Composite Naval Brigade, under General Paris's orders, and the 2nd R. N. Brigade, under the orders of General D'Amade. The 2nd Brigade was originally intended to advance merely in support of the French, but, at the last minute, a change was made, and on the French left the Hood and Anson Battalions (with which was one platoon of " A " Company Howe, under Lt.-Commander Waller, who did excellent work throughout the day) and the French infantry advanced in alternate lines. On the Composite Brigade front, the advance was carried out by the 1st Lancashire Fusiliers (attached from the 29th Division), the orders being for the Drake (and, if necessary, the Plymouth Marines) to follow up any advance, and consolidate the ground gained.

By 12.30, the Hood and Anson Battalions reported an advance of 600 yards, and had passed the Turkish advanced trenches by the White House ; the Lancashire Fusiliers had made slower progress, owing to shrapnel fire and the necessity for keeping in touch, not only with the 2nd Naval Brigade, but with the 88th Brigade. On the extreme left of our line little or no progress had been made, and the French advance was also disappointing. By 3 p.m. the advance, which at no point had got near the Turkish main positions, seemed to be everywhere held, and at 8.30 p.m. the Hood and Anson were definitely ordered by General D'Amade not to advance further, as the rest of the force could make no progress along the Kereves Dere ridge. An hour and a half later the whole line received the same orders, and the Drake went forward to dig in on a line joining the Hood left with the 29th Division right. This was done and a gap which had existed for some hours between the Lancashire Fusiliers and the 88th Brigade was reported as filled by the Drake at 8 p.m. Fighting between the French and the 29th Division, the Naval Battalions, in their first serious engagement, had actually achieved the most substantial advance recorded, and could look forward with confidence to the renewal of the battle. But from a wider standpoint the day's fighting was disappointing. An Army Corps had been easily held by the Turkish outposts, and we were not yet within striking distance of their main position. The Naval Brigade had encountered plenty of opposition at long range, but each position when reached had been found to be empty, and no connected position had been captured or even approached.

And yet, though the losses had been heavy and the strain severe, the attack must continue.

The next day, the advance began on the left only and, after fluctuating fortunes, looked like failing definitely by 3 p.m. In these circumstances, a general attack was ordered, the New

Zealand Brigade being detached for the purpose from the Composite Division and sent over to the extreme left, where our failure had been most complete. The 2nd Naval Brigade under General D'Amade and the Composite Naval Brigade under General Paris had each the same task in this attack, to keep in touch with each other and with the flanks. The Composite Brigade had had this task before it all day, and, with the object of rendering it simpler, had been reorganized with the 1st Lancashire Fusiliers next to the 88th Brigade and the Drake on the right next to Commodore Backhouse's Brigade (who now held their front with the Howe and Anson, the Hood being in reserve). Commander Campbell was in charge of the Composite Brigade front line.

The new attack opened at 4.45 and, except again on the extreme left, met with some success. The French progress, however, along the Kereves Dere ridge was slow, and no substantial advance was possible for the Naval or Composite Brigades. The Lancashire Fusiliers' front was indeed, in the end, 300 yards in rear of that of the 88th Brigade when the fighting died down at sunset ; the gap was covered by machine guns. The net result of the day's fighting was a slight advance by the French and the 2nd Naval Brigade, and a gain of some 300 yards by the right and centre of the 29th Division : between that Division and the Naval Brigade was the Composite Brigade. Throughout a long and trying day, Commander Campbell had been responsible for maintaining communication between the two forces advancing unequal distances at different times, and, for his successful conduct of this inconspicuous but essential operation he was awarded the D.S.O. on the recommendation of the Composite Brigade commander.

The dawn of May 8th saw yet another advance attempted, and repulsed on our left. The outlook was dark, especially as the French professed themselves for tactical reasons unable to undertake a further attack until the British had achieved a distinct advance; but the battle thus launched was not to be allowed to close with so signal a defeat. To offer battle may have been premature ; but once offered it must be fought to a finish, and Sir Ian Hamilton determined to throw in the last of his reserves, the Australian Brigade, so as to help the French. If the left flank could not advance (though one further effort was to be made, this time by the 87th Brigade), the right must be securely lodged on the Kereves Dere ridge before the troops could rest on their gains.

The final assault was ordered for 5 p.m., the main attack to be delivered by the comparatively fresh Australian Brigade of General Paris's Division in the centre, with the 29th Division and the New Zealand Brigade on the left, and the French on the right. This time only a quarter of an hour's bombardment was possible, but at last the pertinacity of the Commander and the finer endurance of the troops met with their reward. Well might the Turks, called on to resist four general attacks in two days, presume that they had broken their enemy's will to victory. But they presumed in vain. As ever the allied armies were as irresistible in the face of defeat as they were ineffective in the organization of victory.

The chief honour of the fight went to the Australians and the French, the former advancing, with an impetuous courage which recalled and explained the " Anzac " landing, for a distance of at least 600 yards, while the latter swarmed up the southern face of the Kereves Dere ridge, capturing the redoubt which had held them up for nearly three days and consolidating the position on which (though it would have cheered few to realize it at the time) our right flank was to rest throughout the campaign. But the Naval and Composite Brigades had their part to play. The Hood and Howe Battalions, advancing behind the French, came up into line with and prolonged their left, and two companies of the Drake Battalion, under Lieut. Cherry, R.N.V.R., closed the gap between them and the Australians at a critical moment when at 8.15 p.m., the Turks were breaking through in force. At 1.15 a.m., the Plymouth Marines were moved up and came into line between the Drake Battalion and the Australians.

Throughout the night and the next day, the work of con-solidation, the evacuation of the wounded,* many of whom were in, or in front of, our first line, and the replenishment of supplies, had to be carried out under heavy fire and over ground wholly exposed to view.

On the morning of the 9th, the 2nd Brigade suffered a

---

* In this work Surgeon Rivers (3rd Field Ambulance), Surgeon Ballance (Anson), Surgeon Schlesinger (Howe) and Surgeon McCracken (Hood) did most brilliant and gallant service.

severe loss through the death of Lt.-Colonel Maxwell, the
Brigade Major, who was killed from close range while recon-
noitring the Turkish positions in front of our line. To his
experience and enthusiasm, this brigade, during their months
of training as well as in their first engagements, owed incalculably much.

Even now, though we were consolidating our line, the
Turks had no continuous positions within 500 yards of our
front, and to harass us in our work (which they did
with never-failing effect until we had the whole organization
of trench warfare in working order) relied chiefly on concealed
machine-guns and snipers, and on shelling the back areas and
our still open communciations. Some of these snipers had
actually been found behind our lines, but by this time generally
they were a little in front of it. The accuracy of their aim,
even at long range, was amazing. Many fantastic stories were
told of these men, but no very supernatural skill, though the
most undoubted courage, was required for a sniper to conceal
himself in the long grass and scrub which still covered the face
of the peninsula. " Sniper drives " became in these circumstances an essential form of warfare, and many fine exploits,
spoken of at the time, must be omitted here only because in
the confusion and constant anxiety of those days no written
reports of such minor operations were submitted. Particularly
fine work of this kind was done, however, by Lieut. Magrath,
R.N.V.R., and Sub-Lieut. McHardy, of the Drake Battalion ;
and Petty Officer W. Mason of the same battalion was mentioned in despatches for his gallantry on May 9th in bringing
in two men of his battalion wounded in an operation of this
character.*

At dawn on May 10th a counter-attack of exceptional
vigour was delivered by the Turks against the French and
the Naval Battalion on their left. For a time the situation
was critical, but in the end the position was restored, on the
Composite Brigade front, largely through the initiative of
Captain Tetley (Plymouth Marines), who led his company in
a counter-attack when the enemy were on the point of breaking
through.

---

* Distinguished service was also rendered in the May operations by Lt.-
Commander Boissier, R.N.V.R. (Howe Battalion), who received the D.S.C.
C.P.O. Toy, of the same battalion, was awarded the Good Conduct Medal at the
same time.

So ended the first engagement in which the Naval Division took a substantial and determining part on the peninsula. The quality of the services rendered by these inexperienced battalions can best be gauged from the tribute paid to the 2nd Naval Brigade by General D'Amade, in a letter to Sir Ian Hamilton, written on the receipt of the Commander-in-Chief's orders on May 10th that the Brigade was to revert to General Paris's command. General D'Amade himself read his letter to the Brigade when he inspected them in their rest camp a few days later. It ran as follows :—

" In accordance with your orders I am returning the 2nd Naval Brigade to the Composite Division. It is my pleasant duty to place on record how much I have appreciated the brilliant military qualities, the devotion to duty, the courage and the intrepidity of the three valiant battalions—Anson, Howe and Hood—of which it is composed. It is a great honour and a great satisfaction to me to have had during the 6th, 7th, 8th and 9th of May the devoted, active and ever-ready collaboration of Commodore Backhouse, an officer who has inspired his troops with those noble qualities to which every French soldier who has seen them at work renders homage."

Allowing for all the requirements of international courtesy, it is reasonable to assume that the battalions to whom such a tribute was paid, had at the least, shown themselves fully competent to engage in active operations of a character more trying than is even at this date readily appreciated. And the Drake and Plymouth Battalions, fighting side by side with Commodore Backhouse's Brigade, had made almost identical progress under the same conditions.

The evening of May 10th marked our firm establishment on the peninsula, not only south of Achibaba but, as we shall see in the next chapter, at Anzac ; it marked also, and equally definitely, the end of the first phase of the Gallipoli Campaign, and the definite failure of the plan for concentrating the entire force against the Kilid Bahr plateau before either part of it was pinned to its ground by the Turkish reserves.

In these circumstances, a reconsideration by the Government of the chances of the campaign was essential, and Sir Ian Hamilton at once submitted to the War Office a revised estimate of his requirements in men, guns, stores and ammunition. Any precise calculation of our chances of success, had these reinforcements been immediately forthcoming, is merely guesswork, but it is certain that they would have been at least more favourable than at the beginning of August, when the reinforcements ultimately arrived. Before that time in the costly war of positions, which could not, it was felt, be allowed entirely to die down (though some argue that this would have been wiser), and still more from climatic disease which inactivity might only have made worse, our original landing force had been irremediably depleted. At the time, however, prospects seemed less dubious, for our victory had at least, though at a heavy cost, won for us a sort of security failing which we must, without a doubt, have withdrawn. It would have been impossible to keep an army corps indefinitely in an area so exposed as that occupied by us on the 28th April. Now, though our advance had been at the most three quarters of a mile and in places less, we had got astride of the different nullahs, and had won a considerable belt of country, whose occasional trees provided a substantial measure of protection. The result was cover from view for our infantry and guns and reasonably safe communication with our front line positions.

To reach even thus far, the Naval Division, though less hotly engaged than the 29th, had lost heavily. Colonel Quilter of the Hood Battalion, one of the most distinguished and popular officers in the Division, and, of the Anson Battalion, Lieut.-Commander Anderson (who had led the beach party at *Implacable* landing), Lieutenant Duncan, Sub-Lieut. Bryan Melland and Sub-Lieut. Tisdall (whose heroism at the " V " beach landing yet awaited recognition) had been killed early on May 6th, in the first advance of the Naval Division up the Achibaba nullah. Later, in the same engagement, Lieut.-Commander Waller of the Howe Battalion, Lieutenant M. D. Cherry and Lieutenant Edgar of the Drake and Captain B. Andrews and Lieutenant Barnes of the Plymouth Battalion had fallen, the last two in the Turkish counter-attack on May 10th. The losses in non-commissioned officers and men were also severe, and the five battalions south of Achibaba had been reduced to an average strength of barely 500 officers and men when, on May 10th (the 2nd Naval Brigade being then withdrawn from General D'Amade's command), they came once

more under General Paris's command. The battalions could
not, however, yet be withdrawn from the line, and with the
Cyclist Company and some Motor Machine Gun detachments
they were formed, during May 10th, into a new Composite Brigade
and put into the line between the Australians and the French
left which had been withdrawn. This Brigade and the Australian Brigade remained as a composite Division under General
Paris till the whole was relieved by the 42nd Division on the
12th, and the Naval battalions withdrew to bivouacs south-
west of Achibaba nullah.

There, with battalions already so dangerously weakened,
General Paris waited for the long-delayed concentration of his
Division, to be completed by the return of his two brigades
from Anzac, and the arrival of the Hawke, Benbow and Collingwood Battalions and the third field company of Engineers
now on their way from England.

The narrow plain shut in between the sea, the Straits and
the curved lines of Achibaba, which was all that we had won
at the price of so much blood and treasure, was to be the home
of the Naval Division for many months, and the scene of all
the fighting it was to see on the Eastern front.

Recalling the scene in memory, as it appeared from the line
of the rest camps, which now grew up between Morto Bay and
Gully beach, the chief feature was the distinctness with which
all the prominent features of our own and the enemy position
could be noted, in the course of an hour's walk across the
peninsula.

Standing to the north of Morto Bay, a little way inland, you
see only an expanse of rocky plain, broken here and there by a
small patch of cultivated ground leading up to the skyline, which
is the ridge overlooking the Kereves Dere. On the side of the
Straits, the view was bounded, as everywhere on the peninsula,
by the cliff line, so that you could not see the Straits or Asia—
unless you stood on the very edge (a fact which saved many
lives during the campaign); and on the other side, by a belt
of wood beyond a valley of shrub and fruit trees, narrowing
gradually to form the Achibaba nullah. Between the cliffs
and the valley (less than a mile) was the French sector.

Turning to the left to walk across the peninsula, you struck
the end of the valley, where, by the side of the small stream
which runs down from the nullah, the Naval Division made

their first advance on May 2nd, and advanced again, and with greater success, in the battles of the 6th to the 8th. In the later days of the campaign, the men of the Division came up and down the valley daily, going between the rest camps and the trenches. The way from the rest camps was marked for them by a line of ruined towers, ruined before the war, more ruinous now, but which still challenged the assaults of time and the violence of man with mighty memories. For these towers were the ruins of a Roman aqueduct, which had carried the waters of the uplands from the same Achibaba to an earlier Sedd-el-bahr. Coming up roughly along the line of the aqueduct into the green valley, the battalions followed the course of the stream till it wound into the small glade, overhung with trees and memorable for the incessant croaking of frogs, across which lay our front line before the advance on May 6th. Beyond the glade, the earliest regular trench system began ; further on was the White House, and further again the line reached by the Division on May 9th. You could see nothing of these trench lines from the entrance to the valley, but only the sloping uplands beyond, leading, as ever, to the inevitable symmetry of Achibaba. On these slopes lay the main Turkish defences.

Continuing westwards across the peninsula, you reached higher ground, but for nearly half a mile beyond Achibaba nullah the country was more thickly wooded, clusters of olive trees shutting out your view on all sides. Among these trees were the first settled bivouacs of the Naval Division, and, under the largest clump, General Paris's Divisional Headquarters. So small, however, was the area sheltered by these trees that those battalions which arrived last inevitably bivouacked beyond the sheltered zone, in full view of the enemy on the edge of the open plain. Here the scene changes, and you can look across almost unbroken ground to the coast-line of the Aegean sea, two and a half miles ahead. Not only this, but the country is open to the north to Achibaba (except for some trees bordering Gully ravine), and to the south to Sedd-el-bahr. Down the middle of the plain runs the main road from Krithia, the village which can be seen for the first time on the south-west slope of Achibaba, to Sedd-el-bahr on the sky-line in the extreme south.

Walking on a little and then turning to face Achibaba, you could follow the line of the main enemy position along the southern slopes of the hill, through Krithia, and then, turning back again with the curve of the hill, to the coast-line in the western distance. Across that expanse of level and unsheltered country, broken only by the Krithia nullah and Gully ravine, the army had to advance if it was to turn the Turkish position from the left.

At this time in May the plain was still green and smiling in the sun, as when it first burst on English eyes on April 25th. Later, except for the trees and shrubs, the peninsula, worn down by the passing of thousands of men, and the endless coming and going of transport from the beaches to the camps, became a bare sandy waste. In time it was worse than that. On three sides the plain rises slightly towards the coast ; on the fourth side it culminates in the domed height of Achibaba. In this there came to be realized a certain symbolism. The army was indeed caught between the hill and sea ; it could go neither backward nor forward. The plain, for all its openness, was a prison, which became a tomb.

CHAPTER VII

WE must now turn to the northern zone, where the Australian and New Zealand Army Corps, reinforced, as we have seen, by two weak brigades of the Naval Division, had been fighting as desperately to maintain a bare foothold on the peninsula, as had the forces south of Achibaba to extend their gains. The casualties of two Australian Divisions, during the first two days' fighting, amounted to more than 5,000 officers and men. And withal, the generals on the spot were not confident of their ability to retain their hold on the position. They held it, but the result was due only to the fighting capacity of the individual officers and men. For all their gallantry, the Australians and New Zealanders had, even by April 28th, reached no naturally defensible position, and the only alternative to evacuation was to set about the systematic construction, under fire, and in face of continuous attacks, of an impromptu fortress, the garrison of which would have to maintain, in effect, a siege, until they were substantially reinforced; or until such time as the encircling enemy might be diverted by pressure from our forces in the south or elsewhere.

Seeing that it was necessary in any event to remain temporarily on the defensive, it may be thought that the slender reserves available from the Naval Division would have been better employed somewhere else, but the conditions of the first three days' fighting on this front had in fact led to such a measure of confusion, that it had become urgently necessary to rest and reorganize the Dominion divisions unit by unit. Till this had been done there could be no security, and security was essential, at least while we were still fighting for elbow room south of Achibaba.

The position held by the Australians and New Zealanders,

on the evening of the 28th, consisted of a strip of beach (known to history as Anzac cove) more than half a mile south of the intended landing-place at Gaba Tepe, of the ridge dominating it (named Maclagan's Ridge, after the leader of the first assault which had carried it), and of the inland heights on either side of Deep Gully, running north-west from the coast, immediately south of Maclagan's Ridge for a distance of a mile and a half.

The heights on the left of the gully (known as the Sphinx, Walker's Ridge and Russell Top) were in our hands, and between these and the Turkish positions further to the north-west was a wide valley. The left of our position was thus already reasonably secure. Not so our centre and our right. The heights east of the gully, divided by innumerable narrow, but often precipitous, ravines into as many separate features, had been fiercely contested, and on the different plateaux, covered with tangled undergrowth and rock, the Turks and Australians still lay face to face actually within bombing range. Not here, as on the left, had our foothold on the heights forced the enemy to retreat, nor throughout the campaign did we ever appreciably loosen his hold of these, his first positions.

In the centre, at the head of the gully, the position was even worse. About a mile from the coast, the gully is split in two by a spur (known as Pope's Hill), running out from the line of hills, which, facing Maclagan's Ridge, formed the northern defensive position of the Turks. On the eastern edge of Pope's Hill the Turks were entrenched, and they thus commanded the heights on either side of the eastern arm of the ravine as well as the high ground at its head. Only on the western edge of the spur had the Australians a foothold, and even here we had no defensive position covering the head of the ravine, and no cover, even from view, from the enemy position on the heights to the north-west.

The first Naval Division units to land were the Marine Brigade,* the 1st Field Ambulance (Staff Surgeon Fleming, R.N.), and No. 1 Field Company of the Divisional Engineers (Major Morgans, R.M.). The Engineers distinguished themselves in their first nine hours under fire by constructing the main road from the beach to the reserve position on Maclagan's Ridge. The Portsmouth and Chatham Battalions

---

* I.e., the Portsmouth and Chatham Battalions. The Plymouth Battalion was still attached to the 29th Division.

moved at once into the front-line trenches on the right of the gully. The position allotted comprised the posts which afterwards became famous under the names of Quinn's and Courtney's Posts, and covered the approach to the gully from the east. The intention was to relieve the 4th Australian Brigade, but the sector was greater than could be defended by two battalions, even under normal conditions; and all that could be done was to occupy parts of it, and enable a tentative beginning to be made with the Australian reorganization. The next day (the 29th) more progress was made, for General Mercer's 1st Brigade* was landed, and the Deal Battalion was brought into the line on General Trotman's left. The Nelson Battalion remained in reserve.

The general conditions were very different from those which the organizing capacity of the trained Staff of the 29th Division had brought about at Cape Helles. On the beach the crowd and confusion had been astonishing. So great, indeed, was the intermixture of units, and the number of men moving about independently on errands of which they alone knew the nature, that it was extremely difficult to assemble even a platoon and march it off. The difficulty in assembling a battalion, landed in open boats, was correspondingly greater. When it had been surmounted, it was necessary to climb the steep hills leading from the beach to the south of Maclagan's Ridge, and cross the main gully. Here were no organized lines of reinforcement or supply, no resting-places for the reserve formations; but every possible piece of level ground had been appropriated by individuals of different units, many of them resting where they had fallen asleep involuntarily after the exertions of three days' continuous fighting. In the darkness it was impossible to tell what places were fully exposed to the view of the enemy. The result to the Nelson Battalion —the only battalion not in the firing line from the start— was that their labours on the construction of dug-outs during the night of the 29th–30th proved in the morning to be fruitless.

The sides of the gully were rocky, and what, in the wet season, was the bed of a mountain stream, was now the only path which the landscape offered. On the upper slopes, thickly covered with arbutus, dwarf oaks, and other shrubs, the

---

* This brigade also comprised only two battalions. The Drake Battalion was already engaged at Cape Helles.

passage of men had, indeed, worn narrow tracks, but these were not serviceable, and merely showed the least dangerous line of approach for individuals to the firing line. This was nothing but a series of hastily-dug posts, untraversed, unwired, broken with the wreckage of battle, scarred with the marks of intensive bombardment, just a series of footholds on the edge of the plateau, but defending the life-line of the Anzac position. The ground in front of the trenches was covered with thick scrub, broken by small depressions and ravines. Beyond it was another gorge, similar to the gully which formed the centre of the Anzac position. Here were the Turkish reserves, and from here on to and across the plateau there was a constant movement of the enemy. Even when the utmost energy and skill had been spent on the fortification of our trenches, the situation at this point remained dangerous, and this key position could only be maintained throughout the campaign by hand-to-hand fighting of a desperate character.

The three Marine Battalions remained in these trenches till May 2nd, fighting being more or less continuous the whole time. The novelty of the conditions, and the entire lack of a disciplined organization of the defences, imposed a strain on raw troops which led inevitably to one or two unfortunate incidents. There is no room for doubt, however, that in general great resolution and a very high degree of gallantry distinguished the defence of the posts by the Marine Battalions during these days, when the first V.C. was won from the ranks of the Division (by Lance-Corporal Parker, of the Portsmouth Battalion), and very severe losses were incurred. The official record of Lance-Corporal Parker's exploits gives an indication of the character of the fighting on a day when, according to Mr. Philip Schuler, " a comparative calm stole over Anzac." One must presume that it stole so quietly as to be unobserved.

" On the night of April 30th–May 1st, 1915, a message asking for ammunition, water and medical stores was received from an isolated fire trench at Gaba Tepe. A party of non-commissioned officers and men were detailed to carry water and ammunition, and, in response to a call for a volunteer from among the stretcher-bearers, Parker at once came forward; he had, during the previous three days, displayed

conspicuous bravery and energy under fire, whilst in charge
of the battalion stretcher-bearers. Several men had already
been killed in a previous attempt to bring assistance to the
men holding the fire trench. To reach this trench, it was
necessary to traverse an area at least four hundred yards wide,
which was completely exposed, and swept by rifle fire. It was
already daylight when the party emerged from shelter, and
at once one of the men was wounded. Parker organized a
stretcher-party, and then, going on alone, succeeded in reaching
the fire trench, all the water and ammunition carriers being
either killed or wounded. After his arrival, he rendered
assistance to the wounded in the trench, displaying extreme
courage, and remaining cool and collected in very trying circumstances. The trench had finally to be evacuated, and
Parker helped to remove and attend the casualties, though he
himself was seriously wounded during the operation."

Of the two officers in charge of this trench, Lieutenant
Empson was killed, and Lieutenant Alcock conducted a fine
defence for four nights and three days (during which period
no adequate supplies could be brought up), before he was forced
to withdraw, owing to shortage of ammunition. For this, and
other services, this officer was mentioned in Sir Ian Hamilton's
dispatch of 12th June, 1915, and was awarded the D.S.O.
The same dispatch contains the names of Lt.-Colonel Luard,
Major J. A. M. Clark, Major H. G. B. Armstrong,* Captain
D. J. Gowney, D.S.C., and Lieutenant W. R. Sanders, of the
Portsmouth Battalion, all of whom did fine work in these operations. Surgeon Playne, of this battalion, also rendered the
most conspicuous service, and was awarded the D.S.O.

On the night of April 30th, an attack was carried out by
" B " Company of the Chatham Battalion, who had been driven
out of a portion of their line a little earlier. The position lost
was retaken, though with considerable loss. Lieutenant Her-
ford, who had succeeded to the command of the company,
was killed, and Lieutenant Watts (Battalion Machine Gun
Officer) was wounded. The next day (May 1st) the Turks
came back to the attack, but were repulsed.† In this fighting

---

* Major Armstrong was killed in action on May 6th when his battalion was
again in the line on this front.

† In the defence of this position Lieutenant J. Cheetham, R.M.L.I., was conspicuous, and, for his courage and initiative, was awarded the D.S.O.

the Marines suffered a severe loss in the death of Sergeant-Major Hayward, the Regimental Sergeant-Major of the Chatham Battalion.

The Marines were relieved on May 2nd. The reorganization of the Australian and New Zealand Corps was now completed, and the position was appreciably more secure. This was due less, perhaps, to Mr. Schuler's "inexplicable calm" during the period from the 28th to the 1st, than to the relief which the arrival of the two Naval Brigades gave to the main force, at a time when the resistance of the Turks was by no means broken, and when the position, so bravely won, could only be maintained by equally soldierly qualities.*

On May 2nd, after a series of misunderstandings had led to the postponement of a larger scheme, it was arranged to attempt the capture of the heights overlooking the head of the gully. The Naval Division troops were held in reserve for this attack, but were called on early in the operations.

The precise objectives were Pope's Hill and the high ground on either side of it. Two columns were formed for the attack of this position. On the left, the Otago (New Zealand) Battalion was to attempt the high ground at the head of the left arm of the gully, immediately to the west of Pope's Hill. On the right, the 16th Battalion was to scale the two ridges commanding the head of the right arm of the gully. The 13th Battalion, coming up in their rear (there was no possible line of approach up the hillside to the left of that to be taken by the 16th Battalion), was to extend the line to the left, and join up with the centre, where the 15th (Australian) Battalion, garrisoning Pope's Hill, was to make a sortie and push forward an advance line in touch with the Otago Battalion.

In general support in the gully, were the three Marine Battalions under General Trotman. Two companies of the Nelson Battalion were in Brigade reserve to Colonel Monash, who was in command of the Australian and New Zealand troops detailed for the operation.

---

* In this early fighting, in addition to those previously mentioned, Lt.-Colonel R. N. Bendyshe, R.M.L.I., Major G. F. Muller, R.M.L.I., Lieutenant J. F. Moxham, R.M. and Lieutenant K. A. Higgins, R.M. of the Deal Battalion, and Captain J. C. Teague, R.M.L.I., Lieutenant C. J. Black, R.M. and 2nd Lieut. D. H. G. Ferguson, R.M. of the Portsmouth Battalion, were killed. The death of so many experienced officers at the outset of the campaign was a grievous loss to the Marine Brigade. Major Tupman, R.M.L.I. (so well known later as Brigade Major to the 1st R.N. Brigade), succeeded now to the command of the Deal Battalion.

The assaulting columns were timed to reach the fringe of the hills to the right and left of Pope's Hill at, approximately, 8 p.m. From thence, they were to move forward to the assault of the Turkish trenches on the forward slopes.

The shades of night, always so confidently and justly reckoned on to bring relief to troops acting on the defensive, were particularly helpful to the Turks on this occasion, for the position attacked was in the form of a semicircle, with the Australians attacking from the centre. The columns necessarily advanced by routes separated by nearly half a mile, and they found themselves, when they had got within striking distance of the enemy, isolated from each other. The 16th Battalion passed through a line of trenches dug by the Turks on the very edge of the ravine, and took up a position a little way beyond, to enable the 13th Battalion to move to their left and join up with the troops in the centre. The 13th Battalion, late in starting, were late in arriving in position, and appear never to have made touch, either with the 16th Battalion or with the troops on their left. But, without hesitation, the battalions each endeavoured to advance.

We must not imagine the scene as an orderly and well-appointed battle, with the opposing positions clearly defined. On this rugged hill top, thickly covered with scrub and dotted with rock, Turks and Australians, losing all organization, fought a running fight for some hours. But neither the Australians nor the New Zealanders seem ever to have reached the main enemy position, and their hold on the plateau's edge was but precarious by midnight, when a huge bonfire lit by the Turks revealed the most complete and hopeless confusion in the ranks of the assaulting troops on the right of Pope's Hill.

Two hundred yards or so from the edge of the gully, officers had set to work constructing a support line, and this appears to have been manned with some degree of method. Ahead, some hundreds of yards nearer the Turkish position, the assaulting troops, beaten to the ground by a murderous fire, formed what was alternatively a firing line or a covering force for the main body behind. Between the two lines were a confused mass of leaderless men—men from the firing line driven back, reinforcements coming up from the gully, stragglers looking for their units, perhaps a Turk or two caught up in the confusion of the night battle, officers looking for orders, or for men to obey them. The attack had failed, and in the prevailing excitement the failure seems to have passed unnoticed. When the confusion was at its height, at 2 a.m., the two companies of the Nelson Battalion came up under orders from Colonel Monash to support the 13th Battalion. While the rear platoons of the force were still in the gully, an ill-supported local advance was in progress, and the leading platoons of the Nelson became involved. The attack was unsuccessful, but when the two companies were at last concentrated, no attempt seems to have been made to make use of these fresh troops, or of the very numerous army of leaderless Australians wandering between the lines, for a final assault on the main positions.

Instead, the Nelson Battalion was ordered, by the senior officer on the right of the 13th Battalion front, to move to the left and cover the New Zealanders (Otago Battalion), if and when they could be found. Later, however, the Nelson were ordered to prepare a position in rear of the 13th Battalion, the New Zealanders not being in evidence, and no one having any knowledge of their whereabouts (they were actually digging in a quarter of a mile further to the left). This was approximately at 2.30 a.m., and the Nelson companies remained, accordingly, till dawn fruitlessly digging in with entrenching tools in rear of the thinly-held Australian support line. In front, the Australian firing line began to dig themselves in at the same time. On the right of the front of attack no greater success had been won. The position was, indeed, ominously similar. Gallant attacks had been made, but they had failed, and the losses among the men and also, perhaps, to some extent the inadequate preparations, had prevented the construction of any strong defensive line. The overriding weakness of the position as a whole was the isolation of the three assaulting battalions from each other. When dawn broke, this, and the superiority of ground still enjoyed by the enemy, made the situation desperate. In these circumstances the Portsmouth Battalion of Marines, in reserve in the gully, were asked to go forward. Owing to a misunderstanding, the request was not addressed to General Trotman, under whose orders the battalion had remained, and, while the matter was under discussion, the left flank of the 16th Battalion were pushed back into the gully, spreading confusion as they retreated. In the half-light of dawn, amid a hail of bullets coming from every direction (for the trenches in the gully itself were under fire from both flanks, from the front, and in places even from the rear), with an uncertain battle raging on the very edge of the plateau above, the rumour that the Turks were pouring into the gully might have had disastrous results. The men were, however, promptly rallied by the staff of General Trotman's brigade, and those who had been the first to turn were among the first to regain their self-control and to assist in stemming the dangerous panic. Nothing, however, could save the position on the plateau itself but the capture even at this eleventh hour of the main Turkish trenches; and, in the belief apparently that these trenches had, in fact, been captured elsewhere on the battle front, and were still in our hands, the Chatham Battalion were sent forward to attack those opposite the sorely pressed 16th Battalion. Almost at the same time, an ill-fated order was given, in the centre of the battle front, for the Nelson Battalion companies to attempt, by attacking to a flank, to protect the 13th Battalion.

The attack of the Chatham Battalion, brilliantly led by the Adjutant, Captain Richards, R.M.L.I., was extremely successful, and in the face of a very heavy, but not devastating, fire, two lines of trenches were taken and, in the first instance, held. Unfortunately, no support was now forthcoming on either flank, and after a gallant defence of some six hours, during which Quartermaster-Sergeant White and Sergeant Oakey specially distinguished themselves, the position, so finely won, had to be abandoned. With it, went our hold on the improvised trenches dug by the Australians on the edge of the plateau at this point.

The fate of the attack on the other sectors was in the end the same : the Nelson Battalion companies had failed to drive home their flanking attack (directed against an advanced machine-gun position), and were ordered by the Australian Commander to retire. Unfortunately, here, as on the 16th Battalion front, the terrors of the night battle had led to a good deal of disorganization, and here, too, something in the nature of a temporary panic broke out. The position was, however, restored, and the Nelson companies, rallied in the gully by Sub-Lieut. Sowerby, returned to the 13th Australians' trenches. Here from 6 a.m. till dusk a memorable stand was made. By the afternoon, when our positions on the right had been abandoned, it became clear that it was only a useless waste of life to cling on in the centre to a position which could not possibly be held against a determined assault such as its importance to the enemy would certainly produce. But before the position could be surrendered, countless wounded, and stores and ammunition had to be cleared. Under constant harassing from the enemy, this was successfully achieved, and, at 5.80, the garrison were able to begin an exceedingly cool and well-planned retreat, so well-planned, indeed, as to be carried out almost without loss, although it was daylight and the enemy were closing in on all sides.

On the extreme right of the battlefield, the Otago Battalion had, it was learnt later, achieved much the same measure of success and failure as the 18th Australians; in the end they too, though some hours later, had to retreat.

In this unfortunate engagement, the Division suffered many serious losses. The Chatham Marines lost nearly three hundred officers and men, killed and wounded, among the killed being their Adjutant (Capt. Richards, whose services since the early days of the Antwerp expedition to this last assault had been so uniformly distinguished) and Lieutenant Grinling. In the Portsmouth battalion, Lieutenant Sanders, 2nd Lieutenant T. A. D. Deane and 2nd Lieutenant T. H. C. Fulton were killed while the battalion was in support on the gully. In the Nelson Battalion the losses, in proportion to those engaged, were even more serious. Lt.-Commander Gibson (commanding " B " Company), Lieut. P. C. Garnham, R.N.V.R., and Sub-Lieuts. Paton, Bookless, Whitaker and Cooke were killed or mortally wounded, and Lt.-Commander Primrose (second in command) and Lt.-Commander T. L. Price (commanding " A " Company), wounded. The losses in petty officers and men were nearly two hundred.

The local results of this costly and unfortunate affair were intangible. Heavy losses were inflicted, but they were sustained, and the same factors that turned against us the balance of advantage in the indecisive assaults at Cape Helles later in the campaign, turned it against us here. The Turks could relieve their tired troops and replenish their casualties, while we could not. As at Cape Helles, however, the immediate results were good. The Turks were put on the defensive, and our men got breathing space for the all-important work of consolidation and organization.

The next day a definite scheme of defence was drawn up, under which the three main posts covering the front of the position, on the safety of which, in view of our failure to secure the high ground dominating the heads of the gully, our security still depended absolutely, were placed under a united command and organized for mutual support. The responsibility for these historic strongholds (which came to be known as Courtney's, Quinn's and Pope's Posts, after the officers who had garrisoned them in the earliest days), fell, for so long as his Brigade remained on this front (till May 12th), to Brigadier-General Trotman, R.M.L.I., who had under his command the Portsmouth and Chatham Battalions and the 4th Australian Infantry Brigade.

As Mr. Schuler tells us, " it was on the holding of these precarious and well-nigh impossible positions in the early days of the occupation that the whole Australian line depended."

Of the part which the Marine Battalions took in their defence, during these critical days, at the very beginning of the campaign, the records tell little, and published history even less.* But it is a sufficient commentary on the part which they had played in the earlier days of active fighting, that they were allocated to the defence of positions of such importance. The history of these posts throughout the campaign is a history of desperate conflicts, sustained with equal tenacity by the enemy and by the Australian infantrymen and the (dismounted) Light Horse Brigade. It was a style of warfare in which individual gallantry and resource told more than scientific training. Yet gallantry and resource could not do more than just hold out. From Quinn's Post, indeed, a series of abortive assaults were made, often with disastrous losses, and the first of them took place while the Marine Brigade was still at Anzac, on the evening of the 10th May. Like so many which followed it, it failed, owing to the failure to join up of the assaulting parties, each of which gained a lodgment in the enemy trenches. Each party in turn was enfiladed, and forced to withdraw down the

* The Australian sources rightly concentrate on the assistance, invariably forthcoming, which Australian units rendered to the Marine Battalions on more than one occasion.

communication trenches, newly dug from our own to the temporarily captured position.

Two days after this unsuccessful effort, the Marine Brigade was relieved by the Light Horse Brigade, and sailed at once for Cape Helles.*

The lot of General Mercer's Brigade was less arduous and responsible. This Brigade had seen little or no actual fighting, save the two companies of the Nelson Battalion on May 2nd and 3rd; and they were sent, immediately on the conclusion of that engagement, to relieve Australian and New Zealand troops on the left of the position. Here, owing to the lie of the land, the fighting was infinitely less severe; the main enemy positions were some hundreds of yards off, and only in the many saps, which ran out from the opposing lines, did the forces come to close quarters.

The sector first allotted to General Mercer's Brigade was on the extreme flank, partly covered from direct assault by the Australian trenches, slightly to the north on Walker's Ridge. The enemy position was centred on a ridge still further to the north, and the flat ground, immediately off the shore, was held only by rival outposts and wire entanglements. Looking north, indeed, from the shore at this point the whole view was open as far as Salt Lake, and beyond Suvla Point the mainland of Turkey and Bulgaria was visible on a clear day in faint outline across the Gulf of Xeros. If they turned their backs on this view of the promised land, the men of the Nelson and Deal Battalions could see, to the south, the whole western coast of the peninsula and the ships off Cape Helles. To the west, set in the placid water of the Aegean, could be seen Imbros and Samothrace, behind which the setting sun would throw a brilliant glow over the rugged outlines of their purple peaks.

The trenches on the extreme left held by the Nelson Battalion backed on to a sandy gorge opening out to the sea. The sides of the cliffs were precipitous, and cut by the wind and rain of the unequal climate into sharp edges, bare of all vegetation; only birds and insects seemed to abound, and at one and the same time could be seen vultures, pigeons, shrikes, martins,

---

* The period from May 3rd to May 12th was one of severe, if discontinuous, fighting, and the Marine Battalions suffered further losses. Among the officers killed during this period were Major A. C. H. Hoskyns, R.M.L.I., Lieutenant J. F. Hyland and 2nd Lieut. F. A. Erskine of the Portsmouth Battalion, and Lieutenant M. Curtin and Lieutenant A. F. Hayward of the Chatham Battalion.

swallows and small greyish hawks; while the trenches abounded in yellow centipedes, caterpillars, lizards, and brown and blue butterflies.

The firing line was manned throughout by a composite force of the Nelson and Deal Battalions, under the command of Lt.-Colonel Eveleigh, R.M.L.I. No incidents of moment mark this period, though the line taken over had to be considerably extended to release the whole of the New Zealand Brigade, who normally garrisoned the sector, for service in the general engagement at Cape Helles on May 6th to 8th. The Naval Brigade remained in the line till the 13th, when they also re-embarked for the southern front. The 1st Field Ambulance, whose work had won high tributes from all sides, left at the same time.*

By this time, the situation had immensely improved. Most noticeable of all, was the order which had been won from the earlier chaos of the beaches, and the regular system of trench reliefs, which had been worked out in the face of such appalling difficulties. In this transformation, as well as in the offensive of the 2nd and 3rd, the Naval Division brigades (raw as they were) had played a small but honourable part, and had vindicated their courage and their training.

---

* For particularly gallant work during these operations Surgeon Pratt, of this Field Ambulance, was awarded the D.S.C.

CHAPTER VIII

BY May 13th, when the units which had been sent to Anzac had returned to the Achibaba front, the Naval Division (save for the Hawke, Benbow and Collingwood Battalions, by now on the high seas) was concentrated under General Paris's command. The campaign developed very rapidly into trench warfare. In three brief weeks, the order and method imposed by the necessities of a siege came over a scene which heretofore had been expanding, changing, taking fresh colour almost every hour, under the stress of active warfare, its cruel losses, its alternating moods of exultation and depression, the knowledge of triumph or the tacit admission of defeat.

The first salient change was the allocation to different formations of the responsibility for certain sectors of defence. No longer was there to exist that camaraderie of the battle-field, when even divisions cease to exist as distinct units, and the reserves, the supports, and the front-line troops develop, almost, an *esprit de corps* of their own. Now each division found its own supports, its own reserves, and each looked askance on its neighbour. In one sector, sniping and bombing had become a science; in another, sapping and digging in at night ("straightening out the line") was the order of the day, a third excelled in the discipline of its sentries, a fourth in the excellence of its field engineering. And each came to regard the other with a peculiar mixture of admiration and dislike, bred by differences of character and ambition and training.

On the right of the line, standing fast to their finely won position on the ridge of the Kereves Dere, were the French, whose sector was a monument of field engineering, of effective organization of all things material. Next came the Naval Division, with their front stretching from the French left across the Achibaba

nullah to the right of the Krithia nullah : this was the front
to which the Naval battalions of the 2nd and the Composite
Brigade had fought in the earlier battles.   On the left came the
42nd Division, and on their left again, the 29th Division and
Cox's Indian Brigade, stretching across the main gully to the sea.

With the organized sectors of defence, came the rest camps.
Whether a battalion was out of the line for rest and reorganization, or in corps reserve, or in divisional or brigade reserve, the
only place for it except actually on days of battle was the rest
camp.   There were its household gods, in the shape of its
quartermaster's stores and transport, and there, more important,
the laborious dug-outs, which alone offered cover from view of
the enemy and a possibility of shelter from the more than
occasional shells.

The Naval Division rest camps were directly behind their
trench sector, on the broken ground to the left of the lower
reaches of the Achibaba nullah.   Without timber or corrugated
iron of any kind, neither comfort nor safety could be immediately
attempted.   Only through long weeks of scheming and con-
trivance and loot could the former be approached.   The latter
remained beyond reach.

The early camps suffered in another way : they were never
meant to be permanent ; and the Naval Division camps were
dug by young men who still cherished the illusion that what
generals did not intend would not occur.   And so the camps
were carelessly planned, unnecessarily cramped, avoidably uncomfortable in their lay-out.

For these reasons, among others, it would be wrong to suppose
that the reversion to trench warfare carried with it intervals
of rest and that generally peaceful atmosphere which we
ordinarily associate with it.   Every square yard of the peninsula
was under fire ; and in a situation where the safety of the
fighting troops depended absolutely on constant artillery support and a plentiful supply of engineering materials and labour
for extensive digging, there were none of these essentials.   The
days following on the May battles were, in the circumstances,
days of unremitting anxiety and hard work, in which every man
who could be spared had during the brief hours of darkness to be
employed on digging communication trenches, or in pushing
forward our front line to within striking distance of the enemy.
Only, it was felt, by renewing the offensive very soon and driving

Howe Battalion Rest Camp, Gallipoli, June, 1915.

the enemy north of Achibaba could we gain sufficient ground and protection to concentrate the expected reinforcements for a decisive victory.

In pursuance of the prescribed policy, the Naval Division, in addition to providing innumerable digging parties all over the peninsula, carried out no less than four night advances before the end of May. These operations, on the 18th, 23rd, 24th and 27th, the first two of which were carried out by the 2nd Naval Brigade, and the next by the 1st and Marine Brigades respectively, took our front line forward nearly half a mile at a cost of less than fifty casualties, and brought the Division within from two hundred to four hundred yards of the main defensive position across the Achibaba and Krithia nullahs. Incidentally, these operations gained for us almost as much ground as had those of May 6th–8th, without giving any unnecessary chances to the enemy to reduce our strength still further before our next assault. If, however, the losses in specific operations were miraculously few, the daily rate of wastage from shells in the camps and trenches, and overhead rifle fire in the gullies and communication trenches, was high. The 1st Brigade suffered a particularly grievous loss when their Brigade Major, Major Frank Wilson, R.M.L.I., was killed by a sniper only a few days after the 2nd Brigade had lost Lt.-Colonel Maxwell in the same way. Among other fine officers killed at this time were Lt.-Commander P. McCirdy, R.N.V.R., of the Anson Battalion, Sub-Lieut. E. Rennie, of the Drake Battalion, Lieut. Treves, R.N.V.R., and Sub-Lieut. Gilbert, of the Nelson Battalion, Lieut. R. O. Tollast and Lieut. A. M. Oakden, of the Divisional Engineers, and Lieut. White, R.M., of the Chatham Battalion. Major Wilson's place was filled by Lt.-Colonel Moorhouse, and Major Roberts, R.A., took over the Anson Battalion.

On May 28th and 29th, under conditions safer, but more dispiriting, than those which their fellows had faced on April 25th, the three remaining battalions landed on the peninsula. The Division was at once reorganized on the original plan. The Hawke and Benbow joined the Drake and Nelson in the 1st Brigade, the Collingwood joined the Howe, Hood and Anson in the 2nd Brigade, and the Deal with the Plymouth, Portsmouth and Chatham battalions formed a complete Marine Brigade.

For all this, the Division was weaker than on April 25th. Then, the effective strength was 10,500 men. At the end of

May, before the arrival of the reinforcements, it was less than half ; and the arrival of three fresh, but wholly inexperienced, battalions was, as far as the immediate future was concerned, a very moderate compensation. What was needed were not fresh units who had to buy their experience, but drafts for the more seasoned battalions. The urgency arose from the decision to make the next attack on June 4th.

It is easy now to say that this attack was foredoomed to failure. Yet such is the buoyancy of temperament of inexperienced soldiers that to many, at least in the Naval Division, this fateful day seemed to hold the promise of a long-awaited opportunity. Never since Antwerp had the whole been concentrated under the hand of their commander. Then they had been raw troops, untrained and unequipped ; now, save for three battalions, they had had the finest of all training, worth how many years of peace-time manœuvres, fighting continuously for a month, side by side, with some of the finest regular battalions. Even the inexperienced Collingwood, Hawke and Benbow were by no means untrained, were well equipped and well commanded. The more seasoned battalions were indeed thinned by losses, weakened by illness, handicapped by reorganizations under trying conditions. But in the excitement of a concerted advance might not tired troops regain their enthusiasm ? Might not the Naval Division, now for the first time united under the orders of their own commander, set the final seal on their reputation ?

*   *   *   *   *   *   *

The new attack, like those of May 6th and 8th, was to be a direct frontal assault on the whole Turkish forward position. We started, moreover, with three advantages, which we had not previously enjoyed. We were now right up against our objective, not vainly groping for it ; we had limited the objectives of the first waves of the attack, and, finally, our troops, though not fresh, were infinitely more rested than they had been early in May. To this extent, the modified optimism which prevailed was justified ; but there was another side to the picture. The Turks had been strongly reinforced and were deeply entrenched, and their left flank (against the French ; that is, on the right of the Allied line) rested on the Kereves Dere Ridge. This position was unassailable, except to an advance along the line of the ridge. Such an advance the French had attempted on May 6th and 8th, but had only pushed forward for a distance of two or three hundred yards along the crest. Seeing that the ridge ran diagonally to our front, it was clear that any failure to advance further along the crest and the upper slopes in the forthcoming attack must prejudice our chances on the lower slopes, where were the Naval Division. Equally, failure there might imperil any gains in the centre, and must, in any event, reduce their tactical value. On this view the success of the operations as a whole must depend largely—far too largely, considering to what extent we were committing all our resources to the uncertain issue—on the success of the French attack. This made the attack from the outset an incalculable gamble.

On the British front the attack was to be carried out by the 29th, 42nd and Naval Divisions, each attacking the Turkish trenches opposite to their own. The Naval Division, which had the shortest sector (less than a thousand yards of front), had to supply two brigades, less one battalion, to the Corps as a general reserve, and were left, for their share in the battle, only the 2nd Naval Brigade and the Drake Battalion. Holding the last-named in reserve, General Paris arranged with Commodore Backhouse for the Howe, Hood and Anson to attack the first two front-line trenches and the redoubt on the right of the brigade boundary, and for the assault of the Turkish third line to be carried out by "A," "B" and "D" Companies of Commander Spearman's Collingwood Battalion. The remainder of the Collingwood were held in Brigade reserve, under Lt.-Commander West, R.N.V.R.

Next to the Anson (on the right of the Brigade) were French Colonial troops, and next to the Howe (on the left) the Manchester Brigade of the 42nd Division.

At 2.30 a.m. on the 4th the battle may be said to have opened with the departure of the 2nd Brigade from the rest camps. Stumbling across the broken ground into the valley of the Achibaba nullah, the leading battalion walked up the dusty road, past Backhouse Post, where Colonel Quilter and Major Maxwell were buried, into the communication trench alongside the stream. Behind them could have been seen an endless number of small groups of heavily-laden tired men, ten or a dozen in each group, or sometimes less, walking almost as though in their sleep, so well did they know the road, or so little did they care to awake the memories which it held for them. These groups were the platoons of three battalions. Very different must have been the appearance of the Collingwood Battalion, at full strength, confidently going forward to the unknown event. The Turks were very quiet that night, and, save for the frogs croaking, there was scarcely a sound.

After the attacking groups had gone forward, the 1st Brigade Battalions came down from the trenches, the Drake to those round Backhouse Post, and the Nelson and Hawke Battalions to the rest camp.

The attack was timed for noon, and the hours of waiting, from dawn to midday, added a new chapter to the horrors of war. To move with a light heart to the assault in the grey half-light of dawn is difficult enough, but at least there is a shadow over the sun to veil the shadow in men's hearts. Here, hour by hour, the sun beats down more pitilessly. Towards ten o'clock the air grows fetid, and the flies begin to swarm on the filth of the parapets, and maggots crawl over the bodies of the dead but a foot or two below the ground. Even the small comforts of garrison duties in the line seem strangely remote. Everything is still, expectant, uncomfortable. With curiosity, officers and men watch the bombardment, on which their chance of survival so greatly depends. In the rest camps, and near the headquarters of generals, the noise is terrific, and the impression one of a vastly efficient destruction. In the trenches the noise is immeasurably less, and the passage of the occasional shells tells the true tale. A desultory bombardment had begun at 8 a.m., and at 10.30 a.m. the rate of fire was increased, but the results were negligible. We now know that the proportion of guns to rifles was only a third of that allowed in France, and the number of rounds per gun immeasurably less. No statistics were needed to reveal, at 11.20 a.m. on June 4th, the full measure of the weakness of our artillery, for at that moment the first intensive bombardment ceased, and a feint of attack was made along the whole line. In an instant the whole enemy line burst into rapid fire, machine guns swept the parapets of our trenches from end to end, and the Turkish artillery searched our reserve trenches

and our communications. The bombardment, which should
have disorganized the Turkish defences, driven their riflemen
to cover, and destroyed their machine-gun emplacements, had
done—just nothing.

At 11.80 the bombardment was resumed, and at 12 noon
the Howe, Hood and Anson advanced to the assault. Once
again, the Turkish rifle and machine-gun fire swept our parapets.
This time they found a target. In the first seconds of the
attack more than half the officers of the 2nd Naval Brigade
(including Major Roberts, R.A., of the Anson, Major Sparling,
R.M.L.I., of the Howe (who were both killed), and Lt.-Colonel
Crauford-Stuart, of the Hood) were hit. Once the whole of
the men were over the parapet and in the open, the law of
averages came into play, and of the few officers, who still found
themselves standing, about half, with about half their men,
reached the Turkish front line. It was unoccupied, save by
the dead, the dying and the wounded. Without a moment's
delay, the Anson went on, led by Lieut. Stuart Jones,
R.N.V.R.,* the senior surviving officer, and stormed the
redoubt in the Turkish second line ; the Hood and Howe came
up on the flank. Seen through field-glasses, it was an orderly
and dashing advance, particularly on the right, where the
Anson were described by Sir Ian Hamilton as fighting in the
best style of the Regular Army. But in the captured trenches
the impression was different. There was an ominous inactivity
on the right of the line, where the Turks could be seen in force
in their original trenches : there was a still more ominous
volume of fire pouring in on the trenches which had been
captured. To hold the eight hundred yards of line which had
been their objective, and which they had reached, there were
left of the attacking force only some twenty officers and three
hundred men. Every minute took its toll of the slender
garrison. Would the Collingwood come up in time ?

Punctually the Collingwood began their advance. But the
success of their comrades helped them in no way. From the
Turkish left, on the Kereves Dere Ridge, there broke out the
same tornado of fire on a target as impossible to miss as the
first. The Collingwood, afterwards supposed to have suffered
their losses almost wholly in their retreat, actually suffered more

---

* With him was C.P.O. Stear (later promoted to Lieut., R.N.V.R.), who, for
fine work in this attack, was given the D.S.M.

than half of them in their advance, among those to fall being
Commander Spearman, R.N., and his Adjutant, Lt.-Commander
Annand, R.N.V.R., both of whom were killed in the first
moments of the attack. The Turkish positions on the upper
slopes of the ridge were still intact, and our attempt to retain
our hold on the lower slopes of the ridge was foredoomed to
failure. Not more than three hundred of the Collingwood
reached the advanced trenches, where by now the scene was
one of indescribable confusion. On the right, the enemy could
be seen in full command of their second- and third-line trenches,
while parties were coming back even into the front line, where
the French had once been. The Naval Battalions were still in
the enemy's second-line trenches on the Anson and Hood front ;
but on the Howe Battalion front, where there was no dead
ground between our lines and those of the enemy, only a few
of the Howe*, and none of the Collingwood, had reached the
enemy's line ; and here also the Turks were now beginning to
come back. With great gallantry, the Anson and Hood and
Collingwood Battalions actually attempted a further advance,
at 12.30 p.m., but the situation was impossible. With the
exception of Lieutenant Stuart Jones, of the Anson, and Sub-
Lieut. Cockey, of the Hood, all the surviving officers were hit
before the enemy's third line was reached.

With the Turks converging on the captured positions,
a retirement became imperative. This was hardly less
costly than the advance, partly because of a brave but
useless attempt to hold on to a position half between the
Turkish and our own original line. It was at this point that
" B " Company of the Collingwood, who had advanced at 12.30
to dig a communication trench across the captured ground,
were almost annihilated. No more now at the eleventh hour
than earlier, in the first fury of the assault, could gallantry
and self-sacrifice prevail against the enemy's machine guns
on the flank. Any attempt to hold a position in advance of
our front line was, in the prevailing circumstances, merely
quixotic ; and after sustaining cruel losses the surviving officers
rightly decided on completing the retirement.

They were only just in time. At 12 noon the assaulting

---

* Among these were Lieut. P. H. Edwards, R.N.V.R. (wounded), and C.P.O.
Homer, P.O. Smith and A.B. Pierce. These N.C.O.'s displayed the greatest
gallantry and resolution, and each received the D.S.M.

force had consisted roughly (excluding details left in the transport lines, at the Field Ambulance, or at the rest camp) of 1,900 men and 70 officers, almost half the men and a third of the officers being in the Collingwood battalion. Now, at 12.45, there returned to our lines 5 officers and 950 men. But of these not all could now be relied on, for many were of the Collingwood, who in this hour of horror had been deprived of all their officers, save one, and of all stability, and there were none to rally and organize the survivors of this fine, but ill-fated, battalion.*   The situation, if a counter-attack had developed, must have been critical, for, in the audacious hope of a crushing victory, the Divisional Commander had been left with but one reserve battalion.   The Drake Battalion were ordered up at once to the front line, and General Paris was forced to ask for a battalion from the Corps reserve to take their place as a reserve to the Division.   The request was granted, and the Benbow Battalion left the rest camp at 2.30 p.m. and moved up into the gully.

Every effort was made to secure French co-operation for a renewal of the attack.   The first intention was for an attack by the R.N.D. alone at 2.15, with artillery support from the French.   This support was not, however, forthcoming, for the Commander-in-Chief was at the same time organizing and attempting to arrange for a joint operation by the French and the Naval Division.   All his endeavours failed.   The French Commander found himself wholly unable to co-operate, and an unsupported attack by the Naval Division was rightly judged impossible.   The issue of the battle had depended from the start on the success of the first assault, and this in turn had depended, for the reasons given, on the advance of the French Colonial troops along the ridge.   The gamble had failed.

The failure was unfortunately conspicuous.   In the centre of the line, the 42nd Division had achieved a memorable advance, and had captured and held three lines of Turkish trenches.   Their casualties throughout the day had been serious, but not overwhelming, and they had been able to hold on, though with steadily increasing losses, in the hope of

---

* The battalion was actually brought out of the line by C.P.O. Carnall (later promoted to Sub-Lieut. R.N.V.R., and posted to the Hood Battalion).   For his services on June 4th he received the D.S.M.

enabling the attack on the right to be renewed. Now their right had to be withdrawn. Here only the first line of captured trenches could be safely consolidated so long as our left remained where it was. Even then the front line held by the 42nd Division to the west of the Achibaba nullah was nearly 350 yards ahead of the old front line on the east, to which the Naval Division had fallen back. This gap had to be filled, or the last of the morning's gains had to be surrendered.

The Manchester Brigade were still heavily engaged, and could find no troops for what must be not only a difficult but an expensive task. In the circumstances, the Nelson Battalion were sent forward to get their first experience of active operations south of Achibaba.

It was apparently first thought that an attack would have to be made on the Turks who still held on to their old front line on the immediate right of the Manchesters; but Colonel Eveleigh, after discussing the position with the Brigadier on the spot, hit on a wiser, though still hazardous, plan, the execution of which was entrusted to "D" Company of his Battalion (Lt.-Commander H. C. Evans, R.N.V.R.). This plan was to construct a number of separate entrenchments covering the gap between the two front lines, and so sited as to afford the maximum protection for the exposed flank. Protected by covering parties, these posts could be completed before dawn, and could then be joined up during the day into a continuous line.

Throughout the night the Turkish fire was continuous, and casualties were heavy, but the plan was so far successful that digging was able to continue, which would almost certainly not have been possible had the Turks been led to realize our intentions by a formal attack on their flank. When dawn broke, the fire, aimed from close range by the enemy in the front line to the right of the Manchesters, became intense, but enough cover had been won during the night to enable the posts to be not only held but steadily strengthened and extended throughout the day. By four o'clock (when "C" Company of the Hawke Battalion relieved the Nelson Company to carry on the work of consolidation), the trench, though shallow, was almost continuous.

With the safeguarding of the captured line the main battle

of June 4th–5th was at an end.* It only remained for General
Paris to relieve the remnants of the Howe, Hood and Collingwood Battalions, and this was done without delay, the Hawke
Battalion taking over from the left of the Drake (who had
relieved the Anson some hours before), and filling the gap
between them and the Nelson Battalion.

This left as an effective divisional reserve only the Benbow
Battalion, who remained in the neighbourhood of Backhouse
Post.

Having regard to the disastrous reverse suffered by the
French and the Naval Division on the morning of the 4th,
the result was not wholly unsatisfactory. The fine pertinacity
of the 42nd Division during the afternoon of the 4th and the
work of the Nelson Battalion the next night had at least
prevented the enemy from exploiting his earlier success and
had preserved for us some substantial gains.

The price paid by the Naval Division for this very negative
success was, unfortunately, out of all reckoning. More than
sixty officers† and 1,800 men became casualties, and, of these,
nearly half were killed. The losses in senior officers and
in Company Commanders impaired the fighting efficiency of
the Division for some time to come. In the 2nd Brigade,
one Battalion Commander (Lt.-Colonel Collins), one Second
in Command (Major Myburg, of the Hood) and one Company
Commander (Lieut. the Hon. K. Dundas) remained. The
loss of the few regular officers of experience was particularly
grievous. A drastic reorganization was necessary, if those
battalions who had already won for themselves a first-class
fighting reputation (the Hood, Howe and Anson Battalions)
were to retain a separate existence, and it was in these tragic
circumstances that General Paris found it necessary to disband, not only the Benbow, but the ill-fated Collingwood
Battalion, whose cruel losses were due in no way to lack of
gallantry or skill. Under this arrangement, the Hood, Howe
and Anson absorbed the officers and men of these battalions,

* Hard fighting continued, however, on the left front of the 42nd Division
throughout the 6th and 7th of June, and the Chatham Battalion was detached
from the Corps reserve to assist General Firth's Brigade in their efforts to safeguard the most advanced of the captured trenches. Owing to lack of artillery
support the full scheme of consolidation (which necessitated two small advances)
was not carried out, but the position was substantially maintained.

† For a list of officers killed in this disastrous engagement see Appendix D.

and the Naval Brigades were reduced to three battalions apiece.

The veteran Colonel Oldfield, of the Benbow, had been wounded on June 5th, and it was thus his Second in Command, Major Bridges, R.M.L.I., who took command of the Anson Battalion, with Lt.-Commander Stuart Jones, the senior surviving officer of the old Battalion, as his Second in Command. Major Myburg succeeded to the Hood, and Commander West was appointed Second in Command of the Howe. Among other officers transferred to the Anson Battalion were Lt.-Commander Bernard Ellis and Lt.-Commander Gilliland (both from the Benbow), who were to serve this battalion with such distinction in France.

The disaster of June 4th raised wider issues than the organization of the Division which had been most signally involved in it. The battle had been watched from first to last with alternate hope and disappointment by the Commander-in-Chief, and when it was over his mind was made up. He would not seek for another decision at Cape Helles. The strong reinforcements for which he had already asked would be thrown in on a new front. The campaign at Cape Helles would be for the future directed towards the gradual demoralization of the enemy by minor operations, with a view to exhausting his man-power, drawing his reserves, and diverting his attention from other points. To enable this policy to be carried out, one fresh Division, and one only, would be landed at Cape Helles.

With this decision the campaign south of Achibaba entered on a new phase, lasting till the middle of July, during which active fighting was always in progress somewhere or another, but the routine of trench warfare was also continuous,* and attention was ever increasingly concentrated on the strengthening of our defences. The local offensives of this period were not unimportant; if nothing else, they forestalled an attack by the enemy and enforced his respect. But, proceeding continuously, and side by side with the more spectacular happenings, we find constant work on saps, on the deepen-

---

* And brought its toll of casualties: Surgeon Stewart, R.N., Sub-Lieut. C. E. C. Flood, Captain C. G. Bulling, R.M. (Deal Battalion), Sub-Lieut. T. E. Love (Hood), Sub-Lieut. A. C. Iliff (Nelson) and Surgeon F. H. Reas, R.N. (Drake) were among those killed in the last three weeks of this month while on ordinary trench duties.

Inspection of the 2nd R.N. Brigade by General Sir Ian Hamilton, G.C.B., at Imbros, June, 1915.

ing and traversing of old trenches, and the making of new ones, on wiring, on the construction of strong points and machine-gun emplacements, which was at least equally important. At this time, too, trench mortars and catapults (barbaric weapons, manufactured by some effort of inherited memory by—so it was said—Messrs. Gamage) appeared for the first time, to give a superficial touch of science to the primitive Eastern scene.

The reorganized Naval Division maintained throughout this period their old sector astride the Achibaba nullah, slightly extended by taking over a small stretch of line from the French. The sector was held alternately by the Marine and the 1st Naval Brigade, and Commodore Backhouse's brigade were taken to Imbros for an essential rest. A use was found at this time for the Divisional Cyclist Company (Major N. O. Burge, R.M.L.I.), who were trained in bombing and attached to the different battalions to assist them, as far as might be humanly possible, to master the constant and untimely vagaries of these peculiar instruments. Later, when all battalions had developed a section of trained bombers of their own,* the experts returned to Divisional Headquarters, to form the nucleus of the first bombing school founded on the peninsula.

After the battle of June 4th–5th the attention of the Divisional Commander was also directed to the construction of a more advanced firing-line, with a view to the renewal of the attack, should occasion arise, under conditions more favourable than those prevailing on June 4th. It was clear that the line could be pushed forward, without great hazard, to a distance of nearly 100 yards, but, opposite the centre section of the divisional front, was an advanced Turkish trench which it was felt ought to be at once easy to capture and useful to hold, and which, had it been either, would have assured an even more substantial advance. This trench it was decided to attack with the Hawke Battalion on June 19th. A daylight assault was out of the question, since every rifle and machine

---

* The metaphor is not without point. From now onward, till the end of 1917, the Army was subjected to continual epidemics, the first symptom of which was almost invariably the formation of a new section of specialists attached to Battalion Headquarters. When the epidemic died down, the specialists would either cease to specialize or be distributed among the companies—according to the severity of the onset of the particular disease.

gun on the slopes of Achibaba and the Kereves Dere commanded the ground, and Colonel Wilson was left with no
alternative to a night attack.

This was carried out by " A " Company (Lieutenant
Morgan, R.N.V.R.). The first assault, for which the Turks
did not seem unprepared, was met by a very heavy fire ;
Lieutenant Morgan and a number of men were killed round
the enemy trench, and a large number were wounded. Rallied,
however, by Lieutenant Horsfield, R.N.V.R., the company
went forward again, quickly made good their hold on the
trench, and began consolidating. Till day broke, the position
looked secure, though our losses, both in the original attack,
and from rifle and machine-gun fire in the later stage of the
operation, were very high, having regard to the comparative
unimportance of the objective. At dawn, the situation took
on a very different aspect. The captured trench was discovered
to have no adequate field of fire, and to be so sited as to be
subject to direct enfilade from the main Turkish position. This
was not all. In the darkness, the Turks had pushed down a
small party of bombers, who were able from an old communication trench which lay in dead ground to the garrison of
the captured trench, to inflict the most severe losses on them.
Had the bombing attack developed during the night, the
position might have been retrieved by a sortie. By day, this was
impossible. Already, moreover, the garrison was dangerously
reduced. Lieutenant Horsfield, wounded in the first assault,
had been wounded again, this time mortally. Sub-Lieut.
Tremayne, the battalion machine-gun officer, had been killed.
Of the original assaulting party not more than twenty were
unwounded. These survivors had been relieved about 6 a.m.
by a platoon of " C " Company, but within ten minutes of entering the trench half of this platoon also had become casualties.
In these circumstances, it was decided to evacuate the position,
as the only alternative to further and useless losses. In
addition to Lieutenant Morgan, Lieutenant Horsfield and Sub-
Lieutenant Tremayne, Sub-Lieutenant Little had been killed
on his way back to the line after "A" Company had been relieved,
and Sub-Lieutenant Milvaine had been seriously wounded
while in charge of a working party engaged on a communication
trench ; he died of wounds a few days later. Of the petty
officers and men, fourteen were killed and seventy-four wounded.

The next day but one, the French carried out a brilliant advance along the ridge of the Kereves Dere, and captured the key positions which they had failed to secure on June 4th. The Marine Brigade was in reserve for this operation.

On June 22nd, the Marine Brigade relieved General Mercer's Brigade in the trenches, and were called upon to attempt once again the capture of the trench which the Hawke Battalion had, three days before, held for six hours and then been obliged to abandon. This time the attempt was made by " A " Company of the Portsmouth Battalion, under Major Grover, R.M.L.I. The attack again succeeded, but the retribution came even more swiftly; the utmost gallantry and skill could not prevail against the facts, and the position was rightly given up within an hour and a half. In this operation the Marines suffered seriously, Major Grover and 2nd Lieut. P. L. L. Jermain being among the killed. On this day the Drake also lost a fine officer in Lieutenant P. W. Magrath, R.N.V.R.

After these set-backs, the Division reverted to its older and wiser policy of sapping by day and digging in in the open and wiring by night. In these operations the Chatham Battalion (Lt.-Colonel R. McN. Parsons, R.M.L.I.) did fine work, which was carried on by the Drake Battalion (now under Lt.-Commander H. D. King, R.N.V.R., Commander Campbell having been invalided a few days after June 4th).

On July 5th the monotony was relieved by an episode which the available records have dignified by the name of a Turkish attack. This was directed against the French lines, but, despite the blandishments of two extremely smart German officers who were seen urging the Turks to go forward, it never developed. Some twenty Turks, however, impelled perhaps more by curiosity than by zeal for battle, entered the Anson Battalion* lines. A counter-attack was immediately organized by Major Bridges, and the battalion returned to their line. The enemy meanwhile had taken advantage of our timely retreat to return to their own lines, and the officer commanding the Anson Company in charge of the front line had finished his breakfast and had come out of his dug-out. This fantastic episode made an amusing tale in the mouths of the Division's enemies in the peninsula (who were not all

---

* The Anson, having returned from Imbros, were attached at this time to the 1st Naval Brigade.

Turks). The more important thing was that the main attacking force of the enemy had been suitably handled on the parapets of their own trenches by the machine guns of the Hawke and Drake Battalions. Altogether at least a hundred casualties were inflicted by the Naval Battalions alone, and the French undoubtedly accounted for more. Our losses were negligible.

The day following, the Naval Division were relieved by the newly-arrived 52nd Division, who were to undertake our Divisional attack. Behind the scenes, the last act in the drama was being rehearsed ; and it was felt to be essential that the attention of the Turks should be effectually diverted from other fields.

The decision to renew the offensive south of Achibaba on any considerable scale in advance of the larger operations now pending was nevertheless unexpected. A resolute defensive, designed to improve the health of the troops and to lead up to a general attack to be made simultaneously with the major operations, would have been a policy more easily understood. The fact was, however, that the General Staff felt for some reason convinced that we could not risk a purely defensive policy throughout July. The result was a compromise between the need for an offensive as it presented itself to General Headquarters, and the still more urgent need for rest as represented by the authorities on the spot. The compromise took the only possible form of an attack by the only fresh Division, but its results were not fortunate. The attack was the most bloody engagement (in proportion to the number engaged and the nature of the objective) of any fought south of Achibaba, and it led indirectly to the spread of sickness* on this front, on a scale which cannot have been without influence on the final issue of the campaign.

During the days preceding the attack (which was planned for July 12th) the Naval Division, already so severely depleted, and having now an establishment of only ten infantry battalions, was ordered to furnish a battalion at full strength, to be trained in pack mule work in connection with the new landing. The Anson Battalion, reinforced by details from other battalions and from the Divisional troops, were detached

---

* It should be explained that dysentery was already rife on the peninsula in June, 1915. The wastage, however, was only gradual. After the July battles the wastage became very rapid.

Firing Line in R.N.D. Sector, mid-summer, 1915

for this duty, and the Deal Battalion of Marines had to take
their turn on fatigue duties at " W " beach. The strength of
the Division on the eve of the attack consisted thus of eight
weak infantry battalions. General Paris had proceeded to
Mudros on leave, on July 8th. Brigadier-General Trotman,
R.M.L.I., was temporarily in command.

The objectives of the 52nd Division were the same as of
the Naval Division on June 4th, and the French were to co-
operate on the right, in so far as was necessary. The Turkish
positions on the right, which had then made it impossible for
Commodore Backhouse's brigade to retain the trenches which
they captured, had, however, been already taken by the French,
on June 21st ; and to make assurance against enfilade fire from
the right doubly sure it was decided that the 52nd Division
should themselves attack in the first instance only on the right.
An advance from the left of their front was to be attempted
only if the attack on the right succeeded.

The first attack (by the French, and the 155th Brigade of
the 52nd Division, from the right of Parsons Road) began at
7.30 a.m., after an eighty-minutes' " intensive " bombardment,
and was generally successful. The second stage of the operations, when the 157th Brigade were to advance from the left of
their line, was also carried out according to plan later in the
day, although the situation in the centre was not altogether
clear. By the evening the position was that on the left the
attack had succeeded completely, as also on the extreme right
of the French line ; that in the centre the attack had not got
beyond the front two enemy lines, and that parties of Turks
were holding out even here in communication trenches and
shell holes. The day's fighting had been exceptionally severe,
and the whole of the 52nd Division reserves had. somehow
become involved in the attack. In these circumstances, the
Chatham, Portsmouth, Plymouth and Drake Battalions of the
Naval Division had unexpectedly been called up to take the
place of the original divisional reserve, and the Howe, Hood,
Nelson and Hawke Battalions were under orders to move at
ten minutes' notice.

During the night of the 12th–18th the position remained
unchanged (though the Nelson Battalion moved forward to
Backhouse Post), but on the morning of the 18th the communication between the 157th Brigade in the advanced trenches by

the Achibaba nullah and the remainder of their Division, was still extremely precarious; and it appears that an attempt made by this brigade, by working back along old communication trenches, to establish touch between themselves and the right of the position in the enemy's old second line led to a temporary retirement. Major Sketchley, R.M.L.I.,* who was on a reconnaissance when the retirement took place, had no difficulty in restoring the situation, and the Turks, who had followed up the retreat, were soon driven back. But the advanced position, so restored, remained isolated, and the Turks, still in possession of most of their third-line trenches, and consequently of covered approaches to the forward positions of the 52nd Division on the left, appear to have remained masters of the situation.

It seemed certain, from the grievous losses which were being sustained, and from the entire breakdown in communications, that we must either advance further or withdraw. In these circumstances, Brigadier-General Trotman (temporarily commanding the R.N. Division) was asked to clear up the position, and he determined on a general attack on those third-line positions of the Turks which had so far defied capture. This attack, the orders for which were issued at 3.20 p.m., was to be carried out by the Chatham, Portsmouth and Nelson Battalions at 4.30 p.m. The Nelson Battalion was to attack on the left, the Portsmouth in the centre, and the Chatham, in co-operation with the French, on the right. The Drake and Plymouth Battalions remained in divisional reserve.

Owing to an inexplicable congestion in the trenches, the orders did not reach the Chatham Battalion (Lt.-Colonel Godfrey, R.M.L.I.)† till 3.55 p.m., and the thirty-five minutes left before the attack were quite inadequate to the necessary preparation ; more particularly as it was impossible to get any news of the movements of the French. The attack, therefore, was actually carried out only by the Nelson and Portsmouth Battalions, though Colonel Godfrey worked forward into the two lines of previously captured trenches on the Chatham Battalion front, which were held by scattered details

* G.S.O.2 of the R.N. Division. For his forceful intervention on this occasion Major Sketchley was awarded the D.S.O., and Lance-Corporal Way, his orderly, who assisted him in organizing the counter-attack, gained the G.C.M.

† Lt.-Colonel R. McN. Parsons, R.M.L.I., had been wounded on June 28th. For his services with the R.N. Division he was later awarded the C.B.

of the 52nd Division. The Nelson and Portsmouth Battalions, on the other hand, advanced with the greatest gallantry. Colonel Eveleigh's battalion had no difficulty in capturing and consolidating the left of the objective, where they found themselves in touch with the 5th Battalion H.L.I., still clinging on to the gains of the previous afternoon in the neighbourhood of the Achibaba nullah. The Portsmouth Battalion, like the 5th K.O.S.B. before them, found that the enemy third line, further to the right, did not exist in recognizable form (the dispatch puts it, perhaps, less clearly, when it says that the Portsmouth Battalion fell into the same error as the K.O.S.B. at the same place), and they advanced too far. Losing almost all their officers, they had to fall back, but, even then, they dug in on a line in advance of the narrow ditch (not more than eighteen inches deep) which was all that there was of the enemy's third line at this point. One platoon of this battalion (under Lieutenant Murdoch Browne, R.M.L.I.)* remained isolated from the rest of the battalion in a still more advanced position. Only those who actually witnessed the unbelievable confusion of the battle, the sickness of the troops, intensified a hundredfold by local conditions, and the tenacity of the Turkish resistance at this time, can appreciate the brilliant character of these advances, which were, in terms of the operations of these two days, decisive.

The losses in the Nelson and Portsmouth Battalions had, however, been disastrous. Lt.-Colonel Eveleigh and Lt.-Colonel Luard and ten other officers† had been killed. Five other officers and 273 other ranks had become casualties in the Nelson Battalion alone, and in the Portsmouth Battalion Captain Gowney, D.S.C., was the only unwounded officer. For the survivors, moreover, clinging desperately to their gains as night came on, the conditions were well-nigh unendurable. Some of the worst scenes ever experienced on the battlefields of France or Mesopotamia were crowded into this narrow front of half a mile, over which fighting had been continuous for nearly

---

* Lieutenant Browne, R.M.L.I., was awarded the D.S.C. for his services in the Gallipoli campaign. By his death in France (on November 13th, 1916) the Corps lost an officer of exceptional promise.

† Lieutenants Wilmot-Sitwell and Dougherty, of the Portsmouth Battalion, Lieut. Baldwin, R.N.V.R., and Sub-Lieutenants J. M. F. Dickson, W. H. Edwards, W. Lintott, E. V. Rice, B. W. Smyth and F. H. J. Startin, of the Nelson Battalion, Sub-Lieut. Weaver, of the Howe Battalion, and Assistant Paymaster H. Biles, R.N.V.R., of the 2nd Brigade Staff.

forty-eight hours, where many hundreds of men lay dead or dying, where a burning sun had turned the bodies of the slain to a premature corruption, where there was no resting-place free from physical contamination, where the air, the surface of the ground, and the soil beneath the surface were alike poisonous, fetid, corrupt.

The Nelson Battalion were the best off, in tolerably deep and traversed trenches, but they had no safe communications either with our old line or with the Portsmouth Battalion, whose scattered relics were digging in on an undefined line, running back from the right of the Nelson to a point some two hundred yards in advance of the left of the Chatham Battalion. With the Chatham Marines in the old Turkish second line were the confused elements of many units of the 52nd Division, facing gallantly the almost impossible task of organizing the defence of what may have been a trench, but had become a graveyard. Even from here, there were no safe communications with our old front line.

If the brilliant success of the afternoon were not to be thrown away, prompt and energetic measures were needed. They were taken. The Drake Battalion was sent up to take over the whole disputed ground between the entrenchments of the Nelson on the left and the Chatham on the right. Though the battalion came up for the first time in the dark, the correct line was found, held, and consolidated, and by dawn lateral communication had been established along the whole front. For this fine piece of work Lt.-Commander King, R.N.V.R.* was to a large extent responsible. The losses of the Drake Battalion were not inconsiderable. In particular the two senior Company Commanders in the battalion, Lt.-Commander N. Wells and Lt.-Commander Sir J. H. Campbell, both survivors of all the earlier battles, were wounded.

The line now held was still short of our objective, for a portion of the enemy's third line, which had been the objective of the right of the 115th Brigade and of the French left on the morning of the 12th, had, owing to the inability of the Chatham Battalion and the French to co-ordinate an advance on the afternoon of the 13th, not been again attacked. The new

---

* Lieut.-Commander (now Captain) H. D. King, R.N.V.R., was soon after this engagement awarded the D.S.O. and promoted to the rank of Commander His fine work with the Drake Battalion was a feature of the campaign.

line was, however, in General Paris's view* the best from a
purely military point of view which his Division had as yet
been called on to hold, and it was wisely decided to be content
with it. General Paris was thus able to devote his unfailing
energies to the extremely difficult task of reorganization and
consolidation. The first move was to withdraw from the over-
crowded, insanitary and dangerously exposed trenches as
many men as possible of the gallant 52nd Division (the whole
sector had now been handed over to the Naval Division. All,
save one battalion on the extreme left of the sector, were
withdrawn on the 14th from the forward trenches. The new
sector was then divided into two Brigade sub-sectors, with the
Marine Brigade on the left and the 1st Naval Brigade on the
right.

Here, for ten days, hardly less anxious and no less unpleasant than the actual days of battle, the Division laboured
on the essential tasks of burying the dead, reconstructing the
trenches and pushing forward barricades along the trenches
communicating between our own lines and those of the enemy.
The strain on the troops must have been almost unprecedented
in the annals of defensive warfare, but the work proceeded :
battalions worked at high pressure for short spells in front
line, and within less than a fortnight conditions reverted to
normal. The Hood Battalion carried out a highly successful
operation during this period, when they rushed a Turkish
barricade, which had been established too close to our line,
and won another thirty yards of trench. In this operation
Lieut. Charles Lister played a very prominent part, and was
wounded, leading the attack with a characteristic distinction.
Lt.-Commander Freyberg, D.S.O., who had taken over
command of the Hood Battalion from Major Myburg (sick)
earlier in the month, was on this occasion wounded for the
second time. He was temporarily succeeded in command
by Lt.-Commander E. W. Nelson, R.N.V.R.

On July 25th the responsibilities of the infantry, so often
incomparably the heaviest, were at last lightened, the garrisoning of the trenches being taken over, under Naval Divisional
arrangements, by the 33rd Brigade. This was the beginning
of the long promised rest, and on August 1st the Naval Division
handed over the line for a definite period to the 42nd Division

* The General had returned from Mudros on the evening of the 13th

and the French. The long deferred time of rest had come,
but it had come too late. The strength of the Division, even
after the June disaster, had been 208 officers and 7,141 other
ranks. On August 1st, it was shown as 129 officers and 5,038
other ranks. The strain of the July battles and of the subsequent fortnight in the line had definitely broken not the fighting
spirit but the physical health of the men. Even of the five
thousand officers and men remaining at the beginning of August,
not 10 per cent. would have been considered fit in France for
duty in the quietest part of the line. In Gallipoli at this
time all officers and men who could actually walk to the trenches
were reckoned as fit. On any other classification the campaign
must have been abandoned. The plain fact was that the
capacity of the troops to stand the strain of continuous fighting
under unhealthy conditions had been over-estimated.

The only relief which the infantry could find was in bathing
when out of the line. This was not merely pleasant but safe,
since a wise discrimination in the choice of bathing places
ensured the protection of the cliffs against shell fire. The test
of *moral* at this time was the ability to face the walk to the
beaches for the pleasure of bathing on arriving there. Samuel
Butler says somewhere that the essence of morality is that the
pain precedes the pleasure. On this view, bathing in July was
a highly meritorious achievement. It was certainly the only
thing which enabled even the hardiest to survive, though not
to escape, dysentery and jaundice and the other effects of living
on tinned food (shared with swarms of flies), in an almost
tropical climate for a period of months.

The Naval Division had at this difficult time their own
peculiar difficulties to contend with. No sooner had the Division
reached their bivouacs and begun the first tentative reorganization than an order was received that 300 fleet reserve stokers
were to be transferred for fleet service. The first thought
was that the Division was being broken up. It was not far
wrong. The Naval Battalions were being deprived of their
backbone of trained and disciplined veterans, and the task of
reorganization had assumed serious proportions. So severe
had been the losses experienced by the Anson, Howe, Hood,
Nelson and Drake Battalions, that the withdrawal of 300
stokers meant, practically, the withdrawal of every regular
rating from the battalions. The needs of the fleet were no

doubt urgent ; but it is probable that the stokers would have been allowed to remain if adequate reinforcements could have been provided to bring the Division up to full strength. The strongest representations, personal and official, had been made to the authorities at home, pointing out the urgent need for reinforcing the Naval Division after the battle of June 4th, and again after the battle of July 12th-13th. Before this date Sir Ian Hamilton, in a personal letter to Mr. Winston Churchill, wrote that " the Naval Division have really done superbly. They have . . . suffered proportionately heavy losses. . . . The particular brigade I spoke of (the 2nd Naval Brigade) will, if it receive reinforcements within a fairly short time, be second to none as a fighting machine in the service. If, on the other hand, I am forced by circumstances to shove it into another severe fight before reinforcements come, then it will be so pulled down in strength that there will not be enough of the old soldiers remaining to leaven the new drafts." The First Lord of the Admiralty received at the same time the most urgent official representations, and the Army Council were formally requested to assist in the provision of reinforcements on the very grounds so forcibly urged by Sir Ian Hamilton. The War Office were unable, however, to assist in any way, and indeed, stated that they proposed to telegraph to Sir Ian Hamilton giving him *carte blanche*, after consultation with Sir John de Robeck, to make any necessary reductions in the establishment of the Division. The fact that a division was at the Dardanelles had appeared before now to be a sufficient reason for starving it of the ordinary reinforcements, and, in any case, it is arguable that the War Office could not have been expected to go out of its way to help the Naval Division. The fact remains that their decision meant that the Division could be fit for little more than garrison duty for the remainder of the campaign, and that the fighting strength of the whole force was thus avoidably diminished.

With the stokers, went Commodore Backhouse and his staff, and the 2nd Naval Brigade ceased to exist. So also did the Marine Brigade. For the Marines, too, there were no adequate reinforcements, and the Portsmouth, Plymouth, Chatham and Deal Battalions were amalgamated into two battalions under Lt.-Colonel Matthews, C.B., R.M.L.I. (succeeded a little later by Lt.-Colonel Hutchison,

R.M.L.I.) and Captain F. N. White (temporary, pending
the arrival from England of Lt.-Colonel Stroud, C.B.,
R.M.L.I.). With the Marine Battalions were brigaded the
Anson (still on detached duty) and the Howe Battalions. This
now became the 2nd Naval Brigade. The 1st Brigade con-
sisted of the Drake, Nelson, Hawke and Hood Battalions.
Lt.-Commander H. D. King and Lt.-Commander B. C. Freyberg
were confirmed in the command of the Drake and Hood
Battalions and were promoted to the rank of Commander.
Major Burge (from the Divisional Cyclist Company) was
appointed to command the Nelson with Lt.-Commander
Nelson, R.N.V.R. as Second in Command; and Lt.-Colonel L. O.
Wilson, D.S.O., M.P. continued in command of the Hawke
Battalion.

With this reorganization our detailed narrative of the
events on the Gallipoli peninsula must close. The remaining
four months of the campaign surpass perhaps in historic
importance, though assuredly not in dramatic interest, the
days of the earlier struggles. But neither in the great events
at Anzac and Suvla in August and September nor in the
heroic local assaults delivered at Cape Helles in August and
September by the 29th, the 42nd and the 52nd Divisions, did
the Naval Division play a part. Sir Ian Hamilton's prophecy
had been fulfilled at any rate to the extent that the Division
was numerically too weak to be thrown into any severe engagement. How it was that so much had been sacrificed for so
little can never be wholly accounted for in a single page, or even
in a single volume. But it is hardly possible to doubt that,
as things turned out, in the light of the unexpected resistance
by the Turks to the attack from Anzac, and of the unexpected
breakdown in our offensive at Suvla, the battles of June and
July on the peninsula cost more than they were worth. For
they cost much more than the equivalent of the aggregate of
our casualties. The Naval Division in August, 1915, was something very different in numbers, in experience and in their
capacity for endurance from the Naval Division in May. The
same was true of the other Divisions on the peninsula throughout the same time.

And so the only thing that remains to tell about the Naval
Division in Gallipoli is the story of an anticlimax rising
almost, in the end, to the dramatic level. Yet at the same

Gully Ravine, Gallipoli, September, 1915

time we shall be able to trace the Naval Division developing, reorganizing, even under the most depressing conditions, finding within itself and in its reinforcements unexpected sources of strength, and in the end needing but little more than rest and a change of diet before it was ready to take its place in the line once more as a fighting Division trained and equipped for the offensive. New personalities had come and were coming to the front under provocation of the urgent opportunity. Commander King more than upheld the reputation of those officers of the regular R.N.V.R. who had formed the majority of the original officers of the Division, and of whom so few were now left, and the new Adjutant of the Drake, Lieut. Sterndale Bennett, R.N.V.R. was gaining that experience which alone was necessary to make him an equally outstanding figure. Commander Freyberg had enhanced the reputation which he had won by his dashing exploit in the Gulf of Xeros and was showing himself not only a fine soldier but a distinguished leader of men, and Lt.-Commander Asquith, Lt.-Commander W. M. Egerton and Lieut. F. S. Kelly shared with Commander Freyberg the credit for bringing the reorganized Hood Battalion in the ensuing months to that brilliant standard of efficiency which was later to assist the Division to an historic success. Lt.-Commander Stuart Jones, Lt.-Commander Ellis and Lt.-Commander Gilliland were creating at the same time a new Anson tradition, and Lt.-Commander C. S. West and Lt.-Commander P. H. Edwards were setting an inspiring example to the Howe Battalion, which had its own difficulties to contend with.

The new Nelson Battalion under Lt.-Colonel Burge, the Hawke Battalion still under the courageous leadership of Lt.-Colonel Leslie Wilson and Commander Ramsay Fairfax, R.N., and the reorganized Marine Battalions (as finely officered as ever before) were also to show themselves fully capable of profiting by the example of their commanders. In short, the Naval Division as it had sailed for Gallipoli was passing away, but a successor was growing up whose achievements, when the time came, were to challenge, if not to surpass, those of its predecessors. The time, however, was not yet. The force south of Achibaba was no better in its present situation than a beleaguered garrison, and the wind from Suvla bore on its wings no rumour of relief.

CHAPTER IX

NEITHER in the landing at Suvla and in the general offensive from Anzac to which that landing was subsidiary, nor in the diversions at Cape Helles early in August, had the Naval Division, as such, any share. Only the Anson Battalion and the 2nd Field Ambulance were detached for special duty at Suvla, the former in charge of pack transport, the latter as corps troops. Amid the constant fluctuations of the new front these two units carried out their essential if inconspicuous task and won high praise from those in authority, but no account can be written here of the scenes amid which they moved, of the nature of the fighting, and of the day-to-day incidents which marked the different stages of the campaign.* The Naval Division remained south of Achibaba, and it is only in its effect on that front that we can treat of the August and September fighting further north.

Considering all things, the secret of the date and place of the new landing was fairly well kept, but towards the end of July the excitement grew, for all knew that somewhere, and soon, a new attempt was to be made to break through the Turkish cordon and set our armies once more on the move. For those divisions who, with the bitter experience of more than three months' continuous fighting behind them, were called on to suffer the inevitable losses entailed by a demonstration against entrenched positions, or who waited, as did the Naval Division, as spectators, for the news which might restore to them their freedom of action, the early days of August were memorable. The initial disappointment, when it came, was severe.

---

* There is a fairly full account in that excellent work, " On Four Fronts with the Royal Naval Division," by Surgeons Sparrow and McBean Ross (Hodder and Stoughton, 1918).

Lieut. the Hon. K. Dundas, R.N.V.R. (Anson), was killed at Suvla on August 7th by a chance shot. As is known, the landing was virtually unopposed.

The partial failure of the operations of August 6th–11th was not, however, fully realized as involving the final breakdown of the campaign.

From a purely military point of view, the delay at Suvla was as fatal as the delay at Cape Helles in April ; but it was not more so. Just as we had had to take Achibaba within forty-eight hours or fail even to threaten our real objective, so, in August, we had to carry Ismail Oghi Tepe and threaten the flank of the enemy position centred on the historic hills of Chunak Bair and Koja Chemen Tepe, if these vital positions from which our guns would command Maidos and the Narrows were to fall to the assault of what was now the main force operating from Anzac. But the breakdown of this plan was not in itself the ultimate disaster. There was still a chance of victory. New formations were available, and could have been sent to Gallipoli early in September, to exploit the inadequate, but still remarkable, success gained in August. Why they were not; how they were first held up till the perhaps premature offensive at Loos had petered out, and how then they were diverted to Salonica, is told in full detail in Sir Ian Hamilton's Diary. It was for the news of these reinforcements that every soldier on Gallipoli waited during the days following the inconclusive close of the first northern battle.

Slowly the hope of reinforcements faded. Rumour—truly the swiftest of military as of other disasters—spoke of doubts and hesitations at home. Troops returning from hospital in Egypt brought news of the indifference with which their great if unavailing sacrifices were regarded by the hierarchy of conservative opinion which ruled the councils at that rather Capuan base. It was then that the spectre of doubt, which had loomed up first when the authentic news from Suvla came to hand, began to cast a lengthening shadow. As things happened, the failure at Suvla, inexplicable perhaps, perhaps merely unexplained, was indeed the cause of the untimely ending of the campaign. But it was not simply the decent charity of one soldier towards another which made common men hesitate, and in the end refuse, to place the whole blame on the staffs, generals and battalions whose several responsibility for the defeat it is still so difficult to determine. Others, who had intrigued against the expedition almost from the start and who now abandoned it, not in favour of the French front, but in favour of Salonica, must share the ultimate responsibility for the decisive failure, for " a disaster," as Mr. H. W. Nevinson rightly says, " leaving its lamentable mark upon the world's history."

The immediate result of the admission of defeat on the northern front was that, south of Achibaba, the resistance of the sorely tried infantry divisions to physical ills and hardships long endured was weakened by the subconscious realization that the campaign was at a standstill. During the September and October, the war-weary divisions at Cape Helles melted like snow in the noon-day sun. By the middle of October, the effective strength of the division had sunk to 3,200. Since April 25th, out of more than 16,500 men of unmatched physique and still unimpaired determination, over 13,000 had become casualties, killed, wounded, or evacuated sick. But for the splendid work of the Naval surgeons throughout the whole period, these figures—appalling as they are— would have been far higher.

It was when this wave of sickness was at its height that it became known that Sir Ian Hamilton was handing over the Supreme Command. Only a few days before he had visited the Naval Division trenches with General Paris and General Mercer, and spoken to very many officers and men. It was no surprise when this visit became, in retrospect, a visit of farewell. And it was no coincidence that his resignation came at a time when the strength of the Division was at its ebb. For the change in command was no more than the logical and expected result of the change in the opinions of the Government at home. It is one of the ineradicable misfortunes of modern war that the fighting soldier can never get to know his Commander-in-Chief, but it was generally felt that, with Sir Ian Hamilton, went the last hope of an energetic prosecution of the campaign. His departure, in fact, summed up the situation, crystallized it. What everyone had feared, was now to happen.

From mid-August onward, the Division were in the front line, and often actively engaged in the modified offensives peculiar to stationary warfare. The new divisional sector which they took over from the 29th Division on August 15th lay between Gully ravine and the Krithia nullah. The sector, sadly damaged in the costly demonstrations of August 6th and

Bathing from the Beach between Cape Helles and Sedd-el-bahr.

7th (carried out on this front by the 29th Division), was neither healthy nor secure. The front line was a part of the old Turkish trench system, and was joined to the present Turkish line by numerous communication trenches, watched from barricades, generally within hand-bombing distance of the enemy. These barricades marked almost invariably the scene of the most bitter hand-to-hand fighting. The bodies of English and Turks alike were built into the walls of these rough-and-ready fortifications, and others were buried only a few inches below the ground. In the rest of the front-line trenches the conditions were only a little less unhealthy. These conditions accentuated the sickness which was due primarily, as has been said, to other causes. The numbers available for duty in the trenches fell constantly, while the length of the divisional sector could not be correspondingly reduced. In the result, the hours of duty were lengthened, the reliefs were less frequent, the fatigues were more arduous.

If active fighting was at an end, the strain of the defensive war carried on under these difficulties was considerable. Moreover, in face of the possibility of a winter campaign, communications had improved; a trench drainage system had to be prepared, and a new front-line trench had to be dug and wired. Our trenches were so sited as to be extremely open to effective bombardment, and the work of reconstructing the sector was dangerous, as well as irksome, to the depleted garrisons.* Throughout this period, a semblance of an offensive war also had to be maintained, if only to forestall any possible Turkish attack. To this end, saps were pushed out, barricades pushed forward, and intensive trench-mortar bombardments added to the horrors of war.

The incidents of this eventful but unromantic period call for little mention. On August 27th we read of a daring reconnaissance of the Turkish front line by Lt.-Commander Asquith (Hood) and Lieut. Blyth (Drake); two days later, of a Turkish reconnaissance of our own trenches in the neighbourhood of the Northern barricade, which was beaten off with loss by the Hawke Battalion. Again, two days later, we read

---

* And to the Engineers, whose energies were unfailing. It is certain that no division was ever better served by its field companies than was the Naval Division.

of the advancement of one of the barricades by Lt.-Commander Isgar, of the Howe Battalion, in a cool and successful operation. During September and October episodes of this character, so vivid in experience, so drab in retrospect, follow one another almost monotonously. By October 6th, the new firing line was completed, and the rest of the month was occupied with the almost more dangerous and uninspiring task of wiring it. Later in the same month, Lt.-Commander Isgar, assisted by C.P.O. Gray, P.O. Conway and L.S. Townes, pushed forward the Worcester barricade. Early in November, Sub-Lieut. Hancock's platoon of "C" Company of the Hawke Battalion carried out the same operation at the Southern barricade with equal success.

The value of these operations, entailing as they did a constant stream of minor casualties, and aggravating if possible the prevailing sickness, was sometimes called in question. We had, however, to hold on this front a very superior force, fully conscious of the victory which they had won on the Northern front in August. On other grounds, too, the policy of the Divisional Commander had much to recommend it. In these operations, the newly-joined reinforcements, put into the line as they arrived, were able to learn something of war, and to retain something of discipline. The tactics afforded, in fact, the only solution of the most serious domestic problem with which the Division was confronted, the absorption of reinforcements under conditions so circumscribed, that it was actually impossible to parade even a platoon.

Difficulties of organization and discipline were heightened by the heavy losses of officers from sickness in August and September. Brigadier-General Trotman was away ill for the whole of September, and Lt.-Colonel Stroud, R.M.L.I., temporarily assumed command of the Brigade. Lt.-Colonel Matthews, R.M.L.I., was invalided permanently from the peninsula at the same time. Lt.-Colonel Wilson (Hawke Battalion), was invalided on October 7th, and was succeeded temporarily by Commander W. G. Ramsay Fairfax, R.N. Lt.-Colonel Burge, R.M.L.I. (Nelson Battalion), was invalided in October, and was succeeded temporarily by Lt.-Commander E. W. Nelson, R.N.V.R. The rate of sickness among junior officers was correspondingly high. During the period August 15th to November 30th the 1st Naval Brigade

alone, in addition to losing four officers killed* (Sub-Lieut.
Farrow of the Hawke, Sub-Lieut. Bligh of the Drake, and
Lieutenant the Hon. Charles Lister and Sub-Lieut. E. H.
Gibson of the Hood) and two wounded, lost sixty-three officers
evacuated sick.† Among those who left the Division during this
period were three chaplains, the Rev. H. C. Foster, the Rev.
B. Failes and the Rev. F. Pierce, and the medical officers of the
Nelson (Surgeon Parker, R.N.) and of the Hawke (Surgeon
W. Bradbury, R.N.‡), all of whom had done magnificent work
throughout the campaign.

If the health of the officers was bad, that of the men was
no better, and the constant fatigues made their existence
infinitely more burdensome. The result was that in September
and October the Division lost well over four thousand men
(though they received reinforcements which made the net loss
a little less), and even in November, when the colder weather
made the conditions in the trenches more bearable, the loss
was over a thousand.

That work continued without cessation, and that the
sector was very materially strengthened, was to the credit of
the men of the infantry and the officers and men of the
Engineers. Their work was not materially lighter whether
they were in or out of the line. In preparation for winter,
and to make room for the 2/2nd and 2/4th Battalions of the
London Regiment, who came to reinforce the Division in
October, the R.N.D. rest camp was moved during October to
the extreme left of the peninsula, behind the new divisional
sector. The new camp was systematically planned to afford
the maximum protection against the shell-fire, but there was
no available timber, and only a little corrugated iron. Safety
and comfort, therefore, alike, depended on digging. The
idea was to build rows of oblong dug-outs, five feet deep at the
back and six feet in front, each draining into a narrow communicating trench, at least seven feet deep, along which officers

---

* In the 2nd Brigade Captain E. B. Carpenter, R.M. (Plymouth), Lieut.
G. S. Perkins, R.M. (Deal) and Sub-Lieut. Massey (Howe) were killed during
this period.

† Among them were Surgeon D. R. Bedell Sivright, M.B., R.N. (best known,
perhaps, as a Rugby international) and Lt.-Commander W. S. Miall Green
(Benbow), both of whom died a short time after.

‡ For his services in the peninsula Staff-Surgeon Bradbury was later
awarded the D.S.O. and Surgeon Parker the D S.C.

and men could move round the camp entirely unobserved.   In
the event of a heavy bombardment it was thought that these
deep and narrow trenches would themselves afford fairly
effective protection.   The chances of prolonged bombardment
of the rest camp were, however, serious, and it was decided to
ensure against its effects still further by linking up the rest
camp with the cliffs, by a prolongation of two or more of the
internal communicating trenches.   The camp could then be
evacuated, if necessary, under cover.

This elaborate scheme, necessary though it might have
proved itself, entailed an almost heartbreaking task for the
infantry battalions.   Yet this task, too, was well on the road
to completion by the end of November, and the Division was
experiencing the nearest approach to comfort which had yet
been encountered on active service when the weather broke.
The first sign was a torrential downpour of rain on the night of
November 26th–27th.   The next night it turned to snow, and
throughout the next two days a northerly gale blew, while the
frost, which had set in on the 27th–28th, lasted for the best
part of three days, reaching its height on the morning of the
30th, when the thermometer stood at 18° Fahrenheit.   For
three days it had not risen above 22°, and the effect of this
sudden cold on men who were still suffering from the effects
of an almost tropical summer was extremely bad.   Only one
dug-out per company was roofed.   The remainder (four-fifths)
of the men were in the open, or at best under a covering of
worn-out waterproof sheets ; and the supplies of blankets, fuel
and oil were wholly inadequate to the emergency.   Had the
cold continued, the situation must have become as serious at
Cape Helles as it did at Suvla and Anzac, when two hundred
died of cold in three days, and ten thousand men were evacuated
sick.   Even as it was, there were many cases of frost-bite
among the troops whose ill luck it was to be in the line at this
time.   Twenty-four occurred in the 1st Marine Battalion
alone.

To the general surprise, for the Army Corps at Cape Helles
had learnt to expect but little from fortune, the weather
improved (though only for a week or so) on December 1st, and,
though the trenches were temporarily flooded by the thaw
which came as suddenly as the frost, things were normal again
by the end of the first week in December.   In one all-important

respect they were actually better. The frost, unbearable
while it lasted, put an end at once to the lingering summer
sickness.

On December 5th, the Division, just as it was nearing the
completion of the rest camp, received orders to take over a
new sector on the left of the line, from the right of the 42nd
Division to the left of the French sector, which was now to be
shortened. This relief was carried out by General Trotman's
brigade on December 11th. On the 17th, the rest camp was
given over to the 87th Brigade, and the Naval Division moved
into French billets on the coast above Morto Bay.

The first thought of the Division, on learning that they had
to take over part of the French line and a French camp, was
one of dismay. The French artillery and the French wine
were universally admired, but the fact that the new sector
would be supported by a group of " 75's " was regarded
as the one consolation. It was assumed that the French
trenches would be more primitive, less clean, and less well
organized than our own, and that the French camp would be a
poor substitute for that which the Division had built up at so
great an expenditure of energy. No assumption could have
been more incorrect. Though the ground on which the camp
and the reserve lines stood was rocky to a depth of some feet,
the trenches and dug-outs were both deeper than our own.
They were also weather-proof, built round with stones, and
roofed with corrugated iron. The officers' quarters were as
comfortable as could be, with tables and chairs, wooden floors,
firmly constructed stone walls, and doors and windows complete
with everything but glass. This was not Sybaritic luxury.
It merely meant that the French War Office had sent out to
Gallipoli supplies of stores essential to the health and comfort,
and so to the fighting efficiency, of the troops, in quantities
which were proportioned to the numbers of their expeditionary
force. For English troops, corresponding supplies had never
been available.

In the trenches, also, was much that the British Army had
lacked through the campaign. Particularly striking was the
abundance of strong corrugated iron (very different from the
flimsy material of the same name which was doled out in yards
to the British) which formed the material for most of the dug-
outs, and was in itself almost splinter-proof, being more than

a quarter of an inch thick.   The whole of this corrugated iron was of English manufacture.

From a military point of view, the most striking feature of the French organization was the artillery liaison system. The arrangements were no better (at least in theory) than those universally adopted a little later by all formations, but they were in advance of anything yet experienced by the Naval Division.

It was, however, no period of rest or comfort which awaited the Division in this sector.   All that can be said is that the arrangements made by the French made it just practicable for the trenches to be maintained in reasonable security by a numerically weak division, under conditions which were extremely unfavourable.   Two new factors made a profound change in the military situation in December, 1915.   In the first place, the weather settled down by the second week in December to definite winter conditions, which meant heavy, though not continuous, rain.   In the second place, the Turks, for the first time, began a systematic and effective bombardment of our front-line trenches with heavy guns.*

Both these adverse factors were such as could be, and were, overcome on other fronts.   By an army starved of supplies, starved of rest, under-officered, suffering from continual disappointment, hopelessly under-gunned, they could only be endured. †

To offset the obvious hardships and increasing dangers to which the force was exposed there was little but the improved health of the troops, which clearly would not be maintained indefinitely through a winter campaign, and the return to all battalions of not a few tried officers and men who had been evacuated sick earlier in the campaign.

It was in these circumstances that official news came of the evacuation of Suvla and Anzac.   The official announcement naturally did not forecast—rather, it definitely denied—the possibility of the evacuation of the southern beaches, but, from

---

* Captain C. F. Mead, R.M.L.I. (Deal Battalion), Sub-Lieut. C. Bridgland, R.N.V.R. (Drake) and Sub-Lieut. B. W. Kenny, R.N.V.R. (Nelson), were among those killed in these closing days of the campaign.

† I do not intend to suggest that the *moral* of the Division was on the ebb.   It was not.   The truth is that it was only the *moral* of the troops which enabled a resolute defence to be maintained under almost impossible conditions. The mere physical strain, however, made a renewal of the offensive, unless reinforcements could be supplied, impossible.

the point of view of the linesmen, this was immaterial. Whatever happened, the relief of the Naval Division for a period of
rest, if only on the adjacent islands, could not now be long
delayed.

Few military histories, which record so proudly and so
truly the enthusiasm of all ranks of an army at the beginning
of a campaign, give equal prominence to the no less fervent
longing of all soldiers for a period of rest after months of continuous fighting. To live on the Gallipoli peninsula was
to be continuously, not merely within effective range, but under
fire. Not a day passed but that some camp was shelled, and
all the beaches; while the daily fatigues were as often as not
carried out under indirect rifle fire. The prospect of a temporary
change from these conditions could have been nothing less
than joyous in any circumstances. As it happened, the prospect first dawned on the men in the front-line trenches during a
week of exceptionally persistent bombardment, when the
casualties were severe. Austrian heavy artillery, moreover,
was reported to be coming into position.

The first hint of relief for the Naval Division was the
announcement, made on December 29th, before the policy
of evacuation was definitely decided on,* that the 8th Corps
would be relieved by the 9th Corps. This was the alternative
scheme which would have been adopted had it been decided
to remain at Cape Helles; but the purpose of the announcement
was wider. On December 24th, Sir William Birdwood, now
commanding the Dardanelles Army under the supreme command of Sir Charles Monro, had received orders to make all
" preliminary preparations for immediate evacuation in the
event of orders to this effect being received," and it was essential
to make some public explanation of the withdrawal of certain
surplus stores, etc., which had to be put in hand without delay.
The situation soon resolved itself, and on the next day
(December 30th) General Paris received orders to prepare for
early evacuation.

Immediately on receipt of his instructions to make preliminary preparations, General Birdwood had ordered silence
to be maintained at stated intervals each night from the 25th

---

* It is not universally known that among those in high command on the
peninsula and in the Eastern Mediterranean were many vigorous opponents of
evacuation.

onward, and, as far as the front line was concerned, nothing
was required in the way of definitive preparations but to continue in the same way.   But much elaborate organization
remained to be carried out behind the lines.   The first thing
was to complete the relief of the French troops from the right
of the line, and to relieve the 42nd Division from the sector
to the left of the Naval Division, the object in each place being
to reduce the number of separate formations to the minimum.
In place of these, the 13th Division and the remainder of the
29th Division, now at last strongly reinforced, returned to
Cape Helles.   The necessary trench reliefs were carried out
on the nights of December 31st and January 1st, and the lines
from sea to Straits were held thereafter by only four divisions,
the 13th on the left, the 29th and the 52nd in the centre and
the Royal Naval Division on the right.   In support of the
last named, there remained some French artillery, which the
French commander readily agreed should come under our
orders for the remaining few days of the campaign, to " escape
the disadvantages of divided command in the final stage "
of the evacuation.

The Naval Division sector, which had previously consisted
of some two thousand yards of line between the restricted
French sector overlooking the Straits and the 42nd Division,
now ran, roughly, from the centre of the old sector to the coast.
General Mercer's brigade remained where it was before, and
General Trotman's brigade moved across to the new sub-
sector on the left, the 52nd Division taking over the old sub-
sector on the right.   The Hood and Drake Battalions of the
1st Brigade and the 1st R.M. and Howe Battalions of the 2nd
Brigade were now in the front lines, the Hawke Battalion and
the 2nd R.M. in the reserve (Eski) line, and in bivouac the
Nelson and Anson Battalions and the 2/2nd and 2/4th
Battalions of the London Regiment.

The date of the evacuation had been fixed for January 8th,
and the final plans, modelled on those so supremely successful
at Anzac and Suvla, had been made.   The task before the Corps
Commander was, indeed, more arduous than had been the case
on the other front.   The accumulation of stores was more
considerable, the front deeper and the communications more
exposed.   But the problem was still essentially a simple one.
During the days immediately following the reorganization of

the sectors of defence, all troops not required for front line or support duty, and all stores not needed for the maintenance of this smaller force had to be withdrawn. As soon as this was done the final withdrawal, accompanied inevitably by an increasing, but still a very limited, measure of risk, could begin. For the purpose of the final orders issued to the troops concerned, this stage of the operation was defined as beginning on " X " day, " Z " day being, of course, the day on the evening of which our positions on the peninsula would be surrendered. The date of " X " day was necessarily determined by the progress made with the withdrawal of stores, guns and reserve troops.

For this the arrangements were in charge of Major-General the Hon. H. A. Lawrence, then commanding the 52nd Division (later Chief of Staff to Sir Douglas Haig in France).

Progress was, on the whole, as good as could have been expected. The first units to leave were, as has been stated, the French infantry and 42nd Division. Next came the bulk of the artillery, the horses, and the surplus transport of the remaining troops. Then, in the last days, the baggage of the Divisional and Brigade Headquarters, the battalion records and the regimental stores of the units in the line.

By " X " day, first announced as January 5th and then postponed till January 6th, all this had been accomplished, and there was nothing to show that our movements had aroused the enemy's suspicion. On this day the period of calculable risk began. The front line trenches and the reserve (Eski) line were still held in full strength, but the artillery was now reduced to a minimum, and the reserve infantry were preparing for embarkation. Thus, on the night of January 6th–7th, the two battalions of the London Regiment attached to the Naval Division were embarked, and by the morning of January 7th the total strength of the Division (all arms) was reduced to some 4,400. Assuming other divisions to have been similarly thinned, there were not many more than 16,000 men on the peninsula on January 7th, when the Turks opened a terrific bombardment at 2 p.m. The shelling on the left was the heaviest ever experienced on the peninsula; on the right, where the Naval Division were, it was less severe than the bombardments of December 23rd, 24th and 25th. This was extremely opportune, since an effective counter-bombardment

could be maintained on the left flank by the guns of the support-
ing squadron (Captain Dent, R.N.), but on that flank only.
As it was, the attempted attack was broken by the help of the
Navy, and the whole front was quiet again by 5 p.m.

After this episode, the execution of the plan went on un-
interruptedly, and during the night of January 7th–8th the
support battalions (Hawke and 2nd R.M.) of the Naval
Division left the trenches for the last time. They were relieved
in the Eski line by detachments of the front-line garrison.
The final allocation of troops for the divisional sector of the
firing, support and Eski lines was 845 all ranks and 8 machine
guns to the firing line, 300 all ranks and 2 machine guns in
immediate support, and 460 all ranks and 3 machine guns in
the third line, all drawn from the Hood, Drake, 1st R.M. and
Howe battalions. Simultaneously, all other arms of the Division in the defensive zone were reduced proportionately, except
the medical personnel, which was fixed at the proportionately
high figure of 210 all ranks.

The dangers of leaving the defence of a position 2,000 yards
in extent to be defended in depth by nearly 2,000 men were
obvious ; but they were not overwhelming. In bivouac, were
approximately another 2,000 men (the Hawke Battalion, two
companies of the 2nd R.M. Battalion and details of Engineers,
medical personnel and the other infantry battalions), and a
new line covering the beaches had been organized by the G.O.C.
embarkation. To this line had been allotted (from the Naval
Division) 400 officers and men of the 2nd R.M. Battalion.
Even the absence of artillery, though it must have meant
very heavy losses had an infantry engagement developed,
could hardly have meant disaster. The real danger was of
a storm at sea, which would cut off the slender garrison for a
period of days. But against this risk no staff work could
prevail.

By now it was " Z " day. The day's programme was
mapped out in detail. Ammunition had to be buried, control
posts had to be manned ; officers in charge of the different
parties had to familiarize themselves for the last time with
the exact route of their departure, with the posts to which
they must report. The burden of work fell, however, to the
staffs of battalions and brigades. Strengths of platoons
and companies, which are usually left to the computation of

Horses picketed on the road made between Cape Helles
and Gully Ravine.

clerks in orderly rooms, were the key to the whole operation. No margin of error was permissible. The route from the front line to the beach was picketed, and, at stated points, control posts in charge of officers and signallers had to be furnished with exact numbers of the parties which would pass them at different times, each scheduled to the minute. As the parties passed, the figures were to be telephoned to the next post, and so on till the beach was reached. If the strengths were inaccurate, or the parties not up to scheduled time, the embarkation arrangements must break down, for each boat had to be loaded to capacity, and as it became available. There was no margin for men, expected at one time, arriving at another.

The computation of a battalion state is at all times one of the minor horrors of war. In a campaign where it is impossible by parading a battalion to exercise the only real check on the figures supplied, it verges on the major category. Where the state has to be exact, the balance goes over. And so, for many of the officers, this last day on the peninsula, which should have been charged with so many poignant and dramatic memories, was spent in feverishly tracing bombers, signallers, transport men or batmen, detached some months before for some special duty, but electing to appear or disappear at this eleventh hour with a quiet modesty which may have indicated a high degree of personal charm, but which accounted for a regrettable absence of that quality in Brigade Majors, Staff Captains, Colonels and Adjutants. Besides these trifling but urgent anxieties, was the disinclination to be wounded at this last moment of an historic campaign.

The afternoon of January 8th wore on, and as the bright sun faded from the winter sky to sink beneath the still placid waters of the Aegean, a silence fell upon the peninsula. Faded now were those dreams of suffering, of ambition, or of victory, which each man, however humble, or however noble, holds in the secrecy of a mind dominated by trustful humility, or ambition, or the inspiration of patriotism. Beneath the soil of that dedicated peninsula, were many who had experienced all these things ; and by these, who had experienced none, those others were to be abandoned. No longing for rest, for the joys of decent and homely comforts, for the society of friends, could quite remove the impression. The trenches were to be surrendered, and the graves of friends were to be abandoned to the enemy. Nearer home, in battles more vast, and in their material issue more important, something of what had been lost was to be regained. But what was saved, was saved by the material victory of superior force. The chance of a victory against odds, and so of an earlier and a wiser peace, had gone for ever.

Probably the judgment of the rank and file was on the whole a merciful one. Perhaps it was too merciful. But, at any rate, it was amid a silence which it needed no discipline to enforce, that at 6.15 in the gathering dusk of that fateful but uneventful day, the troops in bivouac were paraded for the last time on the peninsula, and marched off along the familiar roads worn by the feet of so many men of their own race now dead or broken in battle. With no more than a look, men passed by landmark after landmark familiar in earlier battles, till they reached those beaches, so nobly won, which it was now so important to abandon with quickness and precision. Hardly a shell came from Asia, and those that did, fell mercifully. Each party, as they arrived, were marched along one or other of the piers, packed into lighters or destroyers, so many, methodically counted, into each, and moved off to the larger transports waiting off the coast.

All this time, the front line garrison remained ; it was no use their leaving till the destroyers and lighters, having taken all the reserve troops, were ready to make their second journey. Then only, between 9 and 10 p.m., did the critical hours begin. For at this time the strength of the trench garrisons was to move off, leaving only a skeleton force capable of a resistance long enough, so it was planned, to enable the main garrison to be recalled, or to be embarked, as the situation might dictate. At 11.45 p.m., as soon as the main garrison had been embarked, the skeleton force was itself withdrawn, and the line was left open to the assault of the enemy. Even now the victory would not have been a bloodless one. As the force withdrew, special parties of Engineers and others connected mines previously laid, and closed up barricades and entanglements, before they, too, passed down to the beaches. With them passed the control posts. So, stage by stage, the procession moved on. The period of extreme hazard seemed over. The bulk of the garrison was already embarked, and no Turkish patrols could have got through the mined and barricaded trenches, in time to worry the slender rearguard on the open road between the trenches and the last line of defence above the beaches.

Here, however, the situation was more disquieting. Ever since seven o'clock the wind had been rising, and though the first and second trips were well up to time, the arrangements for the 11.30 embarkations had had to be altered at the last minute, and the prospects for the final trip were anxious. The last troops were expected between 2 and 3 a.m. By 2.30 a.m. all had arrived, but a heavy surf was dashing upon the shore, and it was only under conditions of great stress and peril that the embarkations were effected. The last of the Naval Division to embark were General Paris and his staff, who left soon after 3 a.m. The last of all were Corps and General Headquarters staff and the Naval and Military embarkation officers.

By 3.30 a.m. the inevitable step had been taken. Never again, till peace had been signed, would British troops revisit the peninsula which they had conquered and held against all assaults of the acknowledged enemy.

CHAPTER X

WHEN the Naval Division anchored in Mudros harbour on the morning of January 10th, 1916, its period of service with the Army was, temporarily, at an end, and the force came under the orders of Admiral Sir John de Robeck. It was not uncharacteristic of the Division that, after being withdrawn unexpectedly from its training under the Admiralty to serve the needs of the War Office in two great emergencies, it should now, when it had become thoroughly seasoned and experienced in land warfare, find itself under Naval command, in a situation which seemed to give no chance of its being usefully employed. If, however, the situation was Gilbertian, it was not unpleasant.

Mudros, at this time, was a scene of a vastly ironic activity. The end of the campaign had marked, here, a veritable climax of preparation. The brain behind the chaos had had a vision (so much at least was clear) of some not distant day when mere huts and tents would be too primitive to have any place in the new township which was to be set up on the shores of the harbour. The shells of huge concrete buildings bore eloquent witness to the simple grandeur of the idea. The foundations of camps, the beginnings of roads, mysterious engines and other mechanical devices lying derelict by the wayside, but still monumental in their challenge to the surrounding simplicity; a flock of turkeys in good time for Christmas, 1916, cases of wine labelled medical comforts and filled with water coloured with an unmistakable ingenuity, well-stocked canteens, beer by the barrel for sale, a clothing depot which could have supplied an army in the field, bore testimony to a really remarkable organization. But the Army was no longer in the field. Soon only the organizers and the Naval Division remained.

It was not in accordance with the plan, this sudden juxta-position of the men and the stores. Admirable, in the circum-stances, was the energy which led to the early ·disappearance of everything which could be moved ; and it was but a matter of weeks before only the concrete structures, the derelict machines and the Naval Division remained.

For a short time, it looked as if the Division and the concrete might share the same fate, fixed for all time on the deserted edge of the almost deserted waters. But the problem resolved itself with unexpected ease. On Tenedos and on Imbros, as well as on Mudros, the hand of the organizer had lain, if more lightly, and it was judged necessary to establish semi-permanent garrisons on the three islands. The duty was assigned to one brigade of the Division,* and the other (the 2nd) R.N. Brigade was lent a little later to the Salonica Army, for duty on the Gulf of Stavros.

The only strictly military duty falling to the garrisons of the islands was at Imbros and Tenedos, where detachments had to take over from the R.N.A.S. three anti-aircraft guns. The crews for these guns were found from volunteers from the Hawke and Drake Battalions. Otherwise, the routine consisted of a certain amount of police work, the examination of persons passing in and out of the small area in occupation of the garrison, the mounting of numerous guards and pickets and the search for hostile snipers whenever someone threw a cartridge into an incinerator. The greater proportion of the garrison was employed on none of these duties, and carried out company, or battalion training.

The Stavros front, impressive to the ear as the description is, was not more dangerous than the islands. After the failure of our attempt to save Serbia from the German invasion in the autumn of 1915, the allied force had retired into Greece and taken up a line, covering Salonica, with its right flank on the Gulf of Stavros. This line, some sixty miles in length, was only thinly held, and between our army and the Bulgarian frontier were interposed a number of Greek divisions. The 2nd Brigade held the right divisional sector of this line, their chief duties being to improve the defensive position on their

---

* The Hawke and Drake Battalions with the H.Q. 1st R.N. Brigade went to Imbros, one company of the Hood Battalion to Tenedos, and the balance of the 1st Brigade remained at Mudros.

front, and to prevent Greek stragglers or spies from the Bulgarian Army from getting behind our lines. In certain circumstances the position held would have been one of importance, since it guarded one of the two routes by which the Bulgarians might, if the acquiescence of the Greeks could be secured, direct an attack in strength against us. There was, however, no likelihood of such an attack, of which, in any case, the cavalry patrols many miles in front of our lines would have given us ample warning.

While the Division was thus peaceably engaged, the authorities at home had been thinking, at intervals, of its future employment. Some thought the Division should remain on garrison duty in the East, that the divisional organization should be scrapped and the force reduced to six battalions. The friends of the Division urged, on the contrary, that it should be reinforced and sent to France. The rival schools of thought must have been nicely balanced, for in April orders for the reduction of the Division to six battalions were issued by the Admiralty. The orders were, however, countermanded, and, when the rumour was circulated that the Division was going to Mitylene, it was felt that its departure in the opposite direction would not be much longer delayed.

The Division arrived in France in May, 1916, and was concentrated, according to what was now a well-established routine, in a back area (near Abbeville in this case), for the issue of stores and equipment, and for such preliminary reorganization as was necessary.

When it was finally decided to send the Division to France, the plan had been to complete it to the strength of twelve battalions, from reserves at the depot. The new battalions were to be the 2nd Hood, the 2nd Anson, the 2nd Hawke, and the 2nd Drake. The nucleus of the 2nd Hood was at once formed (from the 1st Hood) under Commander Asquith, with Lt.-Commander Kelly, D.S.C., as second in command. The other three battalions were to come out as complete units from the depot, the 2nd Anson under Lt.-Colonel Ramsden, R.N. (with Major J. H. Levey as second in command), the 2nd Hawke under Captain Hunter, R.N., and the 2nd Drake under Lt.-Colonel Britten, R.M.L.I.

Throughout June this plan held the field, but eventually it had to be abandoned, owing to the shortage of officers and men available for reinforcements for the existing battalions. It was therefore decided that the Division should be brought up to infantry strength by the addition of an army brigade (the 190th Brigade), consisting of the 1st Battalion H.A.C., the 4th Bedfords, the 7th Royal Fusiliers and the 10th Dublin Fusiliers. The promise of this Brigade marked the end of a chapter in the history of the Naval Division, which was recognized by a change of the official name of the Royal Naval, to the 63rd (R.N.) Division. Even at this date, however, the division in the field was not absorbed definitely into the army machine. The two Naval Brigades, becoming the 189th and 188th Infantry Brigades, remained (after almost hourly notifications to the contrary) unchanged in their composition, and the divisional Engineers, the Medical Unit and the divisional train were not interfered with. The result was that the retention of the Division in France still depended, to a great extent, on the goodwill of the Admiralty, who had the right to withdraw all officers and men commissioned or enlisted in the Naval or Marine forces. The advantage accruing was greater than might have been expected. It was, indeed, most unlikely that any substantial proportion of the force would in any circumstances be withdrawn for sea service. The fact remained, however, that this was always a possible result of any injudicious attempt to abolish those characteristics of organization, rank and discipline, on which the *esprit de corps* and the fighting efficiency of the Division so largely depended.

Rightly, the Naval Division was spared none of the recognized stages of acclimatization arranged for all formations arriving in France for the first time. The first essential was, of course, to fill the vacancies in the Divisional and Brigade staffs and among Battalion Commanders. Brigadier-General Mercer had been promoted and appointed Adjutant-General of the Royal Marines, his Brigade Major (Major Tupman, R.M.L.I.) had been given the command of an army battalion, and Brigadier-General Trotman, C.B.* and his staff had been transferred to the new (190th) Brigade. In their place, Brigadier-General H. E. S. Prentice, D.S.O., was appointed to the 188th and Brigadier-General L. F. Phillips, D.S.O., to the 189th Brigade. Important changes were also made at Divisional Head-

---

* Brigadier-General Trotman had been awarded the C.B. for his services on Gallipoli.

quarters. Colonel Richardson and Colonel Ollivant had both left the Division while it was at Mudros, and their places were now filled (as A.A. and Q.M.G.) by Lt.-Colonel Foster, R.M.L.I. and (as G.S.O.1, after two interim appointments) by Lt.-Colonel Aspinall, C.M.G., D.S.O., who had served on Sir Ian Hamilton's staff at Gallipoli, and who was to be a good friend to the Division for many months. Other changes were necessary to fill the places of Fleet-Surgeon Gaskell, R.N., A.D.M.S., who had taken up an appointment under the Admiralty; Lt.-Colonel Carey, C.M.G., late C.R.E. of the Division, who had become C.R.E. of a corps in France, and Lt.-Colonel Chaytor, who had commanded the divisional train. Their places were taken by Fleet-Surgeon Finch, R.N., Major Harrison, R.M., and Lt.-Colonel Liddell, A.S.C.

Of the Battalion Commanders, Captain King, D.S.O., R.N.V.R. (Drake Battalion) and Major Bridges, R.M.L.I. (Anson Battalion) had left the Division for duty under the Admiralty, and the command of the Howe Battalion was also vacant. Lt.-Colonel Tetley, R.M.L.I., and Lt.-Colonel Saunders, R.M.L.I., were given command of the Drake and Anson respectively, and Major French, R.M.L.I., was temporarily appointed to the Howe.

While these changes were taking place, the battalions and divisional troops (who had left such stores and transport, as were theirs, in Egypt or in Mudros) were completely re-equipped, or, more accurately, completely equipped for the first time. The infantry battalions had never before had horses for their mounted officers (many of whom, incidentally, had very naval notions of horsemanship), and had seen their first line transport only for a few days prior to leaving Blandford in 1915. The transport available on the peninsula had been limited to three limbered wagons and a field kitchen or two per battalion, and the once trained personnel for the ordinary complement had long since become casualties. Now, not only had the battalions to organize their transport but to learn how to use it. This applied with even greater force to other units. The Naval Division had never moved, as a division, except by train or transport till it reached France, and the habit of mobility had now to be hastily acquired.

Equally important were the modifications of organization imposed by the new tactics. The machine gun had, in France

2nd R.N. Field Ambulance at Stavros, March, 1916.

in 1916, been elevated to the dignity of a Brigade gun, and the Lewis gun had taken its place as the battalion weapon. At the same time trench mortars had become standardized, and trench mortar batteries were as recognized a part of the establishment of a Division as were infantry battalions. Yet the Lewis gun and the Stokes mortar were, to the Naval Division, completely new weapons.

The Brigade machine-gun (Vickers) companies were formed at once by withdrawing from the battalions the existing machine-gun sections. The 188th Brigade Company was commanded by Captain MacGeorge, M.G.C., the 189th Brigade Company by Lt.-Commander H. E. Funnell, R.N.V.R., and the 190th Brigade Company by Captain Bastian, R.M. The Brigade trench mortar batteries were formed from volunteers from the different battalions, the 188th under Lieutenant Alan Campbell, R.N.V.R., and the 189th under Lieutenant O. J. Wainwright, R.N.V.R. The infantry battalions were in due course brought up to strength again, by drafts of officers and men from Blandford.

The reorganization progressed by somewhat easy stages, and, in particular, owing to the change of plans regarding the composition of the third brigade, the Division was short of one brigade till the middle of July. As early as the middle of June, however, it had moved from the Army concentration area to the IVth Corps area, to undergo the next stage in the established routine. Here, in pleasant villages north-west of Arras, due west of the IVth Corps line, which ran from Lens to the Vimy Ridge, the Division had a period of battalion and brigade training, during which platoons, companies, battalions, and brigades were in turn attached to the 47th Division in the Angres and Souchez sub-sectors, for preliminary tours of duty in the trenches. This was the practical part of the training programme, and, if the Division had not much to learn about the art of trench construction or trench discipline, it had everything to learn about conditions wholly novel and demanding a radical alteration of the accustomed dispositions. The theoretic training was equally thorough. As soon as the Division passed into the Corps area, vacancies for courses of instruction, especially in the new arms, poured in on the battalions. The system of schools and courses became at later stages a mixed blessing, but at this stage it was essential.

Finally, the Division approached the accepted standard of proficiency, and went forward to its place in the fighting line on the 17th July. On this date General Paris* took over command of the Angres–Souchez sector, from the 47th Division. The 190th Brigade was not yet available, and the sector taken over was thus only a two-brigade front, but the Division was, at long last, in sight of its complete establishment. On July 29th, the 63rd Divisional Artillery,† to which the Naval Division was to be so substantially indebted throughout the rest of the campaign, came into the line. The story was completed on August 30th, when General Trotman's 190th Brigade relieved a brigade of the 40th Division in the Calonne sub-sector, on the left of the Angres sub-sector, held by the 188th Brigade.

The Divisional sector lay between Lens and the Vimy Ridge, through the ruins of two mining villages, Calonne and Angres, and thence southward across the Souchez river. The front line, which ran north and south, had originally been further west; for in the rush to the sea the enemy had carried their line across the Arras–Bethune road (east of which our line now ran) right to the heights of Lorette, a mile or so west of Souchez village. These heights had been won back by the French, in a famous battle in the summer of 1915. Since then, our position on the low ground of the Souchez valley, and across the slag heaps which marked the outskirts of Lens, had never been, nor was likely to be, seriously challenged. It was not naturally strong, but that part of the sector which ran through the mining country lent itself readily to infantry defence, and the Souchez valley, through which the enemy might otherwise have attacked, was dominated by the immensely strong position of Lorette. How the French had captured that position in 1915 by direct assault, none but those who made the attack could say. It was certain, however, that with the enormous increase in the weight of artillery available and with the im-

---

* General Paris had received the K.C.B. for his services in Gallipoli. Among others of the Divisional staff and the Divisional troops who had been decorated at the same time were Lt.-Colonel Richardson, Fleet-Surgeon Gaskell, Fleet-Surgeon Finch and Lt.-Colonel Carey, who received the C.M.G., and Major H. D. Lough, R.M.L.I. (D.A.A. & Q.M.G.), Fleet-Surgeon Fleming, R.N. and Major Teale, R.M., who received the D.S.O.

† The artillery consisted of the 315th (Lieut.-Col. Higginbottom), 317th (Lieut.-Col. S. Gosling) and 223rd (Lieut.-Col. Gemmell) Field Artillery Brigades. Brigadier-General A. H. De Rougemont was appointed C.R.A. of the Division.

provement of defensive tactics the Germans would never retake it.

The trenches taken over from the 47th Division were an eloquent testimony to the reliance now placed on the new methods of defence. The Naval Battalions who had been attached to that Division in their same trenches for instruction had indeed been inclined to scoff at their instructors ; it was certain that such trenches could never have been held in Gallipoli. They came to learn, however, that, though the trenches were certainly capable (like most others in France) of very substantial improvement, their first criticism had been very wide of the mark.

Positional warfare in France was something wholly different from that to which the Division had been hitherto accustomed. The rifle and the bomb were as little used in the day-to-day routine of the trenches as the bayonet. The infantry were neither the first nor the last line of defence, for, by themselves and unaided, they had ceased to be capable (in strict theory) of defending anything. The change had begun with the development of the artillery of the opposing armies, which had been a feature of the war at the beginning of 1915. Before that, in Flanders, as later in Gallipoli, the front line trench had been the main line of resistance, held by an unbroken line of rifles and bayonets. Close at hand were support and reserve lines, from which reinforcements could be sent to the front line—reinforcements of more rifles and bayonets. Under this system of defence, the infantry were beyond all question the most important and therefore the most independent arm. The system, however, did not anticipate, or allow for, such a weight of hostile artillery as would render the massing of infantry in line, on a clearly defined position of no great depth, a futile manœuvre. Yet so it became. Casualties in the strongly-held front line became more and more numerous ; the old-fashioned support and reserve lines suffered equally badly, so close were they to the front line. The system had to be radically altered.

Under the new system of defence in depth, the front line and the support line became in effect only a line of sentry groups and a line of pickets. In 1916, the sentry groups and pickets were still provided with lateral communication by means of a connected trench, but in 1917 this was the exception rather than the rule, and a line of posts became the normal first line of defence. Under either system, the front line was held mainly for purposes of observation, and, when there was a continuous trench, the telephone to Battalion Headquarters and to the Battalions on the right and left was its most important feature. The support line was the line on which a delaying action would be fought or any merely local attack held up. The line of resistance was the third line,* held by perhaps two companies of infantry (for whom special protection in deep dug-outs had to be provided), on a battalion front of five or six hundred yards, and a number of machine guns and trench mortars in fortified emplacements. These, though they never developed, as they did in the German lines, into miniature fortresses, were, nevertheless, more important for purposes of defence than the infantry themselves.

But if the third line was the line of resistance, the main defence for it consisted, not even in the machine guns and trench mortars, still less in the rifles and bayonets of the garrison ; but, now and henceforward, in the protective artillery barrage. Only with those few who might come alive through this were the infantry garrison expected or, indeed, sufficiently numerous, to deal.

These developments alone were sufficient to change very greatly the duties and responsibilities of the infantry. It was not, however, only in defence that the man had become in many ways less important than the machine, but also in the numerous diversions of positional warfare. Raids remained the prerogatives of the infantry, but these were the exception, not the rule. Intensive bombardments of back areas by the artillery, of the front line trenches by " Stokes " mortars, night firing off the map by Vickers guns, mining operations by the tunnelling companies and discharges of gas by the " Special " companies of Engineers were the ordinary forms of that paradoxical product of trench life, the stationary offensive.

These great modifications in the responsibilities of the infantry soldier brought nothing but a heavy increase in his daily burden of work. The very depth of the new defences

---

* This is a generalized statement, subject, of course, to many exceptions. The principles remained, however, substantially unchanged till 1918, when after the March disaster a slightly different system, based on the substitution of " zones " for " lines of resistance," came into use. The function of the different arms remained, however, the same.

meant that there were literally miles of communication and fire trenches to be kept in repair by the infantry. Even the ordinary ration and water parties made a serious call on their energies. Every day the need for emplacements of a more elaborate pattern and deep dug-outs more proof against the enemy's bombardments increased. These had to be dug by the infantry under the supervision of the engineers. The enthusiasm of the tunnelling companies provoked continuous demands for assistance from the infantry in the less skilled but equally arduous task of removing hundreds of filled sand-bags. Trench mortar ammunition and gas cylinders had to be man-handled by the infantry from dumps in the rear of the defensive system to positions near, or in, the front line. Signal wires had to be buried by infantry fatigue parties. All the time, specialist units like trench mortar batteries and machine-gun companies had to be kept up to strength. The infantry was, indeed, the only non-specialist arm (though from time to time enthusiastic staff officers rediscovered the rifle and bayonet), and it might have seemed that its chief function in stationary warfare was to supply the needs of other more important arms. Yet those other arms were, in reality, important only in co-operation with the infantry as a fighting unit. It was this dual rôle of the infantryman which was the difficulty.

Although few battalion commanders ever had under their command, except on the actual eve of battle, more than sixty per cent. of their men, the infantry still had to guard the front. There was no substitute for their physical presence, for the officers who would patrol in no man's land, for the company signallers, who must give the first warning of any attack; for the sentry who alone could prevent patrols from entering the line, for the battalion commander who had to take charge of the situation in any emergency, to decide which line to hold and which to give up, when and where to counter-attack and what directions to give to the artillery, and to all the new and proud varieties of specialists who swarmed round his line. The infantryman was the servant but still, in an anomalous sort of way, the master of all.

It was just here that there was something wrong. It was not one of those characteristic compromises, of which English constitutional historians have so much to say, which cannot be defended in theory but which work admirably in practice.

It worked, because it had to work, but it did not, and could not, work well. To this plain fact, and not to any intellectual or moral deficiencies, was due the much exaggerated but still, to some extent, real unpopularity of "the Staff" in France in 1916.

The life of the Division in the new sector was almost uniformly without incidents of individual importance. The Brigade and Divisional diaries chronicle, indeed, only one which can be characterized as an active operation—a highly successful raid by the Anson Battalion, on September 10th, carried out to secure an identification, badly needed to check enemy movements to and from the main battlefield of the Somme. The raid was carried out by Lieutenant F. C. Mundy, Sub-Lieut. W. B. Moir and twelve other ranks of the battalion at 5 a.m. on an enemy sap opposite the northernmost Angres sub-sector, and the party captured a prisoner belonging to the 103rd Saxon Regiment, 23rd Saxon Reserve Division, 12th Reserve Corps. In the course of the raid Lieutenant Mundy was seriously, and Lieutenant Moir and one man slightly, wounded. But the desired information had been gained.

This incident, apart from the life of the trenches, or in support in Bully Grenay, in Noulette Wood, or on Lorette spur, became a matter of routine,* varied only by occasional activities on the part of the specialists, who would discharge gas, or conduct a ten minutes' intensive bombardment, or blow up a crater, with no very great interest in the result, but just to keep their hand in and annoy the enemy. Not infrequently, the annoyance was equally felt by the infantry, but for them, as no doubt for the enemy, it was all in the day's work, and they endured what they affected not to understand.

Meanwhile, the orgy of instruction continued with results now distinctly less beneficial. Professor Saintsbury has said somewhere that the limit to the progress of education will be found not in any lack of people able to learn but in a lack of those able to teach. In this last respect, as doubtless in others, the Army have, or at least had, the advantage of the civil population; because their difficulty was to keep fully occupied the legion of officers and men who were anxious and available

---

* Yet there were the inevitable losses. Among those killed in the summer of 1916 were Sub-Lieut. S. P. Hancock, R.N.V.R., of the Hawke, 2nd Lieut. J. W. Somerville, of the 2nd Marines, and 2nd Lieut. W. C. A. Elliot, of the 1st Marines.

to teach. To meet the difficulty, the more astute, or less conscientious, battalion commanders kept a strictly limited list of officers, N.C.O.'s and men, whom they regarded as available in any circumstances for instruction in any subject. Even so, the untimely manner in which one course would begin before another had ended made it necessary to go outside this list for at least half the vacancies that were allotted.

The other characteristic feature of the early days in France was equally peculiar to the period. The vast organization behind the lines was as yet growing, but it was growing at this period not at the expense of men of military age in non-essential employments at home, but at the expense of Divisions not immediately needed for active fighting. Demands for Town Majors, sanitary squads, staffs for divisional laundries, salvage experts, bath attendants, batmen by the score, men for making roads, officers who could speak Chinese, N.C.O.'s with experience of acetylene welding, subalterns with a taste for licking boots, came in by every dispatch rider, or, as often as not, in the form of a peremptory signal. The first few demands were often easily met, but the time came when every demand which had to be met was met with a definite loss of efficiency. Protests were unavailing. The war had to go on, so thought the cynical infantryman, even if the front-line trenches were under-garrisoned. The strange thing is that the infantryman was about right. The divisional laundry in a four-years' war was, in fact, almost as important as the sentry in the front line. The ironic point seemed, however, at the time remarkably keen.

How far the process of disintegration had gone, few, even in the battalions themselves, realized, till the Division suddenly received orders, late on the night of September 16th, to hand over to the 37th Division (the support and reserve battalions on the morning immediately following) and to proceed once more to the IVth Corps training area. The next hours were a vivid, and not a particularly pleasant, foretaste of the Resurrection. From all quarters and at all stages of the march to the back areas, battalions were met by officers and N.C.O.'s and men, who had been detached for one duty or another, some on the very day the units had arrived in France, the majority immediately on entry into the IVth Corps area. Some of the officers who rejoined had hardly been with their battalions at all, having gone from one course of instruction to another ever since they arrived in France. The same was true of some of the N.C.O.'s. The results were sometimes humorous, especially when some not over-competent officer or man, having been sent to a course to be cursed into efficiency, returned full of importance as a " qualified " instructor to the unit which had selected him, not without reason, as pre-eminently in need of instruction.

Battalion commanders soon learnt, moreover, that discipline had not improved in the process of acquiring technical knowledge. The work of training had to be begun again, on the very eve of the time of testing. Never had officers greater cause to be thankful that they belonged to a composite and individual formation, whose *esprit de corps* could be trusted to make their task lighter and its fruits more satisfying than could under other circumstances have been expected.

The last days of September were spent once more in the peaceful and friendly villages which lie between Bailleul and Arras. Dièval, La Comté, Hersin, Ourton, held the 188th Brigade, and Marquay, Orlencourt, Bailleul itself, held the 190th, while the 189th went to Fresnicourt, Monchy Breton, Hermin, Magnicourt and Frévillers. The Artillery Headquarters were at La Vielfort, and the Brigades were at Bours (315th Brigade), Calonne Ricquart (317th Brigade) and Chamblain Chatelain (223rd Brigade). The Train Headquarters were at Bruay, with companies at Divion, Hermin and Ourton; the Engineers' Headquarters were at Bajus. Division Headquarters, Echelon B, were at Ourton, and General Paris and his staff at a château near by. The Field Ambulances were quartered at Fresnicourt, Divion and Bruay.

This was the first time in its history that the Division had moved as a complete unit approximately at full strength. It had entered the IVth Corps area still in process of growth ; it left it, as it was to remain for the rest of the war, a division complete in every detail of its establishment. As such, it comprised some forty different units ; twelve only of them were first-line infantry battalions. The other fighting troops comprised nine batteries of artillery, three machine-gun companies, and the different light, medium and heavy trench mortar batteries. The principal accessory formations were, as before, the Signal Company, the three field companies of Engineers, the four companies of the Divisional Train and the three Field Ambulances. In addition, there were the Divisional Ammunition Column, the Ordnance Section, the Sanitary Section, the Mobile Veterinary Section and the Pioneer Battalion (the 14th battalion of the Worcestershire Regiment, who did fine work for the Division from now till the end of the war).

Of these units, the Train, the Signal Company, the Field Ambulances knew no rest, whether the Division was in, or out of the line. If they had less danger (which in the case of the Signallers, at least, was by no means always so), and more comfortable quarters (which was usual), they had unceasing work. The Artillery and the Trench Mortars had, on the contrary, like the Infantry, their periods of peace and quiet. But when they were in the line (and they usually came into the line before, and left it after the Infantry), their lot was soon to be nearly as dangerous,* if less physically exhausting. None of the specialist arms, however, were called on (except in an unprecedented emergency) to supply working parties for other units. This duty fell always to the infantrymen, and as a matter of course.

The Engineers had a wider and more varied set of conditions to face than any other unit in the Division. They would be one night in front of our line, and working the next on an improvement to the lighting at Divisional Headquarters. In France they were perhaps employed rather more behind the line than they had been in Gallipoli, when they were almost constantly in the trenches; but an Engineer officer was always attached to each Brigade sector, and was responsible generally for the construction and repair of all the more important works, though the infantry usually had to supply the labour. Behind the front line, the principal task of the Engineers was the maintenance of communications, which involved the digging, the revetting and the drainage of trenches, the repair of roads, and, in certain sectors, the maintenance or construction of light railways.

When we look back on the Naval Division, resting for a few days in these pleasant Artois villages, we must remember, not only the infantry battalions of whose doings we speak so often, but those other units, with their individual tasks in

---

* Later, particularly at Passchendaele, the lot of the Artillery was fully as dangerous as that of any other fighting troops.

hand, or accomplished.   Above all, we must remember that to the staffs of the division and the brigades, to the divisional train, to the medical personnel and the signallers, these moves from village to village, which meant nothing but a wholesome march and change of scene to the infantry, meant an actual increase of work.

The three weeks' rest now enjoyed was admittedly in preparation for an offensive.   At first it had been intended that the Naval Division should attack some positions on the Vimy Ridge which had been lost in May.   This would have been a minor operation, involving at most two brigades; but the idea was soon given up.   Yet another Division was needed in the south, and it was soon common knowledge that the Naval Division were going to the Somme.   Meanwhile, with the chances of the future so uncertain, the present took on a new value.

It is a simple thing to place on record this note of a few pleasant days, spent by the Naval Division on its way from Souchez to the Somme; it is harder, perhaps, to understand. Yet this much will be clear.   The Naval Division was not an amalgamation of innumerable units, each with its own memories and traditions.   It was one unit, and to get back to older memories and older associations the officers and men in it had to look back to the days of peace.   It was not only themselves—that was the least thing that mattered— but their little world which was moving slowly to the edge of the void.   Battalion concerts, company concerts, card parties, formal and informal gatherings of every kind, took on an atmosphere of hail and farewell.

Much had been accomplished together, many men and cities had become part of the common stock of experience. The fruits of that experience, the reality and the pride of those accomplishments, were now to be put to the test.

The Church, Bully-Grenay, August, 1916.

CHAPTER XI

THE battle of the Somme had opened, on July 1st, with an attack by the Fourth Army, and one corps of the Third Army, on the twenty-eight-mile front from Gommecourt to Fay, the attack being prolonged south of Fay by the French. The first day's fighting had carried us into, and in places even beyond, the enemy's front line system from Albert south across the Somme; but from Albert northward across the Ancre, at Hamel, to Gommecourt, we had suffered defeat.

With a view to keeping available sufficient reserves to enable future attacks to be continuous it had been at once decided to withdraw the left flank of the Fourth Army to the Albert–Bapaume road, to put in Sir Hubert Gough's Fifth Army between the Fourth and Third Armies, and to confine our attention, for the time, at any rate, to exploiting the success which we had won south of the Ancre on either bank of the Somme.

Our progress subsequent to this decision had been considerable but very slow. By July 17th we had secured not only the whole of the enemy's first line system from Ovillers (two miles south of the Ancre) to the British right, but had obtained a substantial lodgment in the enemy's second line system. It was not, however, till September 10th, that the whole of the enemy second line positions from Pozières to La Maisonnette were in our hands, and not till September 25th that the third line positions of Courcelette, Martinpuich, Highwood, Flers, and Delville Wood were wholly ours. Even then, Les Bœufs, Morval and Combles on the right flank of the attack, and Thiepval on the left, held out against us, and were not finally captured till September 30th.

This measure of success had been sufficient to achieve the

most immediate object for which the battle had been fought. This was the relief of the enemy pressure on Verdun. There were, however, other objects of equal importance which we had not attained.

If the reinforcements of men and munitions which would reach us before 1917 were to enable us to force a decision in that year, the enemy must first be worn down by continuous pressure, maintained if possible well into the winter of 1916– 1917. To break off the battle of the Somme at the point reached at the end of September would, on this view, be fatal. There was, also, the important consideration that, if the battle died down, the enemy would certainly transfer substantial forces to the East, where the Allied position, never secure, was now actually precarious.

If, however, it was clearly a matter of very great importance to continue our attacks, the situation produced by the previous three months' fighting made it a matter of extreme difficulty to do so.

There was nothing in our gains which reacted at all appreciably on the enemy's position on either flank. Instead, the boot was on the other leg. The enemy still held to his old front line north of the Ancre, and to the south of the battle front, and so long as he did so, he imposed a very definite limit on the extent to which we could push forward the salient which our success on the Somme itself created in our line. This limit had been wellnigh reached by the beginning of October, 1916. There had been just a chance at the end of September that we should be able to maintain our pressure on the existing front of attack despite these difficulties, but this depended on the weather allowing us to attack before the enemy resistance in his new, improvised defence north and south of the Somme had been consolidated The weather, however, broke; and we found ourselves at the end of the first week in October faced, virtually, with only two alternatives. Either we must widen the base of our salient by attacking and carrying the enemy positions which still stood firm on the flanks of our advance, or we must let the battle die down, and risk the transfer of German troops to the East or a renewal of the attack on Verdun.

The general situation forbade the easier and less expensive alternative. In the circumstances, the almost desperate decision was taken to reopen the battle north, and immediately south, of the Ancre, against Serre, Beaumont Hamel, Beaucourt and St. Pierre Divion, four pivots of the strong first line defensive system which (with Thiepval, now in our hands) had resisted our attacks on July 1st. Attacking these positions, with all the advantages of surprise, in perfect weather, with fresh troops, we had then suffered a costly defeat. Since then, the defences had been greatly strengthened and our resources had been depleted ; the weather conditions, moreover, threatened to be wholly unfavourable. Yet it was judged, and rightly, that the renewal of the attack was essential if the fruits of our earlier victories were to be fully gathered.

The attack was to be carried out by the Vth and IInd Corps of the Fifth Army, the Vth Corps on the front north of the Ancre, and the IInd Corps on the less important front south of that river.

To the Vth Corps, the Naval Division had been assigned when it entered the Fifth Army area on October 4th, and it had at once to prepare for the impending attack.

On October 7th, the 190th Brigade were ordered to take over a sector of the line, starting from Serre and reaching southward almost to Beaumont Hamel, with the 63rd Divisional Artillery in support ; officers of the other brigades made reconnaissances of the enemy position opposite. No definite orders for the operation had been issued, but it was understood that the Naval Division would attack Serre or Beaumont Hamel.

While the 190th Brigade was still in the line, and the two naval brigades were in billets at Varennes and Forceville, the Division was shocked to learn, on the afternoon of October 14th, that General Paris had been dangerously wounded on a visit to the 190th Brigade trenches and that Major Sketchley, G.S.O.2 of the Division for so many months, had been killed.

General Paris had been with the Naval Division since the day when it was first concentrated in Antwerp. He had commanded them in their most unfortunate as well as in their most successful adventures, and he had never failed them. But he was something more, in the eyes of the Division, than a respected commander : he was an institution. He was the last relic of the days when the Division had fought under orders from the Admiralty : he was the last bulwark between the

Division and the Army.   And he was a very effective one.
He was recognized by those in authority as an officer of pre-
eminent caution and prudence.   So long as he remained, there
would be no attempt to interfere with the internal organization,
which meant so largely the fighting efficiency of the Division.
It was not, perhaps, realized at the time, how much the Division
owed to General Paris in this respect, though it did not take
them long to learn it.   If he had never erred on the side of
over-enthusiastic praises, he had shown his unswerving confidence in the capacity of the Division to do credit to itself as a
fighting force, by putting no limit on promotion from within
the Division, and by leaving to his subordinate commanders a
reasonably free hand in the discharge of their responsibilities.
The result had been that it had gathered strength from one
reorganization to another, and yet had always preserved its
identity.   To this achievement General Paris had contributed
in no small degree, and when he left the Division which he
had commanded so long and with such fidelity, the atmosphere of confidence in the future, which had grown up in the
peaceful Souchez days, was suddenly shattered.

The four weeks which were to pass before the much discussed attack actually took place were, partly for this reason,
partly because of the general disorganization and lack of
resources behind the battle front, and partly as the result of
execrable weather, the most wearing which the Division had
ever experienced.   Refreshed by a few golden days of sunshine
and peace in the pleasant villages of the IVth Corps area (days
which seemed now, amid the rain, the mud, the noise and the
bustle of the Somme, to have been spent in some distant fairy-
land), the Division had come south almost looking forward
to the expected battle.   Not even the unutterable melancholy
of the ruined villages, the shell-swept mud of the marshes,
the miserable canvas bivouacs stretched forlornly over puddles
of slime which served for billets for many units, had at first
damped the ardour with which officers and men had surveyed,
from our front, the expected objectives, had made the first
tentative plans and imagined the ultimate success.   But
these plans and these dreams were soon interrupted.   The
change in the accustomed routine, in the manner of dress, in
the mounting of guards, in the discipline of sentries, which
followed on General Paris's departure, engaged much of the

attention of subalterns and gave Colonels and Brigadiers not a moment's peace. A little later, ill-concealed rumours of a growing dissatisfaction on the part of the new Divisional Commander (which led, in turn, to even wilder rumours of wholesale supersessions, ending in transfer to the Army) distracted the fighting spirit of the Division still further from the matter in hand. When, shortly after the change of command, the Divisional sector was changed to that immediately north of the Ancre, and the once novel but already tedious process of studying hypothetical objectives had to be repeated, the battle once so confidently anticipated had become something only to be reached after days of anxiety and exertion to which no immediate end could be foreseen.

It was not for lack of plans or orders that this impression gained ground. Plans for attacks, by any number of Corps on a variety of objectives, poured in on the Division, but delays behind the lines, continuous rain, and not a few expressed doubts as to the efficiency of the troops intended for the attack, gave rise to a ceaseless correspondence between Divisions and Corps, between Corps and Army Headquarters, between Sir Hubert Gough and General Headquarters; and these led to endless variations and postponements throughout October and the first days of November.

Meanwhile, the 188th and 189th Brigades remained almost continuously in the trenches, suffering all the minor but unpalatable ills of trench warfare in winter, and endeavouring at the same time to be ready at any moment for the day of battle. The Hamel sector in the distant days of peace-time war must have been at once unpleasant and unsafe. The trenches had been planned by a short-sighted fool and destroyed by a watchful enemy. There were virtually no dug-outs; the communication trenches, which ran across a conspicuous ridge, were under constant and aimed fire; in the firing and support lines men could only stand and freeze in the mud; there was no room to walk or to lie down, and digging, in the face of the enemy, was nearly impossible. When battalions were out of the line their lot was no better a preparation for the attack, for they would go back no further than Mesnil or Engelbelmer, from where they would go up nightly to the trenches, engaged in the most exhausting working parties. To get round a battalion front at this time was a three

hours' walk, with mud often above the knees. Yet in these
trenches half the battalions detailed for the intended assault
had to live, while the other half had to carry up them and
across them stores and ammunition for the innumerable dumps
which would feed the advancing line of battle. The constant
issue and re-issue of battle equipment and stores added to the
confusion. These stores had to be counted in and counted
out, carried up and carried down, till men would have volunteered, almost, to go out unarmed, if they could be spared the
perpetual juggling with bombs and sandbags, and flares,
and wire-cutters and compasses, which seemed the only available alternative.

The last, but not the least, of the hardships of these days
was the digging of assembly trenches on the slopes leading
down to the valley of the Ancre. Here the front-line trench
went back sharply, and General Shute decided that, if the
battalion in this flank were not to lose direction, they must be
formed up in alignment with the rest of the Division. Therefore, trenches must be dug. The decision was wise, but it
involved a risk, for it added appreciably to the burden and
confusion of these days before the battle, and the burden was
nearly as great as many could bear.

When the final orders came, on November 10th, the limit
of endurance had indeed been reached. Battalions had fallen
from an average strength of nearly seven hundred to the
average of barely five hundred, an exceptionally high rate of
wastage even for the Somme, and the majority of those who
remained were tired men. But they were determined. The
excellent relations of officers and men, which had been
strengthened by recent hardships uncompromisingly shared,
and the *esprit de corps* of a Division which was determined to
vindicate its reputation, just turned the scale, and justified
the confidence which, after so many debates, had eventually
been extended to it.

The plan, as finally adopted, was for an attack on Serre,
Beaumont Hamel, Beaucourt and St. Pierre Divion by the
2nd Division of the XIIIth Corps, the 3rd, 51st and Naval
Divisions of the Vth Corps and the 31st Division of the IInd
Corps. The Naval Division's sector (1,200 yards in width)
was immediately north of the Ancre, at right angles to the
river valley, which ran here almost due east to Beaucourt, while

our trenches and those of the enemy ran roughly north and south.

The Division's objective was Beaucourt and the intervening positions opposite to their front.

At a distance of from 180 to 250 yards from our assembly trenches, on higher ground, was the German front line system, consisting as usual of three lines of trenches. The last of these trenches formed the " first " objective, and was known, for that purpose, as the *Dotted Green Line*. Behind the front line system, and separated from it by a valley, through which ran the road known as " Station Road," was a second ridge, running from Beaumont Hamel to Beaucourt Station. On this ridge was a strongly fortified position, called the *Green Line*. This was the second defined objective. The country immediately behind this line was featureless, except the right front of the Divisional sector, where it slopes up to the hill immediately in front of Beaucourt, which commanded the enemy's communications with his forward systems on this part of the front. On the western face of this hill was a trench, which continued parallel to the front across the more level ground on the left. This trench was known as the *Yellow Line*, and formed the Division's third objective. The final objective, known as the *Red Line*, was a roughly-defined position to be taken up beyond Beaucourt, the capture of which would be, for the Naval Division, the real proof of success.

The first and third of these objectives were to be attacked by the 1st Royal Marines, the Howe, the Hawke and the Hood Battalions, each advancing in four waves. The second and fourth objectives were to be attacked by the 2nd Royal Marines, the Anson, the Nelson and the Drake Battalions. The plan, in detail, was that the first four battalions would rest on the first objective (that is, in the enemy's front-line trenches), and reorganize, while the other four battalions passed through, and captured the Station Road valley and the *Green Line*. They, in their turn, would rest and reorganize, while the first four battalions passed through to the *Yellow Line*. The final assault on Beaucourt was then, after another pause, to be carried out by the battalions, who had reorganized on the *Green Line*. With each battalion, was to go a sub-section of the Brigade Machine-Gun Company, and trench mortars were to follow as soon as possible.

The key to the operation was the great tactical discovery of the Somme, the " creeping barrage." Against the enemy's scientific underground works, the old intensive bombardment had proved useless. The substitute was a barrage which moved with the infantry, and which, if closely followed—the whole success of the method depended on this—allowed the infantry to get into the trenches and block the exits from the dug-outs, before the enemy could come up and bring his machine guns into action. A feature of the scheme was, that when there were two or more trenches forming part of the same system, and all interconnected by underground communications, each was assaulted by a separate " wave," which remained in the trench allotted to it till it was finally cleared. This ensured that the enemy would not come up behind our attacking troops as the battle progressed.

The complicated task assigned to the Division, and the novelty of the method of attack, added to the already grievous burdens of preparation. The smoke and noise of the barrage would make the issue of orders or the control of movements during the advance impossible, except, perhaps, on occasion, by isolated platoon commanders. It was thus essential that not only every officer but every man should know before-hand his different objectives, the time-table of the barrage, the halts in the different lines, and, above all, the direction of his advance. In addition, the whole success of the operation depended on keeping up with the barrage, and attacking the dug-outs immediately the lines were reached. This meant that every man had to be told off to particular tasks, and armed with particular weapons. The organization and re-organization of the different " waves " of each battalion, the distribution of maps and time-tables, and the questioning and cross-questioning of N.C.O.'s and men, to ensure that each knew his part at every step of the attack, which extended, even on the official timing over more than four hours, occupied every minute of the hours immediately preceding the night of the 12th–13th.

The night was reserved for the most important of all essential preparations, the concentration of the attacking troops.

The battalions holding the sector on the morning of the 12th were the Howe Battalion of the 188th Brigade (Com-

mander W. G. Ramsay Fairfax, R.N.) on the left, and the
Hawke Battalion of the 189th Brigade (Lt.-Colonel Leslie
Wilson, C.M.G., D.S.O.)* on the right. On the left, the 1st
R.M. Battalion (Lt.-Colonel Cartwright, R.M.L.I.) had to come
in between the Howe and the 51st Division, and on the right
the Hood Battalion (Lt.-Colonel Freyberg, D.S.O.), with one
company of H.A.C. attached, had to fill the gap between the
Hawke right and the Ancre. Nominally, these four battalions
were to occupy the front-line trench on the left, and the new
assembly trenches on the right; but, in fact, they had for the
most part to lie in the open, so narrow and inadequate was the
available cover. Just behind, also in the open, the 2nd R.M.,
Anson, Nelson and Drake Battalions had to be assembled.
Further back, in the support line, was the station for the 10th
Dublin Fusiliers, the 7th Royal Fusiliers, the 4th Bedfords,
and the 1st H.A.C. (less one company).

To move all these different units by night to assembly
positions in the open called for efficient organization and for
first-class discipline. The slightest hitch in the arrangements
must have spelt confusion, and anything like a breakdown
meant an incalculable disaster. If any sound reached the
enemy, or if any man lost his way and got into the enemy lines,
few of the seven thousand men, lying out within rifle range of
the enemy, could have escaped, and the Battle of the Somme
would have had a different issue which might have left its
mark on history. No one can look back on the anxiety of
that night without emotion. It was not only the culmination
of weeks of agonizing preparation; it was a gambler's throw,
which would give or withhold the chance of putting to the
proof the capacity of the Division to keep that place in the
fighting line which it had won at such a price.

But Fate was benignant. There was no sign amid the
darkness of any watchfulness on the part of the enemy. Men
passed quickly and with confidence to their appointed places,
and the dawn was awaited in silence.

Then, at 5.45 a.m., the full strength of our artillery opened
on the narrow divisional front, and the first wave of our attack
moved out into the gloom. At their pre-arranged intervals
the rest followed.

Within seven minutes the whole of the two attacking

* Colonel Wilson had received the C.M.G. for his services in Gallipoli.

brigades had passed out of sight of our line, where were left only the Headquarters of the Nelson, Hawke, Howe, Anson and 1st and 2nd Marine Battalions (the Headquarters of the Drake and Hood had turned a blind eye to the instruction that Battalion Headquarters should not go forward till their battalions had carried their first objective).

It was abnormally dark, and there was a thick mist. The smoke and noise of our own barrage and the rattle of the overhead fire of our supporting machine guns was such that it was impossible to say whether the enemy retaliation was severe, or even what form it was taking. Within a minute of the beginning of the attack, the enemy artillery undoubtedly opened, but, except on the right of our line, where something in the nature of a barrage fell on no man's land and on our support line, the losses from shell fire cannot have been heavy.

For a brief half hour, the attack seemed to have succeeded with miraculous ease, for during all this time, when our men should have been capturing the German trenches which made up the first and second objectives, the numbers of wounded returning were negligible, of unwounded there were none, and the available reports mentioned our troops as in the 3rd, 4th and 5th German lines.

These reports were true in detail, but the absence of any authoritative messages from officers in command of the attacking waves of the Hawke, Nelson, Howe, Anson and 1st and 2nd Marine Battalions, markedly contrasting with the continuous reports received from the Hood Battalion, told a different tale.

On the right of the line the Hood Battalion, perhaps because they kept closer to the barrage, reached the enemy front line, and passed it without devastating loss, though it is significant, in the light of what happened elsewhere, that having reached the line in safety, all four officers commanding the first wave, Sub-Lieutenants Hart, Hall, Chapman and Cresswell,* were hit in the front trench itself ; here, also, the adjutant of the Hood Battalion, Lieutenant C. A. Edmondson, and Sub-Lieut. Gealer (Signal Officer) were killed by a sniper in the enemy third line.

The battalion was, however, able to proceed systematically

---

* To these four officers, who kept the line well up to the barrage, the initial success of the Hood Battalion was largely due.

with the reduction of each of the first three lines, and the destruction of the dug-outs in the railway cutting on their right. This was of great, perhaps determining, importance, for these dug-outs were part of the vast system of underground works which ran from the Ancre to Beaumont Hamel. If the entrances had been missed, the enemy would have come down from the left, where our attack had been less successful and the enemy were still present in strength, and would have cut the communications of the Hood Battalion. In clearing up the dug-outs in the enemy third line, Lieut.-Commander F. S. Kelly, D.S.C., commanding " B " Company (who had commanded a company of the Hood in Gallipoli), was killed, leading a gallant and successful attack on a machine-gun emplacement which threatened to enfilade the whole advance on this flank.

On the third line (the *Dotted Green Line*) the Hood advance should have stopped, and the next objectives (Station Road, the trench in front of it and the *Green Line* on the ridge behind it) should have been captured by the Drake Battalion. This Battalion, however, in crossing the three enemy lines carried by the Hood Battalion, had been drawn into the battle which was still raging in the first and second lines on the left of the Hood front, and had lost more than half their effectives ; among very many officer casualties were Lt.-Colonel Tetley, R.M.L.I., the commanding officer, and Lt.-Commander P. S. Campbell, R.N.V.R. (killed) and Lt.-Commander Turrell, R.N.V.R. (wounded). Indeed, the only Drake officers who had come through behind the Hood in time to carry out the next step of the attack, were Lieutenant C. C. Constable, Sub-Lieut. Fox, and Sub-Lieut. Beak (who now, for the first time, had an opportunity of displaying his fine quality as a regimental officer). With these three officers were only some seventy-eight petty officers and men. If this small force went on alone, disaster seemed certain. Yet, if they waited, they lost the barrage. This situation was critical. There was only a five-minutes' pause in which to make the decision, and considerable confusion prevailed. The situation was, however, largely determined by the prompt decision of Colonel Freyberg (commanding the Hood) to throw the whole weight of his battalion into the next advance, instead of endeavouring to reorganize in the mist and darkness, with the risk of being drawn into the

costly and indecisive fighting which was going on in the centre
of the enemy first-line position.

The combined attack was brilliantly successful : the dug-
outs in Station Road yielded some four hundred prisoners
(including six officers), and by the scheduled time Colonel
Freyberg was on the Division's second objective with a substantial force of nearly four hundred men and nine officers.   But
of this force, only three officers and some eighty petty officers
and men were of the Drake Battalion.   The rest of this fine
battalion were scattered, and nearly half of the remainder
were killed or wounded.   The explanation is to be found
in the still more tragic events in the centre of the battle
front.

Like the Hood and Drake Battalions, the Hawke and
Nelson had passed out into the mist at 5.45 a.m.   When
the first wave of the attack came within sight of the
enemy, and while the barrage was still playing on the enemy's
first line, a devastating machine-gun fire broke out from a
redoubt midway between the first and second enemy lines
opposite the Hawke Battalion front.   On the flank of the Hood
Battalion, some twenty men of the right (" C ") and support
(" D ") companies of the battalion fought through to the *Green
Line,* keeping up with the barrage, though isolated on their left
flank, and without officers, and for the remainder of the operation they fought under Colonel Freyberg's command.   Separated from this party in the course of the fighting, Sub-Lieut.
Stewart (also of " C " Company) with two men and a Lewis gun,
followed the barrage as far as Station Road, and kept the
gun in action against the enemy on the left of the *Green Line*
till it was reached on the right by Colonel Freyberg's brilliant
attack. On the right of the redoubt, a portion of " B " Company
of the same battalion, finely led by Lieutenant the Hon. Vere
Harmsworth, passed the strong point and followed the barrage
to the second German line ; here Lieutenant Harmsworth,
already once wounded, was wounded again, this time mortally,
and of his party the majority became casualties. Of the
remainder of the Hawke Battalion, all that is known is that
they fell round the redoubt which was in the centre of their
objective.   In all, nearly four hundred of the officers* and

* For a complete list of the officers killed or mortally wounded in this terribly
costly engagement see Appendix E (i).

men of this battalion became casualties, and all within the first half hour of the attack.

Following in the wake of such disaster the Nelson Battalion fared but little better. While the garrison of the strong point were engaged with the Hawke Battalion, the first two waves of the Nelson, whose objective lay beyond, succeeded in forcing their way through the mist and smoke without very severe loss, but even they fell far behind the barrage, and lost at least half their very slender effectives in assaulting Station Road with bombs and bayonets, virtually without any assistance from the artillery.* But the third and fourth waves of the battalion, who should have followed them, suffered the same fate as the Hawke, and fell almost to a man in the front and second line trenches, either because the officers leading their waves felt it their duty to attempt the impossible and storm the redoubt, or because, in endeavouring to follow their first waves who had passed to the far side of it, they were observed by the garrison, then less actively engaged. Probably the latter is the true explanation. General Shute, in his report on the battle, attributed the failure of the attack at this point to the mist, which he thinks must have concealed the whereabouts of the redoubt, and prevented its being mopped up. The whereabouts of the redoubt was all too plain, however, to the advancing infantry, and in the light of what is now known the more probable reason why it was never successfully attacked is because no officers and men got within bomb or bayonet range alive, while the artillery barrage missed it altogether. The almost conclusive proof is to be found in the disastrous losses of the Hawke Battalion.

Next to the Hawke and Nelson were the Howe and Anson Battalions of General Prentice's 188th Brigade. The leading companies of the Howe Battalion, finely commanded by Lieutenant Maynard and Lieutenant de la Motte, had kept well up to the barrage and had entered the German lines. The failure of the attack on the redoubt meant, however, that their flank was uncovered. Despite this, the leading waves of the Howe Battalion passed on with the barrage to the third line, but their losses had been too heavy to enable them to hold

---

* Lieut. Dangerfield, Sub-Lieut. Mecklenburg and Sub-Lieut. E. V. G. Gardner were among others of the Nelson Battalion who did fine work on this occasion. These officers each received the Military Cross.

any considerable portion of it. In the fight leading up to this line, Lieutenant Maynard and Lieutenant de la Motte were killed and Lieut.-Commander Edwards* was wounded. One company commander, Lieut.-Commander Sprange,† and some twenty men were all that reached it alive. In the circumstances, the enemy, moving from their centre behind the redoubt, re-occupied most of this important position, and so cut the communications between the garrison of the two front lines, which were still in our hands, and the detachments of the Anson who had been able to pass through the Howe Battalion and to fight their way successfully to the *Green Line*, their allotted objective. These detachments, nearly 180 strong as they passed through the Howe, crossed the Station Road valley under the active leadership of Lt.-Commander Gilliland, R.N.V.R., and reached the *Green Line* up to time, and without further serious loss.

On the extreme left of the attack, the 1st and 2nd Marine Battalions met with disaster at the start from the enemy artillery, and the four company commanders (Captain Loxley, Captain Hoare, Captain M. C. Browne, D.S.C., and Captain H. H. Sulivan), with very many N.C.O.'s and men, were killed crossing no man's land in the first moments of the advance, before the German front line was reached. The fighting even then was extremely heavy, for the 51st Division on the left, engaged in the historic and ultimately successful assault on Beaumont Hamel, were behind the barrage. In the circumstances, the same fate overtook the 1st Marines as had overtaken the Howe Battalion; the third and fourth waves established themselves in the first two enemy lines, but the relics of the first and second waves, advancing on the third line, melted away before the fire from their flanks and reached their objective only in isolated groups. The 2nd R.M. Battalion, following behind, became involved in hand-to-hand fighting in the third line and fell for the most part behind the barrage. Only a few men joined up with Lt.-Commander Gilliland's party, and a slightly larger detachment was reported about 11 a.m. as in touch with the 51st Division west of Station Road.

---

* This officer, who had served with distinction through the Gallipoli campaign, was severely wounded but continued to direct the advance of his Company to their objective. For his services he was awarded the D.S.O.

† This officer was engaged in the fighting in this line and on the Green Line throughout the day, and was awarded the M.C. for his services.

At 6.30 a.m., the Headquarters of the Nelson and Hawke Battalions went over to endeavour to clear up the position in front of the redoubt, but the attempt failed, and Lt.-Colonel Burge and his adjutant, Lieut. T. H. Emerson, R.N.V.R., were killed, and Lt.-Colonel Leslie Wilson was wounded. On the Howe Battalion front, Commander Ramsay Fairfax was more fortunate and succeeded in establishing a brigade report centre in the second German line. Soon after 7.30 a.m., while waiting reports from the front, he proceeded to organize and consolidate our hold of the first two enemy lines. On the left flank Lt.-Colonel Cartwright and Lt.-Colonel Hutchison, also moved forward, though a little later, to the second German line.

If we take the attack of the first two objectives (the German front line system and the Station Road system) as the first stage of the battle, it can be said that the progress made was not unsatisfactory. Each brigade had effected a substantial lodgment in the foremost objective, the *Green Line*, and, except in front of the Hawke and Nelson Battalions, where, through no fault of the officers or men, the attack had failed, we had secured a substantial and increasing hold on the whole front line system. In addition, the enemy dug-outs in Station Road had been bombed and cleared by the Hood, Nelson and Anson Battalions, and the ill-fated redoubt and the trenches immediately round it thus formed the only serious threat to our chances of maintaining our gains.

Of the two parties on the *Green Line*, however, Colonel Freyberg's alone was secure in its communications, adequate in numbers and adequately officered. Between Lt.-Commander Gilliland's party and our forces in the front line system were a large detachment of the enemy in their third line, and between the 189th and 188th Brigades was the still undefeated garrison of the redoubt. This meant that on the left of the divisional front we had no very secure communication from our old lines even as far as the enemy's front line system* ; the proof is to be found in the fact that, of General Heneker's 190th Brigade, the 7th Royal Fusiliers were still in our old front line, and only isolated detachments of the 4th Bedfords and the 10th Royal Dublin Fusiliers had been able to get

---

* The position would have been no better on the right (for the redoubt was, if anything, nearer to the right than to the left Divisional boundary) but for the fact that on the right the ground drops down to the valley of the Ancre.

forward to join the Howe and Marine Battalions. The remainder of these Battalions were still held up by cross fire from the redoubt. As in the case of the assaulting waves, the original plan, whereby the reserve brigade was to occupy the enemy front line system by 6.45, and so enable the whole strength of the other two brigades to go forward at 7.30 for the attack on the *Yellow Line*, had only been fulfilled on the right flank of the Division's attack. The prospects for our complete success were thus still far from bright.

The pause on the *Green Line* of one hour and ten minutes was observed, but punctually at 7.30 the barrage lifted for the attack on the *Yellow Line*. On the extreme left, where the Marines were in touch with the 7th Gordon Highlanders, no advance was attempted ; the party was already isolated, and there was no sign of any other battalions of the 51st Division.* Colonel Freyberg, however, and Lt.-Commander Gilliland led two independent assaults on the *Yellow Line*, and both parties reached the neighbourhood of the line without serious losses. Colonel Freyberg at once consolidated his position (a little in rear of the actual *Yellow Line*, which, though abandoned by the enemy, was still here being bombarded by our artillery as well as by that of the enemy), and threw back his left flank to the *Green Line*. Once more, by his prompt exploitation of a brilliant advance, he contributed substantially to the success of the whole operation. Lt.-Commander Gilliland's advance was equally successful, but the *Yellow Line* on this part of the front was not, as it was opposite Colonel Freyberg, on high ground of the utmost tactical importance, but on low ground commanded from all sides ; and not until later in the day, when information came to hand of the advance on the right, was it considered safe to risk a prolonged occupation of what was, at this point, a very indefensible position.

While this advance was in progress, no change had taken place in the first and second German lines, but behind, for the brigade and divisional staffs, the battle was beginning in earnest. The battle of the Ancre differs much from some other battles on the Somme, and, indeed, elsewhere, in that, within four

---

* This fine Division fought the battle through to a brilliant conclusion, but the exceptional difficulties of the assault on Beaumont Hamel delayed the advance of the Division for a very long time.

hours of the start, the situation was sufficiently clearly defined to the directing staffs for decisive action to be taken.

The German hold on their third line had prevented any authoritative reports either from the Marines with the 51st Division, or from Lt.-Commander Gilliland with his mixed detachment, or from the Nelson details which had captured a portion of Station Road, from reaching their brigades, but Colonel Freyberg's messages on the right flank and Commander Ramsay Fairfax's reports from the left centre, confirmed by detailed reports from Lt.-Colonel Higginbotham (the senior artillery observation officer) and by numerous wounded officers and men, gave a fairly accurate idea of the situation. General Shute at once and wisely decided that the 188th Brigade, reinforced by the 190th, must fight their way across the German front line system on the left of his front, before he could safely exploit the success gained by Colonel Freyberg. The result of this decision was the postponement of the attack on the *Red Line* (Beaucourt village). Colonel Freyberg and his officers were anxious to press on at 8.30 against this position, in accordance with the original plan, but General Shute was above all concerned with keeping open his communications up the Ancre Valley. If the force advanced to Beaucourt, these communications would be lengthened and the forces available to protect them would be inevitably weakened. The resulting risk was not a justifiable one while the Germans still remained in force in the centre of their old front line system and, as he thought, on Colonel Freyberg's flank.* The attack on Beaucourt was thus definitely postponed at about 9.15 a.m. and the H.A.C. were sent up to reinforce Colonel Freyberg on the *Yellow Line*. Meanwhile, reinforcements were sought from the Vth Corps, with a view to extending Colonel Freyberg's left, with fresh troops brought up through the Ancre Valley, should all attempts to reach the *Yellow Line* on the rest of the front fail.

The Vth Corps at once placed the 111th Brigade (Brigadier-General Barnes) of the 37th Division at General Shute's disposal, subject to prior reference to the Corps staff as to its precise employment.

The next stage of the battle, which may be taken as the

---

* This, of course, was not the case; no message, however, reached the 188th Brigade from Lieut.-Commander Gilliland, though many were sent.

period from 10, a.m. on the 18th to dawn on the 14th, has received too little attention. The dramatic interest of Colonel Freyberg's achievements has held the attention of writers as well as readers, and most accounts of the battle pass straight from the capture of the *Yellow Line* by the Hood Battalion on the 18th to the assault of Beaucourt by the same battalion on the morning of the 14th. Actually, in the course of this day and night, the 188th Brigade were involved in continuous fighting, and by 5 p.m. had occupied sections of all the enemy lines on their front up to and including the *Yellow Line*. Largely they were assisted to this advance by the success of the Hood Battalion, but it called none the less for very resolute and skilful leadership, as the advance was open to enemy attack on both flanks. Moreover, even to maintain our positions in the first three lines of trenches continuous bombing attacks were necessary. The principal reason why so little credit was gained by the Brigade for this achievement appears to be that the reports of their advances only reached Divisional Headquarters spasmodically and after long delays. The nature of the fighting and the precarious communications no doubt accounted for this.

The first move in these operations was made as early as 9.80 a.m. on the 15th, when General Prentice ordered all his battalion commanders to advance from the second German line and push forward if possible to the *Yellow Line*. Commander Ramsay Fairfax was unable to comply, as he was actively engaged in leading a bombing attack against the enemy, who were attempting to move northward along their second line from the redoubt. The other battalion commanders, however, with all the men they could collect, pushed forward to the third German line and held it, along the greater part of the Brigade front, with a party of the Anson and the Marine Battalions under Captain Gowney, D.S.C. Lt.-Commander Ellis himself, with one man, got to the *Green Line*, and found there Lt.-Commander Gilliland with his detachment of the Howe and Anson, and details of the Hawke and Nelson, Battalions. This party, now for the first time learning of Colonel Freyberg's success on the right flank, at once pushed on under orders from Commander Ellis to the *Yellow Line*, and there remained as an independent unit, though suffering severe losses, till nightfall, when they joined up with Colonel Freyberg.

Brig.-General A. M. Asquith, D.S.O.

(From the portrait by Ambrose McEvoy in the possession of the Imperial War Museum.)

Meanwhile Colonel Cartwright and Colonel Hutchison with Captain Gowney's detachment in the third German line had got the benefit of a barrage, put down on this line at 12.20 under orders from Divisional Headquarters, and had to retire for a few minutes. On returning Captain Gowney engaged the enemy who were still in the trench to the right and left, and established blocks which rendered his position tolerably secure.

Not informed apparently, of this lodgment in the German third line to the left of his front, nor of the presence of Lt.-Commander Gilliland's party in the *Yellow Line*, the third line was re-bombarded at 3.45 p.m., with the idea that the Howe Battalion would then be able to get forward. There were, indeed, some enemy detachments still to the front, though mostly to the right, of this battalion, but the orders for advance never reached the Howe, and the barrage fell short. The situation was not finally cleared up till a little later, when Lt.-Commander Ellis, after going again to the *Yellow Line* and seeing Lt.-Commander Gilliland holding the southern position of the trench, with the enemy to his left front (in Muck trench), but not otherwise pressed, returned through the German front line system to our old front line and reported fully on the situation. Captain Gowney, with men of the Marine and Anson Battalions, ultimately advanced and dug in on the *Green Line* at 4 a.m. on the 14th in touch with a battalion of Gordon Highlanders of the 51st Division.

Meanwhile, more decisive action had been taken throughout this day by General Shute in completing preparations for the renewal of the attack at dawn the next day.

Six tanks had been allocated to the Division and then had been within striking distance at Auchonvillers on the morning of the 12th. For some obscure (but unsatisfactory) reason they had been sent back to Beaussart on the eve of the attack : they were now recalled, and it was arranged that they should be brought up under cover of darkness and guided into action at dawn against the redoubt. The details of this operation were left to the 188th Brigade. For the main attack on Beaucourt the 111th Brigade was placed at General Shute's disposal.

In the belief that the enemy were holding out on the *Yellow Line* on Colonel Freyberg's left, this attack was planned, after discussion with Colonel Freyberg, in two phases. At 6 a.m., two battalions of the 111th Brigade, who were sent up at night on to the *Green Line*, were to attack the "occupied" part of the *Yellow Line*. Then at 6.30 a.m., as soon as the barrage lifted, Colonel Freyberg's force, which was to include one battalion of the 111th Brigade, and was to be supported by the 7th Royal Fusiliers from the 190th Brigade, was to advance on Beaucourt.

In the confusion of night, on a battlefield where trenches were almost obliterated and distances were impossible to calculate, it appears that the two battalions of the 111th Brigade, who should have occupied the whole of the *Green Line* to the left of Colonel Freyberg's position, only occupied half of it. The result was, that when they advanced at 6 a.m., they occupied only a further 500 yards of the *Yellow Line* to the left of Colonel Freyberg's force, leaving the remainder still unoccupied and liable to be retaken by the enemy.

Colonel Freyberg had arranged to assault Beaucourt at 7.45 with the 18th K.R.R.C. and the 1st H.A.C., leaving the Hood and Drake Battalions in support; but at the last minute considerable confusion was caused by the unlooked-for arrival behind the *Yellow Line* of the 7th Royal Fusiliers, who evidently expected to find that the advance from there had already taken place. They were, of course, heavily fired on from Beaucourt (where our artillery barrage was decidedly weak) and forced to take cover with the assaulting troops. The result was a considerable measure of confusion and a perilous delay. Again at a critical moment in the battle Colonel Freyberg retrieved the situation by himself leading the assault, followed by a mixed detachment of his own men, details of Drake, Hawke, Nelson and H.A.C., and the 18th K.R.R.C. In a moment Beaucourt was ours, the garrison of eight hundred surrendering, almost without a pretence of resistance.

Meanwhile a separate battle, no less successful, was being fought by the tanks, which had been led against the redoubt by Lieut. Alan Campbell, R.N.V.R.; and by the Howe and Anson detachments in the second and third German lines, against the enemy still occupying the trenches round the redoubt. The leading tank was steered into position by Alan Campbell himself, and a brisk bombardment by six-pounders soon brought this formidable stronghold to reason. The whole garrison, some six hundred strong, were marched back to our lines by a party of the Dublin Fusiliers. At the same time Commander

Ramsay Fairfax* and Commander Ellis* to his left engaged other detachments of the enemy, and 176 prisoners were taken. Both Battalion Commanders then pushed on to the *Green Line*, where the Headquarters of all Battalions in the Brigade were finally assembled by 3.30 p.m.

After the capture of Beaucourt and the redoubt, and the occupation of the *Green Line* on the left, it only remained to consolidate our hold on Beaucourt and clear up the situation on the flanks of the position. In the course of the afternoon, these tasks, though under great difficulties and in the face of a good deal of enemy activity, were accomplished. Particularly good work was done by Sub-Lieut. Hill, R.N.V.R. (Hood Battalion) in arranging the disposition of the eighteen Lewis guns at the disposal of the force. The 189th Machine-Gun Company and L.T.M. battery also assisted in the defence. An officer's patrol occupied the bridge across the railway north of Beaucourt and made touch with the IInd Corps across the river, and the remainder of the 111th Brigade (less one battalion which constituted the only effective reserve and was held in our old front line) pushed on west of Beaucourt and reached the greater part of their objective. The extreme left of the Division's objective was not, however, at this time achieved, perhaps because of some misunderstanding on the part of the 111th Brigade as to the precise position of the western boundary of the divisional front. The situation here was finally cleared up, just as General Shute handed over command to the 37th Division, on the morning of the 15th.

The much-needed relief had been arranged during the operations of the afternoon of the 14th which we have just described. In the second day's fighting the casualties had been far lighter than in the first, except during the bombardment of Beaucourt following its capture. Here Colonel Freyberg had been wounded for the third time, and this time severely. Captain the Hon. Lionel Montagu, who had been at his right hand throughout the operations,† and Major Norris, R.M., the 2nd in command of the Hawke Battalion, who had come up from Hedauville during the night to join the small remnant of his

---

* Both these officers were awarded the D.S.O. for their services on this day. So also were Colonel Hutchison, R.M.L.I., and Colonel Cartwright, R.M.L.I., commanding the two Marine battalions.

† Captain Montagu was awarded the D.S.O.

battalion, were also wounded. The result was that the command of the Beaucourt sector passed to the Colonel commanding the 13th K.R.R.C.,* Lt.-Commander Egerton, D.S.O.† took over the Hood, and Lieut. Sterndale Bennett‡ the Drake Battalion.

At midnight the relief division began, the whole front being taken over by the 63rd Brigade of the 37th Division, the 111th Brigade remaining in support, and in reserve in the old enemy front line the remains of the 189th and 188th Brigades. In the afternoon of the 15th these Brigades were finally relieved and marched back to Engelbelmer, the 190th Brigade remaining temporarily to clear up the battlefield.

The two Naval Brigades had suffered the most severe losses. Of the officers and men of the 189th Brigade who went into the attack, there remained unwounded only Lieutenant Morrison, Sub-Lieutenants Hill,§ Arblaster,§ Carnall,§ Jacobs and Surgeon McCracken and 250 petty officers and men of the Hood Battalion, Lieutenant Sterndale Bennett and Sub-Lieutenants Fox and Beak§ and some 280 petty officers and men of the Drake Battalion, Sub-Lieutenant A. P. Herbert (who had come up to Beaucourt with Major Norris on the night of the 13th–14th), Sub-Lieutenant Rackham and Sub-Lieutenant Bowerman and some 30 men of the Hawke Battalion, and Lieutenant Dangerfield, Sub-Lieutenant Gardner, Surgeon Cox and 100 men of the Nelson Battalion. In the 188th Brigade the losses were equally severe, though the four commanding officers survived to lead out the remains of their battalions. With Commander Ramsay Fairfax there came back of the Howe Battalion only Sub-Lieutenant Forrester§ and less than 100 men. Of the Anson the survivors were Lt.-Commander Ellis‖ and 166 petty officers and men without officers (and 80 reinforcements who had arrived late on the 14th). The 1st R.M. Battalion, under Colonel Cartwright, came out with one officer (Lieutenant Van Praagh, R.M.) and 188 N.C.O.'s and men,

---

* Colonel Freyberg remained, however, long enough to complete his dispositions for the defence of the new positions.

† Lt.-Commander Egerton had received the D.S.O. for his services in Gallipoli.

‡ Lieut. Sterndale Bennett was awarded the D.S.O. for his services as Adjutant of the Drake before and during this engagement.

§ These officers, in addition to others previously mentioned, received the M.C. for their services in this battle.

‖ Who was awarded the D.S.O.

and the 2nd R.M. Battalion, under Colonel Hutchison, with six officers and nearly 150 men. The 190th Brigade had suffered only less severely.

The casualties in the Naval Brigades alone were not far short of three thousand, and the strength of these brigades as they marched back was under six hundred apiece. Of this strength more than a third was provided by the Hood and Drake Battalions, whose successes had been the most distinguished. Such is the fortune of war.

To attempt to describe in any detail an engagement so protracted, so many-sided, as that fought by the Naval Division on the Ancre is only to be reminded of the inevitable inaccuracy of historical records. So much must be omitted because so much can never be known, and, of what might be known if all the actors could be assembled and examined, and if memories were more perfect, only a small part can actually be discovered. Even the official records are imperfect guides, where so many of the principal actors on the scene became casualties and could not tell their stories before the official reports were submitted.

Yet a fuller description of this engagement than has yet appeared had to be attempted, for such accounts as have found their way into the larger histories give a rather distorted picture, and hardly do justice to the Division as a whole. The battle (or rather the Naval Division's share in it) has been represented as a failure, redeemed by one brilliant, even astonishing, success. The success of the Hood and Drake Battalions was both brilliant and astonishing, and it was decisive. Yet by the time the assault on Beaucourt was made at 7.45 in the morning of the 14th, the redoubt had been captured, the 188th Brigade were on the *Green Line*, and there was a road through to the *Yellow Line* on the right as well as on the left of the attack. Colonel Freyberg's brilliant and gallant leadership will remain the outstanding individual achievement of the Battle of the Ancre,*

---

* Colonel Freyberg was at once recommended for, and received the V.C. The official account of his now historic achievement is as follows :—

"For most conspicuous bravery and brilliant leading as a Battalion Commander.

"By his splendid personal gallantry he carried the initial attack straight through the enemy's front system of trenches. Owing to mist and heavy fire of all descriptions, Lieut.-Colonel Freyberg's command was much disorganized after the capture of the first objective. He personally rallied and re-formed his men, including men from other units who had become intermixed.

"He inspired all with his own contempt of danger. At the appointed time but, as ever, it was the patient, the unbelievable, obstinacy, courage and endurance of the private soldier along the whole line of battle which turned the scale.† Had the attack really failed on the rest of the divisional front, had the men of the Hawke, Nelson, Howe and Anson, and of the Marine Battalions fallen back to their own lines in the face of their appalling losses, which left them often entirely without officers, the history of the Battle of the Ancre would beyond a doubt have been different. As it was, the whole division won in this battle not only a reputation, but a confidence in its own fighting capacity which contributed much to its future efficiency. Such confidence is not bred of a vicarious success.

Of the results of this battle on the general position, we shall speak in the next chapter, when we shall find the Naval Division once more alongside the Ancre under vastly changed conditions which were largely the product of its own earlier success.

Yet if there had been a triumph there had also been a tragedy. In the month of November the Division had lost a hundred officers and more than 1,600 men killed, and a hundred and sixty officers and 2,377 men wounded. Almost the whole of their casualties were in the twelve infantry battalions and the machine-gun companies, and more than three-quarters of these were in the two Naval Brigades, whose allotted task in the Battle of the Ancre had inevitably exacted higher casualties than those suffered by the four Army battalions. In the face of such losses, congratulatory messages had an empty ring.

---

he led his men to the successful assault of the second objective, many prisoners being captured.

"During this advance he was twice wounded. He again rallied and re-formed all who were with him, and although unsupported in a very advanced position, he held his ground for the remainder of the day, and throughout the night, under heavy artillery and machine-gun fire. When reinforced on the following morning, he organized the attack on a strongly-fortified village and showed a fine example of dash in personally leading the assault, capturing the village and five hundred prisoners. In this operation he was again wounded.

"Later in the afternoon, he was again wounded severely, but refused to leave the line till he had issued final instructions.

"The personality, valour and utter contempt of danger on the part of this single officer enabled the lodgment in the most advanced objective of the Corps to be permanently held, and on this point d'appui the line was eventually formed."

† Unfortunately it has been found impossible to trace any complete records of the numerous decorations conferred on non-commissioned officers, petty officers and men of the R.N. and R.N.V.R. battalions in respect of this engagement.

Those to whom they should have been addressed were beyond reach of the benisons of distinguished generals.

For all, during many months, and for many, always, the valley of the Ancre remained in the background of their thoughts. Here, and on the now deserted shores of Gallipoli, had fallen the flower of the Naval Division. And the valley of the Ancre was the more symbolic resting-place. Over Gallipoli, at any rate in the spring sunshine, there lingered some faint illusion of romance ; over the valley of the Ancre hung, like a pall, the unutterable ruin, the pitiful desolation, of modern war.

CHAPTER XII

A FTER the Battle of the Ancre the Naval Division was withdrawn from the battle area for two months' rest in the
neighbourhood of Rue. The opportunity afforded by so many
casualties among the senior officers of the 189th Brigade was
used to attach to the Division a number of senior Army officers
as Battalion Commanders and Seconds-in-Command. Lt.-
Colonel D. Munro* was appointed to the Hood, Lt.-Commander
Asquith being detached for staff duties; Lt.-Colonel Annesley,
later succeeded by Major Freeland, was appointed to the Drake,
and Lt.-Colonel Whiteman to the Hawke. Commander E. W.
Nelson, R.N.V.R., succeeded Lt.-Colonel Burge in command of
the Nelson, and was now the only R.N.V.R. officer commanding
a battalion in this Brigade. In the 188th Brigade Lt.-Colonel
Kirkpatrick took over the Anson Battalion. Other and more
sweeping changes were in the air. The comings and goings of
Army officers at this time were indeed so frequent that it is
impossible to detail them, and if the continual interchange and
supersession of senior officers which marked this period was at
all characteristic of the methods usual in army divisions, there
is little reason for wonder that the achievement of the Naval
Division on the Ancre had been genuinely unexpected.

The policy of infusing indiscriminately officers from other
formations was perhaps unfortunate. The battalions of the
Division had evolved their routine and their administrative
machinery under the stress of active service conditions. They
came under the army machine for the first time when they were
already in France. Odd scraps of naval routine and naval drill
and the whole naval system of ranks and ratings remained.
Added to this, the Division had never attained any exceptional
standard of proficiency in parade ground drill, a fact which,

---

* Actually Lt.-Colonel Creagh-Osborne was Lt.-Colonel Freyberg's immediate
successor, but his period of service with the Division was brief.

perhaps more than anything else, roused in the minds of the newly-attached officers suspicions of a deep-seated inefficiency. The remedy for this deplorable state of affairs was at first sought in proposals for the gradual militarization of the Division, assisted, if possible, by voluntary transfers of officers and men from Navy to Army engagements, and enforced by the gradual removal of the majority of the senior Naval officers and N.C.O.'s from responsible positions. The advantages to be derived from this proceeding were highly speculative, while the disadvantages were glaring. It was, perhaps, in the circumstances, fortunate that, for whatever reason, the zeal of the reformers suddenly abated and allowed the work of training and re-organization to proceed along more traditional lines. The result was that, by the middle of January, the Division was again ready to take the field, and the battalions fell short of their newly-won reputation only in experience of the ever-changing conditions of war, and in that mutual confidence between officers and men which had been so marked a feature of the Division for more than two years. Such confidence, bred of long experience, could hardly be expected to spring up spontaneously between the reinforcements and their newly-appointed leaders but recently transferred from the army.

The situation as the Division moved back to the line at the beginning of 1917 was one of profound expectancy. In particular, the question of the tactics to be pursued in the exploitation of what had been publicly announced as a decisive victory on the Somme was, at the beginning of 1917, of burning interest to the infantry.

There was no weakening of the will to victory, but there was without doubt a spirit of inquiry abroad. A return to the methods of the Somme, involving as they did the over-straining of fighting troops in innumerable fatigue duties, the costly offensive, the fatal delay while the enemy rebuilt his line, spelt for the infantry an indefinite period of discomfort broken only by hours of extreme danger. Incidentally, it was safe to say that no man could hope to come out of two battles of the Somme type unhurt and that one man in three would lose his life. We cannot wonder that the question whether it was possible, by new methods aiming at a swifter decision, to avoid the sombre prospect of unending battles of attrition, was one frequently and keenly debated.

The fact that new methods were ultimately adopted with disastrous results does not in itself prove conclusively that an escape from the policy of attrition was impossible at this stage in the campaign. The actions now to be described, which followed on the return of the Naval Division in January 1917, to face a beaten enemy in the desolate valley of the Ancre, are of historical importance chiefly for the light they cast on this intricate problem. What was the situation created by our victories of 1916, and was it exploited to the best advantage ?

The battle of November 13th, had, as will be remembered, been planned to dislodge the enemy from his positions between Serre and the northern bank of the Ancre, which had threatened the flank of our salient south of that river and had thus made it impossible for us to continue our advance. The battle had been wholly successful on the front from Beaumont Hamel to Beaucourt, and when it was broken off, the enemy positions in front of Bapaume depended for their security, no longer on three successive positions opposing an advance north of the Ancre, but only on the one line from Serre to Puisieux and thence through Beauregarde Dovecote to Miraumont and Pys, with an outpost at Grandcourt. The reduction of this line was thus all that appeared necessary to give us a chance of dislodging the enemy from his positions on a considerably wider front. The prospect was all the more attractive since the depth of the advance necessary to shake the enemy's hold on the Pys–Miraumont line was not very great. Any substantial advance from Beaucourt would give us the ridge which commanded Grandcourt, and, if Grandcourt fell, it needed only a further short advance on either side of the Ancre to carry us on to the two spurs which commanded the eastern and western approaches to Miraumont, and covered also the enemy artillery positions which alone enabled him to retain his hold on Serre and Puisieux.

Since the Division had been relieved on the morning of November 15th our line north of the Ancre had been pushed forward some distance beyond Beaucourt, but was still below the crest of the ridge which commanded Grandcourt. On the southern bank of the river the line was already on the outskirts of Grandcourt. To ensure the protection of the river crossings, the Vth Corps had handed over the brigade frontage immediately north of the river to the IInd Corps, and the trenches opposite Grandcourt and across the river in front of Beaucourt now formed one divisional sector. It was this sector that the Naval Division took over from the 11th Division, on the nights of January 18th and 19th, the 188th Brigade going into the line south of the river, with the 189th Brigade on their left in front of Beaucourt. The 190th Brigade remained for the time in reserve.

Since the middle of December the frost had been continuous, and, as they had worked their way forward up the hill from Beaucourt, our outposts had had to use and maintain themselves in such cover as the frozen shell-holes of the battlefield provided. No digging and no movement by day was possible, and by night the ration parties visiting the outpost line were the objects of continuous shelling. Virtually the occupants of these shell-holes were isolated, dependent on themselves for their security, and on the hope of early relief for their only consolation. The lot of the support and reserve companies and of the artillery was little better. The spacious dug-outs of Beaucourt provided for some, indeed, an estimable shelter, but they were too far behind our front for any save the reserves, whose duties of fetching and carrying over the shell-swept valley and up the open slopes to the outpost line were inconceivably arduous, and deprived them of leisure to profit by them. The support companies in trenches beyond the village were tied to their inadequate cover as closely as the outposts, and, like them, were condemned merely to freeze in silence till relief came. The artillery, in gun positions well known to the enemy, suffered almost as severely, and the conditions were above all fatal to the horses, for whom the rations, in the unprecedented severity of a happily abnormal winter, were pitifully inadequate.

Conditions such as these are, in their kind, if not in their degree, the inevitable lot of many infantrymen in many winter campaigns. They are worthy of note here because it was in this winter of 1917, and at this very time and place, that the first and last winter offensive by our armies in France was launched, and because it was in spite of these conditions that it succeeded. These facts are of the first importance as an indication of the demoralization of the enemy by the battles of 1916, of the determination of the different British divisions which took part in the renewed offensive, and of the very real chance that existed at this date of proceeding to an even more substantial, possibly to a decisive, success.

The concluding days of January were marked by only two incidents outside the normal routine of stationary war. The first occurred on the night of January 24th, on the left brigade front, where the Hood Battalion posts in the Ancre Valley were attacked and the enemy, coming down the frozen river, effected a lodgment in our line. The attack was eventually driven back, though with loss, Sub-Lieutenant McCormick, R.N.V.R., and seven men being killed in an anxious engagement. The other incident occurred on the front held by the 2nd Marines, across the river, when a German advanced post was captured by Lieutenant Spinney (a Corps intelligence officer, temporarily attached to the battalion) and two bombers from the Marine Battalion. A similar attempt was made the next night by Lieutenant Spinney, accompanied by Lieutenant Wren, R.M.L.I., but the results inevitably were less satisfactory, and, though many casualties were inflicted, the brave organizer of these adventures was mortally wounded.

Towards the end of January, the first move was made, and with a view to the renewal of the offensive at an early date on the Beaucourt front, the 189th Brigade was relieved by the 190th Brigade. The sequel was the issue of orders for an attack by the former Brigade on the two enemy trenches on the ridge commanding Grandcourt. The attack was to take place on February 3rd, and the Hawke and Hood Battalions were chosen by General Phillips for the task. To make the final preparations, these battalions returned to the front line on the night of the 1st–2nd February.

In the hope of effecting a surprise, the attack, which was a simple trench-to-trench affair, was planned for 11 p.m. The Hawke and Hood Battalions had each three companies detailed for the attack and the fourth in support, the four companies in the centre being in two waves of two platoons each and the flanking companies in three waves on a narrower frontage. The left Battalion (Hawke) had perhaps the harder task, as their advance uncovered their flank and a defensive flank had to be formed. " A " Company of the support Battalion (Nelson) was detailed to assist the support company of the Hawke Battalion in this work. The Hood Battalion had no appreciably lighter task, since their objective consisted not only of a well-

Scene of the Hood Battalion advance in the Ancre Valley,
November 13th, 1916.

defined sector of the enemy trenches, but of an ill-defined group of posts in the valley. The capture of these necessitated a half-right turn, an obvious source of confusion in a night advance, by the platoons on the right.

An effort had been made to link up the line of shell-holes, which constituted our first line, into a continuous trench to form an assembly position for the first two waves, and, though the shelter provided was negligible, it was here that the attacking companies lined up at 9 p.m. on the evening of the 3rd. There was a keen frost and a brilliant moon.

The distance to the first enemy line (Puisieux trench) was three hundred yards, and to the second line barely another hundred yards. The whole attack, from the time when the barrage opened to the time when it lifted off the enemy's second line, was to last only eight minutes. In a local operation of this character, the duration of the advance is no index of the difficulty of the operation. With no advance attempted on either flank, the enemy reaction must be easier and more immediate, and the difficulties of consolidating the captured position correspondingly greater. So in fact it was found.

Following close behind the barrage, which was exceptionally accurate and effective, the leading waves entered the first trench without great opposition except from a machine gun in a fortified emplacement opposite the centre of the right (" D ") company of the Hawke Battalion. This machine gun proved, as it turned out, the pivot of a very vigorous defence by the enemy. The chief lesson of the battle of November 13th had been the futility of attempting to carry " strong points " by frontal attack, and the simple corrective urged was to go round them and so, by establishing positions ahead, to compel their surrender. This method was carefully followed by the leading platoons of the Hawke Company under Sub-Lieutenant Blackmore and Sub-Lieutenant Wilkes, but the result was unsatisfactory. Partly owing to the darkness, and partly to the fact that Sub-Lieutenant Blackmore was wounded, these platoons failed to join up in the enemy second line. Instead, the platoon on the right got carried away by the Hood Battalion, who by mistake had turned half-right and followed their right company in the attack on the posts in the valley. The result was that the whole Hood Battalion and two platoons of the

Hawke ended up on an alignment parallel with, instead of at right angles to, the river.

Meanwhile the Hawke had scored a distinct success on the left flank, where " C " Company, under Lt.-Commander Shelton, R.N.V.R., had captured and were consolidating the important flank position at the juncture of River trench and Artillery Lane, where the enemy reaction was likely to be, and in fact became, most severe. The consolidation of the defensive flank was, however, proceeding under difficulties. The Nelson company had failed to obtain a junction with the Hawke left, and the enemy retained a lodgment between the two battalions.

Such was the situation half-an-hour after the attack, when Lt.-Colonel Monro, commanding the Hood Battalion, was wounded, and Lt.-Commander Asquith,* who had gone forward on the heels of his old battalion in the slender disguise of staff learner studying the effects of the artillery barrage, took command. To his energy and enthusiasm the success of the 189th Brigade's operations on this occasion was largely due. Well before 8 a.m. on the 4th, Lt.-Commander Asquith had got the Hood Battalion back to their correct alignment, and although touch could not be gained with the Hawke Battalion (who had probably by now edged further to the left, assuming the attack to have failed on the right) the situation was no longer critical. Dawn saw us with a fair hold on all our objectives, but with an awkward gap in the first and second enemy lines, and a machine-gun post still obstructing the consolidation of the essential defensive flank.

The history of the rest of the battle is soon told. Several attempts to subdue the two strong points and to close the gaps were made during the morning of the 4th, but without success. At 3.50 p.m., however, the enemy post on our left was rushed by the Nelson and Hawke after an effective bombardment from a Stokes gun, skilfully handled by Leading Seaman Wheeler,† of the 189th L.T.M. battery. This rendered our position virtually secure on the flank. The enemy still held out between the Hawke and Hood Battalions, and General Phillips decided to send up the Drake Battalion. Two companies were to assist the Hawke to capture the strong point, one company was to

---

* Lt.-Commander Asquith had been, against his wishes, detached for staff duties a few days before the battle of November 13th.

† This N.C.O. was subsequently awarded the D.C.M.

reinforce the Hood right (where the position was then obscure), and one company to fill the gap between the Hawke and Hood in River trench.

These last companies went up together to the Hood right, about 7 p.m., but, as soon as the first of their companies arrived in the line, a counter-attack developed, the enemy breaking through on the right of the Hood and bombing our communications up the valley. At the same time an intensive bombardment fell on each flank of the captured position. The casualties were heavy; the rear company of the Drake was caught crowded up in a narrow communication trench, and there was a certain inevitable confusion. Meanwhile, one post on the flank of the Hood had been surprised and captured by the enemy. On the left, the situation, thanks to the screen of Lewis and Vickers guns in front of the consolidating party, was more satisfactory. Although the remaining company of the Hawke Battalion had to be called on to assist in the defence, no footing was secured by the counter-attack at any point on this flank.

By 8 p.m. the situation was quiet, and Lt.-Commander Asquith proceeded to a fresh effort to join up with the Hawke Battalion in River trench, and so cut off the garrison of the strong point. This time " B " Company of the Drake (Sub-Lieut. H. K. Lunn) was chosen for the task and was led some distance up River trench without encountering opposition. Unfortunately Commander Asquith, who alone knew well the lie of this trench, now bombarded out of all recognition, and the direction in which the Hawke right must be expected to be, was wounded just as he was starting off to lead the Drake company into position. Sub-Lieut. Lunn, taking on a patrol to find the way, lost direction and found himself in the German lines, where he was cut off, and the gap, though much reduced, remained.

At dawn on the 4th, a final, and this time successful, attack was made against the enemy who still held out in this gap ; the original strong point was captured by Sub-Lieutenant Bowerman, M.C.,* and a party of the Hawke Battalion, and the remaining posts were dealt with by the Hood and Drake Battalions. It is interesting to note that the " strong point " turned out to be a dug-out with a garrison thirty-two strong, though the Brigade staff had reported almost hourly

---

* This officer had received the M.C. for his work in the attack of November 18th.

that there was only a machine gun in a shell-hole, and no dug-out and no garrison at all.

At 5.30 p.m. on the same day a counter-attack was organized by the Hood on the right of their front, and the post which had been lost was retaken without difficulty.

Throughout the day, the enemy infantry had delivered several counter-attacks, especially against the Hood Battalion's front, but they had been beaten off by a very effective series of artillery barrages (for which the 317th R.F.A. Brigade—Lt.-Colonel Gosling—was responsible) and Lewis and machine-gun fire.

The success of these operations, which were planned to take eight minutes and were carried through in no more than fifty hours' continuous fighting, was due as usual pre-eminently to the stubbornness with which the petty officers and men clung on to the captured positions, without regard to the positions on either flank.   Secondly, it was due to the resolute leadership of Lt.-Commander Shelton on the left flank, and to the initiative and skill of Lt.-Commander Asquith in carrying out his self-imposed task in command of the right flank of our attack. Both these officers were awarded the D.S.O.   Captain Barnett, Brigade Major of the 189th Brigade, received a bar to his Military Cross, and Sub-Lieutenant Fernie and Sub-Lieutenant Robotti (the Brigade bombing and transport officers) and Sub-Lieutenant Rackham (the Lewis gun officer of the Hawke, to whose dispositions the defeat of the attacks on the left flank was in no small measure due) were awarded the Military Cross.*

The nature of the fighting, calling as it did for the greatest initiative and endurance on the part of the N.C.O.'s in command of the posts which formed our line of defence, is best reflected, however, by the long list of awards of the D.C.M., among the recipients being P.O. Bettridge, P.O. Callender and A.B. Price of the Drake, P.O. Rosewarne of the Hawke, P.O. Simpson, P.O. Blair and A.B. H. G. Macaulay of the Hood, P.O. Edgar and L.S. Punton of the Brigade Stokes Mortar Battery, and P.O. Buckman, L.S. Tillings and A.B. Schol-field of the Machine-Gun Company.

* Other officers to win this distinction were Sub-Lieutenants Blackmore and Lyall of the Hawke; Bennett, Hilton, Clark and Ablett of the Hood, and Pound of the Drake Battalion.   Surgeon Lieut.-Commander Padwick of the Hawke Battalion was awarded the D.S.O.

The conditions of the attack necessarily placed an almost impossible strain on the administrative staff. The small area of the attack was the chief difficulty, since our communications were known and the enemy had nothing to do but shell them consistently. In these circumstances very few men got adequate rations, and as their iron rations and the water in their water-bottles were frozen, the energy of the attack and the subsequent defence were extremely remarkable. Even more difficult than the supply of rations was the evacuation of the casualties, and the high proportion of killed was perhaps in itself due, to some extent, to the limitation of the front of attack. The stubborn resistance of the enemy lessened the advantage which it had been hoped to gain from a night attack, but the experiment was on the whole successful, and the gaps which occurred in our line were probably inevitable in the light of the stubborn defence put up, which had, without a doubt, been under-estimated. In any case, the test of the fighting quality of troops is the ability to retrieve their mistakes.

Even taking into account the vigour of the enemy resistance over more than two days, the casualties in the Brigade, which amounted to 24 officers and 647 petty officers and men, were exceptional, and the proportion of killed was lamentably high. Among the officers killed were Lieutenant Ellis and Sub-Lieuts. Collins and Rorke of the Hawke, and Lieut. Oliver and Sub-Lieut. T. Jacobs of the Hood, Sub-Lieuts. W. J. Travers and R. A. W. Robinson of the Drake, and Sub-Lieut. A. F. Wolfe, of the Nelson Battalion. Our captures amounted to one officer and 185 men unwounded, one officer and forty men wounded, and two machine guns.

The success achieved, however, had been complete, and its results were immediate. On the night of February 5th–6th (the next following on the complete capture of our objective), while the relief of the 189th Brigade by the 190th was in progress on the battle front, the Howe Battalion, on the other side of the Ancre, pushed two patrols in Grandcourt under Sub-Lieut. H. M. Graham and Sub-Lieut. Bunce.* They found it deserted, and returned with captured rifles and

* Sub-Lieut. Bunce was severely wounded by a chance shot on the way back to our lines and died the next day. The Howe Battalion lost two other officers of fine promise on the previous and following days in Lieutenant Humphries (commanding "C" Company), and Lieutenant Ellis (the adjutant of the Battalion).

equipment.   Commander Ramsay Fairfax immediately notified
his Brigade, and Lt.-Colonel Hutchison, on his right, and the 2nd
Marines entered Grandcourt at 9 a.m. on the 6th, and confirmed
the retirement of the enemy.   The message to the 188th
Brigade on the night of February 5th–6th is of historical
importance as the first notification of the beginning of that
German retreat, which was so profoundly to modify the whole
strategic situation on the Western front.

The next day (February 7th) the H.A.C., after a successful
reconnaissance by 2nd Lieut. Finch (who was awarded the
Military Cross for his exploit), advanced their line up the
Ancre Valley to Baillescourt Farm (some six hundred yards
ahead of the left of the line reached by the Hood Battalion in
the battle of the 3rd–5th).   In this highly successful affair the
H.A.C. captured eighty-one prisoners, besides effecting a gain
on ground which enabled us to make good our hold on a line
in front of Grandcourt; but they suffered two severe losses in
the deaths of Colonel Boyle and Captain Bryant.   Colonel
Boyle had commanded the H.A.C. from the time they landed
in France, and his loss was a severe blow to this fine and almost
uniformly successful battalion.   He was succeeded in command
by Major Osmond.

Whether or no the retreat from Grandcourt was regarded
as of local significance only, it was not till February 17th that
a serious attempt was made to exploit our successes by launch-
ing an attack in force on Miraumont.   The main operation was
to be undertaken by the 18th and 2nd Divisions south of the
Ancre, who were to attack roughly in a northerly direction,
and capture in three bounds the enemy position on the forward slope, the crest and the reverse slopes of the hill covering
Miraumont from the west.   Simultaneously, the Naval Division
had to complete the capture of the spur on the southern face
of which they had won a footing on February 3rd.

The advance was planned for 5.45 a.m., under the now
inevitable creeping barrage.

The Naval Division's attack was carried out by the Howe
and 1st R.M. Battalions of General Prentice's 188th Brigade,
which had handed over the Grandcourt sector to another
division a few days before.   The Anson Battalion held the
already advanced posts on the right of the divisional front
next to the river, and the 2nd R.M. Battalion and two

companies of the Hawke Battalion held the left flank, which rested still in Artillery Alley (the trench consolidated by Nelson and Hawke Battalions in the first advance of the month). The reserve battalion was the Hood. Two companies of the 2nd Marines were specially attached to their first battalion, to help them in consolidating the extension of our defensive flank.

The attack was brilliantly successful, and in the case of the Howe Battalion (on the right) the casualties were extremely light, the flank of their objective being already covered by the advanced posts of the Anson Battalion, who had relieved the H.A.C. at Baillescourt Farm. The 1st Marine Battalion had a harder task, with an open flank to protect, and with the enemy resistance more formidable. While consolidating their objective they experienced rather heavy losses, and they had also suffered severely from the enemy's barrage before the attack began. The result was that two companies of the Hood Battalion had to go up to reinforce them. Nevertheless, they consolidated their objective, and the difficulties which had arisen on the 3rd in safeguarding the left flank were on this occasion avoided.

It remains a significant commentary on the evenly-balanced chances of war that the casualties in this immediately successful operation were almost precisely the same as in the earlier engagement, when severe fighting had extended over a period of more than two days. In that case, moreover, the enemy's resistance was appreciably more vigorous. The moral, perhaps, must be drawn in favour of night operations, especially if it is remembered that the risks of these are mainly due not to any inherent difficulty but to the fact that they are so rarely practised.

On the morning of February 18th, a counter-attack developed, but it was annihilated before it reached our lines by the extremely effective barrage of the divisional artillery and the 188th and 190th Machine-Gun Companies. On the night of the 21st–22nd, the 188th Brigade handed over to the 190th the new position consolidated and intact. In the course of the operations the Marines had lost severely in officers and men. Lieutenant L. W. Robinson, 2nd Lieut. A. A. O'Kell, 2nd Lieut. C. R. Burton, 2nd Lieut. F. W. A. Perry, 2nd Lieut. H. C. Brown and 2nd Lieut. T. Swale were killed, and the casualties in N.C.O.'s and men were over four hundred. The

Howe casualties were fortunately lighter, yet two officers (Sub-Lieut. Shea and Sub-Lieut. Haines) and some twenty N.C.O.'s and men were killed.

Like the earlier operation, that of February 17th had a decisive result, and the enemy at once evacuated his positions at Serre, Miraumont and Pys. When our patrols went forward on the 23rd and 24th they met with no resistance, and the 190th Brigade actually occupied Miraumont on the 25th without firing a shot. Even on the 26th, when the H.A.C., the 7th Royal Fusiliers (Lt.-Colonel Hesketh) and the 10th Dublin Fusiliers (Lt.-Colonel Seymour) had orders to occupy Gudgeon trench, a prepared position between Puisieux and Irles, on which the enemy rearguard might be expected to stand, they succeeded in capturing the position (and a few prisoners) before nightfall.

The success of this operation was largely due to the skilful work of 2nd Lieut. Baines, of the H.A.C., and 2nd Lieut. H. W. Taylor, of the Fusiliers. The next day Gommecourt and Puisieux were evacuated, and, by March 2nd, the enemy had fallen back to the Le Transloy–Loupart line, except in the neighbourhood of Irles.

At this point in the advance the Naval Division were relieved from duty in the line, and their frontage was taken over by the Vth Corps, who extended their line once more to the Ancre.

The almost unbroken successes, achieved in turn by each of the Brigades of the Division, makes this period a memorable one. Unfortunately, they had been bought at a heavy price, and were destined to bring no such striking return in the long run as seemed, and perhaps might have been, possible.

These successes, and those of the other divisions on the flanks, appeared, indeed, to have created a situation for which we were unprepared, and which had to be met as far as possible by eleventh-hour efforts. We had forced the enemy to retreat at a time when, in any case, effective pursuit must have been peculiarly difficult. The frosts, which had prevailed through the first three weeks of February, had given place to milder weather, and the older roads behind our front were now virtually impassable. Once it was decided that, as a measure of precaution, our advance must keep pace with our ability to move forward the normal proportion of guns, ammuni-

Railway Station at Beaumont Hamel, November, 1916.

tion and other supplies, the absence of preparation meant that, before the advance could begin, new roads and railways had to be hurriedly constructed.

To assist in this work the Naval Division were attached during the first fortnight in March to the Canadian Railway Company. No finer men could have been found for this work than the north-country miners who formed so high a proportion of the men of the division, for they possessed that rare combination of skill and energy which is essential when work has to be done against time. All the same, it was a curious irony which made it necessary to call on the Division to do the spade-work necessary to exploit their own hardly-won victories, especially when it is recalled that the February victories had been planned as long before as October.

As it was, despite the most continuous calls on the division in the matter of working parties, the IInd Corps was not in a position to move against Irles, the one outpost held by the enemy in advance of the Le Transloy–Loupart line, till March 10th, and, by the time we were ready to attack that line itself, the enemy were equally ready to retire from it.

By the middle of March, the Division was desperately in need of rest. The camp near Ovillers, where they had been since they came out of the line, had nothing to recommend it. It was, in fact, in the battle area, as remote from all the decencies of civilization as the lines of shell-holes which had served them for trenches in February. When, about this time, a distinct movement of men and guns away from the Ancre front became noticeable, men's spirits rose. Movement on this scale, for heavy guns in particular were being withdrawn daily, heralded indeed a new offensive in some other part of the line, but such is the mood of fighting troops that any reversion, even for a matter of two or three weeks, to comfortable surroundings, any relief, however short, from the nervous strain of the battle zone, is a thing so welcome that ultimate consequences are not considered.

When the order came for the Division to move back to Hedauville on the 18th March and to march thence behind the lines to Busnes, north of Arras, there was nothing short of rejoicing. As the Division set out on its first day's march from Hedauville to the neighbourhood of Contray Château, the Battalion bands were heard for the first time since January at the head of the line of march, sick men began to recover their health, and tired men to feel once more that life was good.

The Division at this time was commanded by Major-General C. E. Lawrie, D.S.O., who had succeeded Major-General Shute on February 19th, and the 189th Brigade was much strengthened by the return to the Hood Battalion of Lt.-Colonel Freyberg. Major Freeland also had left the Drake Battalion to take up a staff appointment and had been succeeded by Commander Sterndale Bennett, D.S.O., R.N.V.R., who had served with such distinction as Adjutant to Commander King and Colonel Tetley in Gallipoli and France.

Going forward under these favourable auspices to the new adventure, the Naval Division had no reason now to fear for its future.

CHAPTER XIII

THE SPRING OFFENSIVE OF 1917

A S the Naval Division reached the front north of Arras, in the spring of 1917, popular expectation was at its highest point, since the days of the Marne. The great German retreat, of which we have told the beginnings was, by the end of March, drawing to its close, and uneducated opinion had not hesitated to draw conclusions the most favourable from its speed, its extent and the absence of effective opposition to the later British attacks. Military history will probably be less complacent in its judgment. It is at least not the whole explanation of our almost bloodless advance that we were reaping at long last the fruits of our victories on the Somme and the Ancre. It was inevitable, however, that this first substantial advance achieved by the British Armies since 1914 should be regarded by many even at the front as a favourable omen for the spring offensive, and that the troops concentrated behind our line should have been looking forward, if not to an equally bloodless, at any rate to an equally successful achievement.

Recent disclosures suggest that the optimism of the staffs was less definite and that no very great results were expected from the Arras offensive. This contrast between popular and informed opinion reflected justifiable doubts of the merits of new plans not wholly military in their inspiration. It must indeed be emphasized that, contributing to the allied defeats of this unfortunate year, there was, as far as the British Army was concerned, no weakening in the fighting spirit and no strategic misconception calculable in its results. There was perhaps an unfortunate lack of elasticity, of originality even, in our tactics on the Ancre, at Arras and at Passchendaele, but for the real cause of our failure throughout the year we must look elsewhere. The 1917 plan of campaign as designed by General Joffre and Sir Douglas Haig had been thrown contemptuously on one side,

and the rôle of the British Armies had been subordinated, with
the consent of the new British Government, to the requirements
of a great attack planned by General Joffre's successor, General
Nivelle.   This attack was fixed for May, 1917, and, to give it
the best possible chances of success, the Arras offensive had
to be pressed forward despite the new situation created by the
German retreat.   Later, it had to be continued in spite of the
strengthening of the German resistance following on the French
defeat.

It was in these circumstances and for these reasons that
the British Army, for all their optimism, were to find themselves
engaged once more in what, virtually, was a holding battle,
and not sweeping forward to a decisive trial of strength.   That
no better use was made of our superior resources and our
heightened *moral* at this critical date was nothing less than
a tragedy, but it was a tragedy for which, according to present
information, the British High Command was not even mainly
responsible.

The first attack on the Arras front was planned for April
9th, exactly a week before Nivelle's major operation which
was to open on April 16th.   The British front of attack ran
from Givenchy en Gohelle (a little to the north of Vimy Ridge)
to a point about eight miles south of Arras, the whole front
of attack being approximately fifteen miles.   Our lines and
those of the enemy opposite lay, as on the Somme, almost due
north and south.   The direction of our attack was thus from
west to east.

The enemy defences as far as Tilloy les Mofflaines, three
miles south of Arras, were of the type to which we were
accustomed on the Somme, and perhaps no stronger except on
the Vimy Ridge.   There were three (and in places four) prepared
positions, one behind the other, forming a defensive zone
of from four to five miles, and each position consisted, again
as on the Somme, of a complete trench system providing lateral
communication between endless " strong points," fortified
villages, and a number of more important miniature fortresses.

At Tilloy les Mofflaines the older positions joined the new
Hindenburg system.   This historic fortification consisted of
two continuous trenches, at a distance from each other of
approximately 1,000 yards, with a chain of machine-gun posts
in concrete emplacements, in rear.   The system had been built

German Barbed Wire at Beaucourt-sur-Ancre, November, 1916.

to meet the lessons of the Somme. It was, to all intents and purposes, proof against bombardment ; the machine guns were in ferro-concrete emplacements, and the bulk of the garrison lived beneath the support line in a continuous tunnel some forty feet below ground, with exits to the trench every thirty or forty yards. At the traverses of the support line were 9-inch trench mortars in concrete emplacements, supplied with ammunition from below ground. The whole system was so sited that every part of the front line was enfiladed from some other part of the system (a device first systematically employed by the Turks).

The attack north of the Vimy Ridge was to be made by the Ist Corps, and on the Vimy Ridge itself by the Canadian Corps, of the First Army. South of the Vimy positions, the XVIIth Corps of the Third Army was to carry on the attack on a front extending to the Scarpe (which flowed at right angles to our line a mile north of Arras). Below the river, the line of battle was carried south by the VIIth and VIth Corps. In general reserve was the XIIIth Corps, held behind the lines, on the north of the battle front, in the Bruay–Barlin area. If any exceptional success was achieved, this Corps was to go through the Ist Corps in the direction of Lens.

The Naval Division was curiously dispersed on the eve of the attack. Directly they came north from the Ancre, the Divisional Artillery, though badly in need of rest and without fresh horses (which, after the experiences of February and March, were essential), joined the 3rd Canadian Division and went into position behind Vimy Ridge. Almost at the same time the 188th Brigade was attached to the 5th Division of the Ist Corps and went into the line opposite Lievin. The balance of the Division—two infantry brigades without artillery —was attached to the XIIIth Corps. Not since the early days of Gallipoli, and then with greater justification, had the Division been subjected to such a dispersal. The incident is small but significant. The comparative immobility of our armies was never more noticeable than in the early days of the Arras offensive. It was not only the civilian soldier who had to unlearn the paralysing lessons of defensive war.

The attack opened at dawn on the 9th in threatening weather. Our maximum success was in the centre in front of Arras, where the XVIIth and VIIth Corps carried the first two positions on either bank of the Scarpe and effected a breach in the enemy's third position (their final objective) at Fampoux and Feuchy. On the left and right we were less successful. The Canadians could not at once complete the capture of the German positions on the Vimy Ridge (the enemy were holding out on the northern end of it), and the VIth Corps made little headway against the Hindenburg line in the south. The intention had been that, directly the enemy's third position had been carried on a sufficiently wide front, the reserves should go forward. As things were, the Germans clinging to the north of Vimy Ridge denied us that full protection for the left flank of our advance which the Canadian attack had been designed to secure, and the enemy's resistance at other points in his second position was still to be reckoned with. The gap through which our reserves must pass was in these circumstances judged to be too narrow. This decision, certainly defensible and perhaps inevitable, determined at this early stage the future of the battle. Once it was decided to renew the battle on the whole front and proceed methodically to the capture of the original objectives before attempting to go beyond them, the issue of the battle was left dependent on the fate of the impending French offensive. Without effective support on another front, the methods of the Somme could yield no immediately striking results.

The definitive nature of this decision was placed beyond doubt by the decision reached the next day to take the XIIIth Corps out of general reserve, and bring them down to relieve the left of the XVIIth Corps on the front south of Vimy. The Naval Division was of course affected by the change of plan, and moved south on the 12th, leaving behind the Anson and 1st Marine battalions still in the line in the Angres sector, and the Divisional artillery heavily engaged and earning warm tributes from the Canadian infantry.

Meanwhile there had been steady progress on the front. On April 10th and 11th, our capture of the first two enemy positions was completed except for three miles on the right, where we were still held up by the Hindenburg line. More notable, however, was our success in capturing Monchy le Preux, a strong position behind the German third line south-east of Feuchy. Many thought that this success, at least, should have made it possible to force our way beyond the enemy's defensive zone. The weather, however, had now broken. We had not sufficient troops available for an immediate renewal of the attack on a wide front, and our artillery found it difficult to get sufficiently far forward to give the infantry the necessary measure of support.

In these circumstances, April 12th also was devoted to clearing up the situation. The operations were again satisfactory within their limits. We extended our hold on the Hindenburg line in the south, and in the north we captured two important heights on either side of the Souchez river, which directly threatened the defences of Lens. The result was a further retirement by the enemy, first detected on the 5th Division front by patrols from the 1st R.M. Battalion, under 2nd Lieut. Kenny and 2nd Lieut. Marsh, who were the first to penetrate into Angres and Liévin. Colonel Cartwright moved his battalion forward to the abandoned positions on the night of the 13th–14th.

The first unit of the XIIIth Corps to go into the line was the 2nd Division on the right of the Canadians. On the night of the 14th–15th April, the Naval Division came in on the right of the 2nd Division and took over from the 34th Division the sector due west of Gavrelle, a village in the third German position which had so far resisted all attacks.

The new front was taken over by the 189th and 190th Brigades on the right and the left respectively. The brigades were covered by the 34th Divisional Artillery. The outposts on the 189th Brigade front were already within striking distance of the German trenches, and the first task of the Division was to bring the outposts of the left Brigade sector into line. The first attempt was made on the morning of the 15th by the 10th Dublin Fusiliers and the 4th Bedfords. The opposition had, however, been under-estimated, and rather heavy losses were incurred in an audacious attempt to advance our line in broad daylight across ground commanded by the enemy. On the night of the 16th–17th these battalions were relieved, and a more successful attempt was made by the H.A.C. and 7th Royal Fusiliers, who on this and the two following nights not only pushed their outposts forward but made them into a connected line, within two hundred yards of the German positions. The 189th Brigade on the left had done the same and the two brigades were now in touch.

Our position was still unenviable. The weather was bitterly cold, snow alternated with sleet, and the new front line lay on the forward slope of the hill looking down into the plain of Gavrelle. On the crest of this hill was the captured German switch line from Fampoux through Point du Jour (a miniature fortress now in the 189th Brigade sub-sector) to Farbus, and our support troops in this line and our reserves on the reverse slope (in what had been the second enemy position) were screened from all observation. The position of the front line troops was, however, deplorable. From the crest of the hill to the enemy's line in front of Gavrelle was a perfectly open belt of country, more than 3,500 yards in depth. Not only, therefore, our front line but our communications were at the mercy of an observant enemy who allowed no interval of immunity to ration and carrying parties, engineers, signallers and runners, on whose attentions the infantry in the trenches so implicitly rely.

Facing a beaten enemy, the position would have been hard enough, but the tidings from the south were not of victory. The great French offensive, the most audacious effort of the allied armies during the war (if we except the Gallipoli campaign) had failed. The reaction on the Arras offensive had been immediate. The enemy resistance was now vigorous, our patrols reported that their front line was held in force, and it became clear that no further success would attend the policy of " peaceful penetration " and local offensives. We must get on or get out. Strategy suggested that we should abandon the offensive in this now unprofitable field and turn our attention to Flanders. But the needs of the alliance and the fear of a German counter-stroke on the Aisne were considerations which could not, it was felt, be ignored. The German reserves must be held at whatever cost on our own front for some days at least, and there was nothing for it but a renewal of the frontal attack on the enemy positions, now once more continuous, formidable and extensive.

The attack was ordered for April the 23rd. The XVIIth Corps (37th Division) was to co-operate on the right flank, and the three objectives of the Naval Division were the enemy trenches in front of Gavrelle, a clearly defined road running roughly north and south through the centre of the village, and a line three to six hundred yards beyond Gavrelle in touch with the 37th Division, whose final objective was Greenland Hill. Further south, the attack was to be continued by the 51st Division of the XVIIth Corps, whose objective was Roeux, and by the VIth Corps, whose objectives included Cherisy, Guemappe and Infantry Hill east of Monchy. The Naval Division was to attack with the 190th Brigade on the left and the 189th Brigade on the right. After the capture of the first objective (the trench system in front of Gavrelle), the 189th Brigade only was to proceed to the further objectives, while the 190th Brigade was to form a defensive flank.

The battalions allocated to the attack were, from right to left, the Drake, Nelson, 7th Royal Fusiliers and 4th Bedfords, with the Hood Battalion in close support. This battalion had to follow behind the Nelson to the second objective and capture the third objective in conjunction with the Drake. The 1st H.A.C. were in support to the 190th Brigade, with orders to go forward as the situation might require. The carrying parties were found from the Hawke and 10th Dublin Fusiliers.* The Howe Battalion of the 188th Brigade was attached as a reserve battalion to the 189th Brigade, the remaining three battalions of the 188th Brigade being held in divisional reserve. Two sections from each of the 189th and 190th Machine-Gun Companies were to go forward with the infantry, and the remainder were to cover the advance with overhead fire. Medium and light trench mortars were to follow up the advance. The attack was to begin along the whole front at 4.45 a.m.

Two days before the attack, the news arrived that Colonel Freyberg had been appointed to command a brigade of the 58th (London) Division. The news afforded reason alike for pride and dismay. No promotion could have been more richly earned, but the gain to the Army was the Naval Division's loss. Who was to command the Hood Battalion in the forthcoming attack ? General Phillips decided at once that the appointment of an officer strange to the Division and battalion at this juncture might have unfortunate results, and, at his instance, an urgent request was sent to Commander Asquith (who had recovered from his wounds received on the Ancre and had been appointed to the Intelligence Staff of the Third Army) asking

* The Drake, Nelson, Hood and Hawke battalions made up the 189th Brigade (still under Brigadier-General Phillips), and the 7th Royal Fusiliers, the 4th Bedfords, the 1st H.A.C. and the 10th Dublin Fusiliers made up the 190th Brigade (now commanded by Brigadier-General H. W. E. Finch).

him to get permission to rejoin his battalion. The permission was granted, and, barely twenty-four hours before the attack opened, Commander Asquith arrived to take over the battalion which had such implicit confidence in his leading.

By midnight on April 22nd–23rd the troops were reported in position, but the Drake patrols discovered that the wire on their right front was mostly uncut, and a characteristic message back to Brigade Headquarters announcing the fact ended with the bland inquiry: "Is the attack cancelled?" The message, so say the official records, was repeated to the XIIIth Corps with the last sentence deleted. Commander Bennett lost no time, however, in issuing amended orders to his battalion. He decided to attack on a company front only, and to cover his right flank with an intensive Stokes mortar and machine-gun bombardment.

This manœuvre proved entirely successful, and the Nelson and Drake Battalions, advancing at zero under the creeping barrage, reached and captured the first objective in ten minutes with comparatively few casualties. Next to the Nelson, the Bedfords were equally successful, but on the left the 7th Fusiliers were held up by the enemy wire and by severe fire from the flank where the enemy were not attacked. This battalion secured, nevertheless, a small lodgment in the enemy front line.

The Hood Battalion had been ordered to wait till the Nelson Battalion reached its first objective before leaving the assembly position. This arrangement meant that it must almost certainly fall under the enemy's defensive barrage, and suffer ruinous loss. To avoid this, Commander Asquith, with great promptitude, decided to lead his battalion forward before the scheduled time. The Battalion reached the German lines on the heels of the Nelson Battalion.

The advance into the village began a quarter of an hour after the capture of the first objective. The Nelson and Drake Battalions led the attack with the Hood in support. The Bedfords and the Royal Fusiliers should have remained on the first objective, but actually not a few of the Bedfords followed the Hood, and in the smoke and confusion of the fighting through the village all units were considerably intermixed before the advance was brought to an end on the second objective (the street running north and south through the middle of the village) by the halt in our barrage.

Major-General C. E. Lawrie, C.B., C.M.G., D.S.O.

(From the portrait by Ambrose McEvoy in the possession of the Imperial War Museum.)

Following the practice usual in trench-to-trench attacks, this halt on the second objective was a prolonged one, designed to facilitate reorganization. In the vastly different conditions of village fighting the halt in our advance was of greater benefit to the enemy than to ourselves. Effective reorganization was indeed impossible. The continuous sniping and machine-gun fire from close quarters, the dense cloud of smoke and dust which clung round the ruined houses, the danger from falling masonry, as the buildings crumbled beneath the indiscriminate bombardment of the heavy artillery of two armies, made it impossible to find most of the men, or to concentrate and reorganize even those who could be found. The most that could be done was to keep the scattered groups where they were, and even this was difficult. It was largely due to the personal initiative and example of Commander Asquith and Commander Bennett that the advance was resumed successfully when the barrage lifted.

From the middle of the village to the final objective, the distance was nearly six hundred yards.

For the first 250 yards the advance continued through the debris of the village, and without much further loss the Hood and Drake Battalions reached the main Oppy–Gavrelle road, which here crossed our line of advance. Beyond this road was open country on the right, where the Drake Battalion were, except for a walled cemetery just across the road at their point of junction with the Hood, and an abandoned German trench running from that point to the right. On the left the position was very different. On the flank of the Hood Battalion the Fresny road crossed the Oppy road, and on the further side was a ridge commanding the exposed flank of our advance. The chief tactical feature here was the famous Gavrelle windmill on the highest point of the ridge. The capture of this windmill, which was essential if our advance was to be pressed any distance across the Oppy road, had been one of the tasks assigned to the Bedfords, who were to carry their defensive flank back from this point to our old front line. There was, however, no sign of the Bedfords, and the enemy, confident of the strength of his position, not only held the ridge beyond the Fresny road but clung tenaciously to two trenches immediately to the front of the Hood Battalion.

Partly as a result of the unfortunate pause on the second objective, partly as the result of casualties, mainly because the flanking movement by the 190th Brigade appeared to have failed, Commander Asquith thus found himself with a very small force in a perilous position, on the flank not only of the Division but of the whole attacking force.

To push forward at once would, in the circumstances, have been rash to the point of folly. Our barrage was as yet feeble (we were beyond the effective range of our field guns) and the men, tired in the unexpected heat, choked with dust, and not yet fully rested after four strenuous days in the line immediately before the attack, were strangely lethargic. The utmost that could be done was to safeguard the gains already won.

Our position was precarious. The enemy not only held the ridge over our flank and the trenches immediately to our left front, but on the right of the Hood, and on the Drake front they were holding an undefined line, not more than three hundred yards distant, from which all movements on our front could be observed. Even consolidation was extremely difficult. The first essential, if we were to hold our position, was to safeguard our left flank. To do so, however, without unnecessary calls on the troops was equally essential, if we were to win a tenable position before a counter-attack developed, and having won it, to hold it. Commander Asquith set out at once with Lieutenant Astbury (commanding "A" Company of Hood) to reconnoitre the most advanced enemy trench, some hundred and fifty yards to the east of the Oppy road on the left of his front. Towards the right of this trench ran a narrow ditch which he hoped might afford sufficient cover for a bombing party to get forward unobserved, and up this ditch Commander Asquith and his party crept forward. Unfortunately the ditch, after some fifty yards, became too shallow to afford any cover, and the party was observed by the enemy. It was here that Lieutenant Astbury was killed. Failing to find a way forward on this flank of the advanced position, Commander Asquith returned and took his party to the left flank up the Arras–Fresny road. A hundred yards up this road was the Mayor's house, assumed to be occupied by the enemy and certainly commanding our own positions. Commander Asquith made his way in, however, found the garrison asleep and made them prisoners. He at once installed a Lewis gun and some snipers in the top of the house, with orders to cover our flank and to keep down the fire of the enemy in their trenches to our front, while we pushed on the work of consolidation. In charge of this garrison of the house he placed Sub-Lieutenant Cooke, R.N.V.R., Brigade Intelligence Officer.

Returning to the main body of his battalion along the Oppy road, Commander Asquith found the position appreciably more insecure. His two senior Company Commanders (Lieutenant Morrison and Lieutenant Tamplin) had been killed, and the enemy shells falling along the line of the road with great regularity were causing continuous losses both in his own and in the Drake Battalion. He decided to send back Sub-Lieutenant Matcham* with one company to the German second line (west of Gavrelle), and sent orders to his adjutant (Lieutenant Hilton, R.N.V.R.) to hold that line at all costs. The remainder of his men (now no more than a hundred) Commander Asquith disposed in shell-holes, as far forward of the road as our hold on the Mayor's house rendered possible. The line was covered by machine guns which had been brought forward by Sub-Lieutenant Exton and Sub-Lieutenant Barrow Dowling.† The move forward, so essential to the safety of the garrison, was greatly assisted by the vigorous action of Lieutenant Cooke and the Lewis Gun crew in the Mayor's house, who came out and engaged the enemy advanced position at close quarters. Lieutenant Cooke and the whole gun's crew except Leading Seaman Charlton‡ were picked off by snipers and killed or mortally wounded in the course of the morning, but the gun remained in action and the enemy eventually withdrew. To this gallant action undertaken on the initiative of Lieutenant Cooke, and maintained by the men under his command, after he was killed, with the utmost fidelity, the delay on the part of the enemy in delivering their counter-stroke must be in no small part ascribed.

The delay was all-important to us. The position on our immediate front was indeed much clearer by 7 a.m. (the Mayor's house was captured at about 6.45 a.m.) and gradually improved, but there was for some hours no real protection against an enemy attack in force from the direction of the windmill. It was

---

* This officer for his work throughout these operations received the M.C.

† Both these officers received the M.C. for their skilful handling of these machine guns.

‡ L.S. Charlton was awarded the D.C.M.

this, indeed, together with the inadequacy of the available cover on the eastern outskirts of the village, and the uncertainty as to the general situation (for the view was bounded on the north by the high ground on which the windmill stood), which had led Commander Asquith to withdraw one company to the far side of the village. What had happened is easily explained.

The 4th Bedfords (on the left of the Nelson Battalion in the original advance) had, as we have seen, experienced no difficulty in reaching and capturing their portion of the first objective, but the 7th Royal Fusiliers on their left had been less successful. " A " Company of the H.A.C. in close support of the Fusiliers had done something to remedy the situation, and when they sent back a message asking for further assistance, Lt.-Colonel Osmond sent up " B " Company of the battalion just before 10 o'clock. By this time, however, the enemy had poured reinforcements over the railway line from the left, and the fighting had become a matter of bombing and counter-bombing in which the 190th Brigade was only slowly driving the enemy along his trenches to the left. The result of this check had been that only the right of the Bedfords had been able to advance in accordance with plan. This small party lost direction and followed the Hood Battalion to the middle of the village instead of making their way to the flank. There, suffering heavy casualties, the party remained till found by Lt.-Colonel Collins Wells, who at once went to the front to find out the situation.

At 9 a.m. Colonel Collins Wells met Commander Asquith at the cross roads near the Mayor's house, and at once arranged to take charge of the left flank with such men as he could find. It seemed clear, however, that any attempt to carry the windmill, though in accordance with the original plan, would fail, unless substantial forces could be brought together, and that if it failed the essential weakness of our position would become obvious and would invite retaliation. This part of the original scheme was therefore abandoned. Colonel Collins Wells could only muster some fifty or sixty men to cover the flank of the 189th Brigade, and two platoons of the Nelson Battalion were lent by Lt.-Colonel Lewis, at the instance of Commander Asquith, to strengthen the line. Not until noon was the position stable. At that time, however, thanks to the energetic but prudent steps taken by the Battalion

Commanders on the spot, we had secured a position which could be defended, and had still sufficient men with which to defend it.

We had done so only just in time. At 1 p.m. the enemy made their first counter-attack, principally on the Drake Battalion front. The attack was broken up by rifle and machine-gun fire and our artillery barrage, but the enemy throughout the afternoon kept throwing reinforcements forward into their improvised front line positions, and the slender garrison holding the village had its work cut out to keep the enemy from concentrating even nearer to our position. All the time the Hood and Drake were suffering severe and continuous casualties from the enemy's heavy artillery, in dealing with which our counter-battery organization proved for once ineffective.

The intricate and continuous fighting put a heavy strain on the Drake and Hood Battalions, and when, at 4.30 p.m., a belated order arrived for a further advance to the originally planned objective, Commander Asquith and Commander Bennett, after consultation with Lt.-Colonel Lewis, decided to ignore it. Their action was approved, and, on getting a full report, General Phillips decided to put in the Howe Battalion in the evening, and to withdraw the Hood to the old reserve position. The Nelson Battalion at the same time took over the left of our new line from the cross roads by the Mayor's house to the railway line, where they joined up with Colonel Collins Wells on the flank. The Drake Battalion remained in their original position on the right of the cemetery.

This relief was completed about 1 a.m., and the remainder of the night was unexpectedly quiet.

At dawn, a few of the enemy surrendered to our advanced posts, and a good many more from cellars in the village, where they had remained concealed during the fighting of the previous day.

During the morning of the 24th the enemy continued to mass opposite our right, and from noon onwards the heaviest shelling so far experienced by the Division developed along our whole front. At 2.55 p.m., this increased to a maximum intensity, and runners from the front line reported that the enemy were advancing. This was a serious and determined counter-attack, and between 3 p.m. and 4 p.m. the enemy barrage noticeably lifted to the old German front line and many attempts were made to enter our front line. The enemy were in strength, and though they suffered under our barrage,* their first wave being almost wiped out, they reached, and at one point on the Howe front actually penetrated, our posts. The prompt and energetic action of Commander Bennett and his officers on the Drake front, and of Lieutenant Mackinlay and Sub-Lieutenant Lawrie of the Howe Battalion prevented, however, any loss of ground and inflicted heavy casualties on the enemy. Only once did the enemy look like breaking through, at the junction of the Howe and Nelson Battalions, when the position was safeguarded by " A " Company of the former Battalion. By 5.40 p.m., the Battalion Commanders were able to report definitely that the attack had failed and that all our positions were held.

In the meantime the H.A.C., who had relieved the 7th Royal Fusiliers on the night of the 23rd–24th, had consolidated a flanking position, which followed approximately the line of the railway, and had established touch with the 2nd Division at 2 a.m. The position on the flank was now as originally intended, except that the original German first and second lines had only been carried to within fifty yards of the intended left limit of our advance, and that, on the flank of the advanced position, the Bedfords had, as we have seen, been forced to abandon all thought of capturing the windmill position. Much excellent work of an individual character was done by Lieutenant Pollard of the H.A.C. in these operations.

On the night of the 24th–25th the command of the battlefield passed to the 188th Brigade, and the Drake and Nelson Battalions marched back to rest. The 190th Brigade was withdrawn at the same time.

So ended a battle which, if it served no great strategic purpose, proved once more the superiority, man for man, of the English private to the German, and still more the superiority of the English regimental officer to the German professional soldier. The engagement was a remarkable vindication of the reputation which the Naval Division had brought with it from the Ancre, and of the policy and practice of its new commander. Village fighting by time-table was, indeed, a deserved

---

* The work of the Divisional Artillery on the 24th was described by the infantry as extremely fine.

failure; but the success, from first to last, was largely due to the initiative of the newly-appointed leaders of the Hood and Drake Battalions. This is not to say that the plans for the attack were bad. It was once more, however, made clear that the most careful preparations, the most precise instructions go only a small way, and sometimes no way at all, towards the final goal. But for the timely variations made in the original plans, and for the exceptional resolution of many individuals, the success would certainly not have been achieved. The chief honours went without a doubt to Commander Asquith and Commander Bennett, but their efforts were finely seconded by many other officers and men, among whom Lt.-Commander Funnell (commanding the 189th Machine-Gun Company), Surgeon McCracken, R.N.* (both of whom were awarded the D.S.O.), Lieut. Mackinlay of the Howe, Lieut. Hirschfield and Sub-Lieut. P. R. H. Fox of the Drake, Sub-Lieut. Grant Dalton of the Hood, and Sub-Lieut. Crosland Taylor of the Nelson (all of whom were awarded the M.C.), in addition to others previously mentioned, did especially well. The individual achievement of L.S. Charlton has already been told. Others who equally distinguished themselves were P.O. Ross, L.S. Gilgrass and A.B. Baldwin. A special feature of the later operations had been the fine work of the medium trench mortars under Captain Campbell.

In close fighting of this kind, with enemy resistance exceptionally vigorous, casualties† were necessarily heavy.

Among others, the commanding officer of the Hawke Battalion (Lieut.-Col. Whiteman‡), the Second-in-Command of the Nelson (Major Wilkie), three company commanders in the Hood, two in the Nelson and one in the Hawke had been killed. The total casualties were over fifteen hundred, and this price

---

* Surgeon McCracken was working under heavy fire in Gavrelle throughout the 23rd with the survivors of his own stretcher bearers and a party of German Red Cross men whom he had captured. He removed to a cellar for first aid and thence evacuated more than 120 officers and men who would otherwise, in all human probability, have been killed either during the long-continued bombardment or by the falling debris. He was recommended by Commander Asquith for the Victoria Cross.

† For a full list of the Naval and Marine officers killed in the two actions of Gavrelle see Appendix E (ii).

‡ The Hawke Battalion had been moved up to the first objective during the 23rd and had suffered rather heavy losses. Among the wounded was the adjutant, Lieutenant A. P. Herbert, R.N.V.R., whose wit was already famous outside the Naval Division.

had been paid for what was but little more than a moral victory. For more than a year, our line was to run where it had been drawn in front of Gavrelle in the early hours of April 23rd.

The battles of April 23rd and 24th south of the Naval Division had been equally severe, and not in all cases equally successful. The lesson of the battle was clear : the enemy was in adequate strength and fighting with an unimpaired *moral* along the whole length of the line, and the battle had unmistakably assumed the characteristics of a battle of attrition. These characteristics, favourable in 1916, when our strength was increasing while that of the enemy was diminishing, were unwelcome in the late spring of 1917, when the probability of the ultimate defection of Russia was growing every day, and when already German divisions were being transferred without any risk from the East to the West.

Nevertheless, the situation produced by the French failure in Champagne was such that it was decided to continue the battle, and to postpone still further the Flanders offensive.

The next attack was planned for the 28th, and was directed against the enemy positions on the front from Monchy le Preux to Arleux. The main objectives were the enemy position on the left of Gavrelle through Oppy to Arleux, and his positions on Greenland Hill on the right of Gavrelle (it was from behind this hill that the majority of the enemy counterattacks had developed during the fighting of the 23rd and 24th).

The attack on the left of the Division was to be carried out by the Canadian Corps and the 2nd Division (on Oppy). On the right, Greenland Hill was to be attacked by the XVIIth Corps. To assist these two operations, the 1st Marine Battalion was to attack on the flank of the 2nd Division, and the 2nd Marine Battalion had to push forward north-east of Gavrelle. These attacks were separate and independent operations, and to this the fact that they were not wholly successful should, perhaps, be ascribed.

The battle of the 23rd and 24th had left the Naval Division in a very pronounced salient. The left of their line, as consolidated by the 190th Brigade, ran at an angle of nearly sixty degrees from the line held by the 2nd Division, for a distance of nearly 2,000 yards to the Mayor's house. From there, the line ran more or less parallel to the 2nd Division line to the

junction with the 37th Division when it bent back behind
Greenland Hill. To push forward any distance from this line
till some progress had been made by divisions on the flanks
was clearly impossible, but it was hoped to secure the ridge
north-east of Gavrelle, and, in particular, the Windmill position.
This was the objective of Lt.-Colonel Hutchison's battalion.
The attack by the 1st Marines was to be launched from the
2nd Division front, the first objective being the enemy trenches,
to the left of those which had been the Naval Division's first
objective on the 23rd. The second and third objectives were
provided by enemy trenches further to the east, the capture
of which would, if all went well, bring the attacking troops
into rough alignment with those engaged north-east of Gavrelle.

The dangerous feature of the scheme was, of course, that
neither attack gave any effective support to the other, and
that in each case the battalions must find themselves, as they
advanced, with one flank in the air. Whether this would prove
fatal or not depended ultimately on the strength of the enemy
in the pocket between the two attacks.

The Brigade was in position for the operation at 2 a.m. on
the 28th, and, at 4.25, the advance began all along the line.
The 2nd Division (with parties of the 1st Marines on their
right) carried, it is believed, the whole of the German front line
system opposite them, but the main body of the 1st Marines
were held up on the German wire or killed in the German front
line trench, which was enfiladed from the right by the same
strong point on the railway which had held up the Fusiliers on
the 23rd. The position had perhaps been missed by the first
wave of the attack, but, more probably, the troops who attacked
it had been annihilated. At 8.50, a further attack on this
strong point was organized by 2nd Lieut. Hawes (commanding
" C " Company of the H.A.C.), which was successful, but there
had been some delay, and, by the time it was in our hands, the
Marines and the 2nd Division had fallen back. The enemy
advanced in their turn, and shortly before 10 a.m. re-entered
their original line. They then bombed the H.A.C. back from
the strong point along the first trench, captured by the Division
on the 23rd, for nearly a hundred yards, before a block could be
formed. The position by noon was that the attack had
definitely failed, and that we had lost some fifty yards of our
own line.

The 2nd Marines, fighting independently, had been more successful. Though it is improbable that our full objectives were ever secured, the most important of them, the Windmill position, was captured and held by a platoon under Lieutenant Newling, R.M.L.I. Especially vigorous counter-attacks were made against this position at 11.50 a.m., at 2 p.m. and again at 4 p.m., but each time they were beaten off, and, though the remainder of the 2nd Marines, after suffering disastrous losses, was forced to withdraw almost to our old line in front of the Mayor's house, the windmill was held. The with-drawal of the main body of the Marines took place at dusk on the 28th, and during the night of the 28th–29th, and was, in the circumstances, unavoidable. The casualties in the many counter-attacks had been heavy, and the enemy opposition entirely miscalculated. The withdrawal, none the less, nearly spelt disaster for the Anson Battalion on the right. " C " Company of this battalion had gone forward, immediately the first success had been gained, to consolidate a defensive flank for the new position. The company (commanded by Sub-Lieut. C. S. Walker) found themselves isolated on the morning of the 29th, and had to fight hard to extricate themselves. They did so, however, and brought back with them a party of 250 Germans, whom they drove before them into their original line. This ingenious operation was planned and carried out by P.O. Scott* and no more than fifteen men.

While these events were taking place, a new attack had been organized, by General Lawrie and the G.O.C. 2nd Division, on the objectives which the Northern attack had failed to hold. The Naval Division's share in this attack, which took place at 4 a.m. on the 29th, was carried out by a composite battalion of the 4th Bedfords and the 10th Dublin Fusiliers lent to the 188th Brigade for the purpose. The attack met with an early success, but, as before, the strong point on the railway was not at first carried, and, until the H.A.C. captured it for the second time, at 7.15 a.m. on the 29th, and sent a company across the railway to assist the composite battalion, the issue was very much in doubt. Even later in the morning, there were lodg-ments of the enemy not only in the line captured by the Naval Division but in that held by the 2nd Division, and not till 12.30 p.m., when the H.A.C. sent a bombing party right up

* This Petty Officer was awarded the D.C.M.

The Ruins of Gavrelle.

this line, which was very broken and ill-defined, was the position definitely reported clear of the enemy.*

The result of these operations was not wholly satisfactory. We had captured another stretch of the German trench system, which had once been their third and last line of defence, and, by the capture and defence of the windmill (a very brilliant operation), we had appreciably strengthened our hold on Gavrelle itself. Our losses, however, had been heavy and our gains not wholly proportionate ; while the blow to the enemy's *moral* dealt by an operation which fell so obviously short of what had been intended cannot have been severe. The plain fact is that the enemy's strength had been under-estimated, and that, in an attempt to engage the maximum number of the enemy, we had taken on more than we could deal with. Probably another Brigade, operating on the ground between the right boundary of the Northern attack and the left boundary of the Southern attack, would not have proved too strong for the task. As it was, despite the continued excellence of the artillery barrage, both Marine Battalions suffered disastrous losses. In the 1st Battalion the commanding officer, Lt.-Colonel Cartwright, D.S.O., R.M.L.I., was mortally wounded. Six other officers were killed, and the total casualties were more than 500. In the 2nd Battalion ten officers and more than 200 N.C.O.'s and men were killed, and the total casualties were nearly 600.†

* This successful issue was largely due to the remarkable personal gallantry and initiative of 2nd Lieut. A. O. Pollard, M.C., of the 1st H.A.C. This officer was awarded the Victoria Cross. The official account of his exploit (taken from the *Gazette*) is as follows :

2ND LIEUT. ALFRED OLIVER POLLARD, M.C., H.A.C.

" For most conspicuous bravery and determination. The troops of various units on the left of this officer's battalion had become disorganized owing to the heavy casualties from shell fire ; and a subsequent determined enemy attack with very strong forces caused further confusion and retirement, closely pressed by hostile forces.

" 2nd Lieut. Pollard at once realized the seriousness of the situation, and dashed up to stop the retirement. With only four men he started a counter-attack with bombs, and pressed it home till he had broken the enemy attack, regained all that had been lost and much ground in addition.

" The enemy retired in disorder, sustaining many casualties.

" By his force of will, dash and splendid example, coupled with an utter contempt of danger, this officer, who has already won the D.C.M. and M.C., infused courage into every man who saw him."

† As in the case of the engagement of the 23rd and 24th, the fighting on these two days was marked by many instances of personal gallantry. Lieutenant Newling's exploit has been mentioned. Captain Huskisson, R.M.L.I. (2nd R.M. Battalion), was awarded the M.C. for his services in the Southern attack,

On the night of April 29th, the Naval Division handed over to the 31st Division along the whole of their front and retired to the Roclincourt area for a brief period of rest and some very necessary reorganization. The total casualties of the Division, in the almost continuous fighting from April 15th to the time of their relief, were 170 officers and 3,624 other ranks, of whom upwards of 40 officers and 1,000 other ranks were killed. The majority of these losses, actually greater than those sustained in the more important and successful battle of the Ancre, were incurred during the operations of the 23rd–24th and 28th–29th, but the explanation is to be found not in any greater severity of the infantry battle but in the strength of the enemy's artillery, the activity of his aircraft and the exceptional length and exposed character of our communications. With the enemy in strength against us, the first necessity appeared to be to remedy this defect, and, on May 4th, the decision to discontinue the offensive was definitely reached.

The Naval Division was employed at once on the new Corps and Army defence lines ; the defence of the ruins of Gavrelle, captured and held with such determination, became in the changed situation of no more importance than that of any other outpost of a position dictated to us by an unbeaten enemy.

The successful German retreat to the Hindenburg line, the decision of the Allies to persist in the face of a changed situation in the ambitious offensive on the Aisne, the failure of that offensive, and, above all, the now definite breakdown of the Russian defensive, had turned the confidently awaited victory into an unexpected defeat.

The battle would be renewed elsewhere. But meanwhile, trench warfare re-established its reign, and on May 19th the Naval Division re-entered the line in relief of the 31st Division on its original front.

The trench strength of the three Brigades of the Division (with the pioneer battalion) numbered at this date 203 officers and almost exactly 6,000 men, an average of fifteen officers and 460 men for each battalion. Among the leaders of the

and Lieutenant Barclay, R.N.V.R. (188th M.G.C.), Lieutenant Goldingham, R.M., Lieutenant Westby, R.M. (190th M.G.C.) and 2nd Lieutenant Godfrey, R.M. (190th L.T.M. battery), won the same distinction. Sergeant Booth and Private G. Davies, R.M.L.I., were awarded the D.C.M.

Division, one or two important changes took place about this time. Lt.-Colonel·Hutchison, C.M.G., D.S.O., R.M.L.I., who had commanded the 2nd Marine Battalion with such distinction in Gallipoli, on the Ancre and in the recently concluded engagements, was appointed to command the 190th Brigade, being succeeded in the command of the 2nd R.M. Battalion by Lt.-Colonel Ozanne, D.S.O., R.M.L.I. Brigadier-General Phillips, D.S.O., who had commanded the 189th Brigade from the date of their arrival in France, was transferred to a higher appointment, and was succeeded by Brigadier-General Coleridge. Lt.-Colonel Cartwright, D.S.O., R.M.L.I., whose death in the action of the 29th was a great loss to his battalion and Corps, was succeeded by Lt.-Colonel Wainwright, R.M.L.I., and Commander Ramsay Fairfax, C.M.G., D.S.O., R.N.,[*] commanding the Howe Battalion, was invalided during May, and was succeeded by Commander C. S. West, D.S.O., R.N.V.R., who had gone out to Gallipoli as second in command of the unfortunate Collingwood Battalion. Another important change was effected when Commander B. H. Ellis, D.S.O., R.N.V.R., was appointed to command the Hawke Battalion in place of Lt.-Colonel Whiteman, who had been killed on April 23rd. Under this brilliant officer, the Hawke Battalion was to prove itself second to none in the Division. Lt.-Commander Lockwood, R.N.V.R., left the Hawke Battalion at this time to take up an appointment under the Admiralty, and was succeeded as second in command by Lt.-Commander Shelton, D.S.O., R.N.V.R. The Hood, Drake and Nelson Battalions remained under Commander Asquith, Commander Sterndale Bennett and Colonel Lewis.

So organized, so commanded, the Division entered on the last prolonged period of trench warfare which they were destined to enjoy. The conditions of the warfare a twelve-month earlier have been already described, and in this curious anti-climax of the summer of 1917, the conditions reverted almost to those prevailing before the opening of the Somme campaign. Noticeable, however, was the still greater depth of the defences, and the greater thoroughness of the arrangements for meeting attack, arrangements which entailed heavy and systematic work for any first-line troops who might be sent to rest behind the lines. In the front line too the work was

* This officer returned to France in command of a battalion of tanks.

arduous, it being necessary at once to consolidate and fortify the rough line won from the enemy in the April fighting. At no point on the divisional sector had we fully gained the objectives of the second battle, and the task was therefore not easy, but the success of the 2nd R.M. Battalion in winning and holding the Windmill position, and the no less valuable and more spectacular performance of the H.A.C. in the same engagement in clearing the enemy from their posts on the north-western flank of the Gavrelle position, made the task possible. By the end of the Division's first tour in the line, which lasted till June 10th, the defences of what remained an awkward salient had been sufficiently completed to win a compliment from Lieut.-General Congreve, V.C., then commanding the XIIIth Corps. On their relief by the 31st Division, the Naval Division returned to work on the Corps and Army lines of defence and on the improvement of rearward communications.

Such was the position when, on the morning of June 12th, the bombardment to the north reached its climax, and the reverberation of the explosion of fifty mines told of the opening of the Flanders offensive.

CHAPTER XIV

THE news of the splendid victory of Messines reached the Naval Division while they were still behind the lines, but it brought them no release from the prosaic tasks in which they were employed. It added rather to their burden.

With the object of holding the enemy in strength on the front north of Arras while the sequel to Messines was being staged, an attack was to be made on the front from Gavrelle to Oppy by the 5th and 31st Divisions on June 28th. For the preparatory work of digging communication trenches down the long forward slope which led from the Army line of resistance (the old Fampoux–Farbus switch) to the forward system the Naval Division infantry and engineers were responsible. Meanwhile the 63rd Divisional Artillery remained in the line and took their full share of the artillery preparation. The attack was in great measure successful, and gave us the enemy's first line from the left of Gavrelle to Oppy Wood, forcing him back to the village of Oppy itself and to an ill-defined secondary position between Oppy and Gavrelle.

It was now that the importance of the successes achieved by the 2nd R.M. Battalion and the H.A.C. on April 28th became evident, for as long as we held the high ground north of Gavrelle, which we won in that engagement, the enemy could not counter-attack from Oppy with any hope of success. The line won on June 28th was thus easily consolidated, and the position was appreciably stronger when the Naval Division took over, on July 4th and 5th, not only their old sector (from the 31st Division) but (from the 5th Division) the brigade sector immediately to the left of it. This new line was divided into two brigade sectors, the left to be held by the 189th Brigade with three battalions in the line, and the right (Gavrelle) sector by the 188th Brigade on a two-battalion front. To the

189th Brigade were attached the 7th Royal Fusiliers and the 4th Bedfords. The 190th Brigade as a fighting organization was temporarily out of action, for the 10th Dublins had left the Division after the Messines Battle to provide reinforcements for the 16th (Irish) Division, and the Artists' Rifles, who had arrived on the 2nd July to take the place of the H.A.C., were short of training. The reorganized Brigade was to be completed by the 5th King's Shropshire Light Infantry, but this battalion did not arrive till July 20th, and special arrangements had even then to be made to give the men leave. They had had none since mobilization.

The Flanders offensive was still unaccountably delayed, and the XIIIth Corps was required to keep the enemy in expectation of a further attack on Oppy. Their operations thus took a form with which the Division had become very familiar in the autumn of 1915 in Gallipoli, the orders being to push out the line continuously, by the familiar methods of establishing posts and consolidating sapheads in front of the line, and then digging in at night.

The Divisional front was shortened after a week, when the 31st Division returned to the left of the Corps front, and the 5th Division again took over the sub-sector handed over by them on July 4th. All three Divisions of the Corps were now in the line, and the confidence bred of a prolonged occupation of the same front enabled the Naval Division to carry out a number of minor operations with complete success. On the night of July 14th–15th, a new front line was dug in Oppy Wood by the Hawke and Hood Battalions and in front of the windmill by the 2nd R.M. Battalion, while on July 20th a very successful raid was carried out on Gavrelle Trench by the Howe Battalion. The raid was carefully planned and rehearsed under the supervision of Commander C. S. West, and commanded by Lieut. W. Marlow, R.N.V.R. Only in one place did the enemy put up a vigorous resistance, and our reported losses (seven men killed and one officer and 25 men wounded) were sustained mostly before and after the operation. The enemy losses in killed and prisoners alone exceeded our total casualties. The raid had found the enemy generally listless and ill-prepared. Their trenches were ill-constructed and badly tended, while many of the garrison were caught without arms or equipment.

On July 23rd, the 189th Brigade were relieved by the 190th Brigade, and on July 30th they, in turn, relieved the 188th Brigade; the object of this triangular arrangement, which was repeated at intervals throughout the following weeks, was to keep the 188th Brigade in the Gavrelle sector whenever they were in the line. It was important to garrison the line with troops thoroughly familiar with it, as the front was very thinly held and there were few reserves. Our mastery of no man's land could also be better maintained.

Towards the end of the month, the Division was asked urgently to secure an identification of the enemy opposite them, and on the night of 30th–31st an enemy post on the left Brigade front was rushed by a battalion of the 189th Brigade, but found to be abandoned. Fighting patrols could do no better; the enemy remained strictly on the defensive, and it was necessary to organize a minor raid, which was carried out with complete success by thirty men of the Anson Battalion, under Sub-Lieut. Russell* on September 7th.

Throughout this time the activities of the infantry had been greatly assisted by the co-operation of the Divisional Artillery and the machine-gun companies. A feature of their operations was a series of hurricane bombardments, keeping the enemy in constant anticipation of attack and destroying his trenches. The Corps Heavy Artillery had by now gone north, and to do their work two batteries of the 223rd Brigade (Lt.-Colonel the Rev. W. E. Wingfield, D.S.O.) were sent some two thousand yards forward. For every bombardment, and, indeed, for every other offensive activity, the enemy retaliated on our position round the windmill, and still more on the artillery themselves. The infantry avoided serious loss by the method, familiar from Gallipoli days, of pushing forward our line too near to that of the enemy for them to bombard it effectively. The artillery, however, had no remedy except a constant change of gun positions, and after a time the most forward sections, only maintained for so long by a miracle, had to be withdrawn.

An interesting and fruitful experiment was made at this time in the organization of the machine-gun companies (now increased to four). These were now grouped for tactical

* In recognition of his fine leadership this officer was awarded the Military Cross.

purposes as a Divisional unit, and the organization subsequently adopted throughout the Army was thus anticipated by some months. Lt.-Colonel Macready, who had commanded the 190th (Marine) Machine-Gun Company with distinction since December, 1916, was the first Divisional machine-gun officer.* Hitherto, the Army organization had operated through too many different administrative units, a Division being thus deprived of the cohesion which a war of movement would demand. The system of brigade groups, which was adopted whenever the Division had to move behind the lines, met the difficulty administratively, but only by ignoring the tactical requirements. The Divisional grouping of the machine-gun companies, decided on by Major-General Lawrie in September, 1917, was a timely recognition of the need for a more scientific organization.

Meanwhile negligible progress only had been made with the Flanders offensive. The initial success at Messines had been followed by a delay of six weeks, partly explained by difficulties among the Allies. At last, on July 3rd, the offensive had been resumed against the front east and north-east of Ypres, the objective being the famous Passchendaele ridge. By the middle of September we had not reached our objective, and further progress was getting hourly more difficult as our reserves became exhausted, the continuing bad weather and the ordinary wear and tear of battle and bombardment made our communications more difficult, and the ground to be covered by the advancing infantry became more impossible. On September 20th we did indeed make an appreciable advance, which was followed up on the 22nd, but if the results were sufficient, in the opinion of Sir Douglas Haig, to warrant the continuance of the offensive, they made it also clear that fresh divisions must be brought into the battle. One of the fresh divisions was the Naval Division, who were relieved by the 47th Division on September 24th–25th, and entrained for Cassel† and the neighbouring villages on October 2nd.

* Just before this the two R.N.V.R. Machine-Gun Companies (188th and 189th) were disbanded for lack of reinforcements and their places taken by the 223rd and 224th Companies of the Machine-Gun Corps under Captain Gants and Captain J. O. Dodge, D.S.C. (who had won the D.S.C. serving with the Hood Battalion in Gallipoli). The officers of the disbanded companies returned to the base, but all in time succeeded in rejoining the Naval Division.

† The scene of their earliest activities under General Paris in 1914.

For a brief moment the front was quiet, but the final
collapse of Russia and the knowledge that a German offensive
against Italy was impending made it necessary to continue our
pressure on the Western front, and the difficulty of changing
the direction of our attack is the justification for the tragic
scenes which accompanied the remaining stages of the offensive.
History may judge that what appeared to be necessary was
not really so, and that what was admittedly difficult was not
impossible.   Nevertheless, the official military view that the
decision to continue our advance along the Passchendaele
ridge throughout October and November was inevitable, must
be given due consideration.

The situation on the evening of October 4th was a simple
one.   Before the battle opened, the allied line from the northern
arm of the Ypres salient ran almost due north to Nieuport,
and the German line was parallel to our own.   Both lines were
drawn across flat country intersected with innumerable dykes
and small streams, uniformly marshy and liable to flooding in
the event of heavy rains.   Behind our lines the country was
equally flat, but behind the enemy's front was the Passchendaele ridge, not parallel to their line but running north-
east from a point on their line opposite Ypres.   This ridge had
thus menaced the flank of any advance from our line north of
Ypres, while it afforded corresponding protection to any
German attack on that line.   Our advances since July had
been directed along it, our line to the north being brought
forward as far as possible in sympathy.   By October 4th,
the main advance had reached a point 9,000 yards along
the ridge, and from here to the north our line was bent back
roughly north-west.   Granted that, for reasons of high policy,
we had to continue our pressure on this front, it was clear that
a further advance along the ridge offered the best prospect of
embarrassing the enemy, while at the same time improving our
own defensive position.   To secure the whole ridge, we had to
advance along it for another four thousand yards, and to the
north of it as far as was necessary to secure a tenable line.
The most difficult task was the advance across the western
slopes of the ridge and the particularly marshy country at the
bottom of those slopes.   Unless, however, we could press
forward here, any advance along the ridge itself must have
created an almost impossible salient.   On the ridge and down

the western slopes lay the Canadian Corps. In the marshes at the foot lay the XVIIIth Corps, to which the Naval Division was attached. It was to assist the XVIIIth Corps in the advance necessary to cover the flank of the Canadian Corps that the Naval Division had come north, and for this advance they were now to prepare.

The sector allocated to the Division was on the flank of the Canadian Corps, where our front line of posts ran north-west from Wallemolen Cemetery to the Lekkebokkerbeek. This front was held on October 4th by the 9th Division, and small advances were made by them on October 9th and 11th. The depth of the advance of the 9th Division was, however, less than that achieved on the flanks, and on the evening of October 11th the 9th Division line formed a rather pronounced re-entrant, our line, across the Passchendaele ridge on the right and towards Poelcapelle on the left, having gone forward without any corresponding gain in the centre. A further effort here was judged imperative, and the Naval Division was asked accordingly to arrange for three successive attacks, each by one brigade. The first attack was to be made on October 26th by the 188th Brigade, and the second on October 30th by the 190th Brigade; the Division was to relieve the 9th Division on the front of attack at such date, prior to the first attack, as they chose.

It is safe to say that the Division was never confronted with a task which, on the lines laid down for them, was more impossible of fulfilment. Flanders mud had become pro-verbial, and even under ordinary conditions exposed the troops in the front system to exceptional hardships. Front line and communication trenches were non-existent. The forward system consisted of posts isolated from each other by a sea of mud, and the support line of another line of posts, the elements of a trench, or, more probably, of a ruined farm-house and outbuildings where a company or so could be con-centrated. These forward positions were scattered in depth over a wide area, and each was dependent on itself for pro-tection. The enemy posts lay often between our own, and every ration and water party had to be prepared to fight its way forward. Communication with the reserve positions was equally dangerous, if less difficult. All supplies and reinforce-ments had to be brought up on duckboard tracks, which with every advance stretched further and further forward. Off these tracks progress was impossible, yet the reliance placed on them was an evil necessity ; they marked to the enemy, as to ourselves, our line of supply, and, though used only at night, they were a perilous substitute for the old communication trench. From an accurate bombardment of these tracks no party using them could escape. To turn aside by so much as a yard was to plunge waist-deep in a sea of mud, where the bodies of the dead were rotting unburied as in the primeval slime.

The enemy positions were equally precarious, and we know from General Ludendorff's memoirs how bitter their experiences were. The fact remains that the advantage lay overwhelmingly with the defence. No comparable strain fell on the enemy in these operations. Their lot was to live in shell-holes or in verminous ruins, inadequately clothed and fed, and to open fire periodically on an enemy vainly endeavouring to move towards them across a sea of mud. The lot of our troops was to suffer, under conditions hardly less revolting, the risks of a continuous offensive across ground which made our barrage virtually useless as a protection against the enemy's machine guns. Our barrage was slowed down, and the most careful preparations were made whereby every known enemy post, in the area to be crossed, was attacked by a separate and self-supporting unit with no other objective. The mobility, however, of the enemy posts, which were seldom where they were expected to be, the impossibility of keeping down by any barrage the enemy fire from positions scattered haphazard over perfectly level country to a depth of a thousand yards, and the difficulty of keeping up with our barrage, in those exceptional cases where everything else proceeded in accordance with plan, had in all the previous attacks neutralized, to a very great extent, every modification of our tactics.

Training behind the line, learning from carefully-constructed models the supposed location of every enemy post and trench on their prospective front, the 188th Brigade was looking forward with confidence to the impending battle. The Divisional Artillery, however, in the famous St. Julien "triangle," and the 189th Brigade,* who had been working

* The Brigade, while engaged on this work, had suffered rather heavily. Among those killed were Sub-Lieut. S. G. James and Sub-Lieut. F. J. Newell, both of the Hood Battalion.

on forward communications since October 10th, knew better. Every gun position, every shell-hole, was under fire, and the physical impossibility of a rapid advance made any very substantial success unattainable.

The chief tactical features on the intended front of attack were the Paddebeek, a flooded streamlet running parallel to our front at a distance of some five hundred yards, and some higher ground a thousand yards to the right front, on which stood the ruins known as Tournant Farm. This side of the Paddebeek, the main enemy posts were believed to be in five groups of ruins and pill-boxes known as Berks Houses, Bray Farm, Banff House, Sourd Farm and Varlet Farm, and in an isolated trench, near our junction with the Canadians, known as Source Trench. Across the stream to our right were Source Farm and Tournant Farm, and on the right a number of isolated pill-boxes and fortified shell-holes. The first objective of the 188th Brigade included all the enemy positions this side of the Paddebeek except Sourd Farm ; the second objective comprised the remaining position, as far as a line drawn north-west through Tournant Farm. The first objective was to be attacked by the Anson Battalion on the right and the 1st R.M. Battalion on the left. Through these battalions, the Howe and the 2nd R.M. Battalions were to advance across the Paddebeek to the second objective. The attack was fixed for dawn on the 26th.

General Prentice decided to take over the front line on the night of the 24th–25th, thus giving his battalions a day to study, at first hand, the ground over which they had to advance. The time was, of course, too short, but this was only another instance of the impossibility of the conditions ; no troops could stay longer in the line and be fit for an advance.

The morning artillery barrage had become a matter of habit for both armies, and this routine had the advantage that we could make a good guess where the German counter-barrage would fall and could fix our assembly positions accordingly. When, however, we intended a serious attack the addition of the machine-gun barrage relieved the enemy of any uncertainty as to our intentions, and there could thus be no question of surprise.

By 2 a.m. on the morning of the 26th, all battalions were

in position. The inevitable rain had begun at midnight and continued steadily, and when the time for the advance was notified to the enemy in the usual manner the ground was as impassable as had been expected.

The advance was on a very wide front, the 1st Marines having a frontage of nearly nine, and the Anson of nearly six, hundred yards. Each battalion adopted much the same formation : two thin lines of skirmishers went in front and behind them were small columns of sections or platoons, according to the objective to which each was detailed. Two platoons from each battalion were required for duty as stretcher-bearers, the normal complement being inadequate to the nature of the fighting.

At 5.45, in heavy rain, the advance began. Our bombardment of the enemy positions during the previous forty-eight hours had turned the ground over which our troops had to advance into a mass of shell-holes, flooded to a depth of several feet ; between them, a path had to be picked over ground only less impassable. Despite these difficulties, the first waves kept fairly well up to the barrage, and especially on the left (the 1st Marine Battalion) substantial gains were recorded. Banff House (the last objective of the 1st Marine Battalion) was reported at 7.20 a.m. as having been captured by Lieutenant Careless, R.M., and the Anson Battalion were reported in Varlet Farm.* This last report was in fact incorrect, although, unknown to their battalion Headquarters, Sub-Lieut. Stevenson and a platoon of the Anson Battalion had occupied another group of ruins two hundred yards to the east. These successes were, however, no indication of the nature of the battle. The enemy machine-gun fire from across the Paddebeek was extremely severe, and almost all the Company Commanders of the attacking battalions had become casualties. They were but small parties who had reached such of the enemy posts as had fallen, and there were other posts, notably in the centre of the German outpost position, which we had never reached. Here was the unsolved tactical problem. The rigidity of our attacking formation was opposed to a fluid defence. The troops who had reached their

---

* Varlet Farm itself was practically invisible and was only identified at the close of the operations. It was never occupied, either by the enemy or by the Anson Battalion.

objectives had, according to explicit orders, accomplished their task. They expected to be isolated, and had no means of knowing, under conditions which made swift movement of patrols impossible, whether the parties detailed to capture the other posts had succeeded. Company and Battalion reserves were in a better position, but, by the time it was clear that the enemy at a given point was still in possession, and a fresh movement had been organized, we had lost the barrage. And so by 8 a.m. the attack in the centre had died down, and only on the flanks did the Howe and 2nd Marine Battalions effect an advance towards the second objective.

One of the finest exploits of this second stage of the attack was the crossing of the Paddebeek, by Captain Ligertwood's " A " Company of the 2nd Marines. The platoons of this company had gone into action under their own flags, strips of red canvas nailed to a stick cut from the woods where the company had done their training, solemnly blessed by the Battalion Chaplain, Father Davey, and taken into action with honour and reverence. These flags were carried through the battle. Captain Ligertwood, three times wounded, led his company to within sight of their goal, when he fell mortally wounded, to rise only once to direct his men to their objective. But on this front and at this time success was denied even to the bravest. This company, staying on their objective throughout the entire day, were powerless to lift a finger to assist the main battle still being fought on the first objective where the enemy centre held their ground.

So merciless was the position in the centre at 8 a.m. that Commander Asquith, watching the attack from our old front line, ordered up two companies of his battalion, which had been attached for these operations to General Prentice's 188th Brigade as a " counter-attack " battalion. Their function was to be in a position to deal effectively and without delay with any counter-attack which the enemy might deliver against the (possibly disorganized) assaulting troops. A little later, a fine reconnaissance by Lieutenant Barclay, R.N.V.R., showed that the enemy were still holding their ground, and threatening to get between our advanced troops and our old line, and a third company was ordered up at 8.30 a.m. When no reports came back from the 188th Brigade, and the Canadians reported that they were not in touch on their left

Commander Asquith and Lieutenant Garnham, R.F.A. (forward
observation officer), with one man went forward to investigate.
Now for the first time the presence of Sub-Lieut. Stevenson's
party near Varlet Farm was discovered, and the enemy who
were closing in on the party were dispersed. Stevenson was
promised relief, and Commander Asquith and his party, going
on to get in touch with the Howe and Anson on the right,
were able to inform them of the position and to establish touch
between them and the Canadians. This reconnaissance was a
decisive incident in the day's fighting, for it enabled our
artillery to safeguard the line won, and prevented any incursion on the flank of the Canadians, who were thus able to make
a more appreciable advance. Plain facts are often obscured
by technical terms. A reconnaissance on this front meant
a two hours' walk in full view of the enemy under heavy fire,
and such a prosaic description of the achievement of these
officers, with their solitary rifleman, gives a truer idea of the
quality of mind and spirit necessary to support it, than do the
more hackneyed phrases of the official reports.

No further advance was attempted in the afternoon of
the 26th. To renew the attack it would have been necessary
to bring up fresh troops, which could only be done by night,
or to throw once more against the enemy the disorganized and
cruelly depleted units clinging to their slender gains. This
would have meant risking the little that we had won. At
5 p.m. the wisdom of the decision was seen, for the enemy
counter-attacked in force on the right, and only the prompt
intervention of " C " Company of the Hood Battalion under
Lieutenant Arblaster averted a retreat. As dusk fell Commander Asquith moved up his whole Battalion, which had
suffered heavy casualties during the day, to relieve the Anson
and Howe Battalions, and the Hawke Battalion was ordered
to relieve the two Marine Battalions. The situation on the
left flank was by now less satisfactory. The party which
had crossed the Paddebeek with such gallantry had been
forced to retire, being almost surrounded and without ammunition or water, and in their retirement had carried with them the
garrisons of Banff House, Bray Farm and Berks Houses.
Commander Ellis, however, quickly restored the position
this side of the Paddebeek, and " C " Company of the Hawke
Battalion (Lieutenant Bartholomew, R.N.V.R.) recaptured all

three positions and established touch with the Hood Battalion. It was only, however, thanks to another exploit by Commander Asquith that this Battalion had established itself with equal security. Scouts sent forward to see if Lieut. Stevenson was still holding out, reported that they had been fired on from the position formerly held by him. If so, our front must in the long run have been untenable, but Commander Asquith* was determined to investigate the situation. He made his way personally to the position and found there Sub-Lieut. Stevenson and seven men, all that were left of the party which had rushed the post in the first minutes of the attack. He then went back and led up the relieving platoon.

This incident, and the temporary confusion on the left flank, were characteristic of the prevailing conditions. The policy of delimiting the objectives deprived the attack of all cohesion, and produced a sense of isolation. Many men were lost through mistaking enemy posts for our own; only investigation could show the truth; many, it is feared, reached their objective and were cut off because no one knew of their success. Only under cover of darkness could communications, inevitably severed in a daylight advance against irregular and discontinuous defences, be re-established. Yet without the maintenance of communications enabling local success to be exploited, nothing could in the prevailing conditions enable us to reach and consolidate our objectives.

Nevertheless, the line finally won by the relieving battalions comprised at least five strongly fortified enemy posts and represented an advance of from three to four hundred yards from our old front; and this in spite of the fact that, in the words of Sir Hubert Gough, "no troops could have had to face worse conditions." Success achieved under such conditions had to be bought dearly, and the four assaulting battalions lost heavily in officers and men. Captain Pipe, 2nd Lieut. F. C. Balcombe, 2nd Lieut. D. J. Aldridge of the 1st Marines, Captain Edwards, Captain Ligertwood and 2nd Lieut. T. W. Brogan of the 2nd Marines, Lieutenant F. C. Mundy, M.C., R.N.V.R., Sub-Lieut. W. Fraser and Sub-Lieut.

---

* For his fine exploits on this critical day Commander Asquith received a second bar to his D.S.O. Lieutenant Bartholomew (Hawke Battalion) was awarded the M.C. Others who won this distinction in the course of the Passchendaele operations were Surgeon R. G. Morgan, R.N., Sub-Lieut. N. de B. Browning, Sub-Lieut. W. H. Clarkson, Sub-Lieut. C. M. Perry, Sub-Lieut. E. A. Elson, Sub-Lieut. K. I. M. Fegan, and Sub-Lieut. K. M. Evans.

J. S. Russell of the Anson, Lieutenant F. L. H. Jackson, R.N.V.R., Sub-Lieut. W. Douglas, Sub-Lieut. W. J. Shaw, Sub-Lieut. E. C. Bonnet and Sub-Lieut. G. H. Hinde of the Howe, were killed on the morning of this attack. Very many more officers were wounded, among them Father Davey, the Roman Catholic Chaplain of the 188th Brigade, Surgeon McBean Ross,* the Medical Officer of the 2nd Marine Battalion (who happily recovered to write a graphic volume of reminiscences of the Naval Division), and Lieutenant Newling, the hero of the Gavrelle " Windmill " attack. The losses in N.C.O.'s and men were equally severe, averaging more than five hundred a battalion in the 188th Brigade.

The Hood Battalion was relieved on the night of the 27th–28th by the Nelson Battalion,† but, before the change was over, the Hood patrols had got in touch with yet another party of the Anson, who had been isolated for more than thirty-six hours in front of the line taken by the Hood the previous evening. These men were relieved and the new posts handed over to the Nelson Battalion. A notable feature of almost forty-eight hours' continuous fighting by the Hood Battalion had been the work of Surgeon McCracken, D.S.O.,‡ who saved the lives of very many wounded, lying out exposed to view on the forward slopes of our position under aimed fire from the Passchendaele ridge. From here the enemy had direct close-range observation of all that was happening on the scene of the attack of the 26th (and of the next attack also). The German field guns were indeed firing over open sights at every sign of movement.

Notwithstanding the disastrous losses of the 26th, it was felt impossible to modify our plans for the next attack, for which the 190th Brigade had been training for the past three weeks. This attack was launched accordingly at 5.50 a.m. on October 30th, virtually against the same objectives as those assigned to the 188th Brigade. Fate, however, which had been hard before, was this time harder, for the enemy unexpectedly

---

* Surgeon Ross was awarded a bar to his M.C. for his services on this occasion.

† It was during this tour in the line that Sub-Lieut. W. E. Jerring, R.N.V.R., of the Nelson Battalion, was killed.

‡ Surgeon McCracken had been with the Hood since the start of the Gallipoli campaign, and his gallantry was a tradition of the battalion. For his services on this occasion he received a bar to his D.S.O.

altered their barrage line on the morning of the battle, and our troops suffered cruel losses in the opening seconds of the attack. When, after the initial disaster, the assaulting battalions were reorganized, they had lost the barrage.

On the left of the front, the Artists' Rifles, despite cruel losses, advanced on Source Trench, but were held up in front of it, knee-deep in mud, by close range machine guns. Here one company of this fine battalion was annihilated. In the centre, and on the left, the 7th Fusiliers and the 4th Bedfords could do no better; movement was in many places literally impossible: in all, it was futile. The enemy's machine guns merely picked off the infantry one by one. Through the day the Brigade had a hard struggle to hold their own, but they gave little ground, and by holding on enabled the reserve battalion, the 5th K.S.L.I., fighting their first battle in France, to perform valuable work which redeemed the day from complete failure. The object of the attack, like that of those that preceded and followed it, was primarily to protect the Canadian flank. By some miracle of endurance and courage, a small party of Canadians had reached the right of Source Farm, a German strong point some four hundred yards east of Source Trench. If this gain was to be held, the Canadians had to be reinforced and their flank secured. When the Artists had done all that was possible by frontal attack, the Division was asked early in the afternoon to try an attack from the right. Two companies of the Shropshires were at once sent off through the Canadian lines, and were at one time reported to have captured the trench: this was not the case. They had, however, joined up with a third company of their battalion which had gone to reinforce the Canadians* at Source Farm, and, at dusk, established a defensive flank from that point to the Artists' right at Varlet Farm.

The total casualties of the Division in their two advances had been 32 officers and 954 men killed or missing, and 83 officers and 2,057 men wounded; and their task was still uncompleted. Without some further advance on their front, the pressure of the Canadians on the Passchendaele ridge could not be maintained. In these circumstances, it was the turn of the 189th Brigade, who had relieved the 190th Brigade on

---

* What had once been a company in this position consisted at the end of the day of one officer and eight men.

the night of the 30th–31st, to make a third attempt to get across the Paddebeek.

This portion of the front had now been taken over by the First Army, who gave instructions that the crossing was to be secured under divisional arrangements before November 6th.

The operations of the next four days and nights, which carried the Division's task almost to completion at a negligible cost, and resulted in gains greater than had been achieved in the two previous attacks, form a dramatic chapter in the history of the Naval Division. For the genesis of these operations we must go back to that tragic morning of October 26th, when the Hood Battalion, from our old front line, watched the pitiful slaughter of the men of the 188th Brigade struggling vainly in the mud to find each other and their objectives. Commander Asquith had watched one earlier attack made over practically the same ground with the same disastrous result, and his conclusion, after seeing and experiencing himself the conditions of fighting, was definite. Absolute mobility, prior reconnaissance, surprise, and personal leading by senior officers were, he was convinced (and so suggested in his official report), the indispensable elements of success against the enemy's new system. These conditions could not be secured so long as the normal tactics of attack at dawn under a barrage were persisted in. The ease with which, on the occasion of the relief of the 188th Brigade on the evening of the 26th, the line handed over had been secured and extended, suggested, however, that night operations might provide a satisfactory solution.

The consent of the XVIIIth Corps to an experiment in the new tactics was readily given.

The 189th Brigade moved into the line, in relief of the 190th Brigade, on the night of October 31st, with the Nelson Battalion on the right and the Hawke on the left. The Hawke had the same experience as on the relief of the 188th Brigade, our advanced post at Banff House being found to have been abandoned. The essential feature of the new tactics was, however, prior reconnaissance, followed by a surprise attack, so the night of the relief was devoted to a thorough investigation of the enemy posts on the front of the battalion and no immediate attempt was made to restore the line. The Nelson Battalion patrols at the same time located the enemy defences in the neighbourhood of Source Trench.

The next night, at 6.10 p.m., operations began. On the right, Sub-Lieutenant Brearly and eleven men of the Nelson advanced in extended order on the German concrete position, which was the centre of their resistance at Source Trench. When they were about eighty yards from the position, they came on wire entanglement and trenches (the same, no doubt, which had held up the Artists in the daylight attack, but which at night were not manned). Here the party divided into three, one N.C.O. and three men going round to each flank while Sub-Lieutenant Brearly and two men found a way through the wire in front. After making another twenty yards the party on the left were fired on, but the enemy had not observed those in the centre and on the right. Lieutenant Brearly* at once decided to draw the whole of his men on to the right flank, and to attack the position from there. The enterprise was a complete success, the post being surprised and carried without a casualty. One under-officer, eleven men and one machine gun were captured, the remainder of the garrison being killed. So fell a post which, through no fault of their own, two battalions had failed to capture in the attack of October 30th.

Meanwhile, on the left, Lieutenant Stear's "D" Company of the Hawke Battalion had achieved an equal measure of success. Here, the first enemy post attacked was on the left of the battalion front, and was probably the same that had held up the left of our attack on October 26th and had compelled, twice already, the evacuation of Banff House. Sub-Lieutenant Perry, with one and a half platoons, carried out the initial operation, which followed the same plan as that adopted by the Nelson Battalion and with the same results. Nine men and a machine gun were captured and two men killed. Four hours later the enemy ration party arrived and were also captured. When the first post was secured, Lieutenant Stear pushed out posts on either flank, and to the north of the long-disputed Banff House, which was now definitely ours. The only misfortune of this night's operations was the enemy retaliation with gas shells on the headquarters of the Nelson Battalion. Lt.-Colonel Lewis, who had been gassed a few days before, had been succeeded in command of this battalion

---

* This officer was awarded the Military Cross for his "conspicuous gallantry."

Passchendaele

by Commander Shelton, D.S.O., R.N.V.R., and he and the whole of his staff became casualties on this night.

The next night, the Hawke and Nelson Battalions were relieved by the Drake and Hood Battalions and, as before, the night of the relief was devoted to patrolling with a view to the next day's operations.

On the night of the 3rd–4th, the Drake Battalion (" C " Company, Lieutenant Harris)* attacked and captured Sourd Farm, the only remaining enemy post of importance this side of the Paddebeek. The advance was made from the neighbourhood of Banff House at 9 p.m., the main attack being carried out by two and a half platoons. A smaller force of one and a half platoons had to advance from the left of Banff House to a position on the left of the objective, from which they could give covering fire to the main party.

In this instance, the attacking parties were observed at a fairly early stage of their advance (no doubt because our previous success had made the enemy more vigilant), but the advantage of darkness still remained decisive. The enemy fire was unaimed, and the bulk of our men, keeping under cover in shell-holes till Lewis gun and rifle grenade fire temporarily silenced the enemy, sustained hardly any casualties as they closed in on the position and finally rushed it. One prisoner was captured, but the rest of the garrison escaped. This operation, as successful as its predecessors, was in some ways more remarkable. It showed that, even under the most difficult conditions, comparatively large bodies of men could be easily handled in the dark, and that, even where the enemy are on the alert, the protection of darkness is often worth immeasurably more than that of a barrage.

The same evening, the Hood Battalion, on the right of the Divisional front, pushed their line forward to the Paddebeek in touch with the Drake at Sourd Farm, and the first and most important part of the Division's task was accomplished.

Before dawn, as soon as the success of the Sourd Farm operations was assured, Commander Asquith and Lieutenant Harris reconnoitred the Tournant Farm position, which was to be attacked the following night. This position was found to be held in considerable strength with the main garrison in the

---

* Lieut. W. K. Harris was awarded a bar to his Military Cross for his share in this successful operation.

ruins and in pill-boxes on the flanks, and the outposts in shell-holes a hundred to a hundred and fifty yards in front. The difficulty of the operation lay in the certainty that the capture of these advanced posts—an easy matter if the tactics of the previous nights were followed—would give the alarm to the main garrison, who were in greater strength than at any other point yet reconnoitred.

When the position was reported to the Corps, the Division were instructed not to press on with the attack if, in the course of the preliminary operations, it became clear that the enemy would put up a strong resistance. With the line of the Padde-beek secured, a further advance on the main ridge was to be attempted shortly, and such an advance would afford, it was thought, an easy opportunity of attacking the main position. In the circumstances, the operations of the night of November 4th–5th were started in no very determined spirit, and when the enemy posts in front of Tournant Farm had been success-fully dealt with (a number of machine guns were captured), and our line had been pushed forward round the right flank of the main position, the attack was called off. The enemy showed great activity throughout the operations and the decision was, in the light of the Corps instructions, inevitable.

The next day the Naval Division were formally relieved (though the artillery remained in the line), and the command of the front passed to the 1st Division. The 188th Brigade actually relieved the 189th on the night of the 5th–6th, but were relieved by infantry of the new Division within forty-eight hours.*

So ended (as far as the infantry were concerned) the ex-periences of the Naval Division at Passchendaele. The total casualties in the 189th Brigade during their advances in November were no more than three officers (Sub-Lieut. Bolton, Sub-Lieut. T. S. Collins and Sub-Lieut. R. Wyard, of the Hood Battalion) and 14 men killed or died of wounds and 14 officers and 134 men wounded, contrasting with casualties substantially in excess of 8,000 during the shorter period from October 26th to October 81st. The maximum advance achieved during the former period by the Naval Division was, moreover, materially less, apart altogether from the fact

---

* Shortly before his battalion was relieved, Lieut. G. W. W. Denman-Dean, R.M. (2nd R.M. Battalion), was killed.

that the most important tactical objective, the line of the Paddebeek, was only secured on November 3rd. The 188th and 190th Brigades had an impossible task, and though they fulfilled no small part of it in the face of conditions wholly unfavourable, it is altogether beyond doubt that the 189th Brigade were right in insisting at the eleventh hour on a drastic modification in tactics. Of this experiment, which saved, without doubt, hundreds of lives, too little has been said in published accounts of the battle, probably because, devised to meet peculiar local conditions, it was not supposed to be capable of wider application. The need for meeting peculiar conditions by peculiar methods is, however, above all else, the lesson of the Flanders offensive of 1918.

Hardly had the 189th Brigade reached the camp behind the lines for a long overdue period of rest (this Brigade had had only ten days' rest since January 21st, 1918), than the news came that Commander Sterndale Bennett, of the Drake Battalion, who had been wounded during a hostile bombardment on the 4th, had died of his wounds at a casualty clearing station behind the lines. Sterndale Bennett possessed in rare degree the qualities, so seldom associated, of energy and judgment, and his death was a great loss. He was succeeded in command of the Drake Battalion by Commander Pollock, R.N.V.R. At the same time, Commander Jones, R.N.V.R., who had commanded the Anson Battalion in Gallipoli, in the autumn of 1915, was given the command of the Nelson Battalion.

While the Division remained resting in the neighbourhood of Ledeszeele, the Divisional Artillery (the 223rd Brigade still commanded by the Rev. Lt.-Colonel Wingfield and the 317th Brigade by Lt.-Colonel Crofton) remained in their cruelly-exposed positions in the St. Julien–Poelcapelle area. Movement to the artillery positions was impossible except by trench-board routes which were constantly shelled, and the range of the gun positions was accurately known. Before the 188th Brigade came into line, the artillery had had to cover an advance by the 9th Division, and had earned a warm tribute from Brigadier-General Tudor. Through the Naval Division operations, the artillery had continued in the line without respite, and now they had to cover the advance of the 1st Division on November 10th. Only by keeping one-third of the gunners at Brigade Headquarters and another third at the wagon lines had sufficient officers and men been kept alive to carry on. As it was, the strain of keeping the guns in action with depleted teams under heavy shell fire was almost too much. Yet they continued to fire. Major Hale's " D " Battery of the 223rd Brigade was, perhaps, the worst sufferer, Lt. Keeping, R.F.A., and one N.C.O. being the only unwounded survivors in the gun positions at the close of the operations of November 10th, yet the one howitzer still in action continued to fire till orders to cease fire came through in the normal course. The casualties of the two artillery brigades in this period were heavier proportionately than those of the infantry in the most disastrous battles of the war.

Not till December 6th were the artillery relieved, and even this relief was not in accordance with the original intention. The Naval Division had been meant to go back into the line in front of their artillery on this date, but developments in the south involved a new disposition of our forces.

Since the relief of the Division on November 6th, important events had been taking place on the Cambrai front, where a tactical experiment of the most far-reaching character had achieved a sensational success. The keynotes of the new tactics were the substitution of surprise for preparation, the use of tanks in advance of the infantry, with a view to the seizure of tactical points being followed by immediate exploitation by fresh troops, and, as a logical corollary, the abandonment of the gospel of the limited objective.

Unfortunately, this daring and fruitful experiment, which might, in happier circumstances, have opened the way for the first time to a war of movement, was ill-timed. Perhaps, as in the case of the second and third battles for Passchendaele in October and November, the necessity for taking the offensive was judged to be imperative, but the fact remains that the ill-luck which had made 1917 the most disappointing (having regard to our opportunities and the relative strength of the opposing Armies) of all our years of war held to the end, and our one overwhelming tactical triumph (if we except the local offensive of Messines) was made at a time when the troops available were insufficient. Not only did we fail to exploit our gains, but even to maintain them. The German counter-stroke on November 30th and the following days had been definitely successful. The vigour with which the enemy pressed home their attack over a wide front took us, indeed, by surprise. This was not unnatural, for, since the second battle of Ypres, no determined attack had been made against our lines by an enemy possessing anything but a local superiority in numbers. German counter-attacks had come to be derided as a characteristic display of racial insincerity. The lesson of the Arras and Passchendaele offensives had not been absorbed. The renewed vigour of the German resistance had been too largely attributed to fortuitous circumstances, to the French failure (in May), to the weather (in the autumn), to indifferent staff work (according to the infantry in the line), or to inadequately trained troops (according to the directing staffs). This tendency to explain away one of the most remarkable incidents in military history was, probably, not confined to subordinate commanders and regimental officers. This is suggested, not only by the facts of the case, but by Sir Douglas Haig's suggestion at the close of his Passchendaele dispatch that, as a result of those operations, the additions to the enemy strength (due to the Russian defection) had been " already largely discounted."

What is more important to our purpose, the very general conviction among the front line troops that they had nothing serious to fear from a German reaction was directly challenged by the news of the set-back at Cambrai. When the full extent of our losses became known, the Naval Division, who were on the point of returning to the Passchendaele front, were ordered on December 6th to entrain for the Third Army area, with a view to taking over a sector of defence on the shattered front. When they arrived, they found an atmosphere of disquietude bordering on alarm, which was new in their experience, and which reflected the gravity of the disaster by which the fighting troops had been so nearly overwhelmed.

The gains remaining to us, after the German counter-attack, from the Cambrai offensive, were represented by the Flesquières salient. Our offensive had opened with the capture of the Hindenburg front and support lines on a front of six and a half miles, south-east of Cambrai; this gain had been exploited with a considerable measure of success on the left. After the German counter-attacks, we still held four miles of the Hindenburg front and support lines running east from a point half a mile north of Demicourt, in front of Flesquières. In advance of this position we held a discontinuous line of posts. On our right, however, the Germans had achieved a break-through, and had penetrated in part beyond our old front line. We had been saved from a general withdrawal only by improvising a defensive flank running south-west along Welsh Ridge, at right angles to those sectors of the Hindenburg lines which we still held. The result was that the residue of our gains formed a very sharp salient which, in the event of a serious attack, could hardly have been held. As, however, the position was one of great natural strength, and as it com-manded the approaches to Masnières and Marcoing, two im-portant enemy centres, it had been decided to maintain and fortify it. This was the new task of the Naval Division, who, between December 15th and 20th, took over the front of the 31st and 62nd Divisions.

The distance along the new front line was 6,800 yards, held by three Brigades, each with two battalions in the front line, one in support and one in reserve. The sector taken over included the apex of the salient, where our line was on the northern slopes of Welsh Ridge, and the whole length of the eastern face of the ridge. On the right of the Division, the southern slopes of Welsh Ridge ran down into a valley, across which our front line, continuing on the line of Welsh Ridge, fell behind our old front line. Approximately at this point was the right Divisional boundary, which was also the Corps and Army boundary. The Division on the left of the Naval Division, who held the captured sectors of the Hindenburg line forming the northern arm of the salient, was the 19th Division. On the right, holding the re-entrant formed by the German incursion behind our original front, was the 9th Division of the 5th Army. The new front, representing, as it did, a position hurriedly improvised in the stress of battle, was almost lacking in material defences.

The only incident of great note in the first fortnight of the Division's tenure of this line was the promotion of Commander Asquith, R.N.V.R., to the command of the 189th Brigade on the 18th December.* Unfortunately, on December 20th General

* The vacancy occurred owing to the invaliding of Brigadier-General Prentice, of the 188th Brigade, whose place was taken by Brigadier-General Coleridge, from the 189th Brigade. When Brigadier-General Asquith was wounded he was succeeded, after a short time, by Brigadier-General Bray.

Asquith was severely wounded. His loss was a serious blow, not only to the Brigade. It was an open secret that for many months his abilities had been generously appreciated within the Division. Now, as the severest time of testing was approaching, the Brigade had to lose his services. The loss was greater than that merely of a supremely competent officer. It was the loss of an officer whom everyone recognized as supremely competent, and who, for that reason, would always get more out of his officers and men than anyone else. Above all, he was a fighting soldier. His whole experience had been gained, not in war, which is an affair of business where credit may go far without much backing in realizable assets, but in battles, which are affairs of art where none but the best can retain a reputation.

The command of the Brigade passed temporarily to Lt.-Colonel Kirkpatrick, Lt.-Commander Buckle taking command of the Anson during his absence. The last fortnight of December was bitterly cold, with many successive days of severe frost, but work on the construction of a continuous front support line on Welsh Ridge was pressed forward,* and, at one point, our line was even extended on December 22nd, through the enterprise of a company commander of the Drake Battalion. From Christmas Day onwards, however, the enemy shelling markedly increased, and at dawn on December 30th the enemy launched a not unexpected attack against our whole front.

Every effort was made to effect surprise, the enemy even going so far as to dress the leading waves in white to match the snow. Nevertheless, the measure of success which the attack met with was due rather to a stroke of singular misfortune than to any display of cunning on the part of the enemy.

Our line was held, from left to right, by the 190th, 189th and 188th Brigades, the battalions in the line being the 1/5 K.S.L.I., 7th Royal Fusiliers, Hood, Drake, Howe and 1st Royal Marines. Under cover of the barrage, the leading waves effected a lodgment in the front line of the 190th Brigade and at the junction of the Hood and 7th Royal Fusiliers and of the Drake and Howe Battalions. The right flank battalion, and most of the Hood and Drake Battalions, stood fast. Elsewhere, on the right and in the centre, the enemy penetrated only to the front line.

---

* During this period Sub-Lieut. C. R. Barker, of the Anson, and Sub-Lieut. F. Hill, of the Hawke Battalion, were killed.

The Hood Battalion at once counter-attacked, although their commanding officer, Lt.-Commander Patrick Shaw Stewart, R.N.V.R. (who had rejoined the Division from the staff at his own request, and had assumed temporary command of the Hood when Commander Asquith was promoted), had been killed during the preliminary bombardment, and some disorganization might have been expected. Instead, the greatest coolness marked the operations of the support companies of this battalion, to whom the first news of the initial success of the attack had been brought by the appearance of two German officers in their line. These were met and killed by A.B. Brown, the " B " Company cook, who gave the alarm. Sub-Lieut. Weir and P.O. Brown,* of the same company, at once led a bombing attack up the communication trench to the front line, and the remainder of the support companies moved up across the open. By 8.25 a.m., the situation was completely restored† on this front and one company of the Hood Battalion was actually available to reinforce the 7th Royal Fusiliers. Very severe losses had, however, been suffered by the Hood, whose front line companies had been virtually annihilated; Sub-Lieut. Lawrie, Sub-Lieut. Roberts and Sub-Lieut. Watkins were among those killed in the course of the morning's fighting.

The situation on the flank of the 190th Brigade was less satisfactory, but the Brigade were able to hold the enemy on their second line and the loss of their front line did not seriously weaken their position.

On the Howe front, through no fault of the men on the spot, the situation was more serious. Simultaneously with the loss of the front line, a shell falling outside Battalion Headquarters had killed Commander West and Lt.-Commander Alan Campbell. Though Captain Pitcairn, Sub-Lieut. Kessen and Sub-Lieut. Neal took very prompt and energetic action to localize the attack (and thus prevented an irretrievable disaster), the support companies could not be organized for a counter-attack quickly enough to prevent the enemy securing a lodgment in the second line, on the crest of the ridge itself. This

---

* This Petty Officer was later awarded the D.C.M.

† Lord Alexander Thynne, writing to a friend about these operations, refers to the Hood Battalion as remarkably organized and with " a splendid fighting spirit."

Commander A. W. Buckle, D.S.O., R.N.V.R. (Anson Battalion).

(From the portrait by Ambrose McEvoy in the possession of the Imperial War Museum.)

made the position of the right of the Drake Battalion* in the front line untenable, and that position too had to be given up to the enemy. Once the crest of the ridge was lost, the organization of a daylight counter-attack became impossible, because of the long, steep slope up which an advance would have to be made, and Colonel Kirkpatrick wisely decided to postpone further action till dusk, when his support Battalion (the Anson) would make a carefully prepared counter-attack. In this the Nelson Battalion were to co-operate, but unfortunately the detailed orders failed to reach Commander Jones in time, and a premature and partial, though very gallant, attack† was launched at 2.15 p.m. by this battalion against the positions lost by the 189th Brigade. Despite excellent work, particularly by Sub-Lieut. Clerk and P.O. Winn (of " C " Company), the attack failed. Everything now turned on that to be made by the Anson Battalion under Commander Buckle, with which the co-operation of the 189th Brigade must now inevitably be less effective. General Hutchison arranged for the Artists' Rifles to make a simultaneous attempt to regain the front line, lost by the 190th Brigade on the left.

The Anson attack, led by " A " Company, with the Nelson Battalion " B " Company (Lieut. Biggs, R.N.V.R.) and elements of the Drake on their immediate left, was a brilliant success, and " A " Company of the Anson reoccupied the vital position on Welsh Ridge with the loss of only three men. To Commander Buckle and to the officers and men of this company belongs most of the credit for what Sir Douglas Haig in his dispatch described as an " admirably executed counter-attack . . . " which " regained all the essential parts of our former positions." ‡

---

* This battalion suffered serious losses throughout this engagement ; among those killed were Lieut. A. A. Johnson, R.N.V.R., Lieut. C. J. Woodford, D.S.M., R.N.V.R., Sub-Lieut. W. L. Burnett, Sub-Lieut. W. H. Clarkson, M.C., and Sub-Lieut J. W. Cookes.

† In this attack, and in the subsequent fighting, Sub-Lieut. R. Taylor, Sub-Lieut. G. J. Robertson, Sub-Lieut. H. B. Cannin and Sub-Lieut. C. A. Clerk, of the Nelson Battalion, were killed. Lieut. F. D. Purser, R.N.V.R., and Sub-Lieut. T. White, of this battalion, had been killed in the days immediately preceding the attack.

‡ Commander Buckle, Commander Pollock and Lieutenant Harris of the Drake and Lieutenant Donaldson of the Hood each received the D.S.O. for their work in the organization and leadership of the many counter-attacks on this day. Lieutenant Maudsley and Sub-Lieutenants Hall and Kessen received the M.C.

On the left the situation was still obscure. The Hood had been forced earlier in the afternoon to withdraw their left company in order to maintain touch with the 190th Brigade, and the counter-attack by the Artists had failed to make any appreciable headway. The troops on this flank were, indeed, only able with difficulty to hold the second line position to which they had been driven back. On this line, which had been reinforced by "D" Company of the Hawke Battalion (Lieut. Stear, R.N.V.R.), at the point of junction of the two brigades, a more or less continuous fight raged, till noon on the 31st December, and during the night one or two posts were lost and retaken by the Hawke company, to whom fell much severe fighting. Substantially, however, the position was maintained against very superior forces, and by the afternoon of the 31st the enemy attacks died down.

From an analysis of the many prisoners captured on different parts of the Division's front, it appeared that the attack had been made by at least fifteen battalions and a quota of storm troops, and the defence of a very indefensible position against such heavy odds was a creditable achievement. In particular, the operations of the Anson and Hood Battalions provided model examples of the organized and the improvised counter-attack, each undertaken in appropriate circumstances with wholly successful results. But if the Division had maintained its reputation, it had done so at a heavy price. The casualties in killed, wounded and missing were 68 officers* and 1,355 men, and among them two battalion commanders and the second in command of the Howe Battalion. Such losses in defensive warfare impose a far heavier strain on the nerves of fighting troops than losses in an attack, however unsuccessful. The deaths, moreover, of Commander West, of Patrick Shaw Stewart and of Alan Campbell, were in the nature of a grievous personal loss to innumerable officers and men of the Division. They had all served with the Division in the earliest Gallipoli days, and had each contributed much to its reputation, not only as a fighting organization but as the gathering place of so many men who were at once remarkably good com-

---

* In addition to those already mentioned, Sub-Lieut. W. A. St. A. Clarke, R.N.V.R., and Lieut. T. Westby, M.C., R.M., of the 190th M.G.C., Sub-Lieut. W. Hunter, of the Anson, Sub-Lieut. W. Wilson, M.C., of the Hawke, and 2nd Lieut. W. Jaques, R.M., of the 1st R.M. Battalion, were among those killed in this costly engagement.

pany and of brilliant attainments. Of Patrick Shaw Stewart's end a full account is contained in a letter from Lord Alexander Thynne, published in Father Ronald Knox's biography. In the first moments of the barrage preceding the German attack, Shaw Stewart was slightly wounded, but he insisted on going round his line and seeing for himself that everything was ready in case the enemy attacked. Then a shell burst on the parapet close by him, and death was instantaneous. Commander West and Alan Campbell were killed by a shell falling at the entrance of their headquarters as they too were moving up to their front line.

Shaw Stewart was less well known to most of the Naval Division than was Alan Campbell, who, with his genius for friendship, his invariable high spirits, his audacious temperament, equally auspicious on the battlefield and at the card table, was a tradition in a division where personalities were not rare. Shaw Stewart's death meant less, perhaps, to those in France at this time, but it closed a brilliant and tragic chapter in the history of more than the Naval Division. Of that small band of scholars, musicians, poets and men of letters who had served in the Naval Division in Gallipoli, he had been almost the last survivor.

CHAPTER XV

THE bitter fighting of the closing days of 1917 was a truthful presage of the impending struggle. For some weeks the prospect of a vigorous German offensive in 1918 had been defining itself ever more clearly. The lesson of the attacks on our front at Cambrai was nevertheless more unpleasant than we were prepared for. If we could hold our own so hardly and with such heavy losses when confronted with a local attack, the results of the expected offensive on a broad front, thinly manned by exhausted divisions, almost all of whom had endured the full strain of the spring, summer and autumn offensive of 1917, could not be anticipated without anxiety.

The danger of the situation was many-sided. In the first place the fighting strength of the British armies in the West was inadequate to their responsibilities, and only by depleting the long line from Arras to the French left of any reserves effective to meet more than a purely local attack could the safety of the Channel ports be in any way ensured. Whether more troops were available at home or on other fronts is one of the great controversies of the War from which the historian of a Division will prudently stand aside. The facts as to the inadequacy of the numbers available in France are no longer in dispute.

In the second place, the front held by the Third and Fifth Armies, though it had been held by the Allies since the close of the spring offensive, had not, by the late autumn of 1917, been fortified with anything approaching German method and science.

In the third place, if the fighting quality of the infantry remained in many formations unshaken, the experience of many of the junior officers was very small. Between November 1917 and the opening of the German offensive the Naval Division alone had lost five of its most brilliant battalion commanders ;

in the course of the retreat it was to lose four more. This rate of wastage was typical of what was going on throughout the army. The Naval Division had perhaps foreseen the officer problem earlier than had the army as a whole, and certainly, to the end of the war, it was never short of qualified senior regimental officers. But of platoon officers the supply was infinitely shorter. The army cadet schools, on which all formations now had to rely for junior officers, appeared, perhaps because of their system of mass training, to produce efficient soldiers rather than efficient officers. Cadets were trained more in the execution of orders than in the exercise of initiative, the tactical handling of independent forces and the formation of plans of attack and defence. In retreat even more than in the offensive the initiative rests, time and again, with very junior officers, who by an error of judgment may render vain the highest personal gallantry.

At the eleventh hour (the opening weeks of 1918 took on this character in the light of the reports of ceaseless enemy concentrations) little that was effective could be done to mitigate these conditions, so threatening to the prospects of a successful defensive.

The Naval Division was unable, after its heavy losses on December 30th and 31st, to continue responsible for a three-brigade sector, and on January 2nd the 190th Brigade, which had suffered the most severely and had put up what was, having regard to the difficulty of their position, a very fine defence, were relieved by the 53rd Brigade of the 19th Division. On the narrower front the Division spent a comparatively quiet three weeks,* concentrating on the strengthening of their defences. The enemy, equally engaged in preparing for the coming battle, were inactive. On the 22nd and 23rd January, the Naval Division was relieved by the 2nd Division, and put in a month's work on the strengthening and extension of successive defensive positions, all of them unfortunately too close to our front to be of much value when the crisis arose. Nevertheless, they added something to the local security and so to the confidence of the front line troops. It was otherwise with another departure from practice which was made at the end of January,

---

* During which period, however, Sub-Lieut. H. B. Cannin, of the Nelson, Sub-Lieut. W. Wilson, of the Hawke, and 2nd Lieut. R. H. S. Bailey, R.M., of the 1st R.M. Battalion, were killed, and Lt.-Colonel G. L. Parry, R.M.L.I., sustained wounds from which he died in hospital on the 2nd February.

when infantry brigades were reduced to a strength of three battalions apiece. This involved for the Naval Division the disbandment of the Howe and Nelson Battalions, and the transfer of the 5th K.S.L.I. to the 19th Division. The Nelson and Howe personnel were absorbed in the four remaining R.N.V.R. battalions.

In the middle of February the Division, strongly reinforced, returned to the Vth Corps' line, and after a series of inter-brigade and inter-divisional reliefs found themselves in a three-brigade sector on the Flesquières ridge, the northern arm that is of the Flesquières salient, with the 47th Division (the right Division of the Vth Corps) between themselves and the Fifth Army. All three Brigades of the Division were in line, each with one battalion in front, one in support, and one in reserve. The 190th Brigade was on the right, the 189th in the centre and the 188th on the left.

Till the end of the month things remained quiet, but the early days of March made it clear that the enemy preparations were almost complete. On the 8th March test barrages were put down by them on the right and centre brigades, and on March 12th a prolonged gas bombardment of the divisional sector marked the final stage of the enemy's methodical preparation.* The whole of the Flesquières salient was drenched with gas shells for more than a day (200,000 shells was the official calculation), and the resulting casualties, which had risen to more than 2,000 by the day of the attack, were without doubt as effective an aid to the enemy's plans as our screen of tanks had been in the Cambrai offensive. The gas used was chiefly Yellow Cross (" mustard ") gas, and its greatest tactical value was that the results were not, as a rule, instantaneous ; it hung round every trench, every dug-out, every headquarter for an indeterminate period, and no amount of gas discipline could prevent a growing casualty list among troops bound to remain in the infected area and to carry on their ordinary and laborious duties. The chief sufferers among the different units of the Division were the Hawke Battalion and Drake Battalion (which lost respectively 15 officers and 582 men and 21 officers and 408 men from gas between the 12th and 21st March), the 223rd

---

* During the period to March 18th the Division lost many fine officers, including Sub-Lieutenant A. E. Maloney (Hawke), Sub.-Lieut. G. J. Mitchell and Sub-Lieut. J. F. St. C. Barton (Hood) and 2nd Lieutenant H. Fielden, R.M. (2nd Marines), who were killed.

Brigade R.F.A.* and the 189th Brigade Headquarters, who lost not only the Brigadier (Brigadier-General Bray) and the Brigade Major (Major Barnett, D.S.O.) but the entire subordinate clerical staff and signal section. On the eve of active operations, these losses were singularly inconvenient and added immeasurably to the difficulties of the new Brigade Commander (Brigadier-General de Pree, C.M.G., D.S.O.) and Brigade Major (Captain Wright). Among the other casualties was Commander Pollock, D.S.O., R.N.V.R. (Drake Battalion), who was succeeded by Commander Beak, M.C., R.N.V.R., on the eve of the enemy's attack.

On March 21st the storm broke.

" At 4.50 a.m.," writes General de Pree,† " a terrific bombardment of gas and high explosive began along the whole front. There was no mistake about it, this was the real thing. It included the front line, the gun positions and the back areas. The roar and scream of the shells passing over and the explosions all around were deafening and continuous, and to them in a few seconds was added the still more terrific noise of our own guns and their shells passing over in reply. The night had been foggy and in a short time the gas and smoke of the bombardment added so much to the fog that even when daylight came fully it was impossible to see more than a few yards."

At this time the Battalions in the line were, from right to left, the 4th Bedfords, the Hawke and the 2nd R.M. Battalion : in support were the 7th Royal Fusiliers, the Drake and the 1st R.M. Battalion ; in reserve were the Anson, the Hood and the Artists' Rifles. The reserve battalions were under the orders of the Divisional Commander in Havrincourt Wood, nearly three miles behind the front line. Between the reserves and our outpost lines were the second system (our original front line prior to the Cambrai Battle) and the intermediate system (the Hindenburg front line), in which were the support Battalions, and the Hindenburg support system, which was the main line of resistance for the front line battalions.

At 5.15 a.m., the bombardment lifted at certain points along

---

* Who lost their Brigade Commander, the Rev. Lieut.-Colonel W. E. Wingfield, D.S.O. He was succeeded by Lieut.-Colonel McClarety, R.A.

† I am very greatly indebted to Brigadier-General de Pree for many of the details which appear in the following pages as well as for permission to quote freely from a written account of the operations which he kindly prepared for my information.

the front, and the enemy attacked. He effected a lodgment in a small subsidiary salient (called the Premy salient) on the 189th Brigade front and at their junction with the 190th Brigade on the right. Communication between the front line and Brigade Headquarters was cut in the first few minutes, and it was not known till 11 a.m. that the enemy had penetrated our front. The commanding officer of the Hawke (Commander Ellis, D.S.O.) was, however, in touch with the situation and organized the defence of a new position.

At 10 a.m. the Divisional reserves were moved up into the second system, and a company of the Drake was moved up in close support of the Hawke Battalion : a third company was moved up in the afternoon. When, by 4 p.m., the fighting had died down, arrangements were made for the Drake to retake that part of the outpost line which had been lost. This counter-attack was, however, cancelled, on instructions from the Vth Corps, and Commander Beak was ordered to relieve the remnants of the Hawke Battalion in the Hindenburg support line ; the Hawke was withdrawn to a position in rear.

The loss on the divisional front as a result of the day's fighting was not serious. A small local salient (always a danger rather than an advantage) was gone, and the new front could have been held with ease. The Corps on the right of the Vth Corps had, however, fallen back slightly, and the IVth Corps on the left had been very heavily attacked, and had been driven in along the Cambrai–Bapaume road as far as Beaumetz.

This news spelt not only a substantial enemy success on the Third Army front, but the beginning of the historic retreat of the Fifth Army. It was at once evident that, in the absence of strong reserves to counter-attack on both flanks of the Flesquières salient, the retreat could not be localized, but must involve also the whole of the Vth Corps. The conclusion, though obvious, was unwelcome, and it was reached only by stages, and in each case (in the absence of earlier orders from the Corps) very late. Not till midnight on the 21st was the Naval Division ordered to withdraw to the intermediate system (the Hindenburg front line), and even then the movement was delayed, owing to the relief of the Hawke by the Drake Battalion, which was in progress. Although it was clear that the intermediate line could not be held, a further retreat to the second (our old front line) position was not ordered till late in the afternoon of the 22nd, and, before this withdrawal could be effected, a withdrawal to a switch line further back became necessary. This line was to be held by the 188th and 190th Brigades. A position still further in rear was taken up by the 189th Brigade, with a view to covering a further retreat to the Green line, a tolerably prepared position covering the whole of the Third and Fifth Army front. The sector of the Green line behind the Naval Division front was some six thousand yards in length, covering the villages of Bertincourt and Ytres (the latter an important corps centre with large dumps of ammunition and R.E. stores). The Green line to the left and right of the Naval Division was to be occupied by the 2nd and 47th Divisions of the Vth Corps, in touch with the IVth Corps and the Fifth Army respectively.

The move to the Metz defences occupied the night of the 22nd–23rd, and was not carried out without incident. In the confusion of continuous movement, the orders for a retreat beyond our old front line never reached the Drake Battalion, and there they remained until, in the gathering darkness, the German patrols came forward on the flanks. At this juncture, Commander Beak came across a demolition party from the Divisional Engineers, preparing with the utmost zeal to blow up his battalion. In the special circumstances, he felt justified in withdrawing, and, to prevent the enemy following up, he himself stayed behind with a Lewis gun mounted on a limber, and kept up a steady fire on those few of the enemy who showed any zeal for the attack. Moving down the road from Trescaut to Neuville by easy, if anxious stages, he repeated the performance sufficiently often to enable his battalion to get clear without casualties. By the time the Drake arrived at the line held by the 189th Brigade, it was 7 a.m. on the 23rd, and General Lawrie had just ordered all three brigades to withdraw to the Green line. The withdrawal was carried out at once by the Drake and three companies of the Hood Battalion. The Hawke and the remainder of the Hood remained in position in front of Neuville, and covered the withdrawal of the 188th and 190th Brigades from the Metz switch. The retirement was completed by midday on the 23rd, when the rearguard was withdrawn. The Hawke retired to Brigade reserve on Bus, and the Hood company rejoined their battalion in the Green line. Here, from left to right, were now the 1st and 2nd Marines, the Hood, the Drake, the Artists' Rifles and the 4th Bedfords.* The Anson were in reserve covering the Bertincourt–Bus road, and the 7th Royal Fusiliers in reserve at Lêchelle. Covering the Bertincourt and Ytres line, were the 317th and 223rd R.F.A. Brigades (the 63rd Divisional Artillery) and the 88th Brigade R.F.A. (attached).

From the local point of view nothing could have been more satisfactory than the position on the morning of the 23rd. Heavily attacked on the morning of the 21st, the Division had held its own, losing only a portion of its outpost line. Its casualties, though exceptionally severe prior to the attack, had been light. When the Vth Corps found itself, as a result of the withdrawal of the IVth Corps and the Fifth Army, in an impossible salient, the Division had withdrawn, covered at each point by its artillery, and had inflicted heavy losses on the enemy ; the Divisional Artillery in particular had found fine targets, at 8 a.m. on the 22nd, when the enemy reserves of infantry and artillery attempted vainly to advance west from Marcoing. Now the whole Division were in touch with the 2nd Division of the Vth Corps on the left, and, so they were assured, with the 47th Division on the right, and were standing on a prepared line organized for defence.

It was, indeed, an excellent manœuvre, and but for the interference of the enemy it would have been successful. As early, however, as 10 a.m. on the 23rd, the enemy were reported in Fins, a small village near the boundary between the Fifth Army and the 47th Division, and within sight of the Green line at that point. The arrival of the Naval Division on the Green line to the left at noon, and the activities of a detachment of the Divisional Machine-Gun Battalion (Lt.-Colonel Macready, R.M.),† sent out at 3 p.m. to keep the enemy from moving from Fins against the infantry brigades, kept the enemy quiet on the divisional front during the remaining hours of daylight. The efforts of the divisions on the right appear, however, to have been less successful. As early as 5 p.m. on the 23rd, the

---

* I.e., two battalions of the 188th, two of the 189th and two of the 190th Brigade.

† A fourth M.G. Company (the 223rd) had been added to the Divisional establishment in October, 1917, and at the beginning of March the four companies in every division were formed into battalions and recognized officially as Divisional troops. The new company was commanded by Lieutenant Dewhurst, R.N.V.R., and largely officered by officers of the disbanded R.N.V.R. companies.

7th Royal Fusiliers (Lt.-Colonel Malone) at Lêchelle were attacked from their right, and forced to fall back on the Bus–Rocquigny road, in touch with the Headquarters of the 189th and 190th Brigades. These activities of the enemy, several thousand yards behind our front line troops, put a different complexion on the situation. From now onward it grew hourly worse.

After dusk on the 23rd, no effective touch could be maintained with the 47th Division, even on the Green line, though several battalions of this division marched back past the division's flank, directed, it was learnt, towards a destination further west. To meet the situation, the battalion commanders of the Drake, Artists and Bedfords decided to withdraw from the Green line on the right of the divisional front and to form a defensive flank in front of the R.E. dump in Ytres, and thence along the Ytres–Bus road. The Marine Battalions, the Hood, and the right companies of the Drake Battalion held their ground in the Green line. The left flank of the Division was covered by the 2nd Division, while the Anson and the reserve brigade of the 2nd Division were in position to the north of the Bertincourt–Bus road, facing south* (like the 190th Brigade) against an attack from the direction of Lêchelle.

By 10 p.m. on the 23rd it was discovered beyond doubt that the 47th Division had withdrawn, and that the Naval Division flank was exposed. Almost at the same time the R.E. and ammunition dump in Ytres was blown up (whether under Corps arrangements or not is uncertain), and the Artists' Rifles suffered severely. This disaster, terrifying as it was to troops compelled to hold the line in front of the dump, probably prevented the enemy from exploiting their success on the right by a frontal attack in the full light of the blazing wreckage. They penetrated, however, into Bus, when the Hawke Battalion Headquarters, who had been kept uninformed of the situation, were inconsiderately interrupted at dinner, and forced to withdraw their battalion to the outskirts. Here they took up a position covering the exits from the village to north-west, in which they were to do valuable service a few hours later.

Such, then, was the situation at midnight on March 23rd.

* See map. The Green line, of course, faced east.

Deprived, without notice, whether by superior force, faulty dispositions or the errors of subordinates, of all protection to their right flank, the Division still held a line of retreat north of Bus along the Bertincourt–Barastre road. All parties of the enemy striking northward against this line were temporarily held by the Drake Battalion and the 190th Brigade on the Ytres–Bus road, by the 7th Fusiliers on the Bus–Rocquigny road, and by the Hawke Battalion, north-west of Bus, covering the road from Bus to Barastre. Nor were the infantry unsupported; with the Fusiliers and the Hawke were the 249th and 248th Field Companies of Engineers, and some of the 14th Worcesters (Pioneer Battalion); the 247th Field Company with the balance of the Worcesters were at Barastre. The Divisional Artillery were still in action across the Bus–Rocquigny road, and the Machine-Gun Battalion had most of its guns in the Green line itself.

Nevertheless, as was pointed out to the Vth Corps, the position, momentarily secured owing to the initiative and tenacity of the officers and men on the ground, could not be indefinitely maintained. On the other hand, a strong and determined counter-attack in the direction of the exposed flank might not only relieve the pressure on the Division itself, but materially assist the 47th Division and the left of the Fifth Army. The Corps' answer was an instruction to the Division to hold on, with information that the 17th Division would counter-attack in the morning.

And, indeed, some such relief was sorely needed. The men had been fighting, marching and digging since dawn on the 21st. By reason of the tactics decided on, and the fidelity with which they had been carried out, the successive retire-ments had all been difficult and dangerous, and the pressure of the enemy constant. Now, sleep and hot food were the essentials, and they were out of the question, with the enemy attacking from the east, the south and the west, while only the 2nd Division stood between the Naval Division and the enemy to the north.

Seldom can any more dramatic change of atmosphere have been experienced in war. The note of these days is not the breakdown of the infantry resistance but of the elaborate organization behind the lines, for which the fighting strength of the front line troops had been ruthlessly sacrificed and on which the infantry had been taught to rely. From a military point of view the explanation was simple enough. The enemy had cut across our communications. But it is worth while, none the less, to try to realize what this actually meant to the fighting troops. In the first place there were no rations : but for the fact that a reasonably stocked canteen at Ytres had been abandoned by the men in charge, the shortage of food would have been serious. More important, there were no working parties, and no carrying parties. The trench mortar batteries simply faded out of the picture, buried their guns, and joined up as infantry. There was no place for them in the warfare of the moment. The 47th Division Machine-Gun Battalion had been able to cover the Division's flank for some hours on the 23rd because Commander Beak, by force rather than persuasion, induced some infantry from another division, who were retiring, to carry up ammunition to them. But from now onwards, even machine guns could only operate within distances over which men could carry ammunition and remain fit, at the end, for active and continuous fighting. The difficulties of the artillery were even greater, for they were cut off from their reserves of ammunition* and could not in the circumstances put down barrages with the frequency or intensity to which the infantry had grown perhaps too much accustomed. Still more extraordinary in its effects was the breakdown of communications, either by telephone or runner, which left the local commanders in ignorance of the situation on the flanks, to their front and to their rear. Even brigade staffs could not get in touch with higher formations. From a great railway centre like Rocquigny the whole of the administrative staff had withdrawn, taking everything portable, and leaving not even a telephone behind. The result was that the only people who knew from observation what the situation was could neither direct their own troops how to meet it nor enable those with troops still under their control to do so.

At 8 a.m. on the 24th, orders did indeed reach the Division from the Vth Corps to withdraw, the intention being that the line Rocquigny–Barastre should be held by the 17th and

---

* The Divisional Ammunition Column had lost their wagons at Etricourt, which had been entered by the enemy before the Naval Division had retired. The loss was in part due to the system, here proved to be mistaken, of having the wagons and horses of the D.A.C. separate.

47th Divisions, while the 2nd and Naval Divisions withdrew to an undefined position in the rear. The orders were issued too late. At 5 a.m., long before they had reached the front line troops (they never did reach the battalions of the 189th and 190th Brigades in the Green line and only reached the 188th Brigade at 8 a.m.), the Germans put down a barrage on Ytres, and a machine gun firing through the Nissen Hut where the 189th Brigade Headquarters were breakfasting at Rocquigny showed that the enemy meant to roll up the flank of the division, long before these nicely calculated moves, which looked so opportune from Corps Headquarters, could be carried out.

The situation in the Green line was critical. On the left of the line, the two Marine Battalions, though attacked only from the front, had suffered heavily through the night, from artillery and machine-gun fire at close range.* In the centre and on the right the situation was even worse, for the enemy were closing in on all sides, and the Hood Battalion, in the Green line itself, were enfiladed from their right, and forced to retire behind the village. By 7 a.m. on the 24th, as no orders had been received, it was decided, at a conference of the six battalion commanders, that a withdrawal could not be longer delayed. How impossible the situation was can be seen from the fact that an enemy observation balloon was actually over Ytres at this time, and his artillery were able to fire at our infantry over open sights at a few hundred yards' range. The decision arrived at was that the 190th and 188th Brigades should retire first, moving north of Bus and Barastre in the direction of Villers au Flos. The 189th Brigade would follow after acting as a rearguard. Whether the enemy were north of Bus was uncertain (as a matter of fact they were not, except for an isolated patrol), but it was evident that, even from Bus, the retreat would be seriously interfered with. The battalions of the 190th and 189th Brigades, moving from Ytres, had to cross a very open stretch of ground north-west of Bus, where in happier days the divisions in this part had been in the habit of holding their race

* Lieut.-Col. Farquharson (commanding the 2nd Marines) and Captain Gibbins were killed at this time. 2nd Lieutenant E. W. Collier and 2nd Lieutenant S. N. Witting of the same battalion had been killed during the retreat to the Green line. Lieut.-Commander Coote, R.N.V.R., succeeded temporarily to the command of the 2nd R.M. battalion.

meetings. To give what protection was possible to the retreat, Colonel Macready sent eight machine guns under Major Moir on to the Bus–Rocquigny road, and twelve guns under Lieutenant Anderson, R.N.V.R., to the cemetery between Les Bœufs and Le Transloy to prevent any sudden incursion of the enemy from the east should the Corps fail, as might be expected, to hold the Rocquigny line. The Anson, Hawke and 7th Fusilier Battalions were also still in a position to assist the retirement of their brigades, although the 14th Worcesters and 247th Field Company of Engineers had been ordered back from Barastre (where they had driven off the enemy patrols from Bus at 2 a.m.) to Villers au Flos. The three Brigade Headquarters had, while the fighting at Ytres was in progress, moved to Beaulencourt, where was General Lawrie with his staff. The Brigadiers themselves, north-west of Bus, were waiting to direct their battalions to an appointed rendezvous between Beaulencourt and Le Transloy.

It is curious to note that these dispositions, which enabled the whole division to withdraw with no effective assistance from other formations, were the result of no general orders, but rather of independent action taken by many local commanders, and by the Divisional and Brigade Staffs, acting at the time independently, and in touch only with isolated bodies of troops. The Commander-in-Chief singles out for special mention the work of Lieutenant Anderson's machine gunners* at Les Bœufs. This detachment did heroic work, and not only assisted their own division but covered the retirement of the guns, transport and infantry rearguards of at least two other divisions. But for the resolution of this detachment, a serious disaster would have been inevitable. Equally important, however, was the stand of the infantry in the Green line and on the Ytres–Bus road ; and the work of the Fusiliers and the 249th Field Company on the Bus–Rocquigny road, to which position they were withdrawn by General Hutchison, must not be forgotten.

From 8 a.m. till noon on this morning of the 24th an observer stationed on the outskirts of Bus could see small bodies moving north-west from Bertincourt and Ytres in companies, platoons, or sections, fired at by enemy machine guns from Bus and other points to the north, but moving

* From the 190th Machine-Gun Company (Major Lindsay, M.G.C.).

steadily away from the immediate point of danger. To his front in Bus and in the Green line, to his right in Lêchelle, and on the outskirts of Rocquigny, were the enemy ; those in Rocquigny, engaged till now by the 109th Brigade, being held in check only by the individual efforts of a number of tanks, and of isolated parties of the 47th Division and the 99th Brigade. Behind him, near Barastre, were the 17th Division, through whom the retirement was to take place. Gradually, during the morning, the whole division was concentrated near the Le Transloy *sucrerie*, the last to come in being the Hawke Battalion, from their position on the outskirts of Bus, which they had been ordered by General de Pree to maintain, till the Drake and Hood Battalions had filed past to the north of them.

All three brigades of the Divisional Artillery had by now, like the infantry, been forced to fall back, as the enemy were active in all directions round their positions, and they were short of ammunition. The 317th Brigade extricated themselves from their positions covering Ytres with the loss of only one section, and took up a position covering Beaulencourt and the appointed concentration area. The 223rd and 88th Brigades, retiring across the exposed right flank by Le Transloy, were less fortunate and, coming under machine-gun fire, lost all their horses, suffered heavy losses and had to abandon many of their guns.

The Hood, Drake, Artists and Bedfords had also suffered serious losses, as the actual withdrawal had taken place in full view of the enemy, and those wounded in the course of it could not be brought away.* Moreover, at least two parties moved away in the direction of Bus, and found themselves caught between two fires and unable, at close range, to make good their escape. Such incidents were, of course, almost inevitable, since the enemy's position and strength behind the Green line was not known, and the first efforts to find a line of retreat were in the nature of a leap in the dark. The Hawke Battalion, too, had their own troubles, for in rear of their position was a steep bank on which the enemy's machine guns in Bus were trained. The battalion crossed it,

---

* Lieutenant Nobbs, R.N.V.R., Sub-Lieutenant F. A. Taylor and Sub-Lieutenant W. G. Simpson of the Hood Battalion were killed on the morning of the 24th. Very many officers also had to be left behind wounded, among them being Lieut.-Commander Turrell, R.N.V.R., of the Drake Battalion.

however, in single file under cover of their Lewis guns with hardly a casualty, and were not otherwise pressed.

Between Villers au Flos and Le Transloy, covered by the 17th Division and 2nd Division, the different Brigades were reorganized and re-formed. Men were able to fill their water bottles and draw on an opportune dump of rations. A rest of two hours was snatched by the rank and file and the junior officers, while the next move was considered.

No definite plan appeared to have been formulated by the Vth Corps, to whom General Lawrie telephoned and so, at 3 p.m., when the 17th and the 2nd Divisions were already planning a further withdrawal, and the noise of firing from Les Bœufs (where Lieutenant Anderson's guns were in action) showed that the enemy were pressing ever further to the south, General Lawrie himself ordered the division to fall back. The new line was to run from Martinpuich to Bazentin le Petit, a defensible position six miles to the rear, on which it was hoped to make touch with the right of the Corps and the left of the Fifth Army. Optimistic though this view turned out to be, the orders saved the division. The long distance across the old Somme battlefield, which was covered in the next four hours, could not later have been crossed without paralysing loss, and if the Division had turned to fight far short of the Thiepval heights it must have been cut off.

The march began at 3 p.m. with the three brigades in parallel columns at 1,000 yards interval, the 188th on the left, the 189th in the centre and the 190th on the flank, with the 7th Royal Fusiliers as flank guard. The columns moved straight across country, passing just north of Gueudecourt and Flers. Throughout the march, the enemy could be seen pressing forward on the open flank, and, but for the machine guns at Les Bœufs, which fired more than 25,000 rounds during the afternoon and held up the enemy's advance for at least three hours, the bold manœuvre would have been less completely successful.

As the Division was halted about 5 p.m. in the neighbourhood of High Wood, General Lawrie received orders from the Vth Corps to take up a position, not in front of Martinpuich, as he had proposed, but in front of High Wood. The 189th Brigade happened to be halted almost exactly on the spot, and were ordered at once to choose and take up a position.

The 188th Brigade were to come up on their left and get in touch with the 17th Division round Eaucourt L'Abbaye. As the 189th Brigade, with whom were still the 248th Field Company, R.E., were moving forward, they were met by a crowd of six or seven hundred men of more than one division, retreating with more haste than discretion, and threatening to spread a general confusion. General de Pree, who was standing by talking to Commander Ellis and Commander Beak, stopped an officer who was occupying a leading position in the retirement, and asked him where he was going. The officer's reply was that he was looking for his revolver. His need was supplied, and he and his party were fallen in on the left of the Division. Hardly had this difficulty been overcome, when a large patrol of the enemy crept up quite close to the 189th Brigade— it was now dusk—as they were waiting to move off to the new line, and began firing into them with machine guns and shouting in the hope of spreading panic. The patrol was apparently working in conjunction with enemy aircraft, for they sent up coloured lights, and immediately their planes swooped down and dropped six bombs on the brigade, causing a good many casualties.

The manœuvre, however, failed of its main purpose. The patrol was driven off and the brigade got into position, the Drake on the south-east corner of High Wood and the Hawke on the left, in touch, in the early morning, with the Anson Battalion of the 188th Brigade. With the Drake, in the front line, were the 248th Field Company R.E., and, in support, the Hood and 1st and 2nd Marine Battalions. The supports with the Brigade Headquarters spent the night at Martinpuich, but advanced at dawn to a position on a ridge half-way between Martinpuich and High Wood. One company of the Hood was detached to cover the Drake right flank, as the 47th Division had retired during the night. The 190th Brigade, who had continued their march the previous afternoon to Courcelette, were in divisional reserve.

So disposed, the Division was to sustain, again virtually unaided, the second attack in force directed against this part of the British line.

" At 6.30 a.m.," writes General de Pree, " the enemy could be seen advancing from Flers towards High Wood, and at 9 a.m. considerable movement was seen behind the enemy's

line, and patrols were seen moving forward round our right
flank. At 10 a.m. the attack became general.

" At this time there was very little artillery fire, and it
was quite possible to ride about on a horse fairly close up to
the front line, and to keep horses fairly close up under cover
in folds of the ground.

" The advance of the German Army was very interesting
to watch and was exceedingly skilfully carried out. The front
was covered by large patrols each carrying one or two light
machine guns. The use of light signals by these patrols was
most remarkable. They signalized each stage in their advance
by sending up a Verey light, with the result that the general
effect given was the advance of a line of light signals going
up as far as the eye could reach. There may have been some
slight disadvantage in this, in that it showed their position
to their enemy, but on the other hand it showed every man
that he was supported on his right and left, and this was a far
more decisive factor.

" The large patrols mentioned above everywhere probed
our front, and if they found a gap, they at once pressed through
it and sent up a success signal. The troops in rear at once
moved to it and poured through the gap, and in a few minutes
our flank was turned at that place. So far as could be seen
the majority of the enemy's infantry on this part of the front
had abandoned their rifles and simply acted as ammunition
carriers to their numerous light machine guns. This seems to
be borne out by the extraordinarily persistent volume of fire
which they kept up from these guns. In no other way could
it have been accomplished. In keeping up this persistency of
fire they were aided by the very slow, but amply sufficient
rate of fire of their guns."

At the beginning of this action, one of the most determined
and well-defined engagements of the many fought by the
Division in the retreat, they were supported on their left flank
by another division. About 9.80 a.m., this division withdrew,
and from that time till nightfall the infantry brigades of the
Naval Division were unsupported, except by their own machine
guns and the divisional artillery, who did fine work from their
new positions on Thiepval ridge. It remained none the less
an infantry battle of an old-fashioned character, with the
Divisional General and his staff directing operations from a

hill behind the front. In the earlier engagements the enemy
had been working round the right flank only and the brunt of
the battle had fallen on the 190th and 189th Brigades. Now
there was a gap in the British line on both flanks, and when
the Division on the right retired, " C " Company of the Anson
Battalion (Lieutenant Walker, R.N.V.R.), on the extreme left
of the Division, was immediately surrounded. A brilliant
counter-attack organized and led by Lieut.-Col. Kirkpatrick
enabled this company to fight its way out, but by 10.15 a.m.
the Brigade had had to fall back, and take up a position,
facing north-east, on the left flank of the Artists' Rifles and
7th Royal Fusiliers at Courcelette.

On the right of the line, the enemy, though in equal strength,
could not get round the flank so easily, since the earlier development of the situation had enabled full precautions to be taken.

At 10 a.m., four Vickers machine guns from the Divisional
Machine-Gun Battalion had been placed at the disposal of the
189th Brigade, and sent forward so as to cover the open flank,
and, at 11 a.m., the 4th Bedfords (190th Infantry Brigade)
were also sent by the Divisional commander to reinforce the
brigade. The Battalion was ordered to prolong our line,
echeloned behind the right of the Drake. The Drake and Hawke
carried out a local counter-attack to assist the advance of
the Bedfords, and captured two machine guns and some
prisoners, besides effecting an advance of some 250 yards.
This success was bought, however, at heavy price, as Commander Ellis, R.N.V.R., here received a wound from which he
died a few days later. His work for the Hawke Battalion and
for the Division had been memorable, and is remembered.

For an hour and a half the 189th Brigade and the Bedfords
held on to these advanced positions. Though hard pressed,
they could have maintained themselves longer, but the situation on the left flank was more serious, and General Lawrie
ordered a withdrawal to a position in front of Courcelette, where
a further stand was to be made in conjunction with the 188th
Brigade. Owing to the conditions of the fighting, the exhaustion of the men, and the shortage of officers, the arrangements for mutual support and withdrawal in stages proved
difficult to carry out, and heavy losses were experienced, but
the Brigade, halted on the Albert–Bapaume road with its
left at Courcelette Mill, was quickly reorganized, and another

stand was made, this time by the 188th Brigade.* Not until
8.30 p.m. was a further retirement on Thiepval decided on, as
there was no sign of support on either flank. In this retirement the 190th and 188th Brigades bore the burden of the
fighting, the 189th Brigade being withdrawn first. The
rearguard to the 190th Brigade was formed by the 4th
Bedfords, the 249th Field Company (Major Edgar, R.E.) and
" C " Company of the 14th Worcesters.

While the infantry and engineers took up their new positions
at Thiepval, at last unmolested by the enemy, the Divisional
Artillery retired across the Ancre, and, at 2 a.m. on the 26th,
under orders from the Vth Corps, the whole Division followed.
They found themselves, by a curious stroke of irony, once more
in Hamel, from which they had advanced to their first victory
on French soil in November, two years before. The enemy
did not press the retirement and did not even attack our old
position at Thiepval, till noon the next day, but the retirement
was dictated by the position to the north, arising, in the words
of Lieut.-Col. Boraston, from " the hurried falling back of
individual units " between Hamel and Hebuterne, " in what
came to be known among the irreverent as the Pys to Pas
Point to Point."† To the south, moreover, the enemy were
already on the outskirts of Albert and threatening to repeat
their old manœuvres of the early morning of the 24th, when
they had advanced from the south to strike at the Division's
line of retreat. This movement had to be forestalled. We had
reached the limit beyond which anything in the nature of a
further general retreat was impossible, if the unity of the allied
line was to be maintained. A counter-attack in force was
out of the question. We had no alternative, therefore,
but to fall back to a position in which we could co-operate,
effectively and at once, with the divisions on the flanks in a
resolute defensive. Such a position was evidently the line of
the Ancre.

The line taken up by the Naval Division on the early
morning of the 26th was, on the left of the divisional front,
our 1916 front line running from the Ancre in front of Hamel,
and was held by the 189th Brigade. From Hamel, south, our
1915 line had crossed the Ancre on to the Thiepval Plateau.

* It was here that Lieut.-Col. Kirkpatrick was mortally wounded.
† " Sir Douglas Haig's Command." Vol. II.

The new position followed the line of the Ancre, and the outpost line of the 188th and 190th Brigades was in Aveluy Wood. The Divisional Artillery were in position at Engelbelmer, save for one 18-pounder, concealed in the grounds of Mesnil Château close to General de Pree's headquarters. This gun carried out effective sniping over open sights at any of the enemy who showed themselves on Thiepval ridge.

About midday a very powerful attack from the north-east was made on the 2nd Division, on the immediate left of the divisional front. " The attack," says General de Pree, " must have been carried out by a large force, as it stretched as far as the eye could see and came on in two or three lines. It was preceded by large patrols, and each line appeared to consist of battalions with a wide interval between them, some moving in a sort of scattered, irregular crowd, others marching in fours down a road, as suited them best. On the high ground on their right near Auchonvillers they seemed to come on well, and to come right up to the New Zealand Division who had just come fresh into the line there. Down near the river they came on till they reached the crest of the ridge between Beaucourt and Beaumont Hamel. There one of our Field Batteries got on to them and burst some shrapnel in their faces. At once the leading men ran back under cover. This happened once or twice and they never came on again in numbers. They kept behind the ridge and from there for several hours they dribbled their men in ones and twos into what was known as the Station Valley. That seemed to finish the attack for the day on this side."

Another enemy attack had been delivered, and with greater success, to the south near Albert, and the clear intention of the enemy was to hold us on the Ancre front round Hamel, and push out north-west from Albert and cut our communications once more. The plan almost succeeded, as we shall see.

On the night of the 26th–27th the Naval Division handed over their line to the 12th Division and retired to Engelbelmer (189th Brigade) and Martinsart (188th Brigade), while the 190th Brigade took up a defensive position from Aveluy Wood to Bouzincourt with the 17th Division on their left. The object of this manœuvre was to hold the enemy should they attempt to debouch north from Albert, where the situation was

Thiepval Ridge.

still obscure. The 188th and 190th Brigades, while in these positions, were under the orders of the 12th Division.

By 1 a.m., all three brigades were in position, and General de Pree, having handed over to the G.O.C. 37th Brigade, started off on horseback with his Brigade Major for Engelbelmer. What followed can best be told in his own words.

" We rode to the corner where the road turns out of Mesnil village towards Engelbelmer, and as we reached it a party of men, evidently a German patrol, fired into us from the bank at about five yards' range and began shouting. Fortunately, no one was hit, and the party charged round the corner only to find themselves held up by a wire stretched across the road. We drove our horses into the wire and it gave, and our whole party clattered down the road towards Engelbelmer. On reaching that place it was found that one battalion had already gone into billets, but that the other two were still waiting to go in. Orders were issued to these to stand to, and to put outposts on the roads coming into the village from the east, as the situation was by no means clear. In a short time an agitated officer, with thirty men of the brigade which had relieved us, arrived and said that there were 2,000 Germans in Mesnil, and that they were marching on Engelbelmer. This was very awkward, as the whole brigade had less than a quarter of this number of very tired men. Still, the situation had to be met, and the two battalions were ordered to line up on each side of the Mesnil road a short distance outside the village, with orders to let the enemy up close in the dark and then fire into him and charge with the bayonet. As it turned out the enemy never came on, owing to a most gallant feat of arms by the 188th Brigade.

" The enemy had crossed the Ancre in small parties at Authville about 1 a.m., and penetrated to Martinsart and Mesnil. The news reached Brigadier-General Coleridge (188th Brigade), whose troops had been concentrated in Martinsart in support of the 36th Infantry Brigade. He at once aroused his brigade and arranged a counter-attack. The Anson Battalion (Commander Buckle, R.N.V.R.) were to advance on Mesnil, the 2nd Marines (Lt.-Commander Coote, R.N.V.R.) were to clear Aveluy Wood on their right flank and the 1st Marines (Lt.-Colonel Fletcher, R.M.L.I.) were to move in

19*

support. The attack was launched at 2.50 a.m. and met with immediate success. The enemy, in spite of their numerous machine guns, broke and fled in disorder, many screaming and climbing the trees in Aveluy Wood in their panic. Fifty prisoners and thirteen machine guns were taken and many were killed. This frustrated the most dangerous attempt which the Germans made to get through on this front. It showed what could be done by a sudden and vigorous counter-attack, even under the most depressing circumstances. It also spoke volumes for the men of this Brigade, that, worn out with fatigue, after days of retirement in which there had been little cause for encouragement, they could turn on their pursuers and drive them before them like chaff."

When the news of this success reached General de Pree at 7 a.m. on the 27th, he withdrew his outposts from the approaches to Engelbelmer, and his brigade was able at last to enjoy a few hours' rest. So also were the 188th Brigade when they returned to Martinsart. It was far otherwise with the 190th Brigade, who at 7.10 a.m. were called out, in conjunction with the 17th Division, to drive back the enemy from the Aveluy–Bouzincourt road on Albert.

The enemy were not in any great strength, but the confused situation favoured their tactics, and they had moved out of Albert in small parties, which were endeavouring to turn the flank of our position on the Ancre. The ability of the Vth Corps to spare troops to deal with the manœuvre without any pre-occupation for the continuity of our line determined the all-important issue. In the course of a day's fighting, severe at times but not continuous, the enemy were driven back nearly two miles to the very outskirts of Albert. The burden of the fighting, as far as the Naval Division was concerned, fell on the Bedfords* and the Artists' Rifles, brilliantly supported by machine-gun detachments under Major Denroche and Lieut. Pearson, R.N.V.R.†

The importance of the success achieved in this part of the front was made clear when the enemy, at 5.30 p.m. of the same

---

* In this attack the 190th Brigade suffered a severe loss in the death of Lieut.-Col. Collins Wells, of the Bedfords. For his heroism throughout the retreat this resolute officer was awarded the Victoria Cross.

† For his brilliant work on this occasion Lieutenant Pearson was awarded the Military Cross.

day (the 27th), delivered a strong attack on our position in the centre, in the neighbourhood of Hamel. Here the line was held by the 36th and 37th Brigades of the 12th Division. Had the flank of this division not been already safeguarded, our whole line would have been involved in disaster. Even as it was, Hamel was lost, and the enemy got within 1,000 yards of Martinsart, but for the second time in twelve hours General Coleridge's brigade came to the support of the front line troops and the enemy were finally held on the Mesnil ridge.

After the fighting of the 26th and 27th, it was felt advisable to relieve the 12th Division. After the 2nd Division had done a brief turn in the line, the sector was taken over on April 3rd by the Naval Division. On April 15th, however, the reorganized 17th Division was ready to take its turn in the line, and the Division marched back to the Puchevillers area to renew its acquaintance with civilization.

Almost at the beginning of their turn in the line, on April 5th, the Division had been subjected to a fierce attack, in which the 7th Royal Fusiliers sustained very heavy losses, and had to be reinforced by the 1st Marines. The next day the enemy returned to attack, and got into our line on the left of the 47th Division, but the 2nd Marines were sent up to reinforce the depleted 1st Battalion, and after a day's hard fighting, in which Colonel Fletcher, R.M.L.I., Major Clutterbuck, R.M.L.I.,* and Captain Newling rendered especially distinguished service, the position was recaptured, and with it fifty-six prisoners and ten machine guns. After this, the enemy's activity died away and the normal conditions of trench warfare slowly re-established themselves. It was an uphill task, much as it must have been in the first days of trench warfare on the Aisne. All reserves of engineers' stores had been lost in the retirement, and trench boards, dug-outs, and all the elaborate paraphernalia of stationary warfare were lacking. The Division, however, had been strongly reinforced, and the line was left more or less defensible by the date the Division was relieved.

So ended on this front, in a return to the earlier methods on the earlier battlefield, the first great German offensive of 1918. Looking back, even over four years of warfare, the

* Who had succeeded Lt.-Commander Coote in command of the 2nd R.M. Battalion.

fifteen days of fighting, from March 21st to April 5th, have an outstanding importance. If our own earlier actions on the same front had indeed been victories, we had suffered a defeat; but there was not lacking the suspicion that we had yet been victorious. The war of movement had opened; and it was clear once and for all that, man for man, officer for officer, the British infantry were superior in tenacity, in resilience, in personality, to the enemy. The Allies had not, of course, by any means regained the initiative. To the north and south, on the Arras front, on the Lys and in Champagne, the struggle was to be renewed, perhaps even more bitterly. But the air was cleared. The first German stroke had been parried, and on this front at any rate there would be no further retreat.

The individual contribution to the general result, always difficult to identify amid the too voluminous, uncritical and *ex parte* records, is, in the case of the operations under review, almost impossible to appraise. Never was there, however, more scope for personal gallantry and initiative, and it is certain that the hour usually found the man. To bring a brigade, a battalion, or a company through a period such as that which began on March 21st was, indeed, in itself a feat of arms.

Battalion commanders with their headquarters fought in the line, but they did not sacrifice their responsibility, and this dual rôle threw on them an especial strain which merits recognition. The action fought by six battalions on the Green line through the night of the 23rd–24th, and the rearguard action of the Drake Battalion* on the Ytres–Bus road on the morning of the 24th, are instances of initiative which had determining results. The divisional retreat to High Wood and the stand there made on the morning of the 25th were instances, on the contrary, where the Divisional and Brigade staffs personally directed operations " on the ground," a practice too often relegated to field days behind the lines. But always the main burden fell on the junior officers and men of the infantry, the engineers and the machine-gun battalion : on their constancy depended the issue.

Never did the men of the Division show more clearly how

---

* For this skilful operation Commander Beak was awarded the D.S.O. The same distinction fell to Lieut.-Col. Fletcher, R.M.L.I., and Major Clutterbuck, R.M.L.I., for their handling of the two Marine battalions. Commander Buckle, for his fine work in command of the Anson on the 27th and 28th received a bar to his D.S.O.

superior was the quality of their discipline, than when the 189th Brigade were operating round High Wood on the evening of March 24th. Details of at least two divisions came among them in considerable disorder, and enemy patrols, firing on the whole body of troops, endeavoured by every artifice to spread the panic. During the first minutes when the confusion was at its height the brigade, which had been formed up in mass to be marched off to its positions, remained in parade formation, apparently indifferent to its surroundings. Then, under orders, detachments moved off to engage and drive off the enemy. Such a quality is worth everything in the confusion of a retreat, for it enables a battle to be fought to a finish, even where the line of retreat is open. The divisions who did this, saved the British Army; where these divisions were, there were no gaps.

The stand to which this incident was the prelude was one of the two marked contributions of the Division as a unit to the ultimately successful defensive. As Colonel Boraston points out in his chapter on these operations in Mr. Dewar's book on " Sir Douglas Haig's Command," the danger, in the afternoon of March 24th, was acute, not only because of the gaps between the IVth and Vth Corps and the Vth Corps and the Fifth Army, but because of gaps in the line of the Vth Corps itself. The Division on the right of the Drake Battalion retired at 1 a.m. on the 25th; and the Division on the left of the Anson Battalion at 9.30 a.m. The 2nd Division (according to Mr. Everard Wyrall) retired at 1 p.m. The Naval Division, covering the Courcelette–Pozières ridge, the Thiepval plateau and the all-important Ancre crossings at Hamel, was fighting in High Wood till 3.30 p.m., and between that line and Thiepval, till 6 p.m. It is impossible to resist the conclusion that the halt called to the enemy's advance by the Naval Division on this afternoon was of real importance.

The other important incident in the week's fighting was the action of the Division, on the night of the 26th–27th and throughout the following day, in counter-attacking the Germans in Mesnil and Martinsart and the north of Albert, each time with decisive results. These achievements were the more remarkable because they were the climax to five days of incessant fighting, which had left the battalions disastrously depleted. Between the 13th and the 27th March, the losses of the Division (including those from gas) were in the neighbourhood of 6,000 officers and men. In all this time no reinforcements had reached the battalions. The average strength of the battalions engaged in the counter-attacks of the 27th were not more than 250, including transport and other headquarter details ; yet they succeeded.

The price of victory was high. Four skilful, experienced and intrepid battalion commanders, Lt.-Colonel Farquharson of the Royal Marines, Lt.-Colonel Collins Wells of the Bedfords (whose gallantry from the first hours of the offensive until he was mortally wounded in the advance on Albert on the 27th had earned for him the greatest of military distinctions), Lt.-Colonel Kirkpatrick of the Anson, and Commander Bernard Ellis of the Hawke, had been killed. Others who had fallen in the later stages of the retirement were Lt. D. W. K. Hall and Lt. G. Wharf of the 1st Marine Battalion, 2nd Lieut. J. A. Smith of the 2nd Marine Battalion, Lieut. C. G. Walker, M.C., R.N.V.R. (whose company had so distinguished itself in front of High Wood), Lieut. G. J. Ridler, R.N.V.R., Sub-Lieut. A. H. S. Kenny, Sub-Lieut. Caton, Sub-Lieut. Dunning, Sub-Lieut. Mallett and Sub-Lieut. Hepworth of the Anson, Sub-Lieut. D. Beatty, Sub-Lieut. G. H. Powell and Sub-Lieut. R. Pawson of the Drake, Lieut. F. C. Forrester, M.C., R.N.V.R., of the Hawke, and Lieut. Grant Dalton, M.C., of the Hood.

Among the wounded were Lt.-Colonel Malone, D.S.O. (7th Royal Fusiliers), Major Leatham (2nd in Command of the Artists' Rifles, who had done fine service on the flank of the Division in the Green line), Staff-Surgeon McCracken, D.S.O., R.N., of the Hood Battalion, who had served with the Hood from the first days of the Gallipoli campaign, and Lieut. B. B. Rackham, M.C., R.N.V.R., Adjutant of the Hawke Battalion, who had served continuously with the battalion since the autumn of 1915.

With such losses, the work of reorganization was heavy, and was made no lighter by the inevitably constant demands for working parties to construct defensive positions in depth on the new front. The tasks of working parties were even more arduous now than they had been in November, 1916, although the weather was dry ; for the increased artillery activity, the constant menace of the hostile aeroplanes, and the dangers of gas bombardments made it necessary to put reserve divisions much further behind the lines, and so to increase the length of the daily marches to and from the front.   The Division was, however, fortunate to find at Toutencourt the ranges and equipment of the Fifth Army School, and the reinforced battalions (at the end of April they had reached an average strength of twenty-five officers and eight hundred men) were able to get, for the first time since December, 1916, some really useful training.   A divisional musketry competition even was held, and won by the Artists' Rifles, who thus maintained their peace-time reputation.

With the completion of this training on May 8th, this chapter will appropriately close.   With the hardening of the British front west of the Ancre and south of the Somme, the first of the German offensives had ended, and, on this part of the front, the work of organizing the army against the return of the initiative had begun.

CHAPTER XVI

THE ADVANCE TO VICTORY

TO those who watched from across the Channel the tremendous struggle on the Lys at the end of April, and the no less anxious days at the end of May and the beginning of June, when the enemy crossed the Aisne, the menace of defeat first observed in the dark days of the March retreat seemed to grow through the summer of 1918 ever more threatening. The climax of popular anxiety was reached in the middle of July when the enemy renewed their attack on the French on a front of fifty miles east and west of Rheims, and crossed the Marne for the first time since 1914. The eye of the spectator was riveted throughout these months on the threatened areas, and missed the unbroken line of trenches from Arras to Albert, and in the centre and on the right of the French line, where many British and French Corps and the growing strength of the American Armies were resting and reorganizing. In the end these sectors were not the least important, for it was here that the Allies were once more reasserting the superiority of their unbroken determination against an enemy who, as the price of his local successes, was visibly weakening over a wider front in skill, material and resolution.

Among those to whom these summer months, for many so anxious, were months of growing confidence and strength, was the Naval Division, who on May 8th returned to the Hamel–Aveluy Wood sector to relieve the 17th Division.

The period of transition from the resolute defensive, which the enemy was still able to impose on the Division when it first returned to the Hamel sector in May, to the resumption of the offensive in August was not without incident, and it remains of some historical importance even at this date.

Throughout May, Aveluy Wood was the scene of continuous

raids by the enemy against the posts held by the 190th Brigade, and, though no ground was permanently lost, the issue was no better than a drawn battle. The same can be said of the Artillery duels which made up the more serious part of the fighting at this time. During the entire period from May 8th to June 4th the enemy artillery activity was maintained, and frequent and intensive bombardments were put down on the trenches and the back areas. Raids on a large scale were carried out by companies of the Hawke and 1st Marine Battalions on May 18th,* and on the 24th by the whole strength of the Anson, Hood and 4th Bedfords, but though the results achieved by the Hawke and Anson Battalions were excellent, the enemy resistance generally was such as to make raiding a matter of hard fighting, in which the heavier losses fell as often as not to the attacking party. This was particularly the case with the Hood and the Bedfords on May 24th. The results of these determined, if miniature, battles were, however, far more than proportionate to our losses. The enemy learnt that our strength was unbroken, and the knowledge was of far-reaching political effect. In Germany their wives and their children were on the verge of starvation, capable of enduring further, but only within assignable limits of time. The mere recrudescence of our activity, on the very scene of their most striking success, was in the circumstances more fatal to those hopes than many an earlier defeat. To the Division, on the other hand, these raids, costly though they were (the casualties in the raids of the 24th were 18 officers,† and 210 N.C.O.'s and men), represented a substantial achievement full of promise. Actually more than half the effectives employed had been raw recruits with no previous service in France. That such men could take part with effect in night operations of an intricate character against a still vigorous enemy was as great a testimony to their own quality as to that of their leaders. The result was all the more satisfactory, since the heavy losses on the retreat, and still more in the subsequent fighting for the line of the Ancre, had necessitated yet another

---

* In this otherwise successful operation Sub-Lieut. R. S. Kelland of the Hawke, and Surgeon A. L. Pearce Gould, M.B., R.N. (1st Marine Battalion), were killed.

† Of whom Sub-Lieut. J. Crowther of the Anson, and Sub-Lieut. P. W. Dann, Sub-Lieut. E. W. Hulbert and Sub-Lieut. R. L. Stephenson of the Hood were killed.

reorganization and many changes of command. The difficulty
this time had been to find reinforcements for the Marine battalions, and in the end these had been amalgamated under
Lt.-Colonel Fletcher, D.S.O., R.M.L.I., and the 2nd Battalion,
Royal Irish Rifles (Lt.-Colonel Harrison, D.S.O.), had been attached to complete the strength of the 188th Brigade. In the
189th Brigade, Commander Jones succeeded to the command
of the Hawke, with Lieut.-Commander E. M. Lockwood as
second in command, and Lieut. R. Blackmore, M.C., R.N.V.R.,
as adjutant. In the 190th Brigade, Brigadier-General Hutchison, C.M.G., D.S.O., left the Division (in which he had served
with such distinction for almost three years), on his appointment
as Assistant Adjutant-General of the Royal Marines, and was
succeeded by Brigadier-General Leslie, D.S.O.

On June 4th, the Division were relieved and enjoyed three
weeks' rest in the Toutencourt area. Then, moving back,
they took over the line in front of Auchonvillers, immediately
to the left of the Hamel sector. The period from June 28rd to
July 25th, which was spent by the Division on this front, was
noteworthy principally for its uneventful character, contrasting
markedly with the prevalent expectation of a further enemy
attack. To meet this a new defensive system was now in
practice ; the chief feature was the abandonment of " lines,"
and even of chains of posts, and the substitution of defensive
zones embracing a number of tactical features, the defence of
each of which was entrusted to a virtually isolated unit. This
system was, of course, never tested. There was no infantry
attack, the enemy artillery had greatly moderated their
activities, and under our own bombardments their defences
gradually crumbled away. Little or no effort was made by the
enemy to repair them. The culminating point of their demoralization was reached on the night of July 12th, when the
Drake Battalion, in a brilliant raid carried out by no more than
two officers (Sub-Lieut. Bolt and Sub-Lieut. Briddon) and fifty-
four men, captured twenty-two of the enemy and one machine
gun, and put out of action at least as many again, with the loss
of one man of the raiding party.* It was a fitting end to three
months of arduous training and reorganization, and a good
omen for the share the Division might expect to play in greater

* See Appendix F for a graphic account of this remarkable success kindly
furnished me by Brigadier-General de Pree.

The Church at Mesnil.

events. These were now impending. On July 20th, when the Division were still in the line, it became known that General Foch's counter-stroke on the Marne had thrown the enemy back across the river, and on the 21st Château Thierry was retaken. The enemy was in retreat.

From now onwards, the history of the Naval Division assumes a new complexity. It is not only that in the great battles which followed one another unceasingly from August 8th to the end of the campaign the part played by any one Division was necessarily small, but that any over-detailed account of particular advances, however successful, would give a false impression of the march of events. Moreover, the events of these dramatic but laborious days were important rather in their results, than in the manner of their achievement. The days of attrition were over, and, in the face of a beaten enemy, the war of positions had begun.

The historian must bow to the logic of events. His story must move swiftly, and as the background for his narrative must be traced the march of armies.

The first battle of the concluding allied offensive had been directed against the enemy lodgment across the Marne. It was a preliminary operation, fought while the Naval Division were still in the line opposite Beaumont Hamel, with no thought of an early close to the war. The enemy demoralization was patent, but the extent of our own resources was naturally unknown to the infantry in the front line; 1919 was the year to which the British infantry still looked for the final offensive.

The first rumour of more dramatic events reached the Division on August 8th, in the form of unexpected orders to move to the Montigny area, just south of the Albert–Amiens road. On that day the Fourth Army, in conjunction with the French (whose advance, however, began actually a day later), attacked the enemy salient south of Albert. The objective was, roughly, our old 1916 line, the possession of which would restore Montdidier and free the Paris–Amiens railway. By August 12th, the objective had been gained, and the way was clear for the second Battles of the Somme.

The first intention had been that the offensive should continue where it had been begun, against the enemy front south of Albert, and it was with a view to protecting the flank of the further advance that the Naval Division had been moved south. As is now known, this project, after discussion, was abandoned, and it was decided to turn the German positions west of the Somme by striking above Albert, and directing the main weight of our attack, from the north, on Bapaume. This meant an attack on a front extending further north even than Gommecourt (the northern limit of the attack of July 1st, 1916), and involved a few days' respite for the enemy, while the arrangements were completed with a speed, a precision and a measure of secrecy which formed a welcome contrast to the practice of the past.

The Naval Division was among those assigned to the new offensive, and it was transferred for the purpose to the IVth Corps, which held the front to the north of Beaumont Hamel, through Bucquoy. Further to the north was the VIth Corps on the left of the Third Army.

Marching only at night, the Division moved north between August 15th and 19th, and found themselves at Souastre, in rear of the line held by the 37th Division, which ran through the Western outskirts of Bucquoy. Here, for the first time, detailed orders were received for the attack, which was to open on August 21st, at 4.55 a.m. The first objective of the IVth and VIth Corps was to be Bucquoy, Ablainzeville and the Ablainzeville Spur. Here were the German first line positions, which they had held for some months. The next objective was defined as the Irles–Bihucourt line, and then north along the Achiet-le-Grand–Arras railway. The direction of the attack was south-east. The first objective on the IVth Corps front was to be taken by the 37th Division, already in the line, and the 5th and Naval Divisions were to go through to the second objective. On the left of the Naval Division would be the 3rd Division of the VIth Corps.

General Lawrie, with his objective across the Achiet–Arras railway, decided to attempt to reach the railway with the 188th and 189th Brigades, and to send the 190th Brigade through at that stage to complete the operation. An intermediate objective, known as the Brown line, was arranged for the 188th and 189th Brigades a little to the east of Logeast Wood. This line was to be attacked by two companies of the Anson, the Marines, two companies of the Drake and the Hawke. The line of the railway was to be attacked by the remaining

companies of the Anson and Drake, the R.I.R., and the Hood
Battalion. The limit of our barrage was the Brown line, and,
beyond that, the attack would be covered by tanks.

Shortly after midnight on the 20th, the Brigades moved
forward, their march being timed to reach our front line ten
minutes before the attack opened. Punctually at 4.55 a.m.
the advance of the 37th Division began, and immediately
behind followed the two Naval Brigades, a change in tactics
eloquent of the changed character of the German resistance
as experienced further south. There was a thick mist, and the
Division were in unknown country, but they kept their direction, and almost all units reached the Brown line with virtually
no opposition. An unfinished message found by the Hawke
Battalion in a captured dug-out revealed indeed that a very
sudden retreat had taken place, and that the enemy's line of
resistance was further east.

By now, we were out of reach of our barrage, and in the
thick mist one of the tanks went over into the 5th Division
area, taking a company of the Hood Battalion with it into
Achiet-le-Petit, which was captured. Two tanks, however,
maintaining direction, reached the Achiet–Arras railway, on
the right of the Divisional front, and here two companies of
the Hood with one company of the Drake on their left secured
a temporary lodgment. A similar success was achieved on
the extreme left of the Division's front (actually in the 3rd
Division area), where " B " Company of the Anson Battalion
reached the railway embankment, with details of the Marines
and the R.I.R.

In the centre, the advance from the Brown line made less
progress in the face of strong opposition, and " A " Company
of the Anson Battalion, " B " and " D " Companies of the
Marines* (who had gone forward in place of the main body of
the R.I.R., which had lost direction), and the main body of the
Drake Battalion found themselves held up on the outskirts of
Achiet-le-Grand. At this place there was a cemetery, a brick
field, and the remains of one of our old hut camps west of the
railway. The floors of these huts had been lowered three or
four feet below ground level to give protection to our troops
against German aeroplane bombing, and these huts now

---

* The Marines lost very heavily in this advance ; Major R. A. Poland, R.M.
and Captain B. G. Andrews, R.M., were among the killed.

afforded a ready-made entrenched position for the enemy. The Germans had placed machine guns and anti-tank guns in these places, and established a strong line of defence, which could be easily reinforced from the ample reserves which they had in the railway cutting. It was evident that they had thinned out their front lines, and concentrated a defence here, maintained by fresh troops. As our troops reached this place, about 11 a.m., the sun cleared away the mist, and they found themselves coming up against it without the help of a barrage which had been left behind, the effective range of the Field Artillery having been passed. The Tanks, which had come up by now, tried to assist, but were disabled by the anti-tank guns. The infantry made a most gallant attack, as the dead lying out in line after the fight testified, but, in the absence of artillery support, the enemy could not be dislodged except by an enveloping movement, for which no preparations had been made.

The result was that the troops in the centre of the divisional front, falling back to a position a few hundred yards east of Logeast Wood, compelled a retirement on the flanks. Advanced posts were finely maintained, ahead of the general line, by the Anson and Drake,* and the former battalion actually achieved a local advance in the afternoon. By 6 p.m., however, the battle was at a standstill, and the line was consolidated, the front being reinforced by units of the 190th Brigade and held from left to right by the Anson (in advanced posts), the 7th Royal Fusiliers, the Drake (in advanced posts), the R.I.R., the Artists' Rifles and the Hood Battalion. The night was quiet, but on the 22nd, the enemy, still standing to their line on the railway, made three determined counter-attacks at 5.55 a.m., at 10.30 a.m. and at 1.15 p.m. The Divisional artillery had, however, by now come forward, and, thanks to their barrage, to some excellent work by the 189th L.T.M. Battery (in which Sub-Lieut. Telfer, R.N.V.R., especially distinguished himself), and to the effective machine and Lewis gun fire from the flanking positions occupied by the Anson and Hood, our line held. Only on the last occasion was even a temporary lodgment effected in the line held by the 188th

---

* Commander Beak, by his skill and gallantry, contributed in no small measure to the success of the operations in the centre of the line and Commander Buckle rendered no less distinguished service on the left flank.

Brigade, and the position was at once restored by the Marines* and the R.I.R.

During the night of the 22nd–23rd the remaining units of the 188th and 189th Brigades were withdrawn, the front being taken over by the 37th Division.† The 190th Brigade remained in immediate support. Such things as inter-divisional reliefs, which on the Ancre, at Arras and at Passchendaele had marked the definite close of an attack, were henceforward only incidents in a continuing battle. To the left, on the front of the VIth Corps, and to the right as far as Albert, the German front line system had fallen, and from the north and the west we were closing in on Bapaume. August 23rd provided an interval of rest only for the Naval Division, while the 37th Division moved forward in touch with the New Zealand Division and the 5th Division, and captured Achiet-le-Grand.

This drove the enemy back on to a line running through Grévillers, Loupart Wood and Warlencourt. The operations were here reaching their critical phase. Judged by the standards of the past, a dramatic success had been achieved, but our aim now was nothing less than to drive the enemy back at once across the Somme. To accomplish this, it was necessary to cut across the Albert–Bapaume road, before the enemy could consolidate a new position against our attacks from the north-west.

On the morning of the 24th the attack was renewed by the 37th and New Zealand Divisions against Loupart Wood, and for some distance on either side, but the progress was not substantial. The wood, indeed, was captured, but isolated posts were still holding out on the eastern edges, and the enemy remained in Grévillers and Warlencourt, and their front from Bapaume southward was still continuous. The attack had to be pressed further.

At noon on the 24th, the Brigadier-General, General Staff, of the IVth Corps, called at General Lawrie's headquarters just east of Bucquoy and gave verbal instructions for the Naval Division to advance that evening on the right of the New Zealand Division, who were to renew the attack on Grévillers.

---

* For his share in these operations, Lieut.-Col. Fletcher, R.M.L.I., was awarded a bar to his D.S.O.

† A complete list of the officers killed in this and the succeeding operations is given in Appendix E (iii).

The 47th and 21st Divisions would attack on the far right of the Naval Division, advancing, between Warlencourt and Courcelette, from their positions further west. When these instructions were given, General Lawrie was out inspecting the battalions after the recent fighting, and there was some delay in issuing the orders, which, however, were communicated to the brigades concerned at 8 p.m. The brigades had been warned earlier that they might be required to attack during the day, and had moved forward in front of Logeast Wood in the morning. From here they were now moved off to the valley north of Loupart Wood, from which they were to advance, at 7.80 p.m., on le Barque and Thilloy, two villages south-west of the wood, across the Albert–Bapaume road. If the attack succeeded, it was to be pressed home to Riencourt.

The situation, as the brigades approached the assembly position, was one of considerable confusion. No one appeared to be sure whether Loupart Wood was held by the enemy or not, and many even of the different battalion headquarters had no maps showing the objectives. The Brigadier of the 189th Brigade decided, therefore, to ride ahead with his battalion commanders to the edge of Loupart Wood to endeavour to get a sight of the country over which the battalions had to operate, but the party had to cross the wood (which, it had been ascertained, was clear of the enemy) before they could form any idea of the country. Even then they could not see the objective. By now it was 7.15 p.m., and there was no time left to explain the plans in any detail to the rank and file of the brigade. The confusion on the assembly position had, meanwhile, been heightened by a severe bombing attack, directed on the Hawke and Hood Battalions by a swarm of low-flying aeroplanes, and it seemed doubtful if these battalions would be ready to go forward at 7.80 p.m., which was the hour fixed for the attack.

Having regard to all the circumstances, Brigadier-General de Pree, as the senior officer on the spot, decided that it was his duty to stop the attack as far as the Naval Division was concerned, and his decision was conveyed to the 188th Brigade and to the New Zealand Division. In days when the German resistance was still vigorous, the decision would have been inevitable: in the conditions prevailing at the time it is impossible to say what the results of the attack might have been, but it is sufficient to say that high authorities a few days later came to the conclusion that the decision was justified. The immediate result was, however, that Commander Egerton of the Hood succeeded temporarily to the command of the 189th Brigade. As was, perhaps, inevitable when all units were feeling the strain of continuous fighting, the breakdown of the arrangements for the night's attack caused a good deal of unfavourable comment. The hypothetical advance became, in retrospect, an assured success unreasonably prejudiced. For such laborious incursions into the domain of constructive criticism there was, however, no time on this anxious night. With the arrival of maps, later in the evening came orders to advance on the same objectives at 6 a.m. the next morning (August 25th). As in the original plan, the attack was to be carried out from right to left by the Anson and the R.I.R., the Marines, the Hawke and the Hood Battalions. The Drake Battalion was to clear a communication trench, which ran along the right Divisional boundary to the German trenches half way between Loupart Wood and the Albert–Bapaume road. They were then to operate on the exposed flank of the further advance. During the night of the 24th–25th, the 47th Division were reported to have reached Warlencourt and the 21st Division to be between that village and Courcelette; but the enemy certainly held the famous Butte de Warlencourt on the Bapaume road, just to the right of the Divisional boundary.

The total distance from the starting-off point to the first objective beyond Thilloy was four thousand yards.

The advance started punctually, and in a thick mist the 188th Brigade, with the New Zealanders in their flank, pushed forward without much opposition. So, too, did the left companies of the Hawke Battalion. Two companies of the Anson Battalion under Captain Scott and Lieutenant Paterson, R.N.V.R., and two companies of the Hawke under Lieutenant Dodds and Lieutenant Stevenson, actually reached the high ground east of Thilloy and for a time maintained themselves, but, on the right flank, the attack had been held up, and in the centre the Marines had only made slow progress. The enemy trench system facing the south-west corner of Loupart Wood was the scene of a vigorous resistance, entailing grievous losses to the Hood and Hawke Battalions. Here fell the two battalion commanders, Commander Jones* and Lieut.-Commander Fish, both survivors of many more desperate encounters, and Lieut.-Commander O. J. Wainright, R.N.V.R., the senior company commander of the Hawke Battalion. Taking cover in the numerous shell-holes, and reinforced by the Drake Battalion, the 189th Brigade set to work with their Lewis guns to master the enemy's fire. After a time their efforts were rewarded, or else, perhaps more probably, the enemy were fighting a rearguard action by time table : in any case, at about noon the enemy resistance broke, and the three battalions (the Hawke and Hood now commanded by Lt.-Commander Blackmore and Lieut. Maudsley, R.N.V.R.) pressed forward and seized the high ground on either side of the ravine, known as the Yellow cut, east of the Bapaume road. The Hawke Battalion extended the position to the outskirts of le Barque, which the Marines had not yet reached. The Artists' Rifles, advancing on the heels of the 189th Brigade, were probably the first to enter le Barque itself. On the left of the Divisional front, the Anson and the R.I.R. were on the outskirts of Thilloy. On this position fell back the relics of the Anson and Hawke companies who alone had penetrated Thilloy and Ligny Thilloy.

Here the attack died down. In the villages the enemy were in great strength, and only the timely assistance of our heavy artillery prevented a serious counter-attack developing on the afternoon of the 25th. To carry the attack through Thilloy to Riencourt, as had been hoped, was wholly impossible. The success had, however, been a remarkable one. The enemy's communications were cut, and Bapaume was effectually isolated from the enemy positions to the south-west. Particularly remarkable, perhaps, was the achievement of the 189th Brigade, largely due to the resolute leading of Commander Beak and Lt.-Commander Blackmore.† This brigade, well outside the

---

* Commander Jones had been first wounded on June 4th at Gallipoli and had since then served almost continuously with the Division, commanding at different times the Anson, Nelson and Hawke battalions. The loss of an unfailingly optimistic personality was much felt.

Another experienced officer killed in this engagement was Lieut.-Commander E. A. Sprange, M.C., R.N.V.R., of the Anson Battalion.

† For his brilliant conduct of these operations, and of those immediately before and after, Commander Beak was recommended for and received the Victoria Cross. Lt.-Commander Blackmore received a bar to his M.C. Fine work was also done by Sub-Lieut. J. W. Kerr of the Hood Battalion, who was awarded the M.C., and by Lieutenant Biggs and Sub-Lieut. Wood of the Hawke Battalion.

Divisional boundary, and without support in the first instance on either flank, remained unsupported till nightfall on the 25th, when the 21st Division came forward.

In the course of the operations 37 officers and 1,095 other ranks had been captured. The next two days of this battle were, however, less successful, for no fewer than four attacks on Thilloy, by the 188th and 190th Brigades, were beaten off by machine-gun fire. The Divisions on the flanks were no more successful, and, on the night of the 27th–28th, the Naval Division was relieved.

The first impression which is left by the operations is one of great initial success, not carried to its conclusion. Such an impression would, however, be hardly correct. The enemy rearguards were fighting hard and scientifically, and would not retreat until we had so manœuvred as to threaten their line of retreat. The spearhead had been thrust, however, into the enemy position, and the fall of Bapaume, and, with it, the fall of the enemy's positions on the western bank of the Somme, was only a matter of days. Bapaume actually fell on August 29th and Peronne on September 1st.

While the fruits of the successes of the IVth and Vth and VIth Corps were thus being gathered, the Naval Division were transferred, on August 30th, to Sir Charles Fergusson's XVIIth Corps to take part in the new battle which had opened further to the north on August 26th.

The immediate object of the second Battles of Arras was to seize the northern end of the Hindenburg system and the Drocourt–Quéant system behind it. If we could carry these positions, we should have driven a wedge between the new positions to which we were forcing the enemy to retire east of the Somme and those to which the enemy was still clinging on the Lys. We should thus compel him to evacuate the Lys salient and to fall back in front of Cambrai to the lines of the Canal du Nord and the Canal St. Quentin. We should, in this event, press on against the line of the Canals, and endeavour, by seizing Cambrai and pushing forward to the east of it, to drive the enemy back on Maubeuge before he could extricate his forces in the south, which all the time would be pressed back on the Ardennes by the Franco-American offensive.

This plan was fully carried out, and at its two most critical stages, the attack on the Drocourt–Quéant line and the attack on the Canal du Nord–Canal d'Escaut position, the Naval Division, fighting on the front of the XVIIth Corps, played no small part. Their particular doings must be shortly described.

The Hindenburg line as designed had run, it will be remembered, roughly north-west from the Somme front, till it joined the old German position south of Arras at Tilloy les Mofflaines. The line reduced considerably the salient in the enemy's 1916 line, which had run north and south almost to Soissons, and then turned sharply east to Verdun. But it still left a minor salient south of Arras, which had been only slightly flattened by our attacks in 1917. The enemy successes in the beginning of 1918 had brought their line back almost to where it had stood before the first Battle of Arras, but their position was now strengthened by the Drocourt–Quéant line, a second prepared position linking the centre section of the Hindenburg line with the Lens defences. The battle which had opened east of Arras on August 26th, on the First Army front, had carried us, by August 31st, across the northen end of the Hindenburg line and over the old battle grounds of 1917 to this new but formidable position. The decisive moment had now arrived when the right of the First Army was to attempt to carry it from a point two miles north of Quéant on a front of some five miles. To assist in this operation, the left Corps of the Third Army (which was the XVIIth Corps) was to co-operate with the 2nd Canadian Division, who were the right Division of the First Army. The XVIIth Corps had already made a substantial advance, but on the evening of August 31st they were still west of Hendecourt and Bullecourt, and were thus still some two miles distant from the Drocourt–Quéant line. The 57th Division was on the left of the XVIIth Corps front, and the 52nd Division on the right.

The main (First Army) attack was to take place at dawn on the 2nd, and, on the night of the 1st–2nd, the 57th and 52nd Divisions attacked and carried Hendecourt and Bullecourt, and the 57th carried Riencourt, still further east. By the hour fixed for the Canadian attack, the 57th Division was only slightly in rear of the Canadians' right. The plan for the remainder of the attack was wisely indeterminate, but the main feature was that the 57th Division was not to attack to its front, but to follow the flank of the Canadians and exploit their success by bombing south, down the Drocourt–Quéant line from the position at which it was entered by the Canadians,

southward to Quéant. They were then to press forward
north of Quéant. The Canadian objective was Magnicourt,
a mile and a half beyond the Drocourt–Quéant line, and the
57th Division were ultimately to prolong the Canadian left. At
this point, if all went well, came the turn of the Naval Division.

At 6 p.m. on the 31st September the Division* was
6,000 yards west of Hendecourt. On October 1st, the 188th
Brigade, which was to lead the Division's attack, moved up
to Hendecourt and arrived at 1.30 a.m. on the 2nd, just as
the 57th Division were moving off to attack Riencourt. Their
orders from the G.O.C. (Major-General Blacklock, D.S.O.,
had assumed command of the Division in place of Major-General
Lawrie, C.B., D.S.O., on August 30th†) were to pass through
the right of the Canadian Division's area on receiving the word
" Move," and, sweeping round from the north, to cut the
Quéant–Cambrai railway and seize the high ground east of
Quéant. If the line of the railway was reached, the Division
was to press on to Inchy. The other brigades were to move
forward, behind the 188th Brigade, by pre-arranged stages.
Brig.-General Coleridge was in command of the operations
at the front, and was to have a call on the battalions of the
189th Brigade.

The astonishing feature of this battle is that, as far as the
Naval Division was concerned, every detail of this tremendous
programme, involving an advance of more than ten miles from
the first assembly position, was carried out.

The operative word of command, " Move," was given by
General Blacklock to General Coleridge, on receipt of information as to the progress of the Canadian attack, at 7.45 a.m.
The 188th Brigade moved, in the first instance, due east on the
tracks of the Canadians to Callingcard Wood, and then struck
down, almost due south, on either side of the Magnicourt–
Quéant road.

From this point events moved with a bewildering rapidity.
By 1 p.m., the 57th Division had reached all their objectives,
and the 188th Brigade, thanks in great part to the fine leading

---

* Except, however, for Brig.-General de Rougemont and his staff, the Divisional
Artillery remained with the IVth Corps and did not rejoin the Division till
November.

† The departure of General Lawrie was very widely regretted throughout
the Division, who had not only admired his personal gallantry but had experienced his unfailing consideration for the officers and men under his command.

of Commander Buckle, D.S.O., was approaching the line of the Quéant–Cambrai railway. The Drake Battalion was still further east, having been ordered to make a wider turning movement through the Bois de Bouche to assist the 188th Brigade. By the afternoon, this movement had succeeded, and the battalion was on the left of the R.I.R. On the left were the Canadians.

The next step was the advance on Inchy, but, before the orders for this reached the battalions (the 189th Brigade were chosen for this objective), Commander Beak had made, on his own initiative, a dashing advance across the railway to Pronville, actually south-east of Quéant, capturing on the way a substantial portion of the Hindenburg support line. Commander Beak crossed the railway at 4 p.m., and his patrols were in Pronville at 6.30 p.m. The main body of his battalion remained astride the Pronville–Inchy road, thus effectively cutting off the enemy's retreat, and ensuring the capture of a substantial number of prisoners as well as many machine guns, and several trench mortars and field guns.*

* The operations of this battalion were remarkable, not only for these results, but for the brilliant leadership displayed by many individual officers and men. Particularly noteworthy were the exploits of C.P.O. Prowse and Sub-Lieut. T. Simmonds, the former of whom was awarded the Victoria Cross, and the latter the D.S.O. The account of their exploits, taken from the Gazettes, is as follows :—

No. W.Z./424 Chief Petty Officer George Prowse, V.C., D.C.M., R.N.V.R., Drake Battalion (Landore).

For most conspicuous bravery and devotion to duty. During an advance a portion of his company became disorganized by heavy machine-gun fire from an enemy strong point. Collecting what men were available, he led them with great coolness and bravery against this strong point, capturing it, together with twenty-three prisoners and five machine-guns.

Later he took a patrol forward in face of much enemy opposition, and established it on important high ground. On another occasion he displayed great heroism by attacking single-handed an ammunition limber which was trying to recover ammunition, killing three men who accompanied it and capturing the limber.

Two days later he rendered valuable services when covering the advance of his company with a Lewis-gun section, and located later on two machine-gun positions in a concrete emplacement, which were holding up the advance of the battalion on the right.

With complete disregard of personal danger, he rushed forward with a small party and attacked and captured these posts, killing six enemy and taking thirteen prisoners and two machine-guns. He was the only survivor of this gallant party, but by this daring and heroic action he enabled the battalion on the right to push forward without further machine-gun fire from the village. Throughout the whole operations his magnificent example and leadership were an inspiration to all, and his courage was superb.

T/Sub-Lieut. T. Simmonds, M.C., D.C.M., R.N.V.R., Drake Battalion.

For conspicuous gallantry and devotion to duty during an attack. He rallied his company under heavy fire and rushed a machine-gun nest, capturing

Meanwhile, orders reached Commander Egerton (still in command of the 189th Brigade), shortly after 5 p.m., to move the Hawke and Hood battalions from the Bois de Bouche to Inchy. These battalions at once pressed forward in the face of considerable opposition, and, assisted no doubt, indirectly, by the earlier advance of the Drake Battalion, reached the junction of the Hindenburg support line and the Buissy switch at dusk. These lines, which were strongly fortified and manned, covered Inchy from attack from the west or north-west, and it was clear that they must be carried by an organized attack, before the battalions could reach their final objective. In the circumstances, it was decided to take advantage of the night to reorganize the battalions, which were in touch with the Canadian Corps, and to attack the Hindenburg and Buissy switch lines at 9.30 a.m. the next morning. The position on the night of the 2nd–3rd was, therefore, that the whole of the assigned objectives had been secured, and that the Hawke and Hood and Drake Battalions were waiting for daylight to renew their rapid and successful advance. They had advanced already six miles from Hendecourt, which may be taken as the starting point of the operations, and it needed only an advance of another mile to carry them through Inchy to the western bank of the Canal du Nord.

In the morning, the advance was first resumed by the Hawke and Hood Battalions, who carried the Hindenburg support line, and reorganized on the southern outskirts of Inchy. Later in the morning the Drake Battalion, coming forward on the right of the Hawke, moved on Tadpole copse, which was carried by 1 p.m. This battalion then consolidated a position on the western outskirts of Mœuvres, while the Hawke and Hood endeavoured to consolidate their hold on Inchy and to secure a bridgehead across the Canal du Nord. The Marine Battalion and some cyclists went forward, during the afternoon of the 3rd, to support these efforts, but, despite the utmost gallantry, the bridgehead, though rushed by a party under Sub-Lieut. Harris* of the Hawke Battalion at 7 a.m. on the 4th, could not

many prisoners and machine-guns. After taking his final objective, he pushed on and captured a convoy, consisting of two large field guns, ammunition limbers and an ambulance wagon, together with many prisoners. He also captured the whole of a party of one officer and seventy men, with transport. Throughout two days' operations he was continually performing gallant acts, and his courage and cheerfulness were a splendid example to his men.

* For his daring leadership, Sub-Lieut. Harris was awarded the D.S.O.; this fine officer was killed in the attack of October 8th on Niergnies.

be held. A position had thus to be consolidated on a line from 150 yards to 300 yards west of the canal in touch with the Drake Battalion, who had now pushed forward into Mœuvres, and were waiting for the Guards Division to come forward on their right flank.

On the evening of the 4th the Germans came across the canal on the left of the divisional front and re-entered Inchy, but were thrown back, after hard fighting, by the Marine Battalion.

During the night of the 4th–5th, the Hood, Hawke, Drake and Marine Battalions were relieved by the 190th Brigade, and the long-drawn-out battle slowly died down. On the night of September 7th–8th, the Division was relieved by the 57th Division, and was withdrawn for rest, reorganization, and training.

The outstanding feature of these operations was the swift exploitation of the initial success of the First Army in breaking the Drocourt–Quéant line. The reaction on the strategic situation was immediate. The rapid advance of the Canadians and the XVIIth Corps sent the enemy back, in the south, on to the Hindenburg system (east of Peronne and Bapaume), and in the north it compelled him to surrender, not only his gains in the Lys salient, but also Lens. The implications of the success were far wider. It showed conclusively that at any rate the more experienced of the British Infantry Divisions were fully capable of exercising the initiative and the judgment called for by a war of manœuvre. The success of the Drake Battalion was more than a brilliant local operation ; it was a movement directed on the initiative of the battalion commander to an important tactical point, and the fact that its execution was as sound as its conception, showed that it was not only the senior officers of the Division who could be relied upon in the new warfare.

Naturally, the novelty of the conditions had had its influence. Communications had at times broken down, movements had suffered at times from that over-organization which is bred of trench warfare, and the infantry and the machine gunners had at first hardly appreciated the value of their weapons as weapons of offence. But by the close of the fighting these defects had largely been remedied.

If the operations of the Drake Battalion were the most

spectacular, it must not be supposed that the leading of the other battalions was not remarkably good. Commander Buckle* had again shown inexhaustible determination in the final stages of the advance; Lt.-Colonel Sandilands,* R.M.L.I., led the Marines with distinction; and Commander Lockwood, leading the Hawke Battalion for the first time, had contributed in no small degree to the success of that battalion in the later stages of the battle. Other officers whose achievements won recognition were Lieutenant Gibson, Sub-Lieut. E. C. Barras, Sub-Lieut. Brewer and Sub-Lieut. G. H. Carr of the Hood; Surgeon Leake, R.N., and Lieutenant Flowitt of the Hawke ; Sub-Lieut. Barnett of the Anson ; and Surgeon Baxter, R.N., and Lieutenant H. L. Hardisty, R.M., of the Royal Marine Battalion. The losses sustained by the Division were infinitely lighter than in the August battles. Then they had lost 27 officers and 358 men killed, 88 officers and 2,356 men wounded, and 9 officers and 486 men missing. Now their total losses were under a thousand. The chief reason, without a doubt, was that a timely halt was called to local operations on a narrow front as soon as the German resistance hardened. For this wise policy the Corps Commander (Sir Charles Fergusson) was responsible, as he gave instructions, early on the 4th, that nothing in the nature of an organized frontal attack was to be attempted.

The explanation was, no doubt, that the tactical implications of the new situation were more fully realized. On a narrow front, the enemy, still fighting gallantly under what must have been the utmost difficulties, was still capable of a tenacious resistance. On the other hand, his reserves were used up, and his mobility was almost gone, owing to the disorganization of his railways, the wretched condition of his transport, and the physical condition of his troops. It was now definitely clear that by persistent offensives, distributed over wide fronts, we could finally break, not his will, but his capacity to resist.

* * * * * * *

The next stages of the advance to victory are known as the Battles of the Hindenburg line.

The first of these battles was fought south of the XVIIth

---

* Commander Buckle received a second bar to his D.S.O. for his share in these operations, and Colonel Sandilands received the D.S.O.

Corps front, round Havrincourt and Epehy, with the result that, by September 26th, the line of the Third Army to the right of the XVIIth Corps had been brought roughly into alignment with that reached by the Canadians and the Naval Division at the beginning of the month. It was now necessary to launch the final assault on the line of the Canals which, opposite the Inchy–Mœuvres line, covered the all-important road and railway centre of Cambrai. For the new attack, the Naval Division, rested and reinforced, came forward on September 26th to assembly positions in and west of Mœuvres. The attack was to start at 5.5 a.m. on the 27th.

The enemy had never been completely cleared from the western bank of the Canal du Nord on this front, and not even the crossing of the canal could be confidently reckoned on. Behind the canal, parallel to it, lay the Hindenburg support line, and more than three miles east of that line was the Canal d'Escaut (which, unlike the Canal du Nord at this point, was filled). The objective of the first day's operations was a line roughly a thousand yards west of this, the last organized defensive in front of Cambrai. The Naval Division's first task in the operation was to secure the crossing of the Canal du Nord opposite Mœuvres and the high ground immediately east of it, which was the lower end of the spur running south-west from Bourlon Wood. With this key position secure, the Division were to turn south and secure the Hindenburg support system. This was the second phase of their attack. The third phase was an attack from the left of the captured position, in a south-easterly direction against the high ground between Anneux and Graincourt. The first two phases were to be carried out by the 190th Brigade, and the last by the 188th Brigade. The Canadians on the left of the XVIIth Corps were attacking Bourlon, and the 52nd Division were to cross the canal on the right of the Naval Division, but to go no further than the Hindenburg line. The remaining Division of the corps (the 57th) were to go through the 188th Brigade on the Anneux–Graincourt line to the final objective, west of the Canal d'Escaut.

An interesting feature of the plan is its resemblance to that which had been so successful on September 2nd. The frontal attack on the Hindenburg line was avoided, and the exploitation of the success was again to be from a flank.

Punctually at 5.5 a.m., under cover of an efficient Stokes

Mortar barrage, the 4th Bedfords (on the right) and 7th Fusiliers crossed the canal opposite Mœuvres and seized the high ground to their front. In their advance these battalions captured six field guns and much other material. The brigade, now reinforced by the Artists' Rifles, then fought their way south, along the Hindenburg line, and met with a fair measure of success. The enemy still held out, however, in many parts of the line when the 188th and 189th Brigades crossed the canal on the tracks of the 190th at 7 a.m., and the former brigade moved to their assembly position on the reverse slope of the Bourlon ridge. The Anson, in fact, had to deploy almost immediately after crossing the canal, and some prisoners and machine guns were captured.

The attack on the Anneux–Graincourt line was due to begin at 7.58 a.m., and, punctually to the moment, the Royal Marines (on the left) and the Anson went over to the crest of the Bourlon ridge, leaving the Hindenburg system on their right. It was an original and daring manœuvre, and, for a short time, seemed threatened with failure, for it became at once clear that the Hindenburg line was still held in many places, and that the 190th Brigade had not yet finished their work. Moreover, barring the way to Anneux on the Bapaume–Cambrai road was a factory, strongly held by the enemy. In front of this, and suffering badly from a galling cross-fire, the Anson were held up, though one company, with almost reckless bravery, made its way into the factory and for a short time held its position. On the left of the Anson, the Marines along the line of the Cambrai road effected a junction with the Canadians on the south-west corner of Bourlon Wood, but they could go no further without support on their right flank.

The probable cause of the check was that the 52nd Division had been delayed in crossing the canal, and that the resistance encountered by the 190th Brigade had thus been unexpectedly severe. The check, however, was only temporary. The Lowland Division came forward steadily, and yard by yard the Hindenburg system was cleared. While this was being done, between 10 a.m. and 1 p.m., the Drake and Hawke Battalions came up on the right and left of the sunken road leading to the factory, in support to the Anson Battalion.

At 2.15 p.m. a heavy bombardment was opened on the factory, and on Anneux and Graincourt, and in a dashing advance the whole of the objectives were reached, the Drake, Hawke and Anson capturing Graincourt, and the Marines, with the R.I.R. in support, entering Anneux at the same time. A tragic incident of the advance was the death of C.P.O. Prowse, V.C., of the Drake Battalion, in the attack on the factory.

The line so finely won was at once consolidated, and by 6.30 p.m. the Division was reorganized in depth and waiting for the 57th Division to go through them. A counter-attack developed at 6.30 p.m., but was beaten off without loss, and the night passed quietly. At dawn the 57th Division advanced, and by 9 a.m. had secured the remaining objective of the corps.

Sir Charles Fergusson at once decided to push forward, and the 57th Division were ordered to secure the crossings of the Canal d'Escaut. The 189th Brigade were also ordered forward, with a view to passing through the 57th Division on the further side of the canal.

The remaining stages of the battle for Cambrai on the XVIIth Corps front form one of the most splendid chapters in the history of the Naval Division, and the most complete vindication of its training and its organization. The battle had reached its climax and its issue must affect the history of Europe. The success of no one Division, of no one Corps, could determine the result, but the failure of one Division at a critical point might have, indeed must have, involved delay, and delay was fatal to the allied plan. We were fighting forward to Maubeuge, and we should surely reach it. That was no longer in doubt. But should we reach it before the Germans could extricate themselves from their front, west of the Ardennes. If not, we might have to face a reorganized enemy on the Rhine. If, however, we could cut off the retreat of the German left, the capitulation would be signed in France. The answer to this question, so vast in its implications, depended largely on the speed with which we could reduce the German line west of Cambrai. Not the least important part of that line was that still stoutly defended by enemy opposite the XVIIth Corps on the afternoon of September 28th.

When the 189th Brigade went forward, they came on a scene of incalculable and dangerous confusion. Parties of the 2nd Division, on the right of the 57th Division, were reported to be across the canal and the river; parties of the 57th Division had certainly crossed the canal (though it was

feared that they had been cut off); but the enemy still held out
in La Folie Wood, this side of the Canal, on the left of the corps'
front. To clear up the position and to force the crossings of the
canal and river was the task definitely assigned to the 189th
Brigade at 4 p.m. on the 28th.

The Hood Battalion was directed by Brigadier-General
Curling * to La Folie Wood, and the Drake Battalion on
Cantignual Mill, where the enemy had retired from the canal,
but held the river crossings in strength. Here there was a
bridge, and a little further to the south, where the river crosses
the canal, was a lock gate, not at this time wholly destroyed.
At the mill, the 57th Division had already crossed the canal,
and the Drake Battalion moved forward into their position
and at once attempted the crossing of the river. The main
bridge was broken, but a wooden footbridge on a lower level had
escaped destruction. This, however, was commanded by the
enemy's machine guns, and all attempts to cross it failed.
Then suddenly, whether by inspiration or mistake, a leading
seaman with a machine gun set out across the main bridge
which was broken, and, before the enemy had altered the angle
of their fire, had reached the gap : here, by some feat of agility,
he swung himself down and got across the river and brought his
gun into action. For a moment the enemy machine gunners
were silenced, and Commander Beak and a few men also came
across. Here till dusk the party maintained themselves, and,
under cover of darkness a few more stole across by twos and
threes.

Meanwhile, General Curling had sent Captain Wright and
Lt.-Commander Blackmore (again commanding the Hawke
Battalion since Commander Lockwood had been wounded in
the advance on Anneux) to reconnoitre the lower crossing.
This was found to have been secured by the 2nd Division,
and it was decided to bring two companies of the Hawke
Battalion forward to this point, as the Hood were still heavily
engaged in La Folie Wood. By the time the battalion arrived,
the bridgehead had been lost, and it was necessary to defer
the attack till dawn, when better support could be arranged.

At night, while the Drake were crossing in driblets, the
engineers, under a heavy fire (for the Drake had been unable

* General Curling had taken over command of the 189th Brigade from
Commander Egerton on September 3rd.

to reach any commanding position and the general line of the river was still held in force by the enemy), put pontoon bridges across.

At dawn the battle was resumed, and the Drake Battalion succeeded in crossing in force, and advancing to higher ground. The Hawke Battalion crossed by the pontoon bridges and the lock gates at 10 a.m., and extended the flank of the Drake; and the Hood Battalion, whose hard fighting in La Folie Wood, through the 28th, had saved the Division's left flank, crossed on the left of the Drake.

Here, at noon on the 29th, the line was taken over by the R.I.R. and the Marine Battalions, who pushed forward on to higher ground. They were well supported by two companies of the Machine Gun Battalion, who got forward in time to harass the enemy in his retreat on Cambrai and Niergnies.

The position now won was on the very outskirts of Cambrai, and only two positions, neither of them of great strength, barred the entry into the town. It was decided to attack the outlying line, between Pronville and Fog de Paris, on the 30th, and for this advance the 190th Brigade came forward. The Artists were to attack on the right, the 7th Fusiliers on the left, and the Anson were to attack an enemy strong point on the flank.

The first attack, on the morning of the 30th, was not wholly successful, though some progress was made, but at 1 p.m., under a fresh bombardment, the line moved forward and all objectives were secured, except that the enemy still retained a lodgment in a strong point on the right of the line, till they were ejected by the Marines and the Anson at 7 a.m. on the morning of October 1st. The same day the Division was relieved by the 52nd Division, who were understood to be going to attack Niergnies.

In four days the Naval Division had advanced, fighting almost the whole way, for a distance of over seven miles, and had carried four successive prepared positions, the last held by the enemy in front of Cambrai, and each one resolutely defended. In their advance they had captured unwounded 63 officers and 2,138 men, five heavy guns and 51 field guns, 90 trench mortars and 400 machine guns. The Division's losses in killed were 21 officers and some 400 men, and in wounded 83 officers and 1,978 men. Considering the magnitude of the operation, the importance of the results obtained, and the vigorous character of the enemy resistance, it would not be wrong to regard this engagement as one of the most successful ever fought by the Division. As usual, the Division owed much to the different battalion commanders, whose cool and daring handling of their battalions during the August and September operations had been one of the most memorable features. Commander Beak had been awarded the Victoria Cross for his magnificent leadership in the earlier battles, culminating in the attack on the Drocourt–Quéant line ; and his leading in the subsequent battles was no less remarkable.* Lt.- Colonel Sandilands, Commander Egerton, Commander Buckle and Lt.-Commander Blackmore had set an equal example to their battalions. If the regimental leading had been good, so also had the work of the Brigade and Divisional staffs and of the administrative services. To General Blacklock, Colonel Mackenzie and Colonel Smyth (now A.A. and Q.M.G. to the Division, Colonel Foster having been promoted to a Corps appointment), and to the staffs of the three brigades, the general success of the operations was in a large measure due. No longer, as in trench-to-trench warfare, was the quality of the infantry, assuming the effectiveness of the artillery support, the virtually decisive factor. The plan of attack, no longer imposed by the necessities of stationary war, but a matter of

---

* The official account of Commander Beak's exploits, which relates to the engagements of August 21st, August 24th–25th and September 2nd–3rd, is as follows :—

T/Commander D. M. W. Beak, D.S.O., M.C., R.N.V.R.

For most conspicuous bravery, courageous leadership and devotion to duty during a prolonged period of operations.

He led his men in attack, and, despite heavy machine-gun fire, four enemy positions were captured. His skilful and fearless leadership resulted in the complete success of this operation and enabled other battalions to reach their objectives.

Four days later, though dazed by a shell fragment, in the absence of the brigade commander, he reorganized the whole brigade under extremely heavy gun fire, and led his men with splendid courage to their objective.

An attack having been held up, he rushed forward, accompanied by only one runner, and succeeded in breaking up a nest of machine guns, personally bringing back nine or ten prisoners. His fearless example instilled courage and confidence into his men, who then quickly resumed the advance under his leadership.

On a subsequent occasion he displayed great courage and powers of leadership in attack, and his initiative, coupled with the confidence with which he inspired all ranks, not only enabled his own and a neighbouring unit to advance, but contributed very materially to the success of the Naval Division in these operations.

choice, was of supreme importance, not so much in determining the result of the operations, as in providing the successive opportunities without which subordinate commanders,
however able, could not have exercised their initiative. It
was not only the infantry and machine-gun battalion supports
and reserves and the artillery who had to be brought forward
stage by stage, so as to be at hand when the opportunity
presented itself, but the supply and transport services which
had to follow up the advance with complete thoroughness, if
lack of hot food or ammunition was not to call a halt to operations at a critical time. The Engineers had also a determining
part to play, since the immediate repair of roads and bridges
was indispensable if the vigorous advances of the infantry
were to be adequately supported. The responsibility for the
co-ordination of the movements of these different arms lay
with the Divisional staffs, and the credit for the uniform success
with which, in the September and October battles, the requisite
co-operation was achieved, must be divided impartially between
the staffs and the officers of the different departments. It
would be wrong to overlook the fact (alluded to in the very full
reports on these operations submitted by the Divisional commander) that the smooth running of the machine, which surprised even the staffs responsible, was incalculably assisted by
the peculiar organization of the Division, which was here put
to the test and which emerged triumphantly from the ordeal.
It is true that, in name, the Machine Gun Battalion and the
Engineers had ceased to be an integral part of the Division, but,
in reality, their identity with the old independent organization
had persisted, and this fact was of the greatest possible assistance. The psychological factor is often too lightly regarded
by military writers. It should, perhaps, in a world of abstrac-
tion, be a matter of no account that the leader of a section
of a machine-gun battalion, of a section of a field company of
Engineers, of a company of the Divisional Train, should have
joined for service with a particular Division, have been trained
with that Division, and be personally known to the infantry
company commanders, adjutants and transport officers with
whom he has to co-operate. In practice, such a thing may
exercise a determining influence. Above all, the paramount
advantage secured was that, almost daily, the infantry were
receiving reinforcements of officers and men who had come

Commander D. M. W. Beak, V.C., D.S.O., M.C., R.N.V.R.
(Drake Battalion).

(From the portrait by Ambrose McEvoy in the possession of the Imperial War Museum.)

back to their old battalions and companies, and who fitted
at once into the organization. Successive engagements on
the scale attempted could not, but for this, have achieved so
uniform a success. A division filled up day by day with strange
reinforcements would in a week have lost its identity. Battalion commanders would be ignorant of the capabilities of
their company officers, the men would have a diminished confidence in the platoon commanders. The loss of each trusted
petty officer or subaltern would be a blow to the confidence of
the platoon or the company, and, in open warfare, where
platoons and companies must function often quite independently, the result must have been a constantly diminishing
efficiency.

This definite advantage, derived from the Divisional organization, was exemplified, not only in the successes achieved
up to October 1st, but still more in the events of the next
few days.

Before the main body of the Third Army could advance on
the Beaurevoir line, their flank, menaced by the enemy concentration at Cambrai, had to be secured. The difficulty
resulted from the decision not to bombard the town, which
made it hard to get forward immediately south of the city.
During the first days of October, the operations had flagged,
and finally, on October 5th, the XVIIth Corps were informed
that the immediate capture of Niergnies and its defences was
of vital importance, and must be achieved. The Naval Division
was about to entrain for the St. Pol area, and Major-General
Blacklock had started on leave for England, but Sir Charles
Fergusson applied for the temporary return of the Division to
undertake the operation. The request was granted, the
transfer of the Division to the First Army was postponed, and
the Divisional Commander was recalled. No secret was made
of the reason for the decision, and the battalions were promised
relief the day Niergnies was captured.

The attack was carried out, like so many others, by the
188th and 189th Brigades, and, by the night of October 7th–
8th, they were in their assembly positions north-east of Rumilly,
waiting confidently for the opening of the barrage. Every
possible assistance was provided to ensure the success of what
was a difficult and critical operation. The Division was
supported by the artillery of the 52nd and 37th Divisions,

which had co-operated so unfailingly in the previous battles, and eight tanks were to go forward with the infantry.

The first objective, to be attacked by the R.I.R. (on the right) and the Drake Battalion, was the enemy trench in front of Niergnies. The second objective, comprising the village and the enemy works immediately behind it, was to be attacked by the Royal Marines and the Hood. The left flank was to be covered by the Hawke Battalion, and the Anson were to attempt to get round Niergnies from the south-east.

At 4.30 a.m. on the 8th the advance began, and, by 6 a.m., the first objective had been carried. The advance continued, and by 8.40 a.m., the second objective also was in our hands. The Anson and Marine Battalions had achieved the most successful advance, though the Hawke Battalion was well forward on the left flank.

At 9.30 a.m., the enemy counter-attacked in force, seven captured British tanks moving forward against our line. For a time the situation was doubtful, but Commander Buckle* and Commander Pollock* (of the Hood) restored the situation, each personally putting one tank out of action, by turning on it a captured anti-tank rifle and a captured field gun respectively.

By 9.55 a.m., Niergnies was again in our hands, though we were still short of the final objective. After hard fighting all the morning, during which the enemy counter-attacked more than once on different parts of our line, a renewal of the advance was planned for 3 p.m., when, under an effective barrage, the line was once more pushed forward. Well to the east of Niergnies, the battalions consolidated, and were relieved in the evening by the 2nd Division, with the last formidable task which was to be assigned to them triumphantly achieved.† Twelve officers and 61 petty officers and men had been killed in the hardly-fought battle of October 8th, and 27 officers and 513 men had been wounded, but the results were of the first importance. Not only had a strongly-defended position been abandoned by the enemy, with a loss in captured alone of 34 officers and 1,155 men, with 81 machine guns and 9

---

* Commander Buckle was awarded a third and Commander Pollock a first bar to the D.S.O. for their exploits.

† Lieutenant Brackenbridge and Lieutenant Hilton of the Hood, and Lieutenant Edwards and Sub-Lieut. Codner of the Hawke, were especially prominent in this short engagement.

field guns, but the way was now open for the advance of the left of the Third Army. The next morning the whole line south of Cambrai moved forward. By October 10th Cambrai had fallen, and the last of the enemy's prepared positions was definitely and finally broken.

In trying to fulfil the obligations of the historian, in selecting from the constant and even surprising successes achieved by the Naval Division certain episodes which seem to have a special importance in relation to the front as a whole, it is difficult to avoid the appearance of overstating the individual contribution to the general achievement. It must, indeed, never be forgotten that the main task of the British and French armies, the attrition of the armed forces of Germany till their power for resistance was gone, had been, to a great extent, achieved before the final offensive began. Whatever judgment those competent to judge may, in years to come, when all the facts are available, pass on the strategy or the tactics of the Allies in the earlier periods of the war, there will never be any doubt but that it was in the first three and a half years that the foundations of victory were laid. So much for the major consideration. As regards the particular achievements of the Naval Division, they formed but one series of memorable incidents among others equally decisive. What is proper to stress is no more than this, that among the Divisions which in the concluding, as in the intermediate, stages of the Great War made not only a material, but an individual, contribution to its victorious conclusion the Naval Division was one. There was a quality of temper and resolution, of initiative, boldness and self-reliance which even the baldest summary of its achievements makes tolerably plain. The historian of an individual unit is always, and properly, open to the suspicion of bias. But the achievement must be the final test of efficiency in war, and judged by that test the Naval Division did not fail.

NOTE

I have avoided heretofore the quotation of congratulatory messages. Th following messages received by all units from the Divisional, Corps and Army Commanders at the close of the operations described in this chapter are, however, of interest, and I reproduce them in full.

From the Divisional Commander :

"The Divisional Commander wishes to convey to all ranks of the Royal Naval Division his greatest appreciation of the whole-hearted way in which they performed their task yesterday.

" Without the Division taking part, the Third Army would have been unable to have participated in the general battle all along the line— Niergnies being the key to the position.

" The splendid success which the Division attained shows the highest standard of leadership, and a whole-hearted discipline and willingness on the part of the men.

"No better reward could have been asked for than the news published in this morning's communiqué.

"(Signed) R. R. SMYTH, A.A. and Q.M.G."

" *9th October*, 1918."

From Commander XVII. Corps, 8-10-18.

"Warmest congratulations to you and the Division on their success to-day AAA. I told the Army Commander they would not fail and my confidence has been amply justified AAA. It is a fine finish to the exploits of the Division while with XVII. Corps."

From Commander XVII. Corps :

" I wish to express to all ranks of the Royal Naval Division my appreciation of and sincere thanks for the splendid work which they have done since joining the Corps on August 31st.

" The Division has always been in the front of every fight, and has never failed to get its objectives, however difficult the task—its final performance, the capture of Niergnies with 1,000 prisoners, could only have been effected by troops imbued with determination and soldierly spirit.

" I congratulate all ranks, and wish them all good luck and success in the future. It will always be a matter of pride to me to have been associated with the Royal Naval Division during their eventful period of the War.

"(Signed) CHARLES FERGUSSON,
"Lieut-General, Commanding XVII. Corps."

" *9th October*, 1918."

From the General Officer Commanding the Third Army :

" Headquarters, Third Army, B.E.F.

" 10-10-18.

" I cannot allow the 68rd (R.N.) Division to leave the Third Army without expressing my sincerest appreciation of the gallant behaviour during the battle of Cambrai.

" In every operation success has crowned its efforts. This was brought about by sound preparation on the part of its Staffs, by skilful tactical handling by all leaders and by a determined resolve on the part of all ranks to beat the enemy.

" The Third Army's record of ground gained and prisoners and guns captured is a splendid one, and I owe my deepest thanks to all ranks of the 68rd (R.N.) Division for their fine share in the achievement.

"(Signed) J. BYNG, General."

CHAPTER XVII

CONCLUSION

' THE Belgian people will never forget that the men of the Royal Navy and Royal Marines were with them in their darkest hour of misery, as, please God, they may also be with them when Belgium is restored to her own by the Armies of the Allies." So, it will be remembered, ended Mr. Winston Churchill's message to the Naval Division on the conclusion of the Antwerp expedition. The hope which inspired it had been fulfilled, when, on November 11th, the Naval Division, in the forefront of the XXIInd Corps, entered on its first experience of peace in the neighbourhood of Mons.

After a period of welcome rest at St. Pol—never before since they landed in France had they been so far from the battle front—the Division had come forward into the fighting line on the 6th November, in relief of the 168th Brigade of the 56th Division, west of the Bois d'Audregnies. From then onward, the advance of the XXIInd Corps front, as elsewhere, was continuous, and almost unopposed by the enemy infantry. Isolated machine-gun detachments, however, and sporadic artillery fire exacted their toll of casualties in what was no longer a battle, but a pursuit.

The progress of our advance was, indeed, governed mainly by the state of the roads, and the difficulty of getting rations to the troops in the forward area. Nevertheless, the morning of November 8th saw the capture of Witheries, and, in the afternoon, our line was carried east of Blaugies, the first advance being made by the 189th Brigade and the second by the 190th on November 9th. The advance of the 190th Brigade reached as far as the road running north-east from Quévy le Petit, and from there the pursuit was taken up by the 188th Brigade,

directed across the historic field of Malplaquet, past Harmignies, to the villages of Villers Saint Ghislain and Saint
Symphonien. Here, for the first time, the enemy made some
show of resistance, and only the bold handling of their units,
by the subordinate commanders of the Anson* and Royal
Irish battalions, enabled the brigade to reach the Mons–Givry
road by mid-day on November 10th, and the line Harmignies–
Malplaquet by the evening.

The advance was ordered to continue the next day to the
assigned objective on a two-brigade front, and so the 188th and
189th Brigades found themselves, on the day of the Armistice,
side by side in the front line. The advance carried them
through Givry, meeting with little opposition. Here the
189th Brigade outstripped the pursuit to the south, and mounted
troops were dispatched to protect their flank, while " B "
Company of the Machine Gun Battalion came into action at
10.45 a.m. against the enemy rearguards clearly visible to their
front. A quarter of an hour later, hostilities ceased.

*   *   *   *   *   *   *

Here this record, faithful as I could make it, comes to
its close. The Royal Naval Division had been brought into
existence in the stress of a great crisis, and when the crisis
was over it passed out of history. For some months, indeed,
it remained in Belgium, engaged in the humbler pursuits which
are the lot of armies in days of peace : actually after the final
demobilization, the War Office urged the Admiralty to re-form
the Division for service in the Army of the Rhine. It was
not, however, for the routine tasks of such a period of transition that the Naval Division had been formed, or was best
suited. Wider interests were calling to these personalities
who had made the principal contribution to the force and individuality of the Division, and one by one they passed on their
separate ways.

If the Royal Naval Division had not by now ceased to
exist, it would have ceased to be memorable. Its achievements
in war had been remarkable, but it owed its strength to its

---

* Sub-Lieut. J. M. Law, of the Anson Battalion, was awarded the M.C. for
his services on this occasion.

originality, grounded in traditions alien to regular formations. It was always different. There were indeed, not a few* among the officers and men of the Division, even at the close of the war, who had been bred from their youth upward in the Naval tradition, and to these faithful few the Naval Division owed incalculably much. For the most part, however, the Naval Division, alike in its qualities and its defects, was representative of the stubborn individualism of the English character, only moved to active co-operation in the pursuit of a common objective by a great cause making a secret if unconfessed appeal to the latent idealism of our race. The same cause may see the Naval Division once more in the field ; but, without its inspiration, they will never be found on the barrack square. Let no one say that this savours of a complacent optimism, of an unenviable readiness to resign to others the work of study and training which is the essential foundation of success in war. Success in war comes to those nations which devote themselves with energy in time of peace to the legitimate occupations of decent and Christian men. Among these occupations, the profession of arms is but one.

And so it is not altogether with regret that we may contemplate the passing of the Royal Naval Division from the theatre of action into the pages of history.

The Royal Marines, with their older traditions, carry on their colours battle honours which will serve to keep alive, in the memory of that historic Corps, the days when they were a part of a more transient organization. The Royal Field Artillery, the Bedfordshire Regiment, the Royal Fusiliers, the Artists' Rifles and the Honourable Artillery Company may also not be forgetful of an active comradeship which the Naval and Marine Battalions at any rate will remember with gratitude. But for the most part the Naval Division will live as a memory, only to be rekindled when, in another great crisis, old traditions are awakened and the familiar battle-grounds of the British people echo again to the noise and rumour of war. The

---

* It would have been fitting to have placed on record here a full list of the many faithful and experienced officers promoted from the Lower Deck who contributed so much to the *esprit de corps* and to the naval tradition of the Division. Unfortunately the records are not sufficiently complete. Lt.-Commander Turrell, M.C., R.N.V.R. (Drake), Lieut. Charles Hoskyns, R.N.V.R. (Nelson), Lieut. F. C. Hill, M.C., R.N.V.R. (Hood), Lieut. Stear, M.C., R.N.V.R. (Anson and Hawke) are only four among many whose services deserve more than a mere passing reference.

statesman who faces that crisis may be prudent if he weighs the considerations of administrative convenience, and allows the memory to slumber in the archives of his office. If he lacks prudence, but possesses imagination, another chapter will be added to this history.

LIST OF APPENDICES

APPENDIX A

Extracts from Minutes of the First Lord of the Admiralty (The Right Hon. Winston S. Churchill), dated 16th, 17th and 30th August, 1914, governing the formation of the Royal Naval Division.

(I)

Secretary.
First Sea Lord.
Second Sea Lord.

In order to make the best possible use of the surplus naval reservists of different classes, it is proposed to constitute permanent cadres of one Marine and two naval brigades. The Marine brigade has already been partially formed in four battalions, aggregating 1,880 active service men. To this will be added an approximately equal number of reservists, making the total strength of the brigade 3,900, organized in four battalions of four double companies of approximately 250 men. The two naval brigades will also consist of four battalions, each, if possible, of 880 men, organized in 16 double companies of 220. The composition of each battalion should be as follows :—

R.N.V.R.	375
R.F.R.	315
R.N.R. (picked, under 30 years of age)	190

The total numbers required for the two naval brigades would, therefore, be :—

R.N.V.R.	3,000
R.F.R.	2,500
R.N.R.	1,800

The Marine brigade will be commanded by a Colonel, and each battalion by a Lieutenant-Colonel ; each company by a Major and a Captain. The means of remedying the shortage of junior officers will be dealt with separately. About 50 new subalterns R.M. must be entered either permanently or on a three years' or till the war stops engagement.

Each naval brigade will be commanded by a Captain, R.N., five of the battalions by a Commander, or naval officer promoted to that rank, and three by R.N.V.R. Commanders ; each company will be commanded by a Lieutenant-Commander, R.N. or R.N.V.R., or, if these are not forthcoming, by a Major, R.M. The question of making good deficiencies in these and in the Marine brigade will be dealt with separately. There are, however, available 50 R.N.V.R. Lieutenants, 66 Sub-Lieutenants and 12 Midshipmen, total 128. About 50 more officers will be required.

The use of these brigades need not be considered until the organization has advanced sufficiently to allow of their military value to be judged.

The formation of these brigades should be completed, so far as resources allow, in the present week. The officers commanding the companies and battalions must be appointed forthwith. The first essential is to get the men drilling together in brigades ; and the deficiencies of various ranks in the battalions can be filled up later. It may ultimately be found possible in the course of the war to build up all battalions of the Marine and naval brigades to the army strength of 1,070, and the organization will readily adapt itself to this, and it must be distinctly understood that this is the paramount claim upon them. All the men, whether sailors or Marines, while training in the three brigades will be available if required for service afloat ; but in the meanwhile they will be left to be organized for land service.

16. 8. 14.   W. S. C.

(ΙΙ)

SECRETARY AND OTHERS.

The following is an amplification and refinement of my Minute of 16. 8. 14:

A camping ground has been selected near Deal.
The War Office have been asked for 700 tents : 160 marine tents will start to-morrow. The War Office to be asked to assist in camping equipment so far as possible. The Director of Victualling to make arrangements for victualling the men by contract.
The following will arrive at the camping ground on Friday next :—

Chief Petty Officers :
  Active Service 32
  R.F.R... 64
Petty Officers :
  Active Service 128
  R.F.R... 128
Leading Seamen, A.B's and Ordinary Seamen :
  Active Service 128
  R.F.R... 128

                Total................ 608

The whole of the R.N.V.R., except those engaged on Tyne patrol and those already embarked, a total of 3,400 with recruits, to arrive in camp on Saturday. They are to retain their existing formations till the Monday, when they are to be reorganized as follows :
The cadres of 2 brigades, comprising 8 battalions and 32 companies, will be formed. Approximately 106 R.N.V.R. will be assigned to each company and 424 to each battalion.
The following C.P.O's and P.O's will also be added to each company :—

Chief Petty Officers :
  Active Service 1
  R.F.R... 2
Petty Officers :
  Active Service 2
  R.F.R... 4
A.B's and Leading Seamen :
  Active Service 4
  R.F.R... 4

                           17

These are additional to the R.N.V.R. petty officers.
The officers available include 128 Lieutenants, Sub-Lieutenants, and Midshipmen, making 4 per company and 16 per battalion. These are to be distributed accordingly. Eight battalion commanders will be appointed on Thursday next. A military officer will be appointed Adjutant to each battalion. These officers will join on Saturday, the 22nd instant.
Thirty-two Instructors, R.M., will also join the camp on Friday next, the 21st.
Seventeen retired officers are also available and will be appointed shortly.
The appointment of all officers to special positions, like the command of companies and battalions, must at this stage be regarded as provisional and subject to confirmation at the end of the first month.
A band must be provided. The quality is not important. There must be sufficient pupils under instruction at the Naval School of Music to provide for this. The band is to join on Saturday next.
On Wednesday, the 26th, 2,000 R.F.R. stokers and 1,500 R.N.R. (the latter picked and under 30 years of age) will join the camp from their respective home

ports and be distributed equally between the eight battalions. The composition of each battalion will be approximately as follows :—

R.N.V.R. 424
R.F.R. 824
R.N.R. 187

and of each company :—

R.N.V.R. 106
R.F.R. 81
R.N.R. 46

The two brigades, aggregating approximately 7,500 men, should be complete by Wednesday, the 26th, and will be inspected on Monday, the 31st, by the Board of Admiralty.

R.N.V.R. will bring their own rifles. D.N.O. will arrange to issue 4,000 rifles for the use of R.N.R., R.F.R., and petty officers. All these rifles are long rifles. Orders will be placed for short rifles to be delivered at the earliest moment.

Forty Maxims have been ordered from Vickers, which, it is stated, can be ready in 10 days. They are to be divided as follows :—

To each battalion in the naval brigade ....4=82
In reserve 4
To the Marine brigade to complete to full establishment 4

Each company throughout the naval and Marine brigades will detail a Maxim-gun section.

D.N.O. will be responsible for the issue of the rifles, Maxims, and accoutrements. Ammunition will be served out later.

M.D.G. has been directed to submit proposals for supplying each of the three brigades with a brigade field ambulance column according to Army scale.

Major Ollivant will submit the necessary establishment of horses and mules. The mounted officers will be supplied with their chargers and saddlery by the Government free.

The pay of all ranks serving in the brigades will be uniform, and no distinction will be drawn between the various classes of reservists.

The Director of Contracts will order 12,000 khaki kits, of which 4,000 will be military for the Marines and 8,000 naval, according to directions given.

17. 8. 14.   W. S. C.

(III)

Secretary.
Second Sea Lord.
R.N.D. Administration.
A.G.R.M. and others concerned.

*   *   *   *   *   *   *   *   *

All appointments and the relative naval rank in the R.N.V.R. are made provisionally from the 1st September, and are subject to confirmation during the month.

Brigadiers should collect from their Battalion Commandants recommendations as to purging petty officers unsuited to field duties. This process should be gradual during the month. The petty officers not required will be returned to the Royal Naval and Royal Naval Volunteer Reserve depots, and be available for general service.

*   *   *   *   *   *   *   *   *

All military officers attached to the division will be given commissions appropriate to their commands in the R.N.V.R.

Brigadiers are to enforce a selection upon their Battalion Commandants, which is to operate during the month of September, so as to secure the best men being appointed, irrespective of their origin and without regard to seniority, to the non-commissioned ranks.

The junior commissioned officers, up to and including Company Commanders, are to be selected on the same principle, no regard being had to seniority or to the branch in which the officer has previously served, or to his personal feelings.

The sole object will be to secure the command of companies as of battalions to the men best suited to lead the units in war.

Entire discretion in the matter of the Company Commanders is given to the Brigadiers, but they will no doubt consult with the Battalion Commandants.

In the same way Battalion Commandants will deal with the seniority of the junior officers in the companies, consulting of course the Company Commanders in whom they have confidence.

    *   *   *   *   *   *   *   *   *

30. 8. 14.   W. S. C.

APPENDIX B

COMPOSITION OF STAFF OF ROYAL NAVAL DIVISION, 1914-1919.

APPOINTMENT	1914	1915	1916	1917	1918	1919
G.O.C.	Brig.-Gen. Sir George Aston. Maj.-Gen. A. Paris.	Maj.-Gen. A. Paris.	Maj.-Gen. Sir A. Paris. Maj.-Gen. C. D. Shute.	Maj.-Gen. C. D. Shute. Maj.-Gen. C. E. Lawrie.	Maj.-Gen. C. E. Lawrie. Maj.-Gen. C. A. Blacklock.	Maj.-Gen. C. A. Blacklock.
G.S.O.1.	Lt.-Col. A. H. Ollivant.	Lt.-Col. A. H. Ollivant.	Lt.-Col. C. A. Ker. Lt.-Col. C. F. Aspinall.	Lt.-Col. C. F. Aspinall. Lt.-Col. W. G. Neilson.	Lt.-Col. W. G. Neilson. Lt.-Col. T. L. B. Soutry. Lt.-Col. J. H. Mackenzie.	Lt.-Col. J. H. Mackenzie.
A.A. and Q.M.G.	Maj. S. S. Richardson.	Lt.-Col. S. S. Richardson.	Lt.-Col. R. F. Foster, R.M.L.I.	Lt.-Col. R. F. Foster, R.M.L.I.	Lt.-Col. R. F. Foster. Lt.-Col. R. B. Smyth.	Lt.-Col. R. B. Smyth.
G.O.C. 1st R.N. Brigade (renumbered 2nd R.N. Brigade, 7.7.16, and 189th Brigade, 19.7.16).	Commodore Henderson, R.N. Brig.-Gen. D. Mercer.	Brig.-Gen. D. Mercer.	Brig.-Gen. L. F. Philips.	Brig.-Gen. L. F. Philips. Brig.-Gen. J. F. S. D. Coleridge. Brig.-Gen. A. M. Asquith.	Brig.-Gen. A. M. Asquith. Brig.-Gen. E. N. Bray. Brig.-Gen. H. D. du Pree. Brig.-Gen. B. J. Curling.	Brig.-Gen. B. J. Curling.
G.O.C. 3rd (Royal Marine) Brigade (renumbered 2nd Naval Brigade, July, 1915, 1st Naval Brigade, 7.7.16, and 188th Brigade, 19.7.16).	Brig.-Gen. A. Paris. Brig.-Gen. C. N. Trotman.	Brig.-Gen. C. N. Trotman.	Brig.-Gen. R. E. S. Prentice.	Brig.-Gen. R. E. S. Prentice. Brig.-Gen. J. F. S. D. Coleridge.	Brig.-Gen. J. F. S. D. Coleridge. Brig.-Gen. H. Nelson.	Brig.-Gen. H. Nelson.
G.O.C. 2nd R. N. Brigade (broken up July, 1915, replaced in France by the 190th Brigade).	Commodore O. Backhouse, R.N.	Commodore O. Backhouse, R.N.		—	—	—
G.O.C. 190th Infantry Brigade.	—	—	Brig.-Gen. C. N. Trotman. Brig.-Gen. the Hon. C. J. Sackville West. Brig.-Gen. W. C. G. Heneker. Brig.-Gen. H. W. E. Finch.	Brig.-Gen. H. W. E. Finch. Brig.-Gen. A. R. H. Hutchison.	Brig.-Gen. A. R. H. Hutchison. Brig.-Gen. W. B. Lesslie.	Brig.-Gen. W. B. Lesslie.
O.R.A.	—	—	Brig.-Gen. C. H. de Rougemont.	Brig.-Gen. C. H. de Rougemont.	Brig.-Gen. C. H. de Rougemont.	Brig.-Gen. C. H. de Rougemont. Brig.-Gen. W. A. M. Thompson.
C.R.E.	Maj. Carey, R.E.	Lt.-Col. Carey, R.E.	Lt.-Col. G. H. Harrison.	Lt.-Col. S. H. Cowan.	Lt.-Col. S. H. Cowan.	Lt.-Col. J. A. Graeme.
A.D.M.S.	Fleet Surgeon Meeden, R.N. Fleet Surgeon Gaskell, R.N.	Fleet Surgeon Gaskell, R.N. Fleet Surgeon F. J. Finch, R.N.	Fleet Surgeon F. J. Finch, R.N.	Fleet Surgeon F. J. Finch, R.N. Col. R. W. Clements, R.A.M.C.	Col. R. W. Clements. Col. H. A. Davidson.	Col. H. A. Davidson.

APPENDIX C

SUMMARY STATEMENT OF ROYAL NAVAL DIVISION CASUALTIES.

Officers and Other Ranks.

	Killed.		Died of Wounds.		Died.		Wounded.		Missing.		Prisoners and Interned.		Total.	
	Officers.	Other ranks.	Officers.	Other ranks.	Officers.	Other ranks.	Officers.	Other ranks.	Officers.	Other ranks.	Officers.	Other ranks.	Officers.	Other ranks.
Antwerp	6	41	1	10	2	41	2	135	—	—	39	2,332	50	2,559
M.E.F...	102	1,551	26	574	5	283	199	4,838	—	—	—	2	332	7,198
B.E.F...	337	5,510	91	1,882	12	295	1,163	24,555	—	—	80	2,750	1,683	34,992
Died in United Kingdom (other than those above)	—	—	—	2	—	78	—	—	—	—	—	—	—	80
Total	445	7,102	118	2,466	19	647	1,364	29,528	—	—	119	5,084	1,965	44,820

APPENDIX D

1ST ROYAL NAVAL BRIGADE

Nelson Battalion.
Acting Lieut.-Commander H. C. Evans, R.N.V.R.
Lieutenant J. A. R. McCormick, R.N.V.R.
Sub-Lieut. J. W. Edwards, R.N.V.R.
Sub-Lieut. J. P. Robley, R.N.V.R.

2ND ROYAL NAVAL BRIGADE

Howe Battalion.
Major S. J. Sparling, R.M.
Lieutenant H. B. McIntosh, R.N.V.R.
Lieutenant N. H. Miller, R.N.V.R.
Sub-Lieut. W. G. M. Callendar, R.N.V.R.
Sub-Lieut. E. A. Clifford, R.N.V.R.
Sub-Lieut. J. Norman, R.N.V.R.
Sub-Lieut. G. W. Ross, R.N.V.R.
Sub-Lieut. F. W. Stacey, R.N.V.R.

Hood Battalion.
Lieut.-Commander R. S. Parsons, R.N.
Lieutenant the Hon. M. H. N. Hood, R.N.V.R.
Lieutenant J. W. Ferguson, R.N.V.R.
Sub-Lieut. F. Baker, R.N.V.R.
Sub-Lieut. W. D. Browne, R.N.V.R.
Sub-Lieut. C. J. Martin, R.N.V.R.

Anson Battalion.
Major R. A. Roberts, R.A.
Lieutenant J. C. Spencer-Warwick, R.N.V.R.
Acting-Lieut. W. F. Brown, R.N.V.R.
Sub-Lieut. T. M. Crowe, R.N.V.R.
Sub-Lieut. W. J. Henry, R.N.V.R.
Sub-Lieut. J. A. H. Richmond, R.N.V.R.

Collingwood Battalion.
Commander A. Y. C. M. Spearman, R.N.
Lieut.-Commander W. M. Annand, R.N.V.R.
Lieutenant J. B. T. Church, R.N.
Lieutenant F. M. Badham, R.N.V.R.
Lieutenant J. W. Hart, R.N.V.R.
Lieutenant W. F. Hayes, R.N.V.R.
Lieutenant F. A. Lowe, R.N.V.R.
Sub-Lieut. A. G. Bagshaw, R.N.V.R.
Sub-Lieut. W. Bolton, R.N.V.R.
Sub-Lieut. J. E. Davies, R.N.V.R.
Sub-Lieut. O. Freyberg, R.N.V.R.
Sub-Lieut. R. Jukes, R.N.V.R.
Sub-Lieut. A. McLeod, R.N.V.R.
Sub-Lieut. D. Milroy, R.N.V.R.
Sub-Lieut. G. Plunkett, R.N.V.R.
Sub-Lieut. L. E. Tucker, R.N.V.R

22*

APPENDIX E (i)

188TH BRIGADE

Anson Battalion.
Lieut.-Col. F. J. Saunders, D.S.O., R.M.
Surgeon C. H. Gow, R.N.
Sub-Lieut. J. N. Bowden, R.N.V.R.
Sub-Lieut. R. J. Gee, R.N.V.R.
Sub-Lieut. E. A. G. Harvie, R.N.V.R.
Sub-Lieut. O. J. Hobbs, R.N.V.R.
Sub-Lieut. W. Johnston, R.N.V.R.
Sub-Lieut. H. Kilner, R.N.V.R.
Sub-Lieut. C. Lee, R.N.V.R.
Sub-Lieut. J. A. McMillan, R.N.V.R.
Sub-Lieut. G. W. A. Wauchope, R.N.V.R.
Sub-Lieut. F. C. Weaver, R.N.V.R.
Sub-Lieut. W. C. J. Williams, R.N.V.R.

Howe Battalion.
Lieutenant G. R. Airey, M.C., R.N.V.R.
Lieutenant E. R. Aston, R.N.V.R.
Lieutenant C. D. F. de la Mothe, R.N.V.R.
Lieutenant A. F. Maynard, R.N.V.R.
Sub-Lieut. W. C. Hakin, M.C., R.N.V.R.
Sub-Lieut. A. E. N. Chance, R.N.V.R.
Sub-Lieut. C. G. O. Fletcher, R.N.V.R.
Sub-Lieut. H. Fry, R.N.V.R.
Sub-Lieut. H. V. Howard, R.N.V.R.
Sub-Lieut. G. N. Strang, R.N.V.R.
Sub-Lieut. C. H. G. Wagner, R.N.V.R.

1st Royal Marine Battalion.
Captain M. C. Browne, D.S.C., R.M.
Captain H. Hoare, R.M.
Captain V. D. Loxley, R.M.
Captain C. L. E. Muntz, R.M.
Captain J. M. Pound, R.M.
Captain G. H. Sulivan, R.M.
Lieutenant F. J. Hanson, R.M.
Lieutenant J. W. Richards, R.M.
2nd Lieut. C. W. Martin, R.M.
2nd Lieut. H. E. R. Upham, R.M.

2nd Royal Marine Battalion.
Acting Lieut. H. B. Welman, R.M.
2nd Lieut. L. J. A. Dewar, R.M.
2nd Lieut. L. M. Stokes, R.M.
188*th* *M. G. C.*
Sub-Lieut. A. C. Hamilton, R.N.V.R
188*th* *T. M. B.*
Sub-Lieut. L. J. Oates, R.N.V.R.

189TH BRIGADE

Hood Battalion.
Acting Lieut.-Commander F. S. Kelly, D.S.C., R.N.V.R.
Lieutenant C. A. Edmondson, R.N.V.R.
Sub-Lieut. R. J. Apthorp, R.N.V.R.
Sub-Lieut. H. Gealer, R.N.V.R.
Sub-Lieut. A. R. Hart, R.N.V.R.
Sub-Lieut. J. G. Watson, R.N.V.R.

Drake Battalion.
>Lieut.-Col. A. S. Tetley, R.M.
>Lieut.-Commander P. S. Campbell, R.N.V.R.
>Sub-Lieut. C. W. R. Bradley, R.N.V.R.
>Sub-Lieut. H. A. Foster, R.N.V.R.
>Sub-Lieut. J. A. Langford, R.N.V.R.
>Sub-Lieut. J. H. M. Newall, R.N.V.R.

Hawke Battalion.
>Surgeon J. S. Ward, R.N.
>Lieutenant the Hon. V. S. T. Harmsworth, R.N.V.R.
>Lieutenant W. Ker, R.N.V.R.
>Sub-Lieut. J. A. Cook, R.N.V.R.
>Sub-Lieut. R. C. G. Edwards, R.N.V.R.
>Sub-Lieut. H. Gold, R.N.V.R.
>Sub-Lieut. A. R. Knight, R.N.V.R.
>Sub-Lieut. S. G. Poole, R.N.V.R.
>Sub-Lieut. F. A. C. C. Turnbull, R.N.V.R.

Nelson Battalion.
>Lieut.-Col. N. O. Burge, R.M.
>Sub-Lieut. D. R. G. P. Alldridge, R.N.V.R.
>Sub-Lieut. A. L. Ball, R.N.V.R.
>Sub-Lieut. E. W. Cashmore, R.N.V.R.
>Sub-Lieut. J. H. Emerson, R.N.V.R.
>Sub-Lieut. D. Francis, R.N.V.R.
>Sub-Lieut. L. S. Gardner, R.N.V.R.
>Sub-Lieut. E. Langstreth, R.N.V.R.
>Sub-Lieut. G. A. Reddick, R.N.V.R.
>Sub-Lieut. E. W. Squires, R.N.V.R.

189th M. G. C.
>Sub-Lieut. E. M. Aron, R.N.V.R.
>Sub-Lieut. J. D. Black, R.N.V.R.
>Sub-Lieut. J. H. Brothers, R.N.V.R.

190th M. G. C.
>Acting Captain E. Bastin, R.M.
>Lieutenant A. H. Chapman, R.M.
>Sub-Lieut. H. W. Troughton, R.N.V.R.

1st Field Ambulance.
>Surgeon G. A. Walker, M.B., R.N.

APPENDIX E (ii)

NAMES OF OFFICERS OF THE ROYAL NAVY, ROYAL NAVAL VOLUNTEER RESERVE
AND ROYAL MARINES KILLED IN THE 1ST AND 2ND BATTLES OF GAVRELLE,
APRIL, 1917.

188TH BRIGADE

Anson Battalion.
>Sub-Lieut. G. H. W. Hughes, R.N.V.R.

Howe Battalion.
>Sub-Lieut. L. S. Savill, R.N.V.R.
>Sub-Lieut. R. H. Sikes, R.N.V.R.
>Sub-Lieut. W. R. Yeoman, R.N.V.R.

1st Royal Marine Battalion.
>Lieut.-Col. F. J. W. Cartwright, D.S.O., R.M.
>Lieutenant N. T. Lion, R.M.
>Lieutenant E. L. Platts, R.M.
>2nd Lieut. J. Fielding, R.M.
>2nd Lieut. H. C. Holmes, R.M.
>2nd Lieut. F. S. Marsh, R.M.

2nd Royal Marine Battalion.
Captain N. E. E. Burton-Fanning, R.M.
Captain J. Campbell, R.M.
Lieutenant H. E. Markham, R.M.
2nd Lieut. P. E. R. Hardy, R.M.
2nd Lieut. C. H. Kearney, R.M.
2nd Lieut. W. A. Lake, R.M.
2nd Lieut. D. H. Walker, R.M.

189TH BRIGADE
Hood Battalion.
Lieutenant C. P. Astbury, R.N.V.R.
Lieutenant J. W. Morrison, R.N.V.R.
Lieutenant G. H. Tamplin, R.N.V.R.
Sub-Lieut. D. F. Bailey, R.N.V.R.
Sub-Lieut. R. V. Cleves, R.N.V.R.
Sub-Lieut. A. S. Cooke, R.N.V.R.
Sub-Lieut. T. K. Cross, R.N.V.R.
Sub-Lieut. C. C. Sennit, R.N.V.R.

Drake Battalion.
Sub-Lieut. A. H. Banning, R.N.V.R.
Sub-Lieut. G. C. Bowles, R.N.V.R.
Sub-Lieut. C. F. Neale, R.N.V.R.
Sub-Lieut. A. B. Wallis, R.N.V.R.

Hawke Battalion.
Lieutenant F. B. Melland, R.N.V.R.
Sub-Lieut. H. A. J. Burr, R.N.V.R.

Nelson Battalion.
Lieutenant C. A. Truscott, R.N.V.R.
Lieutenant G. K. Turnbull, R.N.V.R.
Sub-Lieut. H. C. Hewitt, R.N.V.R.
Sub-Lieut. E. J. Palmer, R.N.V.R.
Sub-Lieut. H. A. Siddle, R.N.V.R.

190th M. G. C.
Sub-Lieut. F. L. Rees, R.N.V.R.
Sub-Lieut. J. E. Willis, R.N.V.R.

R. N. D. Engineers.
Lieutenant H. Shaw, R.M.

APPENDIX E (iii)

NAMES OF OFFICERS OF THE ROYAL NAVY, ROYAL NAVAL VOLUNTEER RESERVE AND ROYAL MARINES KILLED IN THE CONCLUDING ENGAGEMENTS OF AUGUST, SEPTEMBER, OCTOBER AND NOVEMBER, 1918.

(a) BATTLES OF AUGUST 21ST TO 28TH (ATTACKS ON ACHIET-LE-GRAND, LE BARQUE AND THILLOY)

188TH BRIGADE
Anson Battalion.
Lieut.-Commander E. A. Sprange, M.C., R.N.V.R.
Lieutenant P. S. Luce, R.N.V.R.
Lieutenant G. Paterson, R.N.V.R.
Sub-Lieut. W. F. Hardy, M.M., R.N.V.R.
Sub-Lieut. H. J. Dewdney, R.N.V.R.
Sub-Lieut. N. Nesbitt, R.N.V.R.
Sub-Lieut. T. H. Westbrook, R.N V.R.

Royal Marine Battalion.
    Acting Major R. A. Poland, R.M.
    Captain B. G. Andrews, R.M.
    Captain E. L. Andrews, R.M.
    2nd Lieut. C. A. Barber, R.M.L.I.
    2nd Lieut. W. C. B. Matthews, R.M.

189TH BRIGADE

Hood Battalion.
    Lieut.-Commander S. H. Fish, M.C., R.N.V.R.
    Lieutenant H. T. Ely, R.N.V.R.
    Sub-Lieut. J. Menzies, R.N.V.R.

Drake Battalion.
    Sub-Lieut. F. J. Philp, M.C., R.N.V.R.
    Sub-Lieut. W. Barbour, R.N.V.R.
    Sub-Lieut. G. Hunter, R.N.V.R.
    Sub-Lieut. A. R. G. Love, R.N.V.R.

Hawke Battalion.
    Commander S. G. Jones, R.N.V.R.
    Lieut.-Commander O. J. Wainwright, R.N.V.R.
    Sub-Lieut. C. H. Darrell, R.N.V.R.
    Sub-Lieut. W. L. Willison, R.N.V.R.

(b) BATTLES OF SEPTEMBER 1ST TO 8TH, 1918 (ATTACK ON DROCOURT-QUÉANT LINE, INCHY, AND MŒUVRES)

188TH BRIGADE

Anson Battalion.
    Lieutenant R. Donaldson, M.C., R.N.V.R.

Royal Marine Battalion.
    Lieutenant J. R. Bates, R.M.
    Lieutenant A. C. McAdam, R.M.

189TH BRIGADE

Hood Battalion.
    Surgeon A. R. MacMullin, D.S.C., R.N.
    Sub-Lieut. J. E. Webber, R.N.V.R.

Drake Battalion.
    Sub-Lieut. E. W. Fry, R.N.V.R.

Hawke Battalion.
    Acting Lieut. H. B. Biggs, M.C., R.N.V.R.
    Sub-Lieut. A. A. Leighton, D.S.M., R.N.V.R.
    Sub-Lieut. W. Chapman, R.N.V.R.
    Sub-Lieut. H. S. Strickland, R.N.V.R.
    Sub-Lieut. E. G. C. Unwin, R.N.V.R.
    Sub-Lieut. E. E. Wicks, R.N.V.R.

(c) BATTLES OF SEPTEMBER 29TH TO OCTOBER 3RD, 1918 (ATTACKS ON CANAL DU NORD, GRAINCOURT, ANNEUX AND CANAL D'ESCAUT)

188TH BRIGADE

Anson Battalion.
    Sub-Lieut. F. Southern, R.N.V.R.

Royal Marine Battalion.
    Captain F. G. Eliot, M.C., R.M.
    Lieutenant L. F. Albury, R.M.
    Lieutenant A. W. Gregory, R.M.
    Lieutenant G. R. B. Hollamby, R.M.

Appendix E

Hood Battalion.
Sub-Lieut. L. H. Card, R.N.V.R.

Drake Battalion.
Surgeon F. G. Pocock, D.S.O., M.C., R.N.
Sub-Lieut. C. E. Upson, M.C., R.N.V.R.
Sub-Lieut. C. Attfield, R.N.V.R.

Hawke Battalion.
Sub-Lieut. P. Reeve, R.N.V.R.
Sub-Lieut. J. G. Todd, R.N.V.R.

(*d*) BATTLE OF OCTOBER 8TH, 1918 (ATTACK ON NIERGNIES)

188TH BRIGADE

Anson Battalion.
Acting Lieut. A. E. Ross, R.N.V.R.
Sub-Lieut. P. R. Shinkfield, R.N.V.R.

Royal Marine Battalion.
Lieutenant A. G. Bareham, R.M.L.I.
Lieutenant A. Wallis, R.M.

189TH BRIGADE

Hood Battalion.
Sub-Lieut. J. C. Morley, R.N.V.R.

Drake Battalion.
Sub-Lieut. A. Ross, D.C.M., R.N.V.R.
Sub-Lieut. W. F. Benson, R.N.V.R.
Sub-Lieut. A. J. Loutit, R.N.V.R.

Hawke Battalion.
Lieutenant A. O. Cookson, R.N.V.R.
Sub-Lieut. J. O. Harris, D.S.O., R.N.V.R.
Sub-Lieut. F. C. Harry, R.N.V.R.
Sub-Lieut. J. B. Johnston, R.N.V.R.

(*e*) ENGAGEMENTS OF NOVEMBER 6TH TO 11TH, 1918 (FINAL
ADVANCE THROUGH BELGIUM)

188th BRIGADE

Anson Battalion.
Sub-Lieut. F. E. Brooks, R.N.V.R
Sub-Lieut. C. A. Richards, R.N.V.R.
Sub-Lieut. F. E. Trenholm, R.N.V.R.
Sub-Lieut. H. Young, R.N.V.R.

Royal Marine Battalion.
2nd Lieut. S. Goodwin, R.M.L.I.

APPENDIX F

RAID BY THE DRAKE BATTALION, JULY 12TH–13TH, 1918

" Two German strong points, in which there were always a considerable number of the enemy, were marked down by careful reconnaissance.

" Air photographs were taken of them, and they were laid out with tapes life size on the ground near Mailley–Maillet village. When the Battalion was out in reserve the Company selected to carry out the raid practised it several times on the tapes till every man knew exactly where he had to go, so as to find his way in the dark.

" The raid was under command of Lieutenant Robertson, O.C., 'D' Co., and the actual raiding party consisted of 54 men under 2nd Lieuts. Bolt and Briddon, who commanded the right and left parties respectively.

" On the night chosen for the raid, July 12th, the party moved forward three hours before zero, owing to the muddy state of the trenches. After a rest of an hour and a quarter and a meal of hot tea and meat sandwiches in the front trench, the men started to line out in the assembly position 45 minutes before zero.

" Thanks to the careful preparation of the officers responsible, the spacing out of the men was punctually carried out, and the whole party were in position a quarter of an hour before zero. At midnight, the zero hour, a powerful barrage of artillery and trench mortars opened to the second.

" Besides heavy fire on the points to be attacked, a mine crater and a knot of trenches, a box-barrage of artillery and machine-gun fire was put down on three sides of the scene of operations, to prevent any of the Germans running away or any reinforcements coming up to assist. The men were in excellent spirits and confident of success.

" When the barrage opened they automatically fixed bayonets, and moved forward to within 30 yards of it. In doing this they had to pass through the wire, which, despite a few gaps, caused some difficulty. It was fairly loose, however, with few stakes, and the men were able to tread it down and pass over it.

" At zero and 4 minutes, when the barrage lifted, the men charged the first objective with a lusty cheer. When 'B' party (2nd Lieut. Briddon), on the left, arrived at the trench, they found the Boches ' standing to,' some on the fire-step, and some in the trench. They showed fight and refused to surrender, and were killed. In the trench were six dug-outs, the occupants of which refused to surrender. 'P' smoke bombs, followed by Mills grenades, were thrown down the entrances and the inhabitants killed. Every dug-out was treated like this, and one was actually in flames when the party returned to our lines.

" They moved forward as arranged along Lounge trench until 'A' party was met. Here a Boche was found in the act of firing a light machine gun. He refused to surrender, and tried to turn it on the party. The officer in command of the party killed him with his revolver. Another was found firing a rifle, and he was overpowered and made a prisoner, and sent back to our trenches. This man made two attempts to escape on the way back.

" All the enemy dead were searched for papers useful to the Intelligence Staff, but nothing was found.

" 'A' party (2nd Lieut. Bolt), on the right, on reaching this first objective, found no one in the trench. They carried on half-right ' over the top' to Lounge trench. A bombing party, working up Lustre Support trench, met with opposition and could not get on.

345

" The rest of the party, on arriving at their second objective, met a Boche, who immediately called down a dug-out, and two or three others came out and surrendered. The party then worked along the trench and found 12 dug-out entrances. The inmates were called on to surrender, which they did without resistance.

" When the prisoners had come out, ' P ' bombs and Mills grenades were hrown down all these entrances to set the dug-outs on fire.

" In this vicinity ' A ' party captured 21 prisoners, and destroyed one heavy machine gun.

" The officer in charge and 7 men were actually responsible. It was a fine feat for eight men to bring this number of prisoners out of the enemy's lines, and 2nd Lieut. Bolt and these men deserve great credit for their coolness and pluck. They returned to our lines at zero and 45 minutes, and joined their comrades, who had already returned, the officers minus the greater part of their breeches, which they had left on the German wire.

" The total captures were 21 men and one light machine gun, and a considerable number of the enemy were killed. Our losses were one man missing and five slightly wounded."

INDEX

Index

23

354 Index

Divisions, British Army—continued.
316, 317; relieve R.N.D. 1st
Oct. '18, 320; artillery of, in
attack on Niergnies, 8th Oct.
'18, 323.
56th Division, 168th Bde. of, relieved
by R.N.D. 6th Nov. '18, 327.
57th Division, in attack on Drocourt–Quéant line, 310, 311; re-
liev R.N.D. 5th Sept. '18, 314;
in attack of 27th Sept. '18, 316,
318; position of, 28th Sept. '18,
319.
62nd Division, relieved by R.N.D.
15th–20th Dec. '17, 266.
63rd (R.N.) Division, Royal Naval
Division renamed, 171.
188th Infantry Brigade, formation
of, 171; Brig.-Gen. Prentice
appointed to command of, 171;
position of, Aug. '16, 174; on
the way to the Somme, 180;
conditions experienced by, Oct.
'16, 187; disposition of, before
battle of the Ancre, 191; share
in battle of the Ancre, 195, 196,
199–201, 202–203; losses in battle
of the Ancre, 204; achievements of,
in battle of the Ancre, 205–206;
reorganization of, Dec. '17, 208;
in line south of Ancre, '17, 211;
reports beginning of German
retreat, Feb. '17, 218; in attack
of 17th Feb. '17, 218–219; relieved by 190th Bde. 21st Feb.
'17, 219; attached to 1st Corps
at beginning of battle of Arras,
April, '17, 225; in first battle
of Gavrelle, 229, 236; in second
battle of Gavrelle, 239, 240; in
the Oppy–Gavrelle sector, June,
'17, 245; trench reliefs, July
and Aug. '17, 247; in attack
at Passchendaele, 250, 252, 254;
losses at Passchendaele, 257;
relieve 189th Bde. 5th–6th Nov.
'17, 262; achievements of, at
Passchendaele, 263; on Welsh
Ridge, 267; position of, before
retreat of March, '18, 274; line
held by, 22nd Mar. '18, 277;
withdrawal of, 23rd Mar. '18,
277; withdrawal of, 24th Mar.
'18, 282; action of 24th–27th
Mar. '18, 285, 286, 288, 293; 2nd
Bn. Irish Rifles attached to,
May, '18, 300; in attack of 21st
Aug. '18, 302–305; attack of
24th Aug. '18, postponed, 306;
in attack of 25th–27th Aug. '18,
307, 309; position of 1st–2nd
Sept. '18, 311; in attack on
Drocourt–Quéant line, 311, 312;

in attack on Canal du Nord,
Anneux and Graincourt, 316, 317;
in attack on Niergnies, 323;
advance of, on 10th–11th Nov.
'18, 327, 328.
189th Brigade, formation of, 171;
Brig.-Gen. L. F. Phillips, D.S.O.,
appointed to, 171; on the way
to the Somme, 180; conditions
experienced by, in Oct. '16, 187;
dispositions of, before battle of
the Ancre, 191; action of, in
battle of the Ancre, 191–204
(see under Drake, Hawke, Hood
and Nelson Bns.); losses of, in
battle of Ancre, 204; reorganization of, Dec. '16, 208; in line
north of the Ancre, Jan. '17,
211; relieved by the 190th Bde.,
212; attack by, 2nd–3rd Feb.
'17, 212–216; relieved by 190th
Bde. 217; before Gavrelle, April,
'17, 227; local advance of, on 16th–
17th April, '17, 227; in first
battle of Gavrelle, 229–236; Brig.-
Gen. Phillips succeeded by Brig.-
Gen. Coleridge, 236; trench warfare in the Oppy–Gavrelle sector,
June, '17, 245, 246; trench reliefs, July and Aug. '17, 247;
operations of, on 30th–31st July,
'17, 247; conditions experienced
by, at Passchendaele, Oct. '17,
251, 252; operations of, 31st
Oct.–5th Nov. '17, at Passchendaele, 259–263; Brig.-Gen. Asquith
to command, 18th Dec. '17, 266;
German attack on Welsh Ridge,
Dec. '17, 267–270; position of,
before beginning retreat of March,
'18, 274; casualties from gas,
12th–21st Mar. '18, 275; withdrawal of, 22nd–23rd Mar. '18,
277; actions of 24th–26th Mar.
'18, 282–290; at Engelbelmer,
26th–27th Mar. '18, 290; achievement of, in March retreat, 295;
reorganization, May, '18, 300;
plans for, in attack of 21st Aug.
'18, 302; in attack of 21st–23rd
Aug. '18, 302–305; temporarily
commanded by Comdr. Egerton,
24th Aug. '18, 307; in attack
of 25th Aug. '18, 307–308; in
attack on Drocourt–Quéant line,
313–315; in attack on An-
neux–Graincourt and the Canal
d'Escaut, 317–319; Brig.-Gen.
Curling succeeds to command of,
3rd Sept. '18, (footnote) 319;
in attack on Niergnies, Oct. '18,
323; advance of, on 8th Nov.
'18, 327–328.

360

Index

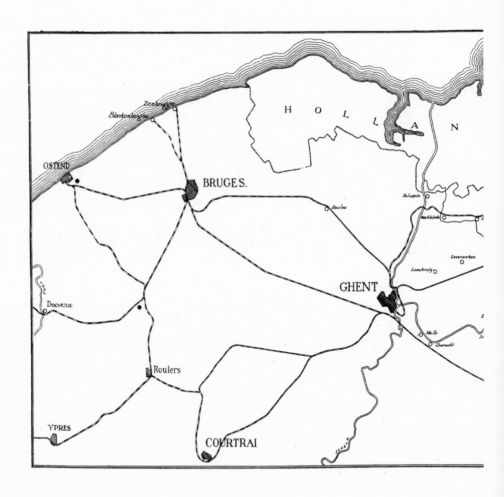

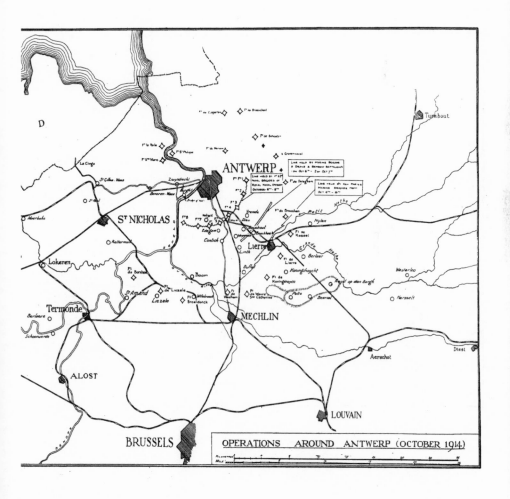

OPERATIONS AROUND ANTWERP (OCTOBER 1914)

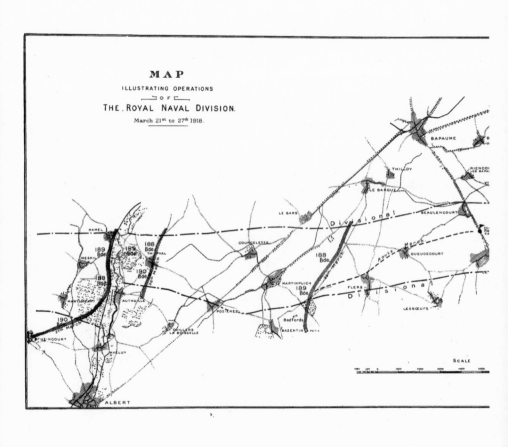

MAP

ILLUSTRATING OPERATIONS

OF

THE . ROYAL NAVAL DIVISION.

March 21st to 27th 1918.

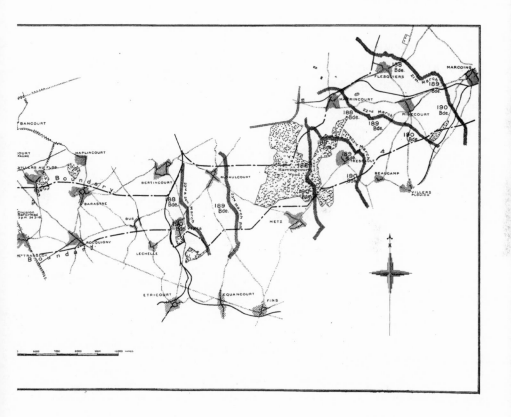

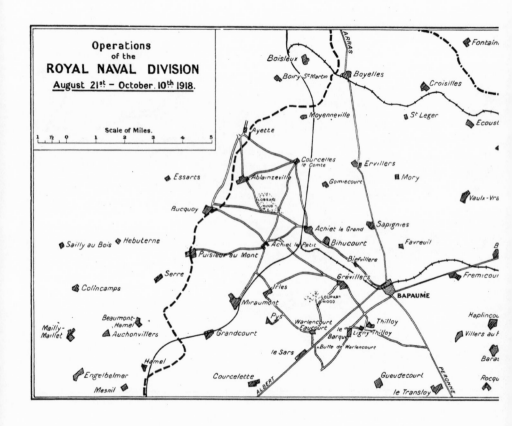

Operations
of the
ROYAL NAVAL DIVISION
August 21st – October. 10th 1918.

Scale of Miles.

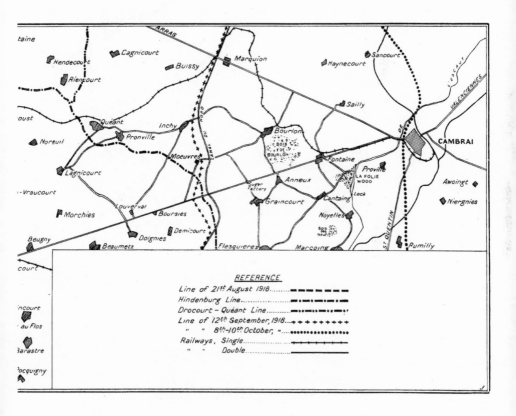

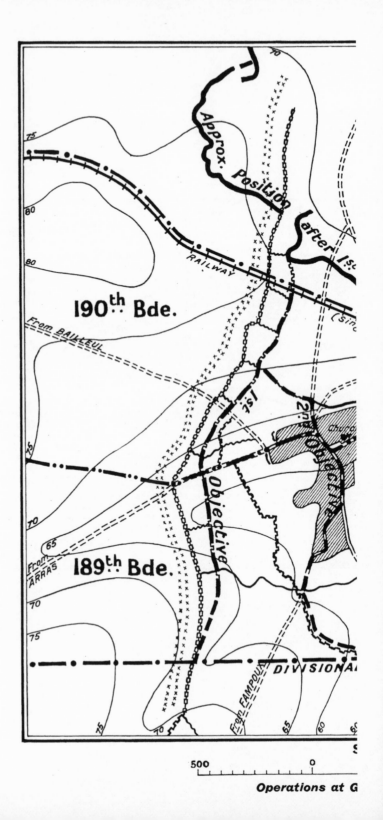

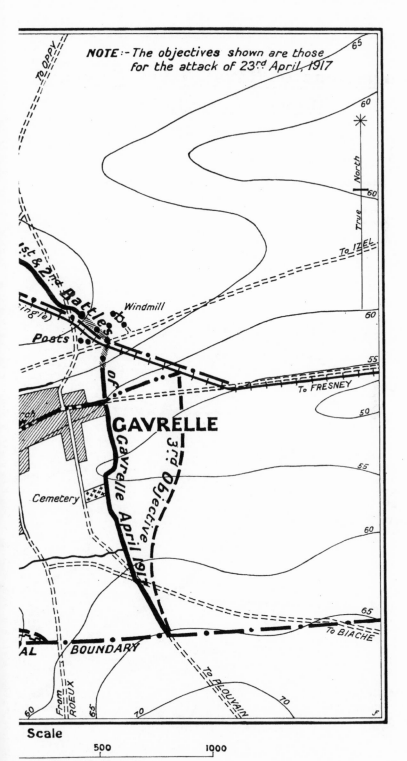

Gavrelle, April 1917.

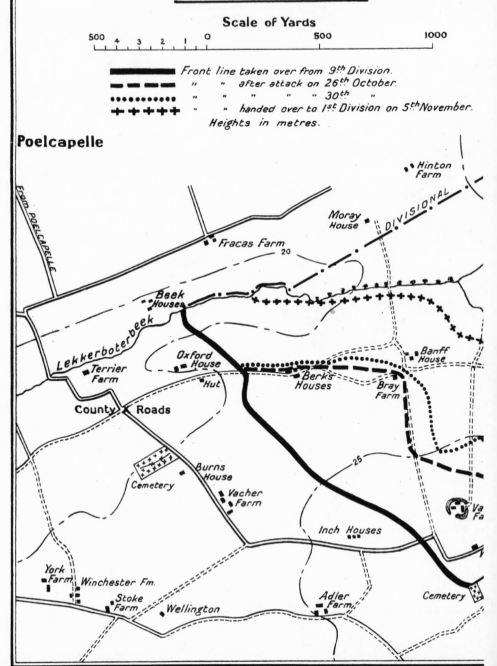

Operations of Royal Naval Division,
October – November 1917.

Scale of Yards

500 4 3 2 1 0 · · · · · 500 · · · · · 1000

— Front line taken over from 9th Division.
– – – " " after attack on 26th October.
•••••• " " " " 30th "
+ + + + " " handed over to 1st Division on 5th November.
Heights in metres.

Poelcapelle

Hinton Farm

Moray House

DIVISIONAL

From POELCAPELLE

Fracas Farm

20

Beek Houses

Lekkerboterbeek

Terrier Farm

Oxford House

Berks Houses

Banff House

Bray Farm

Hut

County Roads

Burns House

Cemetery

Vacher Farm

25

Va Fa

Inch Houses

York Farm

Winchester Fm.

Stoke Farm

Wellington

Adler Farm

Cemetery

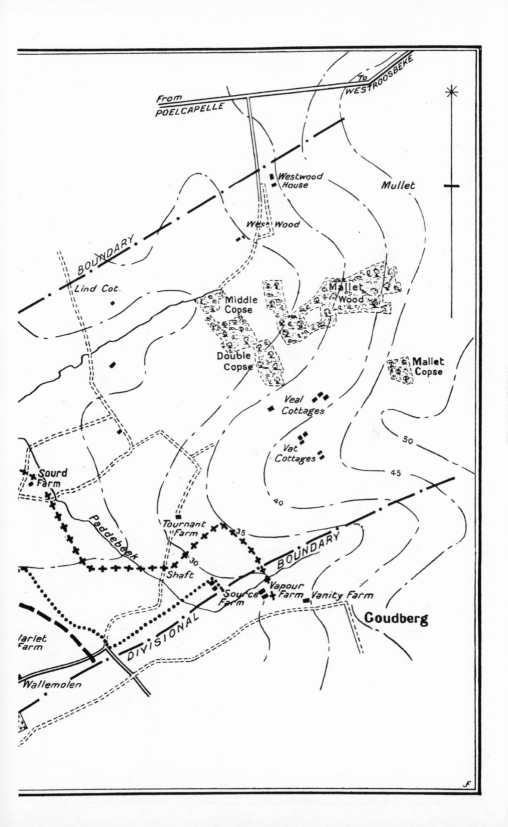

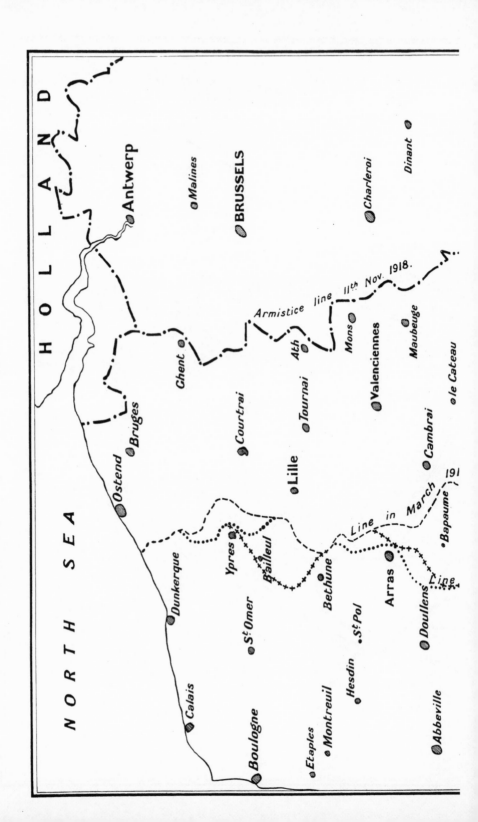

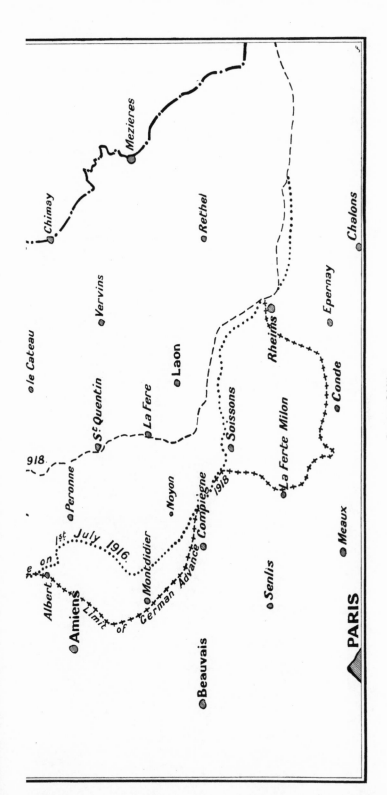

The British Front, Northern France.

Scale of Miles

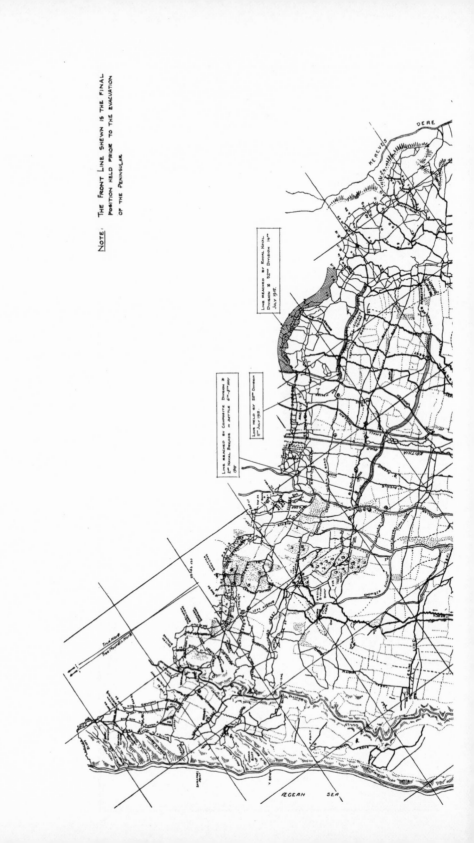

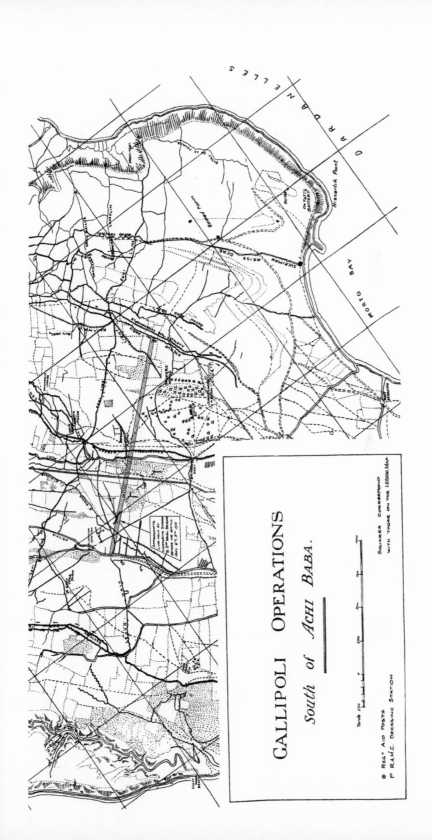

GALLIPOLI OPERATIONS
South of ACHI BABA.

Yards 250

SQUARED CORRESPOND
WITH THOSE ON THE 1/20,000 MAP

⊕ REG'T AID POSTS
F R.A.M.C. DRESSING STATION

Printed in Great Britain by
Amazon.co.uk, Ltd.,
Marston Gate.